P9-DIY-392

Women and the Reformation

I dedicate this book to those most dear to me – Kaleigh Kirsikka and Kristian, David and Benjamin, and Brooks.

WOMEN

and the

REFORMATION

KIRSI STJERNA

Blackwell
Publishing

BLACKWELL PUBLISHING

350 Main Street, Malden, MA 02148-5020, USA
9600 Garsington Road, Oxford OX4 2DQ, UK

The right of Kirsi Stjerna to be identified as the author of this work has been asserted in accordance with the UK Copyright, Designs, and Patents Act 1988.

First published 2009 by Blackwell Publishing Ltd

1   2009

Library of Congress Cataloging-in-Publication Data

Stjerna, Kirsi Irmeli, 1963–
   Women and the Reformation / Kirsi Stjerna.
      p. cm.
   Includes bibliographical references and index.
   ISBN 978-1-4051-1422-6 (hardcover : alk. paper)—ISBN 978-1-4051-1423-3 (pbk. : alk. paper)   1. Women in Christianity—History—16th century.   2. Reformation.   3. Christian women—Religious life.   I. Title.

   BR307.S75 2009
   270.6092′2—dc22
                        2007042450

A catalogue record for this title is available from the British Library.

Set in 10 on 12 pt Minion
by SNP Best-set Typesetter Ltd., Hong Kong
Printed and bound in Singapore
by Fabulous Printers Pte Ltd

The publisher's policy is to use permanent paper from mills that operate a sustainable forestry policy, and which has been manufactured from pulp processed using acid-free and elementary chlorine-free practices. Furthermore, the publisher ensures that the text paper and cover board used have met acceptable environmental accreditation standards.

For further information on
Blackwell Publishing, visit our website at
www.blackwellpublishing.com

Contents

Acknowledgments

It is very much thanks to my students at the Lutheran Theological Seminary at Gettysburg, and their interest in studying the women of the Reformation, that this long-percolating idea has become a reality. Every "Women and the Reformation" class has contributed in many important ways to the project.

From a humble initial vision of preparing a brief textbook, the manuscript has grown thicker with every passing year – just as my children have grown taller, and just as the field keeps expanding and exploding. Enough has been accumulated here for one book, and I hope the stories told within this volume inspire further exploration.

The manuscript took shape in many inspiring places and with the assistance of many individuals.

I am grateful to the staff in the many inviting libraries where I had the pleasure to work: the Library of Congress, Washington, DC, the Herzog August Bibliothek in Wolfenbüttel, Germany, the Finnish Institute of Villa Lante in Rome, Italy, the Helsinki University Library, and, most of all, the A. R. Wentz Library at Gettysburg, PA, where the amazing staff – Susann Posey, Roberta Brent, and (now retired) Sarah Mummert – could get hold of any book in the world.

The final product would not have been possible without the diligent copy-editing of Felicity Marsh, the efficient picture hunting of Kitty Bocking, and the creative production management of Karen Wilson and Louise Spencely, and other Blackwell staff.

The institutional support at the Lutheran Theological Seminary at Gettysburg – especially from Deans Norma Wood and Robin Steinke and the faculty administrative assistant Danielle Garber – and the encouragement and varied assistance of dear colleagues and staff there have been invaluable.

Several student assistants participated in the project – Amy Sevimli, Joel Neubauer, Rebecca Carmichael, and Tim Leitzke. Barbara Eisenhart and Demaris Kenwood assisted with selected French texts, and consultations with colleagues Nelson Strobert, Eric Crump, and Susan Hedahl were most valuable – as has been, most of all, the multifaceted support of Brooks Schramm, my spouse and colleague, a fellow inquirer and lover of words.

I wish to thank Rebecca Harkin, Publisher in Theology and Religious Studies at Blackwell, Scott Hendrix, Professor Emeritus from Princeton University, and Carter Lindberg, Professor Emeritus from Boston University, for their trust, support, and enormously valuable feedback along the way.

I thank Kaleigh Kirsikka, Kristian, and Brooks – for everything, including their untiring optimism and excitement, accompanying me on my travels, and patiently coaching me in the nuances of a language that is not my own.

This research was made possible by the funded sabbatical from LTSG (Spring 2006) and the most generous Theological Scholars Grant (2004–5) from the Association for Theological Schools.

Introduction

The Vision and the Scope of the Book

Teaching courses on the Reformation is no longer feasible without the inclusion of women as subjects in the story of the Reformation and its evaluation. The lack of easily accessible sources has complicated this necessary broadening of the scope of study in the classroom. The vision for this book arose from the need to have a portable introduction in English, and it was hoped that by presenting the best material available the exploration of the lives, thoughts, and contributions of women in different Reformation contexts would be facilitated, broadening the understanding of the Reformation from the perspectives of both genders, and, last but not least, inspiring theological inquiry informed by feminist scholarship.

The initial vision proved ambitious, as a delightful abundance of materials surfaced – and continue to surface. Several principles have shaped the work: First of all, the primary goal is to present stories of several women in varied visible leadership roles in different Reformation contexts. The term "leadership" is given broad meaning, including leadership exercised in politics, religious matters, and households, in writing and teaching and speaking, or in "hosting" and "partnering." Second, the selected women's lives, contributions, and challenges are interpreted in light of the reformers' teachings about women's place in the Church and society as well as in light of the emancipatory potential imbedded in the gospel proclamation that so attracted these women. Third, the chapters rely on the important studies already available (references for which are provided at the end of the book), in addition to leading the reader to the original sources. Only occasional references will be made to the grand pool of Reformation sources in general. It is assumed that the reader has a basic familiarity with Reformation history.

The biographical introductions, which synthesize and interpret information scholars have already made available in different languages, present women in different vocations and examine their different self-understandings, evolutions, and contributions as Protestant believers. Basic feminist-oriented questions organize the biographical material: Who was this woman? What kind of a Reformer was she? How did she understand herself as a woman and as a reformer? What did she write or do about the issues that mattered to her? How did others receive her? What were her options? What role did her gender have in her life? Why is she important in the larger scope of Protestant history (histories) and theology (theologies)? What has been her place in scholarship, and what, with Luther, Calvin and other "great" reformers, can she teach us? In terms of the bigger picture of women and the Reformation in general, we continue to pursue with Natalie Zemon Davis (1975, 66) the questions she posed in 1975 (Davis 1975, 66) of whether the Reformation had a distinctive appeal to women (and if so to what kind of women) and how so, and what Protestant women did to bring about religious change and what impact the Reformation had on their lives and vice versa.

The lives of the women featured in this book shed light on these issues and on women's involvement in religious affairs in general. Their stories call for a reexamination of Reformation history and theology and for a consideration of the actual benefits and losses generated by the Reformation for women in particular. The tragedy and the humor, the sustained suppression, and the occasional freedom from constraints, the costs and the rewards of individual women's faith commitments provide many, perhaps unanticipated, touching points with the lives and struggles of people today. The voices of the women who "mothered" the Reformation for later generations offer an important reality check for the, at times, one-sidedly celebratory appraisals of Reformation theologies and complement the male experiences and perspectives that have so far been the dominant study in the field.

The women in this book come from different geographic, cultural, linguistic, and social contexts. Their leadership roles have differed, but most of them have left a written or otherwise tangible legacy: Katharina von Bora Luther, Elisabeth von Brandenburg and Elisabeth von Braunschweig, Argula von Grumbach, Marie Dentière, Katharina Schütz Zell, Ursula Jost, Marguerite de Navarre, Jeanne d'Albret, Renée de France, and Olimpia Morata are highlighted as exemplary matriarchs of the Reformation who, each in her own way, responded to Protestant teachings, exercised religious leadership, and lived out her religious conviction with a significant effect on the individuals and communities around her. They demonstrate women's instrumental role in the life of the Church, instrumental regardless of and in response to the dominant patriarchal values and norms. Their insights and experiences promise to complement as well as challenge the (predominantly male) perspectives that have shaped Protestant theologies and spiritualities. Understanding women's choices, passions, and vocations in light of the varied factors that shaped women's religious lives allows for a holistic and critical grasp of the Reformation as a whole.

The Term "Reformation" and Inclusivity Concerns

The singular term "Reformation" does not do justice to the different reforming movements of the sixteenth century, as has been demonstrated by Carter Lindberg (1996). With its forerunners and proponents, the Reformation was in many respects catapulted from Martin Luther's vocal and well-published reaction to the institution and practices of the late medieval Catholic church that he perceived to be ailing and incapable of meeting the spiritual needs of the people. He most famously voiced his concerns in his Ninety-Five Theses in 1517 and his reformatory writings of the 1520s, and soon enough he was joined by others on a similar mission.

The corruption in clerical offices culminating in the self-serving interests of the renaissance popes, and the grossly abused sale of the indulgences (letters of pardon for acts of penance and satisfaction and for time in purgatory) in particular became a common starting point for many calls for reform and movements towards reforming the Church, theology, and people's religious practices – reforms that materialized differently in different contexts in Europe. Eventually this turmoil resulted in the formation of distinct denominational traditions (in the Lutheran, Anglican, Reformed, Anabaptist, and/or Mennonite churches), each shaped by distinct visions for the role of the Church and ministry in the world, the purposes and uses of the sacraments, and the interpretation and preaching of the Scripture among other things. This fragmenting of the one catholic church coincided with reforms within the Roman Catholic church, especially a renewed emphasis on its spiritual traditions and resources, sacramental practices, and moral values.

In each Reformation, the importance of education, literature, catechetical materials, sacramental practices, and understanding of vocation were central, as were the Confessions. Lutherans were the first to set themselves officially apart with their united Augsburg Confession of 1530. The word "Protestant" – encompassing the different Reformation traditions, from Lutherans and Calvinists to Anglicans and Anabaptists – derives from a historic moment at the 1529 Diet of Speyer when the evangelical princes, theologians, and clergy "protested" against the proposed reinforcement of the 1521 Edict of Worms, which would have forced evangelicals to return to the Catholic faith. While Germany and Scandinavia experienced a predominantly Lutheran Reformation, elsewhere in Europe, especially in the French-speaking world, Calvin's teachings had more far reaching effects. In England, Reformation theology and practices found their own unique "middle way." Everywhere in Europe the Anabaptists and other charismatic Protestant groups (those practicing believer's baptism in particular) were persecuted.

Regardless of what was originally a shared vision of re-Christianizing Europe and a shared conviction of the primary authority of the Scripture, the questions and strategies about what reforms to make and how to make them varied, leading to the formation of different confessions and confessional groups (as argued by Scott Hendrix [2004a]). Apart from the geographical, cultural, political, and confessional differences, the Reformation took root and shaped lives in different ways for men from women, for clergy and the learned from the laity, for the city people from the country folk and peasants. The Reformation story and its evaluation thus have many versions and there are many perspectives to consider. The very question of "was the Reformation a success or a failure?" is impossible to answer as such due to the plurality of the phenomenon. For instance, just as the Protestants "failed" to reform the Catholic church according to their visions, the Catholic church became invigorated through its own reform but failed to draw the Protestants back. And, although both the Catholic and Protestant Reformation "failed" to bring forth equal benefits for men and women, laity and clergy, they have successfully attracted both men and women. It is thus most appropriate to conceive the Reformation as plural, even if in the text it is the singular term which is mostly used. (See Lindberg 1996; Hendrix 2004a.)

Addressing the roles of particular women in the Reformation movements, this book adds yet one more plural to the term: The Reformation for women was not necessarily in every regard the same as it was for men. The "good news" proclaimed about the gospel and the structures built around it were not necessarily equally good for women and men. At the same time, hasty conclusions about gendered roles, views, and experiences in the Reformation movements are not warranted. For instance, it is not true that men were always active or leaders and women always passive bystanders or receivers, or that women adopted the gendered world with its gender-biased options and parameters without scrutiny. The truth is much more complex.

This book does not claim to present "the truth," but a perspective, and an attempt to interpret under-utilized material. Let it be stated about the perspectives offered in this book that the author's intentional and unintentional biases derive from experiences as a European Lutheran clergywoman teaching in a North American seminary setting. The focus on Protestant women in sixteenth-century Europe is not intended to imply that the Protestant, or more specifically the Lutheran, reforms were superior to the other reforms: had the scope of the book allowed it, Catholic reforming women would have been included.

In terms of language and the spelling of names, whenever it has been reasonable and possible to do so without obscuring a figure's historical identity, the original form of personal names has been used; in some cases, after extensive consideration, it has seemed preferable to use the name by which someone is most widely known than their birth name. Inclusivity is at the very premise of writing this book. When quoting the primary sources or studies about them, however, the text is included as it appears in the source without any attempt at making the language more ideologically correct to the modern reader. Apart from the fact that the inclusive use of pronouns is, to a degree, a language-specific issue, it is not one which concerned our sixteenth-century writers. At the same time, the writers' use of masculine pronouns for the third person singular, according to the conventions of their language, or their references to God nearly exclusively as "He," "Lord," and "Father," and often with masculine images, does not necessarily imply that maleness was understood as superior to femaleness or that God was seen as "more" male than female or neutral. This said, it seems fair to conclude that the centuries of *Wirkungsgeschichte*, or "history of influences," of androcentric assumptions in Christian expressions of faith and theology, so manifest in language, obviously shaped our women's thinking and articulation about God and spiritual matters. In that regard, any attempt on the part of women writers to envision God in other terms than "He" and "Lord" should be noted as extremely bold and modern and be cheered!

Visionary Studies on Women and the Reformation

Much more has been written about the wars, the Diets, and the reformers' assorted treatises than about how the Reformation was experienced and transferred by women. Surprisingly few book-length studies have been published on the subject of women in the lives and theologies of the reformers or assessing their theologies from gender perspectives.

Whereas theological inquiry with a gender perspective has been slow to unfold in Reformation studies, the opposite is true in social studies. Since the 1960s, there has been an "explosion" of research. "Historians have searched for new sources which reveal the historical experience of women, and used traditional sources in innovative ways" (Wiesner 2000a, 1–8 at 1). It has become clear that the socially and theologically constructed limitations on women's options for expressing their faith have to be taken into account when assessing the successes as well as the failures of the Reformation from the perspectives of both genders. In a continuous reappropriation of a historic faith tradition in new times and situations, gender studies promise both continuity and the discovery of renewed "meanings" that can make a particular faith tradition theologically and spiritually sustaining through changing times.

In recent decades scholars have unfolded materials that have identified women in different roles and thus diversified the group of participants and factors in Reformation history. Historians have discovered a variety of rich sources coming from women. The editing and translating of these works has begun, promising an exciting exploration of women's theologies from their own writings. With identities discovered and first-hand sources made available the new challenges in Reformation scholarship will be, first, to formulate a more realistic and inclusive story of the Reformation by placing equal value on the roles and experiences of both sexes, and, second, to let the women writers' theological contributions inform the ongoing critical reevaluation of Reformation theologies and their impact. Simply gathering and adding missing material with old premises will not be sufficient. Just as women's perspectives through the centuries are more than a footnote, so too the women of this period are part of the main text of our history.

The unfolding of the stories of the sixteenth-century reforming women has already brought to light the importance of the role of gender in how, in its different forms, the Protestant Reformation was preached, implemented, received, or rejected. Gender views and norms were also a factor in "what" was being preached and implemented. The recognition of the permeating, inevitable role of gender in human life and history has led to a significant acknowledgment that no history or theology can ever be gender blind or neutral – just as no theology or history can be non-contextual or without a human face. This recognition calls for a new level of inquiry that is inclusive in terms of "who names the reality" and "whose experience and perspective counts" and "what are the important questions to ask." An inclusive approach to the materials will naturally help to correct the gender biases and class biases, as well as race biases and other prejudices that have dominated the interpretations of Reformation history and theology.

Joan Kelly, in her 1977 essay "Did Women Have a Renaissance," was among those setting the course for gender-aware historical scholarship. She called into question the entire periodization and definition of the Renaissance with her observation about the

so-far insufficiently recognized role of gender in evaluating history and human experience and culture: "To take the emancipation of women as a vantage point is to discover
that events that further the historical development of men . . . have quite different, even
opposite, effects upon women. The Renaissance is a good case in point" (Kelly-Gadol
1977, 176). To continue Kelly's theses, we can ask the same question about the Reformation: Was there a Reformation for women, and if so, what was it? For instance, inasmuch
as history is about changes and their interpretation, and as relatively moderate, indirect
changes occurred in women's lives and in attitudes towards women in the Renaissance
and Reformation periods, we can hardly talk about "history" in respect to women
of the period with the same meanings as when we talk about the his-story of men.
Approaches that only recognize "exceptional" women or fail to recognize the impact of
the different forms of subjection on women's history across the board, that are not
informed by the realities and experiences of women of the period in question, are
based on skewed premises of what constituted normalcy or progress for women (see
Sommerville 1995, 8, 39–78, 250).

In the same vein, Gerda Lerner argues that women's long subjection to the other sex
is the history of implicit beliefs shaping social structures and constraints and giving the
force of law and custom to what were mere assumptions. She names patriarchy as the
culprit for the development of different forms of dominance and hierarchical relationships (in reproduction, economics, and human relations). "In the course of the establish-
ment of patriarchy and constantly reinforced as the result of it, the major idea systems
which explain and order Western civilization incorporated a set of unstated assumptions
about gender, which powerfully affected the development of history and of human
thought." Distinguishing between history and his-story is part of coming to terms with
the observation that "it is in recorded history that women have been obliterated or marginalized." According to Lerner, it is because of being deprived of cultural fostering
through dialogue and encounter with educated peers that women have for long lacked
the essential prerequisites for participating in the constructive recording and interpretation of the history of which they have been part (Lerner 1993, 3–5, also 12–13).

With a growing awareness of the complexity of human life, "we stand at the beginning of a new epoch in the history of humankind's thought, as we recognize that sex is
irrelevant to thought, that gender is a social construct and that woman, like man, makes
and defines history" (Lerner 1993, 283). Merry Wiesner-Hanks offers an insightful
metaphor for the interdisciplinary work in progress: in the study of history, the structure
we call "history" is very much a City of Men (or Some Men), and, in order to break
holes into this millennia-old structure and to build a sturdy new structure for a City of
Women, all immigrants are welcomed to the task in which "we may build high towers,
but we need open gates" (Wiesner-Hanks 2001, 16).

In this book women are introduced as history makers and as subjects of their own
history. In inviting the ongoing interpretation of religious history and theological
understandings to take shape from women's varied experiences, there is hope for more
inclusive history writing and theologizing.

This book builds on and draws from the substantial and visionary work of scholars
who have been pioneers in detecting the footsteps of sixteenth-century women and who
have provided both biographical studies and critical editions and translations of the
women's works. The 1885 work by Mrs Annie Wittenmyer deserves special mention as
the predecessor to this present book as an early attempt to provide biographies of several

of the women of the Reformation. The work benefits also from the rich studies on late medieval women's religiosity and from feminist scholars who have prepared the way for understanding the role of gender in history and theology. Their work is reflected in the bibliography.

Critical works on individual women and their writings and theologies are still coming. Just a few women, such as Marguerite de Navarre, have already attracted remarkable amounts of scholarship in different disciplines. Just a few, such as Argula von Grumbach and Katharina Schütz Zell, have stimulated a variety of recent articles and book-length studies. The English women of the Renaissance and Reformation have enjoyed substantial scholarly attention elsewhere, Queen Elizabeth and her father Henry VIII's wives in particular, and, as the primary goal has been to provide a good representation of women of the period in diverse roles, they are not subject to special attention in this study (see Levin, Carney, Barrett-Graves 2003, 1988). Women who were partners with famous reformers, such as Katharina von Bora Luther, have drawn miscellaneous interest, both hagiographical and polemical – as have the humanist noble ladies who sponsored reform from within the Catholic church, such as Vittoria Colonna, Giulia Gonzaga, Caterina Cibo, and Isabella Bresegna. The Anabaptist and "radical" women, for instance, Elisabeth van Leeuwarden and Ursula Jost, remain almost unknown, as do the Scandinavian women, among whom the Lutheran queen Dorothea of Denmark stands out. Theologically oriented women with a public voice, such as Katharina Schütz Zell, Argula von Grumbach, Marie Dentière, Olimpia Morata, and also prominent noblewomen such as Jeanne d'Albret and Renée de France, inspired some book-length treatises as early as the nineteenth century, and even greater interest has been shown in them recently, but mostly what has been written has been in languages other than English.

In English in particular, full critical biographies of many of the Reformation women are still to come. The same is true of critical editions and translations of women's texts, and of in-depth analysis of women's theologies in particular. This work highlights the works of those scholars who have already translated precious pieces into English. When quoting from these sources, the honor thus goes to the original translators and editors, whose works are detailed in the bibliography.

A word about referencing: In the final editing process, it was decided to exclude the heavy references accumulated in the course of the work, to ensure the clarity and the flow of the text. Only when quoting in detail or when a particular scholar offers an especially valuable or distinct interpretation or addresses a specific issue are authors and works cited in the text as well as in the bibliography. Otherwise, the reader is advised to turn to the end of the book and consult each chapter's bibliography where the works of most importance and those which are mostly used are listed, in addition to references for further reading.

Women in this Book

This book introduces women as receivers, agents, and implementers of the Protestant faith in sixteenth-century Europe. The focus is on women who, in writing or in other positions of leadership, publicly confessed their faith, lived out their vocations as Protestant women, and tangibly contributed to the cause of the Reformation in their time and place.

Katharina von Bora Luther exemplifies the newly elevated vocation of mothers and the new calling of the Protestant pastors' spouses as domestic implementers of the faith through home and family. Marie Dentière as an ex-nun turned Reformer and proselytizer gives an astute lay woman's interpretation of the reforms in Geneva. Argula von Grumbach, Marie Dentière, Katharina Schütz Zell, and Olimpia Morata each explicitly defended women's rights to speech and action and articulated their view of the Christian duties of all women. Their stories demonstrate both the competence and the challenges of the few learned, outspoken female theologians and defenders of women, all ridiculed by their male critics but convinced of their right to teach and argue theologically. Their legacy for later generations is a rich assortment of theological writing and courageous witnessing of their faith. Marguerite de Navarre and her daughter Jeanne d'Albret, with Renée de France, demonstrate the precarious political authority and the courageous religious commitment several noblewomen cleverly employed in protecting Protestants under dangerous circumstances. Prophets like Ursula Jost from Strasbourg managed to continue the medieval tradition of charismatic prophets and mystics in a clash with the mainstream Protestant preferences and overall suspicion of such experiences. The Princess Elisabeth of Denmark who became on her marriage Elisabeth von Brandenburg and her daughter Elisabeth von Braunschweig implemented Reformation in their private and public domains, in acts and words of confession and persuasive legislation. Many of the women presented here stand as examples of committed individuals in often precarious positions of authority and as examples of faithful wives and mothers who could pay a dear personal price for their public mission for the benefit of the Protestant faith. Many equally intriguing women were left out of this study due to reasons of space.

Protestant women of the sixteenth century from central and southern Europe rose up as the main subjects of this study. With their publications or otherwise manifest religious leadership roles, the women chosen embodied the different faces of women's vocations, gave those vocations specific meanings in their context, and contributed as private believers as well as public leaders. To set a common framework for the individual women's stories introductory essays and the Conclusion discuss briefly a variety of issues pertinent to women's options and the bearing the reformers' theologies had on women's lives. The hope is that by setting stories of individual women against the complex story of the Reformation, and with intentional attention to gender issues, this work will contribute to the ongoing reconstruction of Reformation history and theology and to the investiture of women as respected leaders in their own church and tradition.

PART 1

Options and Visions for Women

CHAPTER 1

Prophets, Visionaries, and Martyrs – Ursula Jost and her Publisher Margarethe Prüss

Introduction – Medieval Women Visionaries

Did the Reformation offer women new possibilities of embracing religious leadership roles and using their theological voice in public, or did it limit women's options? What happened to the women mystics and visionaries of the medieval world? How well did the Protestants' teaching of the priesthood of all believers apply to women? Did Protestant theology and reforms promote spiritual equality and emancipation for all concerned, including the women? The answers are ambiguous.

On the one hand, a seed of radical emancipation was embedded in the reformers' teaching of justification by faith as a gift from God for humans without a merit of their own. The priesthood of all believers would thus seem like a natural expression of – and a foundation for – spiritual equality. The eagerness with which many a woman joined the Protestant believers tells that they heard in the new preaching a promise worth responding to, without perhaps fully comprehending at first what that promise entailed for them as women in particular. On the other hand, there was no collective voice of women and thus no joint recorded "women's opinion" on this, just documents on individual responses. The number of sources from (and on) the Reformation women pale in comparison to those preserved from their medieval foremothers. The apparent disappearance of women writers coincides with the Protestants' dismissal of the mystics, prophets, and saints who in the medieval religious scene had often been important female counterparts to the otherwise exclusively male clergy and school theologians and androcentric religious imagery.

The late medieval context and women's religious roles there offer a revealing mirror to examine how women's situations changed both for better and for worse. These changes can be understood in light of the basically unchanged gender conceptions, societal factors, and new theological emphases. The most important changes in women's lot arise from the new perspectives on spirituality and vocation.

In spite of the tenaciously preserved Pauline teaching about women's silence and submissive roles in the Church, and the institutionally executed rules against women's teaching, preaching, and public roles, there have been individual women in Christian history who have found ways to break the gender rules. Against the regulations limiting women's theological activity and voice, those motivated to do so have succeeded in establishing themselves as teachers and leaders. They have done so as lay persons and as private believers, more often than not "authorized" by specific spiritual convictions and experiences they have purposefully traced back to God's irresistible calling. The Middle Ages especially produced an astonishing number of female visionaries with "divine messages." Because of the public character of their actions and identities, these women stand out as exceptional, and as disobedient to the centuries-old ideals set for Christian women. Transgressors whose actions could be deemed to originate from God's divine action could win forgiveness and even respect, whereas the same latitude was not afforded the women who broke the rules "on their own," without any claimed or manifest supernatural authorization.

Since the earliest days of Christian history, individual women who have espoused the roles of religious leaders and teachers have typically drawn their justification for such "unwomanly" activity from their transforming religious experiences of mystical nature. In the pre-Reformation context in particular such spiritual experiences were far from uncommon. Quite to the contrary, mysticism flourished in medieval Christianity, as an important counterpart to the official, institutionalized religion dominated by the clergy. It is hardly a coincidence that many of the mystics were members of laity and women for whom mysticism offered the only possible platform for teaching and preaching and religious authority.

"In the first part of the sixteenth-century, as in the late Middle Ages, women were sometimes seen as spiritual authorities because of their visionary and prophetic experiences. They based their claim to authority not on office, but on experience, an extraordinary vocation. Such experience often took the form of prophetic visions" (Snyder 1999, 282). Scholarship has established that the

> visions were a socially sanctioned activity that freed a woman from conventional female roles by identifying her as a genuine religious figure. They brought her to the attention of others, giving her a public language she could use to teach and learn. Her visions gave her the strength to grow internally and to change the world, to preach, and to attack injustice and greed, even within the church. Through visions, she could be an exemplar to other women, and out of her own experience, she could lead them to fuller self-development. (Ibid. See also Snyder and Hecht 1996.)

Only few women would write in their own name (for instance, Marguerite Porete, burned at the stake with her book in the early fourteenth century, and Christine de

Pizan, earning her living as a professional writer from the fourteenth to the fifteenth century). A preferred option was for a woman to identify herself – with the desired affirmation of others – as a messenger and a mouthpiece of God. A "documented" supernatural call would supersede human orders. In a parallel order created by God's spirit, women could see visions, prophesy, teach, and publish.

The tradition of mystical and prophetic writing flourished in the Middle Ages. For instance, Hildegard von Bingen and the visionaries from the Helfta Convent (from the twelfth and thirteenth centuries) and Julian of Norwich, Caterina da Siena, and Birgitta of Sweden (from the fourteenth to the fifteenth centuries) earned a following as holy women who had dedicated their lives to a God-given mission (as they perceived it) to deliver divine messages. They attracted a following among the people as well as suspicion from the ecclesial authorities. In their survival and success the advocacy of male authorities, often confessors and scribes, was instrumental, especially in proving the visionaries' orthodoxy and promoting official recognition of their sanctity. Further proofs of the visionary women's exceptional authority as spiritual leaders came from their extraordinary lives and manifestation of "manly" virtues. In many ways the holy women needed to give up their womanhood and self-identity and annihilate their human needs and relations in order to excel in ascetic and contemplative practices, in the process of becoming non-gendered instruments of God whose jealous love was all-consuming. For the women themselves, it appears, this process could mean spiritual emancipation, within the framework of what was esteemed and considered possible for women in terms of religious roles and experiences.

In the high and late Middle Ages, in the climate of a heightened interest in mysticism, there was an upsurge in the number of lay teachers concerned with the spiritual well-being of people and critical of the rise of clerical power and accumulation of problems in the Church. Numbers of lay visionaries, prophets, and mystics offered their visions for reform, often envisioning spiritual and moral reforms for which they would be the starting point; this kind of transformation would later characterize the heart of the Catholic reform in the sixteenth century. Monasteries and convents, which had multiplied by the late Middle Ages, provided a natural environment and stimulus for mystics and visionaries, many of whom became forerunners for the Reformation, both Protestant and Catholic. In the latter, the mystics continued to function in influential roles as spiritual leaders; in the former, the mystics all but disappeared, and with them women prophets and visionaries.

This speaks of shifting priorities in spiritual life, piety, and theology: spiritual experiences and individual bodily and charismatic expressions of religiosity became devalued while the "extra nos" effectiveness of grace in individuals' lives became emphasized. For everyone, male or female, who took part in the Protestant Reformation both the notion and expressions of spirituality underwent a fundamental change. Excluded from the pulpit and public teaching places, women also lost their role as female prophets and mystics in the Protestant church, where their spiritual life was more or less confined to the domestic world. From now on, women would need to find other callings to make their mark in the "new" church.

To sum up: For sixteenth-century Protestants, the pure proclamation of the Word was seen as key to reform. New emphasis was placed on preaching the Word purely, and living it out in one's vocation; the first aspect was open only to men, the second to women as well. Protestant women gained home and "world" as their new holy land, while they became seemingly (to us anyway) imprisoned in this exclusively preached domestic model for women. With the coinciding loss of the convents, women lost the environment that had most essentially supported women's individual spiritual development and mystical activity and nurtured many a visionary writer. Protestant women were to forget prophesying and mystical experiences and instead embrace their domestic holy vocations as spouses, mothers and caretakers of their households. While some women cherished this interpretation of the gospel, others rejected it. Some endeavored to combine both. In the early years of the Reformation, a minority of women managed to continue in the roles of the prophets while also embracing their marital and maternal duties. The story of these "radical" Protestant women intertwines with another tragic story: that of the martyrs – women and men believing and acting against the prevalent norms. As a tribute to those women who died for their faith, many of whom remain nameless, the discussion here begins with those who were most persecuted.

Anabaptists and Martyrs

The Anabaptist prophets experienced a burst of freedom in the early years of the movement, before being confined similarly to their sisters in the mainstream Protestant traditions. They welcomed the Protestant teaching of the goodness of marriage, and some of them also shared the pulpit, so to speak, with their husbands, in the roles of a prophet.

The activity of the spiritually authorized lay teachers continued among the radical reformers. The term "radical" refers to those Protestant groups (formed from approximately the 1520s onwards), of which the Anabaptists were one, that emphasized the independent activity of Holy Spirit in the interpretation of the Scripture and practiced believer's baptism (that is to say, adult baptism as a testimony of one's faith). With the principle of *sola scriptura*, they rejected earthly authority, refused civil and military service and the giving of oaths, in conformity with their apocalyptic teachings. Diverse groups which coalesced around these basic tenets (the Swiss, the South Germans and Austrians, and the North Germans and Dutch) sought separation from the "world" and were persecuted throughout Europe. The 1685 Martyrs Mirror reported that 30 percent of all martyrs were women.

While there were many reasons for the persecutions of the Anabaptists, the issue of spiritual experiences and the work of the Holy Spirit was of central importance in regards to women. Namely it was the spiritual experiences that carved for Anabaptist women a unique place in Protestant history, and which also caused them great peril.

> The identification of this radical "spiritual" emphasis is crucial to the telling of the story of Anabaptist women. Appealing to the Holy Spirit as the central interpretive agent meant that a spirit-filled, illiterate, or semi-literate woman or man would be a truer exegete of Scripture than would a learned professor lacking the Spirit. This spiritual and egalitarian approach to scripture, which emerged in Luther and Zwingli's own movements, opened the door to the participation of women and uneducated commoners in radical and Anabaptist reform. (Snyder and Hecht 1996, 3)

The magisterial Reformers disapproved: their opposition to the radicals was even fiercer than their prohibitions against women's teaching.

Mainstream reformers preached the good news of justification by faith alone with a renewed emphasis on the work of the Word and the two recognized sacraments. Stressing the importance of the responsibilities of all believers, on the one hand, they also upheld the institutional means of grace and the "right call" to the office of the Word, on the other. Thus, even with the agreed upon principle of *sola scriptura* and the exhortation for the laity to read their Bibles, now increasingly available in the vernacular, the reformers remained suspicious of Spirit-filled individuals sharing their spiritual experiences beyond the ordered church structure and its authorized offices. At the heart of the disagreement was the understanding of the work of the Holy Spirit and of what constituted "spiritual." In the case of women, the dangers were only magnified. Anabaptist women engaged in prophetic activity were doubly disruptive of the order in the new church(es) that had no more tolerance for heresy, disobedience, or disruption of order than the Catholic church had in the outset of the Protestant movements. Anabaptists who did not adhere to the accepted forms of faith, whether Catholic or Protestant (primarily the Lutherans and their Augsburg Confession), and who practiced adult (re)baptism in defiance of the imperial law, were in the position of outlaws and were persecuted throughout the Europe.

Mainstream and radical reformers found agreement in one issue in particular: God would want women to remain subject to men, staying in the home as spouses and mothers. Throughout the early years of the movement, Anabaptist women, however, could espouse exceptional opportunities for religious leadership, especially as prophets. As the movement became institutionalized, though, many of the women's early opportunities for visible leadership roles were lost (just as they had been in the early "heretical" movements, such as the Montanists). That scholars disagree on the degree of women's emancipation among the radicals reflects the ambiguous nature of women's history in general and speaks of the complex reality of the gendered norms that affected every movement. In general, it seems, only the work of the Spirit could disrupt the order that regulated gender relations in church and society!

The degree of women's freedom in Anabaptist circles varied from place to place, and from teacher to teacher (for instance, Melchior Hoffman saw the office of a prophet suitable for women, whereas Menno Simons interpreted the Scripture endorsing women's submission), and, generally speaking, the Anabaptists sent an ambivalent message to women: On the one hand, their break with the church institution and their enforcement of subjectivity in religious matters in the early days suggested the liberating effect of the Spirit in individuals' lives and ensuing religious autonomy beyond institutional control. The theology of the egalitarian pouring out of the Spirit and trust in charismatic experiences allowed both lay men and women to assume the role of a prophet, one with religious authority and a public voice. "The 'calling of the Spirit' which provided the foundation for the Anabaptist movement was radically egalitarian and personal, even though it led individuals into a commitment to a community" (Snyder and Hecht 1996, 8). Eventually, however, Anabaptist women would be subjected to the same gender conventions as others, with an expectation to find fulfillment in a patriarchally ordered marriage and household and church.

While at no time was there full equality, in the beginning of the movement several factors allowed Anabaptist women more opportunities to participate in the life of the church than they could in society at large. Throughout their history, women contributed instrumentally in the Anabaptist communities of faith. They even "appointed themselves to places of leadership. No one asked them. They sometimes became apostles, prophetesses, and visionaries. Their messages were unpredictable" (Sprunger 1985, 53). The activities of Elisabeth of Leeuwarden following what she claimed was just such a call by the Spirit of God made her famous. Before being martyred in 1549, she was a known leader and an associate of Menno Simons in the northern Dutch Anabaptist circles. A learned, independent woman praised for her "manly courage" (Joldersma and Grijp 2001), Elisabeth had come from a convent background and bravely assisted in the Anabaptist network, establishing herself as the first known Mennonite deaconess. Other women, like Elisabeth, performed informal proselytism, crafted hymns, hosted Bible readings and sewing circles, and worked actively at a grass-roots level. Some distributed alms and housed itinerant ministers and refugees. They spread the gospel by word of mouth. In all these activities Anabaptist women gave an extraordinary lay witness. For instance, Aeffgen Lystyncx in Amsterdam, a wealthy lay woman, organized conventicles. At Schleiden, two women notably acted as itinerant preachers: Bernhartz Maria of Niederrollesbroich, with ecstatic visions and Maria of Monjou, executed by drowning 1552. A few Swiss Anabaptist women earned fame as prophetesses: Margaritia Hattinger of Zurich and Magdalena Muller, Barbara Murglen, and Frena Bumenin of St Gall. (See Sprunger 1985, 52–7; Snyder and Hecht 1996, 8, 10–11, 14–15, 97–8; Wiesner 1989, 15–17.)

A particularly tragic chapter of Anabaptist history was lived in Münster, where women found themselves in an abusive situation under the totalitarian rule of Jan Mathjis and Jan van Leiden, who promoted polygamy and women's total subjection to their husbands, with a threat of death or imprisonment. The lives and deaths of the martyrs were documented in *The Martyrs Mirror* (by Thieleman Jansz van Braght [1625–64]), also called *The Bloody Theater or Martyrs Mirror of the Defenseless Christians*. It includes information on 278 women, who constituted one third of all the martyrs, who were drowned, burned, strangled, and buried alive for their faith, with or without their husbands (for instance, Anneken Jans and Weynken Claes.) Their gender made the persecuted women exceptionally vulnerable.

> Each individual woman was put in a position of defending herself against a weight of sanctioned authority and theological learning to which she, by virtue of being a woman, was allowed no access. Still, each Anabaptist woman was empowered by the Anabaptist principles of encouraging every believer, female as well as male, to independently search Scriptures and to share their understanding of the truth with others. (Joldersma and Grijp 2001, 27–36 at 27–8)

Women's answers demonstrated their learning and bravery as well as conviction of faith.

Martyrdom was not limited to the Anabaptists. In addition to widespread witch hunts, stories of female martyrs came from all over Europe. Especially bloody periods marked by the French Wars of Religion and the religious strife in England throughout the Tudor and Stuart period produced martyrs on both sides as the religious adherences and policies of the heads of state underwent successive changes. (See Bainton 2001b, 211–29, 159–209) From England, the telling records of trials against Lutheran, Calvinist, or Anabaptist women portray brave women with convictions they were willing to die for. As an example, English gentlewoman Anne Askew was executed in 1546 after being tortured and scrutinized for her reforming views and activities – and in an attempt to secure evidence of heresy against the queen, Katherine Parr, last of Henry VIII's wives, whose own reformist sympathies were unpopular with the powerful bishop of Winchester, Stephen Gardiner. Anne left a detailed recording of her ordeal in her own writing (the first of which dates from 1545), which provides an autobiographical picture, with a description of her gruesome torture, as well a woman's interpretation of several debated theological issues, such as Christ's presence in the Lord's Supper (see Beilin 1996). As another example, the most famous female Protestant martyr in England was the beheaded second wife of Henry VIII: Anne Boleyn's story exemplified tragically the hazards a sixteenth-century woman, even a queen, faced due to her religious choices, gender, and sexuality (see Warnicke 1989). (Her daughter, Elizabeth I, had her own reasons to remain in public as asexual and neutral in religious matters as possible.) Many of the Reformation women in positions of power sought to intervene with the persecutions and save believers from execution. For instance, Marguerite de Navarre and her daughter Jeanne d'Albret, and their friend Renée de France, were famous for their asylums and protection of the Protestants. With a shared attitude against violence, Katharina Schütz Zell and Argula von Grumbach wrote on behalf of religious tolerance and acted in defense of those accused for their beliefs. While women died for their faith just as men did, many women leaders (with the notable exception of Mary Tudor and Catherine de Médicis) seemed more interested in ending the violence practiced in the name of religion than killing for it.

The perspectives provided by the Anabaptist women and the martyrs demonstrate the ambiguity of the Reformation's promise to women. They reveal, once again, the intertwining of politics and religion, with gender factoring in both. Last but not least, their stories provide evidence for the determination, tenacity, and shrewdness with which women took the roles of leadership, witnessing and confessing, even at times when much less was expected of them.

Prophets in Strasbourg and their Publisher Margarethe Prüss

The tolerant free city of Strasbourg, home of Katharina Schütz Zell, was a central place for prophetic activity and for the publication of many radical and lay works (especially between 1522 and 1534). Many of the city's women were married to Anabaptists or Spiritualists (men and women together accounting for 10 percent of the population). Some of them became known as prophets and were associated with a visiting Anabaptist Melchior Hoffman (1529), who assisted in the publication of the prophetic works he respected. Among the most influential of the illiterate female prophets were Ursula Jost and Barbara Rebstock, the wife of a weaver, who served as an "elder of Israel" in her Anabaptist congregation. Both were close associates of Hoffman and were influenced by Hans Hut. Their visions, filled with zeal and biblical references, were published by Melchior Hoffman and a brave female publisher Margarethe Prüss, one of the most daring and productive publishers in Strasbourg. The daughter of a printer, wife of two printers, and a printer on her own, she was neither a prophet nor a teacher herself, but became instrumental in publishing the prophets' works. Her third marriage to an Anabaptist may, like her decision to publish "forbidden" or potentially scandalous works, reveals her religious sympathies, given the persecuted status of the Anabaptists. (See Chrisman 1972, 159–160 on her role as a publisher in the reformation in Strasbourg.)

In 1510 her father, Johann Prüss, died and she inherited his print shop, which had been in operation since 1504. She then married (1511–22) Reinhard Beck, who became co-owner of the "Prüss-Beck" print shop. Whereas her father had printed Catholic works, Marguerite and Reinhard chose to print reformation materials, such as Martin Luther's and Andreas Bodenstein von Karlstadt's works, along with classical and humanist works in both Latin and German. Limits set by the town guild limited the period for which a woman could operate a business alone, and so, after Reinhard's death, Marguerite's business activities were threatened. She managed to establish another print shop, which she operated alone until she hired Wolfgang Foter, who would become her son-in-law, and then in 1524 she married Johann Schwann of Marburg (an ex-Franciscan), with whom she continued to publish reformation materials until his death in 1526. In May 1527 she married for the third time, this time to a known Anabaptist, Balthasar Beck.

In the 1530s, risking (and in the Balthasar's case suffering) arrest and financial hazards, the Prüss-Beck press published the works of Anabaptists and Spiritualists, including those of Ursula Jost, Sebastian Franck, and Melchior Hoffman, among others considered radical either because of their content or their author. (For instance, they published Katharina Schütz Zell's hymnbook based on Michael Weisse's songbook from Bohemia.)

> Margarethe clearly was aware of the ideological bent of the books being produced by her press. In fact, it appears that Margarethe's choice of husband/printers was coloured by her commitment to the continued printing of radical materials. This woman pragmatically contributed to the movement of the early Anabaptists, and radical reform generally, in the best way available to her in her context." (Snyder and Hecht 1996, 259)

She passed her shop and legacy in equal shares to her eight children, her wishes signed in a will dated May 23, 1542. The choices made by the four children about whom we have some knowledge give a poignant depiction of the religious choices and career options available at the time: her son Reinhard became a printer in Basel, her daughter Juliane joined a Catholic convent, her daughter Ursula married a printer (the same Wolfgang Foter hired by her mother), and her daughter Margarethe married the Spiritualist, Sebastian Franck. (Chrisman 1982, 29–30, 151–69; Snyder and Hecht 1996, 265–70)

In conclusion,

> Key to Margarethe's story was her decision to marry printers that enabled her to continue in this line of work and to retain some measure of control of the Prüss family printing business. She utilized the best means available to her as a woman of her time. Margarethe exercised control over the materials published in her printshop through her choice of husbands.

She married only people in favor of the Protestants and published works accordingly, increasingly radical works, which serves as convincing evidence of her Anabaptist leanings. "As a printshop owner and a woman, Margarethe overcame the limits of the role assigned to women by sixteenth-century culture and as a result, made a significant contribution to the early Anabaptist movement far beyond the city of Strasbourg." (Snyder and Hecht 1996, 270) Her courage and significance and that of other similar printers cannot be over-estimated. Their significance "lay in their control of the printed word. Ultimately their decision to print or not to print a particular book or tract could have an immediate effect on political and religious events and, in a time of rapid change, on institutions." In other words, "printers helped to determine the course of events." (Chrisman 1982, 29, 30.) They were instrumental in opening a forum for lay teachers such as Ursula Jost. Ursula provides a connection to the strong tradition of spiritually authorized women teachers and mystics. She also embodies what was lost, for women and men, with the mainstream Protestants disapproval of the mystics and prophets.

Prophet Ursula Jost and her Visions

A lay woman assuming the office of a prophet, Ursula continued the long tradition of mystics and prophets who had thrived in the Middle Ages. She embodied a challenge to the Reformers' opinion about the office of preaching belonging only to men, and their lack of respect for mystical religious experiences. Ursula unabashedly assumed a position of spiritual leadership and openly spoke of her desire for visions: "After my husband and spouse was released from custody and was let go, he and I together prayed earnestly and diligently to God, the almighty merciful Father, that he would let me also see the wondrous deeds of his hand" (Snyder and Hecht 1996, 282). She wished to be a prophet, and she became one through her encounter with the Spirit, her source of authority. She prophesied from the beginning of 1524, most actively during the bloody period of Anabaptist history and widespread persecutions. Against all the odds, the Anabaptist female prophet who could have faced martyrdom, apparently died a natural death – as did her publisher, Margarethe. (See Snyder and Hecht 1996 for the core information on both women.)

Certain pieces of information are available: we know Ursula lived and prophesied in the early 1500s; that she lived with her husband Lienhard Jost in the Krutena neighborhood of Strasbourg; that he was imprisoned in 1524; that her own visions were published in 1530; and that her daughter married in 1543. However, there is little to flesh out these facts, and Ursula's own birth and death dates and her family background remain unclear.

Lienhard Jost, a butcher by trade, came from the village of Illkirch, south of Strasbourg and was engaged in prophetic activity in the early days of the Reformation in Germany. Because of his prophecies, Lienhard was imprisoned in a hospital; he was released in 1524, the year in which he had already married Ursula. When exactly they became involved with the Anabaptists and their practice of rebaptism is not clear, but Ursula's prophetic activity began following her husband's release. She documented her visions, but did not publish them until 1530, after which date information on her becomes even sparser. From 1537 onwards the name "Agnes" appears in the Anabaptists' records in association with Ursula's husband, and by 1539 she was known as Lienhard's wife. Unless we are to suppose the possibility of divorce or bigamy (neither of which are plausible as divorce on any grounds other than adultery has never been permissible in the Anabaptist church and sexual attitudes in general seem to have been in keeping with contemporary society), Ursula must have died somewhere before 1539, the year the records mention Lienhard's new wife.

Of her 77 preserved visions, she received 58 during the Peasants' War of 1525, whereas in the following three-year period of peace she recorded only one. Her final 18 visions were recorded in 1529, during famine and the persecution of the Anabaptists. By that time, Ursula, her husband Lienhard, and a fellow prophetess, Barbara Rebstock, had established themselves as the "Strasbourg Prophets," with a considerable following. She had also become associated with Melchior Hoffman, one of the fathers of Anabaptism, who had visited Strasbourg in 1529 and met the three prophets.

Hoffmann, a lay preacher exiled for preaching apocalyptic sermons and doing so without an appropriate preparation or calling (according to Luther), resonated well with the other dissidents in Strasbourg, a city tolerant of diverse expressions of faith not in concurrence with the mainstream reformers whose citizens were not interested in killing people for their religion. Strasbourg saw only a few executions take place, and the exile of some individuals. (Writers like Katharina Schütz Zell who applied the principle of tolerance in a time when such concepts were quite foreign had considerable influence in the matter). It was hardly a coincidence that charismatic lay leaders found a home in the city (which, with its heterogeneous population, came to define a unique place in relation to the institutionalized Reformation in Germany and Switzerland). Nowhere else could prophets like Ursula have lasted so long. (See Chrisman 1982.)

Melchior Hoffman's interest in Ursula's visions was pivotal. They impressed him sufficiently for him to lend his support to their publication. The first book was ready in 1530 (with a reprint in 1532), the year of the Augsburg Confession (1530) – the Lutherans' first official joint defense of their faith. In the aftermath of its rejection by the Catholic church and the Holy Roman Emperor, Protestants had no theoretical or legal freedom to express their faith but were expected to return to the Catholicism. Only in 1555 would Protestants, and, even then, only those adhering to the German Lutherans' Augsburg Confession, gain approval for their faith within the bounds of the Holy Roman Empire. Ursula was neither Lutheran nor Catholic; she was an outsider to both. Besides, she was in a compromising position on many accounts: she produced prophetic literature as a lay person, she published her unauthorized visions, she adhered to the publicly rejected Anabaptist theology, and she exerted teaching authority as a woman. Again, this could happen in Strasbourg, where the publication of dissident works coincided the years of Ursula's activity (1524–34). Her visions, her role in the circle of the prophets, and her alliance with Hoffman soon made Ursula famous and an attraction in town.

The first record of Ursula's book dates from April 23, 1530, when Hoffman was accused of having published a woman's visions and was arrested, with Margarethe Prüss's husband Balthasar Beck. Later Ursula's name was mentioned in the introduction to Hoffman's 1532 publication that included a vision (her 22nd) which was attributed to the "prophetess Ursula." Ursula's publication was one of the 14 Anabaptist writings that were sent to the Strasbourg city council in 1537 as a warning of possible uprisings against the church and the pope.

Regardless of unresolved questions about the origins and nature of Ursula's, or any prophet's, visions, they can be appreciated for what Ursula herself wanted to convey with them. The nature of her visions, whether they were conscious or unconscious fabrications of her creative imagination, or hallucinations, or dreams, or revelations of a mystical nature, is less important than discerning their importance to Ursula herself and the people around her, and the window they give to a particular religious context.

The first thing to consider in this respect is that, unlike most of the medieval visionaries, Ursula frankly admitted that she wanted to have visions, and that her prophetic call did not just fall upon her but that she actively sought it. Her visions were not unsolicited, unwanted, or involuntary, and this is where she stands apart from the model of medieval women mystics who often made a point of stating that they were operating under involuntary divine force. Ursula wanted her visions, as she explained in her introduction:

> After my husband and spouse was released from custody and was let go, he and I together prayed earnestly and diligently to God, the almighty merciful Father, that he would let me also see the wondrous deeds of his hand. God's grace and kindness granted this to us, and these visions written down here all appeared to me. I saw all these visions and wonders in the glory of the lord, which always unfolded itself before me. And in it I received knowledge of the meaning of these visions of divine wonders. After that it always came together again and went away and disappeared. (Ursula Jost in Snyder and Hecht 1996, 282)

Her first vision from 1524 reports, "And I saw first that the glory of the Lord came upon me and unfolded and showed itself in such bright splendor that I could not recognize the shape because of the brightness of the glory of the Lord. After that, this same splendor of the Lord became a beautiful wreath above me" (Ursula Jost in Snyder and Hecht 1996, 283). From her own account, she received visions at different times of the day and night, sometimes waking up from sleep, but always in a state of consciousness. She was given an understanding of the meaning of the visions she felt originated from God, which was her primary concern. For a woman, prophecies coming from God offered the best possibility for public teaching and preaching. It remains unclear exactly why Ursula wanted her visions, whether it was for the sake of an experience of God or for the opportunity of teaching.

The second point to consider in respect of the importance of the visions to Ursula and the community in which she was active is that the dark, apocalyptic imagery in her visions echoed the actual context of real danger, whether the enemy was war or famine or persecution. For instance, "On the Sunday after mid-Lent, 1525, I saw in the glory of the Lord that water and fire fell down from heaven" (31st vision, Ursula Jost in Snyder 1999, 284). Images of war, clouds dripping with blood, rainbows, wreaths, toads, snakes, bishops, knights, and virgins filled the visions that conveyed a theological perspective shaped by her vision of the two kingdoms: the kingdom of good and the kingdom of evil in a cosmic battle with one another. The visions of the two kingdoms, with corresponding imagery, portrayed a wrathful but patient God ready to judge the wicked, but also to offer salvation to the faithful elect who would endure their suffering. Ursula's vision wished to convey that God was in control and God's children would endure (Snyder and Hecht 1996, 277–8).

Ursula's visions elaborated on the scriptural verses, especially from the Book of Revelation, and on biblical themes of judgment, repentance, salvation, damnation, and the resurrection of the dead. For instance, she envisioned God shooting burning arrows (38th vision); the Savior leading people in triumph yet chastising them (35th vision); headless men and animals running into each other in panic (52nd vision); rivers of blood filling the sky (67th vision); corpses floating in the waters (19th vision); water, fire, pitch, and brimstone raining down from heaven and burning men (32nd vision); the "great city" being destroyed by wind (51st vision); a bishop with a deformed head being pushed into a dark lake (21st vision); the pope with a rope around his neck, being dragged into the darkness (41st vision); Ursula trying to sprinkle blood on the dead to raise them, but the knights interfering, the invading Turks serving as God's tools (74th vision); a mother with a child, a mother turning into a bird (10th and 13th visions); a large poisonous spider on a branch of a tree (47th vision); and children climbing up and down a sunbeam (49th, 5th, and 76th visions) (see Deppermann 1987, 207–9; Snyder and Hecht 1996, 282–4).

Interpretation of these cryptic visions would be difficult, and something Ursula did not attempt to do in writing (at least, there are no such texts extant). There is no record of her offering an interpretation orally either. Given the context, and the popularity of her prophecies, Ursula's visions as such obviously offered "meanings" to her contemporaries as a visualization of the threats and dangers of life as they knew it and as tools to imagine hope from the God.

Conclusion

What makes Ursula so interesting among the Reformation women is the very fact that made her memory lasting – her prophecies. She continued the genre and office of the medieval visionaries, such as Birgitta of Sweden, who preached with spiritual authority drawing from experiences that evaded empirical explanations. Ursula, like Birgitta and Caterina da Siena and other prophets in the history of Christianity, witnessed a strong personal faith and determined conviction of her call to be a messenger of divine wisdom. The urgency of the situation coinciding with the personal calling and, as the prophets experienced it, the mysterious empowerment of the Spirit, put women like Ursula in a category of their own. The prophet Ursula represented the kind of a woman the mainstream Protestant leaders did not welcome in their midst and did not condone as a model for other women.

Ursula stood as if between two worlds – the medieval religious world that appreciated visions and personal spiritual experiences, on the one hand, and the early modern Church that shifted the emphasis from individuals' spiritual life and experiences to the external work of the Word that did not need to be "experienced," on the other. With the loss of the appreciation of spiritual experiences, and thus of mystics and prophets, the Protestant laity, women in particular, lost a central means for teaching, preaching and theological influence beyond the domestic sphere. (It is to underscore the importance of this that the story of Ursula is placed here at the beginning of the book.)

In fine, Ursula and her publisher Margarethe Prüss were instrumental in the spreading of the radical Protestant views and had a wide ranging impact on the lives of individuals beyond their own locale. These two women, like the numerous martyrs who paid with their lives for a faith commitment that clashed with the majority views, presented a brave model of confessing and of putting one's faith into practice. They were passionate about their own faith and their fellow human beings' spiritual well being, and thus took huge risks in their public confession – all qualities that were venerated in the ensuing Protestant "hagiographies," books commemorating the heroic Christians and defenders of the evangelical faith. Sadly, the mainstream Protestants failed to honor those confessing a faith different from theirs, but rather added to the pool of martyrs with their own intolerance and their fear of losing control.

CHAPTER 2

The Monastic Option – The Struggle of the Convents

Introduction – The Drama of Closing the Convents

One of Luther's most radical reform ideas was his eventual rejection of the celibate monastic life and his sanctification of marriage as an equally important, if not better, religious call. The closing of convents and monasteries was one of the first and most visible institutional changes with the Reformation in most cities, whether it came as a swiftly enforced change or a slower process completed through attrition. Given that a significant percentage of the European female population had been living in convents, in which all-female communities they had experienced the only opportunity for women of a life centered around religious practice, and which were an important alternative to the general path of marriage and motherhood, the Protestants' preaching against celibacy and convent life had immediate ideological and practical consequences in women's lives.

Whereas ex-monks, if converting, could become pastors in the Protestant church, ex-nuns had few other options but to marry, unless they wished to continue their convent life in another, Catholic territory. Out of their convent, unmarried full-time religious women had no established place in society or in the emerging new church life. They had to find both a new calling and a new home. In addition, the closing of the convents stripped women of the opportunities their all-female environments allowed them of higher education and self-expression, as well as of many cherished rituals and ceremonial roles. Coinciding with the dismissal of beloved female figures in religious practice and piety, such as the Virgin Mary and the female saints, the deletion of the offices of nuns and powerful abbesses meant the disappearance of recognizable examples for women's religious leadership and spiritual roles and deeply felt changes in spiritual life. In other words, "the loss of saints affected men and women unequally. Reformed prayer could no longer be addressed to a woman, whereas the masculine identity of the Father and Son was left intact. It may seem anachronistic to raise the matter of sexual identity in religious images during the Reformation, but it is not." "So, if the removal from Holy Mother Church cut off certain forms of religious affect for men, for women the consequences for their identities went even deeper." (Davis 1975a, 88, also 86–9) It is hardly a coincidence that proportionately more of the male religious converted and willingly left their celibate callings than did women (as, for instance, in France), whose concerns failed to be on the radar screens of the male preachers of the reforms: "Indeed, sermons on clerical marriage stressed how the groom would now be saved from fornication and hellfire but said little of the soul of the bride." (Davis 1975a, 89, 88)

Both collective and individual experiences of power and independence for women in the religious realm diminished with the loss of convents and related traditions, with ensuing wide-ranging ramifications for women's self-understanding and spirituality. Women's mixed responses to the Reformation's promises where thus most poignant in the reactions of the convent women. (See Blaisdell 1999, 160; Douglass 1974, 303–9.)

Women who had been placed in convents by their families and who had no particular religious calling to such a lifestyle responded to the Reformers' call differently from those who had theological and spiritual reasons to live as the bride of Christ apart from the "world." "The Protestant championing of marriage and family life, which some nuns accepted with great enthusiasm as a message of liberation from the convent, was viewed by others as a negation of the value of the life they had been living; they thus did all in their power to continue in their chosen path" (Wiesner 2000a, 231, also 228–31). The drama of closing the convents, dispersing their inhabitants, and confiscating the monasteries' assets caused pain on the individual and institutional levels. Hundreds of years of tradition and conviction did not change over night, nor was it easy to replace the centuries-old monastic institution, no matter how enthusiastically the Reformers preached the "gospel" of liberation from the bonds of celibacy and papal-led religiosity.

An Excursion – Monastic Calling

Monasteries had had a central role in medieval society: whereas knights and queens fought and reigned and peasants labored, the important task for monks and nuns was to pray and uphold the Christian virtues, for the protection of the whole Christian community and their birth families. Convents also served as boarding schools and safe places for the daughters of nobility, as much as they provided a context for intellectual and scholarly activity and work with texts (particularly their production and preservation). Much of medieval theology and religious writing can be traced back to the monastics.

For centuries, the monastic option represented the very ideal of Christian perfection as the highest religious path beyond the reach of most citizens. The monastic ideal of

Christian perfection has its roots in the persistent ascetic impulse in Christian faith, enhanced by the historically tense relationship between Church and state. For the early Christians, to follow Jesus and prepare the way for the Kingdom of God on earth had meant difficult choices and leaving the "world" as they had known it; many of them suffered persecution. As time passed and the anticipated second coming of Jesus was "delayed," and as, under the Emperor Constantine in the fourth century, Christianity became accepted as the state religion of the Roman Empire, institutionalized Christian piety mellowed, while the ascetic ideals remained. While the institutionalization of a church helped preserve the Jesus tradition, concerns that the original radicality of Christian ideals would be lost were themselves manifested in various ascetic models and reforming voices.

Monastic orders were typically built around a vision for spiritual perfection held by individuals and groups concerned with both personal and Church reform. Believers fired with the passion for the "original" and pure way of Christian life typically left their homes, possessions, family, and freedom in the world for a godly, ordered life. They inspired others and commonly formed religious communities built on agreed upon principles of worldly personal denial aimed at both imitating and attaining a perfected spiritual state. These principles were usually if not ubiquitously formulated as vows, typically encompassing obedience, poverty, chastity, and humility. In the sixth-century St Benedict established an order whose rule laid a foundation for several later orders, some of the most popular ones being the Cistercians, Franciscans, and Dominicans in the High Middle Ages. Through the centuries the reform movements led to mushrooming of new orders for both women and men. While some orders had always been solely for men, others had welcomed women in associated houses or had even been established as double orders. Most of those which had at first rejected women would subsequently go through modifications to include both sexes in separate establishments. Only a few orders were created especially for women (particularly after the Fourth Lateran Council in 1215 and its ruling against new orders: prominent as an example of female conventual life originating from after the Council is the order established by St Birgitta of Sweden in the fourteenth century. Birgitta intended the order to follow the Regula S. Salvatoris, which, quite exceptionally for a woman, she herself had written – at Christ's dictation, she claimed. The rule was meant specifically for women – in honor of Christ's mother Mary – and invested remarkable power in the abbess as the head of the convent. Still, it accepted men in specific roles, and was approved after a long battle only as a modified rule of St Augustine, being based upon the loose principles for religious life provided in the Church Father's letter of spiritual guidance.

Monasteries made a significant contribution to intellectual life and theology in the West. Throughout the Middle Ages they served as centers for higher education, theological work, and the preservation of theological sources. In addition to the labor of writing theological treatises, biblical commentaries, devotional writings, and copying and preserving documents monasteries fostered spirituality and produced some of the most important teachers and leaders in the Church (Martin Luther, Thomas Aquinas, Bernard de Clairvaux, Meister Eckhart, St Caterina da Siena, St Birgitta of Sweden, St Teresa de Ávila, and Hildegard von Bingen).

Since the time of the Desert Mothers and the famous sister of the Great Cappadocians, Macrina, monastic life has drawn men and women equally, and in the Middle Ages different possibilities for that life emerged. Women could, for instance, choose to live as free beguines (from the late twelfth to early thirteenth centuries onwards): single women who, without taking a vow, without belonging to an order, cohabited and studied theology together and supported themselves with labor. This option was met with suspicion by the Church, which preferred to control women's religiosity, as it did in the lives of cloistered nuns. Women could also choose to live as lay women affiliated with a cloister (as, for instance, did the Dominican penitent women in Italy) or in a freer communal arrangement for religious unmarried women (for example, the Devotio Moderna), as anchoresses living in a cell attached to a church (like Julian of Norwich) – or they could attempt to live a celibate life within marriage (Birgitta of Sweden, Margery Kempe, Angela da Foligno, each doing so after giving birth to several children). Most often religious women were associated with male orders, with modifications to the rule, and in strict cloistering, separated from the world (a model that would be reenforced in the Council of Trent [1545–63]). An appealing option for women was to join one of the canoness houses, which allowed women relative freedom and required a less austere lifestyle. As entry to these esteemed women's religious houses typically required some degree of family assets, the canoness houses typically hosted daughters of nobility and could become independently wealthy and powerful (see, for instance, the Cistercian convent of Helfta).

Of all the religious arrangements for women, the canoness houses were the most independent institutions. Their powerful abbesses exercised considerable authority over a number of people and over property, and fulfilled both administrative and spiritual leadership roles, exerting power typically held by a small group of elite men. These were the women who were most subject to target in ecclesiastical efforts to keep religious women under male supervision. They were also the ones who rebelled the loudest – or who found creative ways to transform their institutions – in the face of the sixteenth-century reformations. "Long traditions of power, independence, and prestige combined with a reinvigorated spiritual life to make reformed convents and canoness houses the most vocal and resolute opponents of the Protestant Reformation." (Wiesner-Hanks 1996, 16, 14; see idem 2000, 228–31.)

Nuns' Fight for Freedom

The strongest female protest against the Reformation in Germany came from the convents where women were used to expressing themselves on religious matters and thinking of themselves as members of a spiritual group. Thus, although the Protestant reformers did champion a woman's role as wife and mother by closing the convents and forbidding female lay confraternities, they cut off women's opportunities for expressing their spirituality in an all-female context. (Wiesner 1989, 26)

The limited opportunities for education and cultivation of the mind provided another reason for the convents' resistance to the Reformation: the universities that had started to replace monasteries as intellectual centers were not open to women, and so for this too women fought to protect the convents. Convent life had offered opportunities for creativity, self-expression, writing, and leadership that were not easily available other-wise. Those convents that housed the daughters of noble families were especially bold in defending their rights – much was at stake for noble families with financial investments in the convents and interest in preserving these "safe" and convenient homes for their unwed or widowed daughters. It is not a coincidence that some of the canoness houses revolted successfully and with more determination against the reformers' closing efforts than did their male counterparts. Everything from burning slippers and blocking doors to refusing to listen to their Protestant visitors and offering vocal resistance was used to avoid forced conversions and deportations. Creatively, some convents accepted Lutheran theology while continuing their communal life and eventually converted their convents into educational institutions. (Wiesner-Hanks 1996, 14–16; Lowe 2003, 397)

Convent women's responses and fates were varied, though. While some were forced to leave, others left out of their own free choice. Many of the nuns, like Katharina von Bora and Marie Dentière, eagerly left their cells for the new life, and most of those who did quickly married. Many found a new calling as new Protestant pastors' wives. Yet others, like Caritas Pirckheimer, Katherine Rem, and Jeanne de Jussie, fought for their right to continue their conventual life. While some women opposed the Reformation on theological grounds, certain convents with a healthy endowment that drew the majority of their sisters from noble families resisted for other reasons as well, fighting for their individual and communal independence. In rare cases, women strove to combine the best of both options by embracing the new theology, maintaining as much as possible the forms of the convent lifestyle, and turning their convent into an educational institution for women. For instance, a free imperial convent in Quedlinburg, under the leadership of its powerful abbess Anna von Stolberg, who supervised nine churches and two monasteries, accepted the Augsburg Confession in the 1540s and became an elementary school for girls and boys. Another independent abbess would follow later, Anna Sophia von Quedlinburg, who defended her convent life style's compatibility with her Lutheranism in writing. A few other brave abbesses took the same route. Protestant nuns and canonesses faced a difficult path, as did the sisters who desired release from their vows in areas not in favor of the Protestant reforms. While it is hard yet to evaluate the full picture, the evidence from particular contexts such as Brunswick-Lüneburg, where 14 convents adopted Protestantism and survived into the nineteenth century, laying the foundations for modern-day women's institutions, is quite telling. (See Blaisdell 1999, 148–9, 156–9; Wiesner-Hanks 1996, 17–18, 22; Wiesner 1989, 9–11; for a case study on the slow closing of convents in Strasbourg, see Chrisman 1972, 163–6.)

The, at times, tense relations between the women on different sides of the convent walls reveal a further dimension to the Reformation battle and provide yet another insight into women's concerns. For instance, a particularly interesting conflict took place in Geneva where a Protestant ex-abbess, Marie Dentière, audaciously led a delegation to convert the convent of Poor Clares by force and was met by equally stern resistance under the leadership of Jeanne de Jussie, whose resistance was so strong she was only removed by force.

Between 1535 and 1547 Jeanne, a nun and later perhaps abbess of the Order of St Clare in Geneva, wrote a revealing chronicle, *The Leaven of Calvinism,* or *The Beginning of the Heresy of Geneva.* In this text, which was hidden until its publication in 1611, she gave her interpretation of the violent attacks of the Protestants, who were trying to pour "venom" on "poor nuns." She reported stories of Protestant women offending the Catholics by doing laundry or handwork during religious celebrations; she knew, she said, of a Lutheran woman being hit on the head in a tussle. Although she refused a public disputation on the issue of monastic life on the basis that this was unsuitable to her sex, she acted with irreverent disregard to the rules regarding women's behavior in her vocal advocacy of the monastic life.

> Our glance at the Reformation as seen by Sister Jeanne gives evidence that Protestant preaching in praise of marriage seemed to unsympathetic contemporaries to be of considerable importance in the new faith and a radical departure from the tradition. We also see that though the Protestants talked of "freedom" to the nuns they were perceived as bringing a new form of constraint, a constraint to marry and be subject to husbands. Furthermore, Sister Jeanne's journal helps to confirm our impression that women played a more active role in bringing about the Reformation than usually has been assumed. (Douglass 1985, 101, see also 98–105)

(See Åkerlund 2003, 106–9, 117–19; Douglass 1974, 310–13)

Extant texts from several women who wished to explain their decision either to defend or to leave their convent lives provide precious insights into the battle and the issues at stake. Their writings demonstrate how women made deliberate decisions about their religion, independently and bravely. Some of the printed apologies were anonymous, others indentify the author. Both Catholics and Protestants used these testimonies as propaganda – for instance, the letter written by Katherine Rem defending her convent life and Ursula von Münsterberg's articulations of her reasons for leaving were both published and circulated with poignant forewords. (See Jung 2002, 41–75.) Various abbesses, such as Elizabeth Gottgabs in Obervesel who published a tract against Luther, mounted valiant battles.

Caritas Pirckheimer, sister of the famous humanist Willibald Pirckheimer and an accomplished Latinist and abbess (from 1503), not only defended her own right to continue in monastic calling in the Poor Clares, but was also successful in securing the safe existence of her convent through the turbulent years of Reformation. She defended the nuns of the Klarakloster and herself in a published text describing the atrocities committed by the Protestants (for instance, by interrupting the delivery of basic supplies, depriving the nuns of the sacraments, physically assaulting them, and intruding into the convent). In her response to the ultimatum of June 7, 1525 which demanded the release of the nuns from their vows, she stated that the vows were not made for her but God, and thus she could not release anyone. She invited an audience to witness the drama as mothers forcefully dragged their daughters out of the convent (see Barker 1995).

Caritas' words are illustrative:

> But when I called them in and told them that their mothers wanted to take them away this very hour, they all three fell to the floor screaming, weeping, and howling and exhibited such woeful behavior, that may God in heaven have pity . . . Likewise, the entire convent wept and wailed, because these were pious and clever children who remained with us willingly and in heart and soul did not want to leave us.

Furthermore,

> the wild wolves and she-wolves came among my beloved little sheep, entered the church, pushed all the people outside, and bolted the church shut, and I unfortunately had to open

up the convent door to the chapel . . . Then they wanted me to forcefully order the children to come out on their own, which I also refused to do. (Caritas Pirckheimer in Bryant 1987)

Caritas points out that "afterward they never spoke ill of the convent, rather, on the contrary, when given the occasion, they said the best of us, and bore within the great yearning and desire to return to the cloister" (ibid., 301).

The impressive resistance of this particular convent impelled Philipp Melanchthon himself to come and evaluate the situation. He actually agreed with Caritas's reasoning that choosing a monastic life was acceptable while not necessary – he disagreed on the binding nature of the vows, though. True to his peaceful nature, Melanchthon did not approve of the violence that had developed. In the end, both sides won: St Klarakloster was allowed to remain open until the last nun died – which was to happen in 1590 – but could not accept new sisters. The community could not attend Mass, receive the Catholic sacraments, or make confession. (Bryant 1987, 292, 287–92; Jung 2002, 44–9, 77–120.)

Another testimony came from Katherine Rem, who wrote to her brother Bernardus defending her decision to stay in her convent. With discernable irritation she wished to demonstrate her informed and well-reasoned decision to stay. "I certainly know that you have said that your daughter and I are to you more as if we were in a brothel than in a convent . . ." (Katharina Rem in Wiesner-Hanks 1996, 29). "It would be better if you mulled this over. You are a good fellow and happy. You have shocked us because you actually wanted to come to us. If you don't come in kinship, stay out. If you want to straighten us out, then we don't want your [message] at all. You may not send us such things any more. We will not accept them. We also [already] have many good books" (ibid., 31). Furthermore, she wrote, "you should not think that we are so foolish that we place our hope in the convent and in our own works. Rather we place our hope in God" (ibid., 29). She insulted her brother, calling him a false prophet. She had reflected on her theology and her response to the reformers' theologies and had concluded accordingly. Based on her reading of Scripture and her theological reasoning, she was better off in her convent. (On Katharina and Veronika see Wiesner-Hanks 1996, 49–51, 22; Jung 2002, 51–3.)

An opposing testimony came from a noblewoman in Saxony: Lady Ursula von Münsterberg (c.1491–c.1534) wrote about her reasons for leaving her convent in correspondence with her cousins the Saxon dukes George (the Bearded) and Heinrich the Pious (his successor), and the elector of Saxony, Johann Der Beständige (the Steadfast). This originally private correspondence between family members for and against Ursula's decision to escape came to provide juicy propaganda material for the Protestant reformers. A granddaughter of King George von Podiebrad of Bohemia and his wife Johanna von Rosenthal, Ursula had lived in the convent of Mary Magdalene the Penitent after her parents' death and there became influenced by Luther's teachings. His message had reached the convent in particular as the result of preaching: two chaplains preaching Lutheran doctrine had been assigned to the sisters, one apparently upon the request of Ursula, and neither had been appointed with the approval of the Catholic Duke George; his younger brother Heinrich, who had control over the town of Freiberg and the convent, was behind this with his Lutheran wife Katherine. (To no one's surprise, after succeeding George, the couple moved on to implement the Lutheran faith in their land.)

On October 6, 1528 Ursula escaped the convent and fled to Wittenberg. Writing about her experience, she stated that she did not come to her decision lightly but through deliberation and suffering over (at least) two years. "I have written this work with my own hand, out of my heart . . . Through this [work], your graces will discover that this has not happened out of thoughtlessness, but because I am accountable to the judgment of God for my soul" (Ursula von Münsterberg in Wiesner-Hanks 1996, 41). She assured her reader that "this has not happened from a foolhardy disposition nor from hasty spontaneity, but that everything has been considered and well thought out. The confidence is in each one who is informed and taught by God, through the divine grace of faith" (ibid., 43). She quoted texts from the New Testament as "reasons for our leaving" (Mark 16:5, 16; John 3:16, 14:16).

In her writing Ursula addressed the differences between baptism and monastic call, her understanding of grace as a gift and of justification by faith in contrast to the monastic expectations. She asserted her Lutheran faith and shared her experience of spiritual turmoil: "You see that our salvation rests only on faith. Our consciences have been greatly troubled and our flesh corrupted . . . Who can withstand God's wrath?" Her solution to her dilemma was a newly defined call as bride of Christ: "We are married to Christ and to seek to be saved through another is adultery. The three monastic vows are the work of men's hands. There is only one way to relieve our consciences and that is to make a clean break. We have suffered such torments of spirit that we could no longer hold on." She signed her writing about her "Babylonian captivity" as a testimony of faith and praise of God. Her motivation for writing was not only her own defense but her concern for her fellow sisters in danger of dying without certainty about their salvation but attaching their hopes to merely human conventions. So useful did the tract become in the propaganda war that it was circulated with Luther's preface (WA XXVI, 623ff. in Ursula von Münsterberg in Bainton 2001a, 51–2, also 45–53. See Wiesner-Hanks 1996, 39–63, 12–18.)

The very fact that so many of the women's texts, Catholic and Protestant, came from the convent women proves the importance of the monastic tradition in providing manuscripts, skills for literary activity, and a nurturing environment for theological reflection. Convent ladies, often from patrician and noble families, were as a rule more educated and theologically sophisticated than the majority of their lay sisters. Convents had fostered women's intellectual pursuits and writing more than any other institution at the time and (especially in urban centers) had provided an "intellectual space" and opportunities unavailable to women elsewhere. In other words, nuns had made many sacrifices for their calling, but gained in return opportunities to develop in areas beyond the reach of married women whose time and energy were consumed by their family and household tasks. It was not at all self-evident that the majority of convent women would eagerly give up what they had for the in their eyes questionable pleasures of marriage with all its dangers, including childbirth mortality and abusive husbands – and yet that was for all practical purposes the only alternative offered by the Protestant reformers. (See Lowe 2003, 263–396.)

Conclusion

On the one hand it can be argued, in Douglass's words, that

The only 'women's liberation' of interest to the sixteenth-century Reformation was the elimination of the monastic view of women, sex, and marriage . . . Protestants wanted to give monks and nuns as well as laymen the freedom to take up their Christian vocation in the world by providing a new theological understanding of life as well as an opportunity to leave the convent. But we see in Sister Jeanne's account that though the protestants talked of 'freedom,' to the nuns they seemed to bring a new sort of constraints, a constraint to marry and be subject to husbands. (Douglass 1974, 314)

On the other hand, as she continues, however, "the protestant doctrines of Christian vocation and the priesthood of all believers, along with a new view of marriage, did in fact tend to change the image and role of women in the direction of greater personal freedom and responsibility, both immediately and over the centuries" (ibid.)

If the Protestant reformers wanted to liberate women from convents to live sacred lives in the "world," the Catholic reformers reaffirmed the ideal of women living in cloistered environments in pursuit of religious calls. On the Catholic front, the convent tradition remained strong with the force of such new religious orders as the Society of Jesus (the Jesuits) and the renewal of existing orders, such as that of St Theresa de Ávila, the Carmelites. The renewed orders in many ways embodied the spirit of the Catholic reformation. Envisioning a company of single women and widows dedicated to serving the poor and the needy, while earning their living with teaching or weaving, Angela Merici founded the Company of St Ursula, otherwise know as the Ursulines, as a women's counterpart to the Jesuits, and so provided a new alternative for Catholic women. It also seems that among Catholic city women, another kind of "organized group action" was taking place (Davis 1975a, 92–3, 85). Any women's movement and especially single women cohabiting without the "protection" of an order and male supervision continued to pose a problem. The Council of Trent (1545–63) thus called for the strict cloistering of women, while the Jesuits among others forcefully encouraged girls to pursue a monastic life, even, if they were opposed, against their parent's wishes. Dispersed cells of women religious with new visions and self-claimed freedom persisted throughout Europe while the rulings of Trent were slowly but surely implemented. (See Wiesner 2000a, 231–40; McNamara 1996.)

The mixed reactions from the convents exemplify how the Catholic and the Protestant traditions both have offered women appealing, albeit distinct, models for religious life. "Both forms of religious life have contributed to the transformation of sex roles and to the transformation of society," but at the same time, in both traditions women continued to struggle with "powerlessness," the Protestant women with less "organizational creativity" than their Catholic sisters (as evidenced in case studies from France; Davis 1975a, 94, 85). With the dissolution of the convents, women lost a forum for a collective voice and religious group action. The convent women's fate demonstrates some of the disturbance and heartache that came with the reformations, and provides a particular lens with which to view the results from women's perspective. The rebelling voices of the conventual women remind us that the Protestant Reformation did not offer exclusively "good news" for all women any more than the Council of Trent proved to do anything other for them than compromise their ambitions.

CHAPTER 3

Marriage and Motherhood –
The Preferred Calling

Introduction – Marriage Only?

Sola scriptura, sola fides, sola gratia – the Protestant slogans emphasizing the priority of grace, the gift nature of salvation, and the renewed relationship with God through faith generated by the Word made their appeal to both men and women. For evangelicals the Protestant theologians' preaching on the mystery of justification by faith and the effectiveness of the Word and the sacraments of Baptism and the Lord's Supper transformed the life of piety and worship. Women and men alike were excited about the changed orders in the Church and the assertion (at least in principle) of the priesthood of all believers, the prospect for each individual of reading the Scripture for him or herself and worshipping in the vernacular (freedoms regulated by the confessional frameworks – for instance, the Augsburg Confession for the Lutherans). However, as much as in the Protestant movement a "Christian woman" was "newly identified by her relation to Scripture," and as much as she had a "new option" to "be engaged in the pure and serious enterprise of reading and talking about Scripture," she nevertheless remained "just" a wife – and unequal both in gender relations and in terms of interpreting and proclaiming the Word. (Davis 1975, 84, 78–9, 88–92) Of all the "new" ideas proclaimed, in comparison with the past reverence for a monastic or celibate life, the declaration of the priesthood of all believers and the spiritual equality of all persons that the reformers espoused, if no more than theoretically, in their preaching of the sacredness of daily "ordinary" life had the most profound promise for women – as well as the most deeply felt pitfalls. While the renewed vision of motherhood and marriage, in particular as holy vocations for women, conveyed through sermons, pamphlets, images, and tavern talks, was enthusiastically preached and proved a promised land to some, it seemed like a prison to others.

With the rejection of the monastic way of life and convents in pro-Reformation cities, women lost significant opportunities for spiritual formation and vocations: "When the women religious heeded Luther's words and gave their hands in marriage, they relinquished roles as leaders of spiritual life and lost the confirming experience of sisterhood found in monastic communities" (Clark and Richardson 1977, 133). At the same time, "for some few women . . . the Protestant Reformation opened up an increased possibility for exercising both a spiritual and a social influence on the world" (ibid.). The down side of the peculiarly Protestant "good news" to women was the exclusiveness of marriage as the basis for the holy vocation. No other options received a theological blessing. Thus Reformation theology, generally speaking, enforced the domestication of women.

The domestication of women to the honorable callings of motherhood and marriage, advocated through theological argument, knitted with the Protestants' valorization of family and marriage as the cornerstones of society, on the one hand, and their reiteration of the Pauline rejection of women teachers and ministers, on the other. Just as the exclusion of women from public teaching roles and official forms of ministry continued, so too a status quo in gender relations was promoted both at home and in society, backed by biblical arguments about the created order of human life and the effects of the first sin. Women's subjection to men, to their fathers, husbands, and male pastors, was instituted in societal laws and defended theologically. The theological principles of spiritual equality and justification by faith hardly disturbed the established gender hierarchy, whether in society, culture, ideologies, church, or theology. An ambiguous message about the limits of spiritual equality and gospel-based liberation was thus communicated to women from the pulpit, in publications, and in formal and informal written, oral, and visual communications. (See Wiesner 1989, 12–15; Wiesner-Hanks 2000a, 222–7, 253–4; Witte Jr. 1997; Witte Jr. 2002.)

The Holy Marital Vocation

Marriage had been valued as a sacrament in the Catholic church and elevated by Christian humanists as one of the moral foundations of society. With their insistent exhortation to both sexes to marry, with their simultaneous spiritualizing and secularizing of marriage, and with their rejection of the worthiness of celibate life the Protestants went further.

> In one sense marriage was demoted because it ceased to be a sacrament; but in another sense its status was elevated because it was deemed equal or superior to celibacy. Reformers, therefore, had to forge a new theology of marriage that took account of both changes, and in light of that new theology they had to reformulate the relationship of Christians to the matrimonial estate. Martin Luther was in the forefront of this reformation of marriage. (Hendrix 2004, 170)

Luther advocated marriage even before he married in 1525. He addressed the subject in many of his writings, also devoting specific treatises to it, most particularly his "Sermon on the Estate of Marriage" (1519/LW 44, WA II), "On the Estate of Marriage" (1522, LW 45, WA X), "On the Babylonian Captivity" (LW 36, WA VI), "Commentary on Genesis 1–5" (in particular [LW 1]), as well as "Sermon on Genesis" (1523/24, WA XIV) and "Sermon on Marriage" (1525, WA XVII/I). He saw the importance of marriage as derived from the creation of human beings in two sexes. Wo-man, in his interpretation of the Old Testament creation narratives, was created as a companion and a helper to the first man, and as someone to love. Until 1519 he considered marriage a sacrament, but already by 1522 he emphasized love as the central constituent of marriage, which belonged to the order of God's creation, while it was also to be viewed as a public, secular arrangement. Its spiritual dimension as a holy estate arose out of its institution by God the creator as the pattern for a genuine religious life (superior to celibacy) in which Christians had a special obligation to live according to the principles of mutual love. Luther, who saw marriage as a natural and honorable calling for most if not all people, wished to "recover the dignity of marriage by emphasizing the divine intention behind it and proposing a specifically Christian appropriation of married life" (Hendrix 2004, 184, 178, 172–4, 181–2). (See Ozment 2001, 1–50; Karant-Nunn and Wiesner-Hanks 2003, 15–49, 88–136)

Women thus had an honorable role in living out a Christian marriage. In addition to this, as the divinely ordained primary purpose of marriage was the procreation of children, motherhood was the most glorious – and natural – calling for women. In the area of sexuality – the original beauty of which had become tarnished in the Fall – women, in their wifely roles specifically, served an important role as instruments and antidote for safeguarding against inordinate (male) sexual appetites. Women's role in the holy calling in marriage was, according to Luther, to be companions to men, to exercise the human responsibility to multiply, and to assist men in regards to their sexual needs. According to this understanding, women would be assisting the creator in maintaining a godly order. A good wife would be a foretaste of heaven, a realization of spiritual living. Luther called it the greatest blessing to have "a pious, God-fearing domesticated wife to whom one can entrust his property, even his body and life, with whom you can raise children" (WATr II, transl. in Karant-Nunn and Wiesner-Hanks, 125–6) (See Karant-Nunn and Wiesner-Hanks 2003, 100–9, 119–2).

In both social and spiritual orders, men were to rule their wives and households. Already implanted in creation as a biological difference between the two sexes, male dominance was reenforced in the Fall and realized in the church order and secular laws: "Every Protestant territory passed a marriage ordinance that stressed wifely obedience and proper Christian virtues" (Wiesner 1989, 14). Women needed to be willingly subject to men, even if the marital relationship itself was based on mutual love and companionship. Men would face the challenge of governing their wives (in the face of their wives' recurrent rebellion) with gentleness, honoring the "weaker" vessel as co-heirs of their eternal life and as mothers. The daughters of Eve were to be redeemed through motherhood, the crowning glory of women. (Blaisdell 1985 16–17; Karant-Nunn and Wiesner-Hanks 2003, 88–9, 93–5, 147–8).

In short, Protestant reformers following Luther's model presented marriage as the preferred and highest religious calling for women, the vocation in which they were to fulfill God's order and will and to redeem the effects of the Fall. Women's true identity and calling were derived from their basic reasons for existence: to assist men in procreation, be companions to men, manage the household, and in this role embody an antidote to lust. The reformers hardly presented anything new in regards to women and gender relations in this regard. Unaware of his unexamined gender notions, Luther did, however, offer a new emphasis in his theological appraisal of motherhood and sexuality, and in the value he placed on mutuality and love in the marital relationship. The novelty of the reformers' views regarding marriage and women's role in that much was demonstrated nowhere more clearly than in the new role of the pastor's wife. (See Blaisdell 1985, 14–16 and Schorn-Schütte 1999 and 1997)

Pastors' Wives

The role of a pastor's wife was brand new. It presented a peculiarly Protestant ideal for women – and families – on the one hand, and it promised a relatively independent religious and social role for women, now charged with the administration of parsonages as well as presenting a model of Christian family life for others, on the other. In reality, the potential of providing a special religious space for women through this role was hardly realized and the status of the pastor's wife remained essentially tied to the pastoral office of her husband. (Schorn-Schutte 1999, 256–7, 276–7.)

The new role of a pastor's wife came with many challenges. Since the eleventh century when a number of synods had attempted to curb the habit of priestly marriage and concubinage, the Western Church had upheld mandatory celibacy for its priests, while in reality many priests continued to have live-in-mates or concubines and to father children out-of-wedlock. Clerical "transgressions" in this matter brought revenue to the Church in the form of punitive "taxes" assigned by the bishop for illegitimate partners and children. This meant that the first generation of Protestant clergy wives were faced with combating the image of themselves as concubines and fighting for the legitimacy of their intimate relationships and children (Katharina Schütz Zell went so far as to write a defense of clerical marriage in general and her own in particular). What made many of the first clergy marriages even more scandalous to contemporary society was the fact that several of the very first pastors' wives were (like Katharina von Bora Luther) ex-nuns, and thus these women, more than the townswomen who married into the clergy, carried a double burden of stigma. Although they were probably the most competent women for the task, with the many skills learned in convent, the ex-nuns also faced the realities of life at a lower social standing than they were accustomed to and many new responsibilities requiring their attention. For the noblewomen, in particular, this was a learning experience. At the same time, their self-confidence and education factored into their competence and their successful contribution to the marital partnership, upon which many expectations were laid in the new Protestant society. (See Mager 1999; Janowski 1984.) Eventually many of the pastors' wives would come from bourgeois city families in positions of jurisdiction, and thus had had important preparation for their new administrative roles; daughters of the existing pastors' families would, in their turn, receive special Christian, even doctrinal, formation for their functions as the future mothers of the church and matrons of the parsonages. (See Schorn-Schütte 1999, 262–5.)

Women like Katharina von Bora Luther, who managed their households, raised their children (and often those of others) under the watchful eyes of the world, and offered endless support to their husbands and generous hospitality to a constant stream of visitors, set an ideal for the Protestant clergy households and parsonage tradition. They created the institution of evangelical parsonage. "Although these ministers' wives were hardly the independent professional women we admire today, they were the first of the non-aristocratic women to have an acknowledged position in secular life. It is true that they held that position by virtue of their relationship with their husbands; nonetheless, their role required some fundamental change in the traditional notion of a wife as having purely domestic status" (Clark and Richardson 1977, 134). (See Nielsen 1999, 128; Schorn-Schütte 1999.)

The duties of the pastors' wives expanded beyond the household. Especially those who married prominent reformers not only opened their houses and provided food, care, and shelter to large changing "congregations," they also assisted in founding and running hospitals, orphanages, schools, offering shelter for refugees and students, and in general participating in the life of the society and the mission of the church. Some of them were engaged in personal and "pastoral" counseling. Popular as godmothers, they sponsored individuals and participated in cultural life and the many aspects in the ministry of the church (in a manner their role resembled that of Renaissance ladies with their salons). "These households became the cultural, intellectual, and social centers of their communities, providing models of human life . . ." (Clark and Richardson 1977, 133, also 134). (As Schorn-Schütte 1999, 260–71 says, with their varied functions pastor's wives contributed greatly to the prominence and public role of the pastor and parsonage in a society where the lines between private and public were fuzzy.)

The main expectations for the ladies of the parsonage were the same as those of other women: to give birth to as many children as possible and to obey and love their husbands, and to care for their family. Pastors' wives, even when seeing themselves as the servants of the Word, were not expected to take on the duty of proclaiming the Word or administer the sacraments or assume any official public leadership. They were to be subjected to their husbands and their male pastors just like other women. (See Schorn-Schütte 1999, 266, 275–7). Moreover, exemplary obedience may have been demanded from pastors' wives who, like Caesar's wife, set the model for others. For some wives, especially those accustomed to the freedoms afforded by their convent life or noble status, this required major attitude adjustment. Some were disappointed and wished to expand their realm of operation and authority. Others found satisfaction in the role of a housewife and excelled in it.

For instance, Katharina von Bora Luther invested most of her energy in supporting her husband and managing their household, her theological interests only implicitly evident. Katharina Schütz Zell exercised a call to public ministry and involved herself in the life of the church as her husband's equal partner, also in theological discourse. Wibrandis Rosenblatt may have set a record in how many Protestant reformers one woman could support by marrying them – she married and was predeceased by three after her first husband left her a widow! Less is known of Anna Reinhart-Zwingli, Katharina Melanchthon, and Idelette de Bure, perhaps because they and their husbands had more reserved personalities. (See Mager 1999, 117, 121–2; Nielsen 1999, 128–9, 147–8 on Walburga Bugenhagen, Elisabeth Cruciger, Ottilie Müntzer, Anna Rhegius, Agnes Roettel-Capito, Wibrandis Rosenblatt [-Keller, -Oecolampadius, -Capito, -Buzer],

Katharina Firn, Anna Reinhart-Zwingli; see also Mehlhorn 1917; Bainton 2001a, 159–62; Bainton 2001b, 87–8, 159–62.)

As "living demonstrations of their husbands' convictions," pastors' wives were expected to model "wifely obedience and Christian charity," and serve their husbands and church in silence and modesty. (Wiesner 1989, 20.) They were instrumental in spreading the evangelical faith even without writing theological treatises themselves. (Those with no children, such as Katharina Schütz Zell and Margaretha Blarer, who remained unmarried and assisted her brother in his ministry, were active also in the extra-domestic area.) The Protestant faith being implemented through homes as much as through preaching, the mothers lived out a holy calling at their homes as bishops and apostles to their children. (Mager 1999, 122, 129; Clark and Richardson 1977, 103–7; Karant-Nunn and Wiesner-Hanks 2003, 17–49, 108.)

To conclude, the role of a pastor's wife did not necessarily ameliorate women's position in Church or society in the long run, but it did offer a particular calling, and quite a visible one. Conclusions about women and the Reformation in the Scandinavian context can be thus generalized:

> by the Reformation women gained a visible and socially acceptable role in the institutional church. The new role was, however, an extension of the domestic aspect of their role in society at large. They were not given a voice in the affairs of the church or in the discussion of faith. That remained a male prerogative. In the long run, this visibility and the emphasis on the domestic role of the minister's wife as a model for other women may have helped undermine the acceptability of women's public role and work outside the family. (Jacobsen 1989, 54)

Motherhood, Prostitution, Divorce

The tightening of control and intensified subjection of women shows in different areas related to marriage, and in all the areas of law. (See Witte Jr. 1997; Witte Jr. 2002; Karant-Nunn and Wiesner-Hanks 2003, 13–47) First of all, motherhood, a significant part of marriage, had traditionally been an area where women had more control. (Ironically, more texts about motherhood and childbirth, and conception, come from men than from women; Luther in particular readily offered his advice and opinions on the matter.) With a renewed emphasis on baptism, and the reinforcement of infant baptism in particular, birthing and related rituals such as baptism became more tightly controlled by male authorities. Midwives came under increased suspicion, as the reformers feared "misconduct" in the event of emergency baptism. (What if the midwife failed to baptize the child properly – or at all, in the case of an Anabaptist midwife?) In terms of religious practices, many of the Catholic rituals that had assisted women in labor, as well as female saints on whom they had called, were dismissed. Calling on the female saints and Mother Mary for help was no longer acceptable; the name of Christ and the triune God should suffice. In many ways, male control was being exerted over women's lives, including their spirits as well as bodies. (Wiesner-Hanks 2000a, 78–89, 171–85; Karant-Nunn and Wiesner-Hanks 2003, 171–2, 183–5; Jacobsen 1989, 60–1; Davis 1975, 88.)

Attitudes towards birth out of wedlock tightened as well, as did intolerance towards prostitution. What had been publicly accepted brothels and similar arrangements were now driven outside the city walls. This did not end prostitution but led to individuals "free-lancing," which was a more dangerous option for single women for whom there had previously been some protection, and bondage, in the brothel. The fear of prostitution and the moral harm it might entail made any single woman a suspect of "lewd" activity (Roper 1989/2001, 89–131).

Given the respect accorded to marriage, and the efforts to monogamize all female–male relationships, the options for divorce remained sparse, as did women's realistic options for single life. Secular courts could decree divorces, but it was never preferred as anything other than the last resort. (The most outrageous example of this was Luther's "confessional" advice to the Protestant prince, Philip von Hessen, to commit bigamy rather than divorce his wife!) Sexual or faith-related complaints were nearly the only valid reasons for divorce, or the nullification of a marriage. If one's spouse was impotent, unable or unwilling to have sexual relations, committed adultery, or was an Anabaptist, divorce was an option. One reason for discouraging divorce – even if secularizing it could have made it more possible – was the rationale of binding women in an orderly relationship with a man, be it their father or a husband, be the arrangement happy or not. A divorcee or a single woman was an anomaly in the social structure, and it was not recommended for a respectable woman to occupy either role. Women whose sexuality was considered uncontrolled, that is, women not in monogamous legal relationships, posed a particular threat to the order. Widows were an exception, with special freedoms and privileges, but often with considerable pressure to remarry. In general, life as a single woman was not presented as a religious option, marriage was. Sexuality apart from marriage – and thus from men – was rejected. (See Karant-Nunn and Wiesner-Hanks 2003, 88–170; Wiesner 1989, 11–20; Chojnacka and Wiesner-Hanks 2002, 113–43, 42–71.)

Conclusion

Bearing and rearing children, supervising the household, and teaching the catechism and Psalms to the children became a respected role and duty of the mother. These duties of Protestant mothers were probably not very different from those of Catholic mothers. But Protestant pastors, with their sermons and homilies, consciously raised the role of wife and mother to a new level of importance and respect. Vocation or Christian calling included more than the religious life of the convent. The vocation of wife and mother gained recognition as God-given with religious and social importance. (Blaisdell 1985, 20, also 22)

The message given to women by the preachers was that marriage was now the highest and most desirable state. Since most women both before and after the Reformation did marry (convent life was for a small group only), this must have sounded pleasing to a large majority of women. But they could not have foreseen that the price for the elevation of the wife was paid by the women who, either voluntarily or involuntarily, did not marry or who were left as widows. And within marriage the superiority of the husband was stressed, perhaps more so than before. (Jacobsen 1989, 56, also 57)

Conclusions from decades ago still carry: "Certainly it is true that the Reformed solution did promote a certain desexualization of society, a certain neutralizing of forms of communication and of certain religious places so that they became acceptable for women"

(Davis 1975, 93–4). These were important gains, bringing about new opportunities for both sexes, as well as losses:

> This-worldly asceticism denied laymen and laywomen much of the shared recreational and festive life allowed by Catholicism. It closed off an institutionalized and respectable alternative to private family life: the communal living of the monastery. By destroying the female saints as exemplars for both sexes, it cut off a wide range of affect and activity. And by eliminating a separate identity and separate organization for women in religious life, it may have made them a little more vulnerable to subjection in all spheres. (Davis 1975, 94–5)

Blaming the Reformers for condoning misogyny and sexist views and practices in their patriarchal context is as unhelpful as expecting them to preach women's liberation, abolish hierarchy in gender relations, and thus alter women's roles in society. The ambiguity regarding the Reformation's promise and failures for women shows in scholars' conflicted assessments. It has been concluded that women were increasingly tied to the home (out of fear of uncontrolled female sexuality, for one thing) and that the marital ideal and practice did not alleviate but continued the oppression of women, with a lasting negative impact on women's lives, identities, and the futures they envisioned for themselves. At the same time, evidence would seem to speak of women's (general yet not uniform) content with the "new" theology.

> Despite the drawbacks of marriage (frequent pregnancy, child rearing, deference to a husband), women of that time give every appearance of having preferred marriage and homemaking to living and working independently as domestics in the households of strangers and relatives. They seem also to have relished the authority they wielded as housemothers, something renegade nuns claimed cloisters had no equivalent for, apart from a lucky few who became abbesses and prioresses. (Ozment 2001, 39; see also ibid., 38.)

Whatever the women's expectations were, they did not collectively rebel against the central teachings and practices – with exceptions.

Women heard, received, and acted upon Reformation preaching and theology in ways compelling and feasible to them.

> In summary, Calvin and Luther did not bring about any major changes in attitudes towards women or the roles permitted them in the early modern period. Women, however, contributed outside the structure of the Reformed Church in spite of traditional male instructions for passive, submissive behavior. They acted as if somehow male prescriptions for female submissiveness did not apply to them, and they seemed to find personal, spiritual, and emotional satisfaction in the movement whether or not it changed their status. (Ozment 2001, 35)

Or, what has been said about the Renaissance women rings true also about the Reformation women: "Something changed during the Renaissance [and Reformation] in women's sense of themselves, even if very little changed or changed for the better in their social condition. That change did have its roots in the spiritual experience of women, and it culminates in the consciousness put into words by the first feminists of the Renaissance [and Reformation]" (King 1991, 238–9.) In sum, the story is complex, as should be the answers.

CHAPTER 4

Learning and Power –
An Elusive Option

Introduction: The Impetus and Obstacles for
Theological Writing

The number of works penned by women writers in Christian tradition has been humble compared to the volumes authored by men. This is especially true with the Reformation period. There have been few women's names among the recognized canon of theologians. There is a reason for that. The odds have been great against women's success as writers, not to mention as theologians. First of all, for a woman's writings to be preserved, or to be published, she needed connections, a noble or convent background, and/or extraordinary religious zeal or gifts evidenced in spiritual experiences and exceptional habits of piety. Second, women wrote in genres not traditionally recognized as theological sources. Third, the deep-rooted beliefs that women's intellectual abilities were less than those of men combined with the ideological and practical barriers against women's use of public voice raised the bar high for women theological writers. As a matter in fact, "the culture imposed silence on women" and women were excluded from public roles (King and Rabil 2006, xxii). Fourth, fascination with "exceptional" or "holy" women's lives and piety has overshadowed women's contributions as theologians, almost creating an illusion that women did not write theology. (For instance, in her examination of Marguerite de Navarre as a theologian, Carol Thysell assesses this frequently raised dilemma: "'Why did women of the sixteenth century not write systematic theology?' 'I am puzzled to account for this phenomenon,' wrote Roland Bainton in 1974. 'Have women refrained from theology because they were not supposed to exceed their sphere or because they were not interested?'" [2001b, 3].) (See also Davis 1975, 80–1, 85.)

Regardless of what first appearances may seem to show, women did write theology and were interested in conveying their theological views to others. We know of a few who did so, and we also know of the supportive work of women who sponsored others' writing (King and Rabil 2006, xxii–xxiii). Religion continued to have a central role in people's lives. The context of intensified piety in the sixteenth century, whether Protestant or Catholic, fostered religiosity in both men and women. Religious culturation happened by many means: books being only one of the ways, people's religiosities and identities were also formed through worship (where women as well as men listened to the sermons and sang the new hymns) and through varied forms of art, religious symbolism, and practices. The reformers invited women as well as men to respond to the new theology, to live out their faith and instill it in their children and "subjects" with their new catechisms and their own example. They did not, however, encourage women to participate in public conversation and theological work, or in church leadership. Women's participation in religious life and their spiritual development were to be channeled through their homes and domestic vocations. With little stimulus to advance beyond elementary learning, and often lacking female networks or forums within which to deepen their theological learning and self-confidence, it is hardly a surprise that so few managed to write treatises recognized for their theological value.

The few Protestant women who left behind theological texts of any kind showed exceptional skill and determination, and were simply fortunate to have the right connections. The challenges for women's public theological work and publishing were many. In a culture that imposed silence on women, "speaking out" was considered "a form of unchastity" (King and Rabil 2006, xxii). "The few women who did write rarely published their works as publishing required money, connections and a sense that what one was writing merited publication. Women's unpublished works, such as letters and diaries, were rarely saved, for they were not regarded as valuable." When published, they were "always judged first on the basis of gender" (Wiesner-Hanks 1998a, 149; 2000a, 223). The issue of gender was ubiquitous.

Views about gender and gender-appropriate roles changed very little during the Reformation. Quite the contrary was the case, with the emphasis on domestic rather than intellectual vocations for women increasing. Consequently, the majority of women were not privileged enough to enjoy the fruits of higher education and therewith the skills and confidence necessary for publishing. Protestant women in particular lacked an important form of authorization that would compensate for their lack of education and status, and their gender: the mystical experiences esteemed in Catholic spirituality but devalued by Protestant theologians. Furthermore, the principle of the "priesthood of all believers," which could have enforced fuller equality, was interpreted with an unmistakable gender bias. Eliminating the convents also deprived Protestant women of an option that for centuries had nurtured women's spiritual and intellectual development, and thus their writing. Last but not least, when women did write, as in the Middle Ages, they used genres that were different from the traditionally revered theological sources coming from the pens of academically trained male theologians. The theological writing of the late medieval and early modern women was typically more experience-based and personal in style; to make a constructive evaluation of their work thus calls for a radical shift in terms of criteria, perspectives, and sources used in theological reflection about the issues of importance.

Writing with and without Visions

Unlike their Catholic foremothers and contemporaries, the Reformation women would need to write without the religious authority granted those who had laid claim to supernatural visions. At the same time, they could not just go ahead and write without an apology, that is, without some form of acceptable justification. Given the Reformers' emphasis on women's domestic duties, from what else would they draw their justification but their maternal vocation? As mothers, holders of a role broadly conceived of as an "office," many of the Reformation writers conceived it as their call to care for the well-being of their children and their dependants, and thus their church. (See Wiesner-Hanks 1998a, 144; Wiesner 2000a, 222, 222–4.) Experiences of a supernatural nature were not typically quoted as justification, as opposed to maternal duty which was, even by women with no children of their own. For instance, in her public role the childless writer Katharina Schütz Zell explicitly presented herself as a Church Mother. Similarly Elisabeth von Braunschweig referred to her maternal duty and office in her writing; she too employed her widow's status, using it both as authorization and as conferring her calling and special responsibilities. Other reasons offered by women as making their writing acceptable would be a particular situation that called Christians to take drastic measures, on the one hand, and simply their Christian faith and calling, on the other. For example, both Marie Dentière and Argula von Grumbach, prompted by a concrete situation, responded with quite feminist arguments about women's rights to preach and teach.

Some of the genres used by Reformation women were similar to those of medieval women writers. The one genre strikingly missing from the canon, with the exception of the radical Protestant women, is that of visionary and prophetic literature. Women wrote a variety of devotional materials, autobiographical texts, prayers, and hymns, also meditations and interpretations on the Scripture, and even occasional speeches (for weddings, baptisms, and funerals). Most of all, women wrote letters that served political, theological, and pastoral purposes, as well as that of personal communication. Letters were the safest and most acceptable writing forum for women as nominally private letters could be published and become pamphlets (Katharina Schütz Zell) or be used as propaganda (Ursula von Münsterberg). In fact, the "private" writings often had a public audience in mind and "the line between public and private writing is fuzzy" (Wiesner 2000a, 189, 191.) Some women (see Elisabeth von Braunschweig and Jeanne d'Albret) were involved in the writing of church orders and other official documents; some (Argula von Grumbach and Katharina Schütz Zell) intentionally published their arguments. Exceptionally, women could offer a commentary on a historical situation or on Scripture, or write an explicitly theological piece (Marie Dentière, Olimpia Morata, Marguerite de Navarre and Katharina Schütz Zell all did this).

In other words, women found creative ways to write when they were convinced that they had a message to deliver, a responsibility to voice their concerns and share their wisdom, and when they were passionate enough to do so regardless of the odds. Gradually their sources and their theological contribution are being identified in a process which requires a stretching of the established methods and criteria. In the exploration "we must also search in the margins for insights about women" (Davis 1995, 151). These margins can offer valuable insights into the writers' lives and thoughts. Given the genre differences and the female authors' different life experiences, training, "Sitz im Leben," and related concerns, simplistic comparisons between women writers and established male theologians have hardly been constructive. First the differences need to be appreciated.

The Education Factor

At times in the Middle Ages, a person with little or no formal education would emerge as a mystical teacher, drawing authority from spiritual experiences and charisma that compensated for any deficiencies in literacy, or status, or, in the case of women, in defiance of their gender role. Almost without an exception, the writings of the women among these individuals were sponsored by well educated, influential male devotees who would assist as scribes and editors. Otherwise, many if not most of the published female writers were either erudite noble ladies with access to education and books, or convent women from an environment that intentionally nurtured women's spiritual identity and intellectual maturation. Education was a central factor for both men and women. Women's education, however, posed a particular problem in patriarchal medieval societies: educated women would disturb the status quo and the existing gender conventions with their actions and their writings.

Broadly conceived, women of the late medieval and early modern period had two basic career options: to marry or to enter a convent. Learning was compatible with the latter option but not the first, and to pursue it would always put a woman in a precarious position "for women who were learned had gone beyond the expectation of their sex" (Labalme 1980, 4). "A woman who excelled intellectually disregarded the boundaries of her sex and mental powers . . . She became an intellectual transvestite." Learned women, who often opted not to marry, interrupted normalcy and were suspect of unchastity. Normal, chaste women married men, not scholarship. The women bound by the vows of chastity but freed spiritually, the nuns, were in a category of their own. For them, chastity "offered psychic freedom. It served as a barrier against the cruel criticism often leveled at learned women." In a complementary class of their own were prostitutes, who most definitely exploded the rules about women's domestic chastity and, in the most fortunate cases, could express their freedom in also other areas of life, including learning. The freedoms of the prostitute and the learned woman may not always have overlapped, and may not be equated in modern society, but in a world in which the norm was for women to be controlled there was a perceptual correspondence between the two. After all, "an eloquent woman was reputedly unchaste; a learned lady threatened male pride" (Labalme 1980, 4, also 5). Neither nuns nor prostitutes were part of the ideal Reformation society in which an adult woman was by definition a happily married wife – both groups represented women free from monogamous sexual relationships with men, and at times with an unusual degree of education (more often so in the case of the nuns than prostitutes, the latter always a tragic option). The combination of uncontrolled sexuality and higher learning in women was intolerable for men invested with the authority to maintain order (Stock 1978, 13; King and Rabil 2006, xxvi–xxvii). Chaste Protestant women were to marry men and find fulfillment in mothering, they were not to flirt with higher learning and other "diversions."

To conclude, in Merry Wiesner-Hanks' words,

> Though learned men in early modern Europe disagreed about many things, they were united in their view that women should be silent. With exceptions one can count on one hand, Italian, English, and German; Protestant, Jewish, and Catholic men agreed that the ideal woman was, to use the title of Suzanne Hull's collection, "chaste, silent, and obedient". That ideal changed little throughout the many centuries of the late Middle Ages and early modern period when so much else about European culture changed dramatically. (Wiesner 1998a, 143)

At the same time, "the Reformation itself provided a tremendous impetus to education throughout Europe. Most important was a first step towards universal education" (Stock 1978, 60).

Protestant towns, according to the vision of the Reformers, used legislation to ensure that every child would learn to read their Scripture in the vernacular and would study the catechism.

> Protestant stress on the Word of God, reading Scripture in the vernacular, and teaching children the Bible and catechism at home accentuated the importance of literacy for men and women in the sixteenth century. Humanism also helped to accelerate a trend toward education . . . With Protestant emphasis on spiritual equality for women, an improvement in female literacy could be expected. (Blaisdell 1985, 21)

This did not, however, mean gender-equal education. The level of literacy achieved in the male population rose faster and the spread of literacy was greater amongst men than women. Boys' education could be more academically rigorous, with a curriculum that was based on a different set of expectations, reflecting their possible future roles in society. For instance, apart from a basic education, it was not considered necessary, with exceptions, to provide girls' with advance knowledge in mathematics (Blaisdell 1985; also Stock 1978, 60–6).

Comprehensive data on the exact curricula girls followed at the elementary level is lacking, but it seems (based on studies in Zwickau and Strasbourg) that the educational provisions of the Protestant Reformation, while nurturing the traditional female values of modesty and submissiveness, etc., limited girls' education to rudimentary reading and writing skills and, generally speaking, provided a poorer standard of basic education than they had received in the convents. Women rarely pursued higher education. Even those benefiting from humanist cultivation would eventually need to choose between scholarship and marriage. "Thus," instead of educational equality, "not only in the realm of basic literacy did the gap between male and female education grow in the sixteenth century, but at the level of higher education, particularly literacy in Latin and familiarity with the classics, it became a chasm." (Wiesner 2000a, 158, also 159.) Was this what the first-generation Reformers had envisioned?

Luther, aware of what women's education had lost with the dissolution of the convents and not seen replaced, had envisioned that girls should be educated not only in religion but also in languages and, his favorite subject, music, as well as in mathematics, literature, and history. He saw it as the responsibility of those with authority to inaugurate compulsory school attendance and education for all children. The aim was to assist young people in finding their roles and equip them with the domestic crafts and skills they would need in their place within the social structure, in which the expectations for men and women were quite different. In line with his vision, in 1533 a maiden school was established in Wittenberg. The same year it was ordered that all towns establish a school for girls to teach them reading, writing, singing, and even arithmetic. Aware, too, of the increased need for female teachers, Luther spoke in favor of the enhanced liberal arts studies for suitably qualified women (Green 1979, 96–7). His collaborator Philipp Melanchthon, who was among those most passionate for educational reforms in Germany, ordered that in addition to Latin schools for boys (a model to be imitated elsewhere) different schools be established for girls, preferably close to their homes, with a solid curriculum of reading, religion, and hymn singing, and with shorter school days when so needed. The requisite female accomplishments necessitated the employment of female teachers, who, moreover, could be hired for less than their male colleagues. As for her more academic abilities, "a potential teacher's intellectual abilities often came third in the minds of city councils establishing girls' schools, after her 'honorable lifestyle' and ability to teach domestic skills" (Wiesner 2000a, 148). Calvin, in his turn, established a praised school program and what would become a famous academy in Geneva. He too believed that girls and boys needed separate schools for primary education; in his opinion only boys would benefit from secondary education. In Strasbourg Martin Bucer helped to establish several girls' schools, as did Johannes Brenz, with a Church Order. Andreas Musculus particularly advocated girls being provided with schools where they would be taught reading, writing, prayer, and songs. Johannes Bugenhagen, via the Church Orders he wrote, was widely involved in the formation of schools in Germany and Denmark. (Church orders with decrees about schools followed the first one from Hesse in 1526; Hamburg 1529, Lübeck 1531, Bremen 1542, Pomerania 1535, etc.) (See Green 1979, 96–103; Luther, Address to the German Nobility 1520; Stock 1978, 60–3.)

Some of these early visions and orders meant little beyond paper, but important steps were taken as the educational evolution progressed. Progress was achieved at a different pace in different contexts, most efficiently in contexts where the states, city councils, princes, and the churches collaborated on a shared vision. "It was in German territories where education was compulsory and sponsored by the state, that the education of girls as well as boys was most widespread by the end of the eighteenth century." In rural areas there was less of a difference between boys' and girls' schooling in terms of curriculum and school hours. No advanced studies in Latin or rhetoric were offered in these schools (see Wiesner 2000a, 148–9). In all, the unresolved gender tensions clashed with the potentially emancipatory vision for general education of both sexes. It would be a while before equal education opportunities would become a reality and more was expected of girls than that they achieve basic reading and writing skills, learn the catechism and some psalms, and cultivate the virtues of modesty and obedience to make them good future wives.

The Educated Women

Beyond elementary education, women's paths for education varied, largely depending on their social standing and family's wealth. Patricia Labalme (1980, 11–17) outlines four types of education from which a woman might benefit: informal and formal moral education (for instance in midwifery or in convents); vocational education in trade (by parents or husbands); intellectual education and character formation (by tutors, parents); and intellectual education for a role in society or at court or for individual fulfillment (children's education in social graces or for a career). Women's birth and marital status generally dictated which path was an option. From the latter category could women emerge with an education in the humanist disciplines, such as languages – Latin mostly, but also Greek and occasionally Hebrew – for instance, Katharina Schütz Zell, Olimpia Morata, Marguerite de Navarre, Jeanne d'Albret, and Marie Dentière were interested in the Hebrew language and grammar.

Mastery of modern languages was not uncommon, especially among royal women married off to foreign lands and trained for dynastic diplomacy (Elizabeth I of England wrote prayers in English, Latin, Greek, Italian, and French; Queen Katarina Jagellonica of Sweden corresponded in seven languages). Some women (for instance, Olimpia Morata) pursued language skills in particular and were engaged in translation, an acceptable literary expression for women. Especially in England several women were occupied in this indirect form of theological writing (Elizabeth I translated Marguerite de Navarre's "Mirror of the Sinful Soul" into English, as did Anne Locke). Some ventured to provide "secular" texts, such as historical commentaries, dialogues, verses, administrative pieces, etc. (Marguerite de Navarre wrote love stories, Elisabeth von Braunschweig "orders," and Olimpia Morata dialogues and verses). (See Bainton 1980, 117–25; Wiesner 2000a, 175–210, 143–58.)

Apart from letters, which women used in multiple ways for political and theological discourse, and pastoral care and spiritual advice, women have provided diverse devotional literature: their religious writings range from Teresa of Avila's mystical compositions and Katherine Parr's "Lamentation of a Sinner," to Marguerite de Navarre's "Chansons Spirituelles" and mystical treatises, Vittoria Colonna's "Rime Religiose," Katharina Schütz Zell's meditations on the Psalms and pastoral letters, and Elisabeth von Braunschweig's songs and "mirrors" to her children. Collectively, women's religious writings reveal their impressive knowledge of the Bible, as well as their deliberate use of that authority. Their biblical acumen shows also in the hymns and poetry they composed (Katharina Schütz Zell and Elisabeth von Braunschweig are notable here). Women's expert use of Scripture was also evident in women's prophetic writing – an activity that all but stopped among Protestants except with the radical women, such as Ursula Jost and Barbara Rebstock – and in the writings of the martyrs like Anne Askew and Elisabeth Leeuwarden. (See Wiesner 1988, 148–51; Bainton 1980, 118–19, 125; Wiesner 2000a, 222–4, also 189–202, 143–58.)

To conclude,

> Women's education had always taken place, even at times when it was available only for a select few and given only by private tutors to daughters of the nobility and the wealthy. After the Reformation, however, schooling for girls became more and more widely diffused, until at length it was placed within the grasp of most females in the west. In the transition

which took place, one may detect a gradual evolution in concepts regarding the role of women in society and of the education or training appropriate to their social position. (Green 1979, 101)

During the sixteenth to eighteenth centuries in particular, primary education of girls was mostly moral education, geared to providing basic reading skills, and occasionally including vocational training. The value of educating women was not considered to be in developing the mind of the individual but rather in ensuring the moral character of future mothers and wives, those fulfilling the noblest calling for all Protestant girls (Green 1979, 80).

The same expectations were true in regards to a particular group of women most privileged in terms of education and means of authority: the noblewomen in positions of (limited) power who either wrote or sponsored others' writing. Themselves often educated and surrounded by learned people, they were in a position to sponsor learned activities and such risky enterprises as spreading new theology. "Women who did not themselves write but encouraged others to do so boosted the development of an alternative tradition. Highly placed women patrons supported authors, artists, musicians, poets, and learned men." Some of the authors wrote for female patrons, or "matrons", at times by invitation. "Silent themselves, perhaps even unresponsive, these loftily placed women helped shape the tradition of the other voice" (King and Rabil 2006, xxiii). The patronage of the sponsoring women was crucial, enabling the production of many works that otherwise would have never seen the light of the day.

The noblewomen's connections and access to resources made them privileged, and often among the first to learn about novel ideas and publications. It is hardly a coincidence that among the most vocal women, and among the women in most visible roles in promoting the Reformation, aristocratic women outnumbered women from other classes. Their privileged status came with its burdens and responsibility, and their personal faith would often have public ramifications, and vice versa (as evidenced, for instance, in the cases of Elisabeth von Brandenburg and Elisabeth von Braunschweig, Renée de France and Jeanne d'Albret, Anne Boleyn, and Elizabeth I, all of whom were subjected to persecution and excommunication threats, and even worse). As much as their roles in protecting the Protestant faith and its implementation cannot be overestimated, neither can the tragedies they endured in their private lives be forgotten.

Apart from enjoying a privileged status of a noble lady or endeavoring to enter the privileged and male-dominated world of higher learning and public writing, what could women in general do in response to and "with" the Protestant proclamation (Davis 1975, 92–3): they could "irritate" their Catholic sisters by publicly not observing the traditions set for the Catholic holy days, they could read Scripture for themselves (in private, at least theoretically), they could offer their house for religious gatherings, they could even produce printed materials if affiliated with a printer, they could break images and customs, march in public and sing Protestant songs with a message, or they could die a martyr's death for their faith. Most of all, as far as was feasible in their own situation, they could raise Protestant children, they could support their partners and friends and associates, and they could transform their own identities and lives with their new faith.

PART 2

Women as Models, Leaders and Teachers of the Reformation

CHAPTER 5

"Herr Doktor" Katharina von Bora, 1499–1552. The Lutheran Matriarch

Katharina von Bora Luther

Katharina von Bora Luther, 1499–1552
PARENTS
- Katharina or Anna von Haubitz, or Haugwitz (dead by 1505)
- Hans von Bora (dead by 1523)

SIBLINGS
- Hans, Georg, and one other, name unknown – and one sister, name unknown

SPOUSE (1525–46)
- Martin Luther (1483–1546)

CHILDREN
- Johannes (Hans) (1526–75) (married Elisabeth Kreuziger, one daughter Katharina, no grandchildren)
- Elisabeth (1527–28)
- Magdalena (1529–42)
- Martin Jr. (1531–65) (married Anna Heilinger)
- Paul (1533–93) (married Anna von Barben, six children)
- Margarethe (1534–70) (married Georg von Kunhein, three of nine children survived)

Introduction

Katharina von Bora Luther, Käthe, wrote no reformatory treatises or preached no sermons from the pulpit. We have only few cues about her theological interests and input, but she made a tangible contribution to the cause of the Reformation as the spouse, partner, and sustainer of one of the most famous religious men of the time. She gave her whole person for the new evangelical, "Lutheran" theology and spirituality that transformed her life. She set models for a particular multidimensional calling for women, that of a spouse and a mother, and did so in a visible place as wife of a famous pastor and professor, as a notorious reformer's partner, and as a "manager" of their unique and innovative parsonage. Like the other reformers' wives, she had an integral role in the successful fostering and implementation of the Protestant Reformation. Katharina's work suggests an unofficial but a very real office ("Amt") for women in the newly structured Protestant religious life. Her personality, gifts, self-awareness, and determination made her more than the remarkable spouse and partner for Martin Luther that she undeniably was.

Katharina made a mark of her own in Reformation history. The double images created of Martin and Katharina by the famous evangelical painter Lucas Cranach the Elder already tell of her unique stature. "The singularity of the portrayal of Katharina von Bora, therefore, has to do first with her public role as Luther's consort, but also, inseparably linked to this, with her individuality, which she asserted at the side of her husband." (Treu 1999a, 175–6; also 1995a, 5.) It has been suggested that "even though she left no scholarly writings, Katie's life may be seen as an object lesson of her husband's theories. 'Had Katherine von Bora been unequal to her role as wife of Martin Luther . . . their marriage might have injured the Protestant cause. But she honored her position and is revered.'" She proved wrong the worries uttered by Philip Melanchthon and Erasmus of Rotterdam about her negative impact on the advance of the aims and principles of the Reformation. (Smith 1999, 767, quoting Edith Deen 1959, 83, also, 754–8, 767; MacCuish 1983, 1.)

Katharina's personality and deeds are known mainly through Luther's writings. Some colorful personal information can be drawn from "Table Talk" and Luther's 21 extant letters to her (especially the ones from Coburg [1530] and Eisleben [1546]). Eight letters dictated by Katharina herself have survived, but none of the ones she wrote to Luther have been found so far. (See Smith 1999, 746 and appendix for Katharina's letters; also in Thoma 1900.) From the time of the Reformation, critical appraisals have portrayed Luther's wife in a negative light. In the eyes of Luther's critics, she could do no right (as is evidenced in Cochlaeus' and Erasmus of Rotterdam's lashing portraits that cast doubt on the new bride's character). In Protestant circles Katharina has enjoyed a particular idolization, however. The reconstruction of a most truthful rendition of her life has been hindered by the lack of first-hand sources. (See Smith 1999, 758–68.)

Katharina – From a Nun to the Ultimate Reformer's Spouse

Katharina von Bora Luther lived from January 29, 1499 to December 20, 1552. She came from a noble family of Boras, or Bore, with a long history as lords in the area of their estate in Lippendorf, near Leipzig. Not much is known about her childhood. Her mother, whose name was Anna von Haubitz, or Haugwitz, was dead by 1505, her father was Hans von Bora, and she had three brothers – Hans, Georg and a third whose name we do not know – and perhaps one sister.

At the young age of five or six, Katharina was sent to a Benedictine cloister in Brehna that provided education for young girls. At the age of nine or ten, Katharina was sent to join two of her aunts in the Cistercian convent of Marienthron in Nimbschen. There, at the age of 16, in 1515, she took the veil of a nun, after one year as a novice. Whether the decision to keep Katharina in the convent was her father's or her stepmother's preference in the long run is not clear. It did not necessarily indicate a personal calling to convent life from her part as it was not unusual for a noble family, especially if impoverished, to send their daughter to a convent for a set period of time or indefinitely. Although many of the convents expected a healthy dowry from the entering ladies, as was the case with the convent in Brehna, others, like the one in Nimbschen, would also accept novices with few or no gifts. In Katharina's case, her family was both impoverished and she had lost her mother when she was still young, just around the time at which she entered the convent. As some of the eighteenth- and nineteenth-century sources suggest, there are indicators in her story of a lack of eagerness on the part of her stepmother to have Katharina return home.

Of the nearly 20 years Katharina spent in convent life, the 15 years she spent in the Cistercian convent with 40 or so sisters from mostly noble families, with her maternal aunt probably as the abbess and paternal aunt as a fellow nun, were especially important for her personal and spiritual formation. As well as learning how to run the affairs of a self-sufficient cloister, in those years she also learned discipline and religious habits, singing, and the art of prayer and reading Scripture. While it is not clear what Katharina's particular office was, her daily life as a nun was ordered from three in the morning until eight at night with prayers, recitation of Scripture, reading, singing, and study. Physical labor did not belong to the daily routine of actual nuns; lay sisters or servants performed such functions. She learned Latin through its liturgical use and, it seems fair to assume, well enough to facilitate her participation in theological conversations (in which Latin was the language of the day). Her reading skills enabled her to become familiar with Luther's writings at first hand. She associated in the cloister and afterwards with women of the highest education, for instance, Magdalena von Staupitz, sister of Johann von Staupitz, and Elsa von Canitz, both of whom assumed careers as teachers in young women's schools after their escape to Wittenberg. Her convent "grooming" and the awareness she carried with her of her family's nobility infused her with a self-esteem that would become manifest later in her new life in Wittenberg. (See Treu 1999b, 12–13; Kroker 1906, 23–5; Rüttgardt 1999, 47–9.)

The story of Katharina's escape is famous. In 1523, on Easter Saturday night on April 4 (according to Thoma 1900, 32, but elsewhere also April 5, 6, or 7), in a plan masterminded by Luther, 12 nuns escaped from the cloister of Marienthron in Nimbschen with Leonard Koppe, a city councilor and merchant. Committing what was in the territories under Duke George's jurisdiction the capital crime of abducting nuns, Koppe drove a fish wagon out of the convent, smuggling in it Katharina, Elisabeth (Elsa) von Canitz, Laneta von Gohlis, Ave Grosse, Ave and Margaretha von Schönfeld, Magdalena von Staupitz, Veronica and Margarete von Zeschau. The brave women did not know for sure what they would be doing or where they would be going, unless their families would welcome them back. The life of the cloister had offered a different "career" from that of the townswomen they were now joining, with opportunities for overall education and religious leadership, and freedom from forced marriages, hazardous childbirths, and domineering husbands. Now, beyond returning to their families, the only conceivable options available to the runaways were to marry quickly or try the precarious lot of a working woman (difficult even as a concept, not to mention in practice), for being "married to Christ" would not provide them support outside the convent walls. (See Köhler 2003, 117–18, 127–34; Jung 2002, 33–40.)

There are no records to give insights into how Katharina herself discerned her religious calling either in relation to joining or leaving the convent or of what it had meant to her to be a nun all those years. Whether the choice to take the veil was a happy one for her, whether a religious or a pragmatic choice, the alternative to the very honorable "angelic" path she had followed would have meant facing the unknown, and leaving what was for all practical purposes her only family since she was estranged from her biological family. These were the women with whom she had grown up, many of whom were cultured members of the nobility, with whom she had learnt more about books than household chores. There is an indication of her overall satisfaction with her years in the convent, though, in that, "there are no negative comments from Katharina about her time in the cloister, even though later, amid Luther's circle at table, the guests certainly would have liked to hear them" (Treu 1999c, 159, 172). The only evidence of any inner conflict regarding her monastic call comes from her actual decision to leave as soon as theological argument gave her a feasible alternative. Her risky decision to leave the only world she knew without firm alternatives, with just the support of her fellow runaways and Luther in Wittenberg, was the maturation of her exposure since 1519 to his writings against monastic life, which had caused unrest among the nuns. (See Köhler 2003, 118; Beste 1843, 14–15, 18. Hansrath 1993, 250; Thoma 1900, 25–32; Rüttgardt 1999, 49–51.)

Katharina may have kept an open mind about her alternatives once she left the Marienthron. Her father was dead by then, and there is nothing to suggest that return to the family home was an option, but there is no indication that she was in a hurry to marry once she was in Wittenberg despite the fact that, with Luther's enthusiastic involvement, speedy matchmaking was to take place for those who arrived in the lively city. Even though, inspired by his writings on the subject, the first reformers had started to marry in 1521, Luther was not about to rush into marriage himself, but he felt responsible for the nuns who had found refuge in his town, and he did become infatuated with one of them – but before he made a move Ave von Schönfeld had married a pharmacist's assistant in the town. (WA Br 6:169; Kroker 1906, 47, 50–2.)

Much speculation has buzzed around the scenario that led to Katharina's and Luther's surprise wedding. Verdicts have varied from "Luther rescued the pitiable left-over nun out of commitment and conviction" to "ambitious Katharina forced herself upon Luther and a marriage of convenience." Katharina's beauty, or lack of it, has also been a topic of interest in attempts to explain the marriage, especially in Catholic polemical writings. (See Kroker 1906, 57–8; Beste 1843, 32–3.) While Luther made it clear that he did not marry out of love or because of Katharina's overwhelming beauty, the initial feelings or calculations of the bride remain unknown to us. Some insights can be gained from Katharina's other options: Luther was not the first to propose, nor was he the first Katharina would promise herself to.

In Wittenberg Katharina initially stayed at Master Reichenbach's house, at Melanchthon's house, and mostly at the painter/pharmacist Lucas Cranach the Elder's house, where she learned important lessons in managing a household. She learned of a lifestyle and duties she was somewhat unaccustomed to as a noblewoman raised in a convent; she needed to attend to affairs that ordinarily would have been dealt with for her. She befriended Lucas' wife and numerous other people, including the exiled king of Denmark Christian III, a young student of Melanchthon called Hieronymus Baumgartner, and Joachim Camerarius, one of Melanchthon's friends.

In an era when most marriages were arranged, Katharina had an exceptional chance to marry a man of her heart's choice. She met Hieronymus Baumgartner (born March 9, 1498), who in early 1523 had returned to study in Wittenberg, and the two developed a relationship with many hopes. When June 1523 came, however, the suitor left for home and capitulated to pressure from his family to surrender his dreams of marrying the object of his affection, Katharina; his family was simply not about to embrace as their new daughter-in-law an ex-nun who was not only poor but also, according to the time's standards, past her prime as a potential bride. Had he carried out his plans it would have been an act that transgressed both the secular and religious laws of the time (albeit a step taken before by others). Anecdotal records from the inner circle in Wittenberg tell that heartbreak made Katharina ill. Luther himself intervened: he reminded the young man in a letter of October 1524 that Katharina's love for him remained, but, if he did not marry her, someone else would. Hieronymus' thoughts on the matter are not known, but the fact is that he married another, younger, and richer girl – Sibylle Dichtel, a daughter of "Oberamtsmann" Bernhard Dichtel. Conspicuously, though, he did so only after Katharina's and Luther's wedding, on January 23, 1526. The couples actually maintained cordial, if distant relations, as evidenced in correspondence and mutual greetings. Luther's occasional teasing of his wife about her "old flame" may suggest that Katharina eventually recovered from her heartbreak, by Luther's side. (Kroker 1906, 57–60; Luther to Hieronymus, WABr 3:358, 5:641, 9:529.)

The "old flame" story serves as a correction to the persistent misconceptions about Katharina's pitiable status and unattractive personality. So does the story of the king of Denmark (whom she first met in October 1523) giving her a golden ring (that, according to another persisting legend, served as her wedding band). Katharina did not act like a woman who was desperate to marry: the self-confident lady could afford to reject a suitor. She did not want the consolation groom proposed to her either: Luther tried his hardest to match Katharina quickly after her heartbreak to pastor Gaspar Glatz (Glacius), who had been a university rector and a pastor in Orlamünde since 1524. He was eager, she was not. This proposal occasioned Katharina to utter her famous words to Luther's close friend Nicholas von Amsdorf, whose help she had solicited in frustrated desperation: declaring herself free from Glatz and other suitors, she pronounced she would consider marrying no other men but von Amsdorf or Luther himself. In other words, she told the well-meaning men to stop trying to fix her up, if they were not willing to do it themselves! (See Kroker 1906, 53, 57–62; Treu 1999c, 161, 21–9; Thoma 1900, 39–42) (On matchmaking and courting, Treu 1995a, 21–9; WABr 3:455)

Could it be that Katharina had had her eyes on Luther as a "great catch"? and, if so, did that seem like a realistic hope for her or an absurdly distant possibility? For Katharina, was Luther the best, the only, or the last possible choice? Did she premeditate as a plausible career path the role of mighty reformer's wife? Since von Amsdorf was apparently a devoted bachelor and not a particular friend of Katharina at first, Katharina got what she apparently wanted. Luther, who as late as early 1525 had not spoken about his own marriage, was ready to walk the talk with the willful woman – as he had been advised by Argula von Grumbach earlier. He would please his parents and irritate the pope and the devils, in his own words, by getting married with the last ex-nun available in town. In May 1525, the 42-year-old Luther was talking about "his" Katharina, and in the spring he had been to home to ask for the blessing of his parents, who rejoiced at the chance of having grandchildren. The match had been made somewhere along the way – and perhaps more by the choice of Katharina than Luther. (See Kroker 1906, 57–8, 67, 72: In his June 1525 letter to Spalatin, Luther was already calling Katharina his "Herr Katharina." See WABr 3:900, 892, 911; WATr 2:2129; Lindberg 2000, 134, 138.)

Nobody spoke of love at first, when on Tuesday, June 13, 1525, the couple contracted each other in marriage and consummated their union. Only a small group of witnesses were present at the Augustinian monastery – just the Cranachs, lawyer Johann Apel, Justus Jonas, and Johan Bugenhagen, the pastor of the Wittenberg city church who officiated at the wedding; Barbara Cranach was the only other woman present. Melanchthon's absence was striking, and something Luther never addressed in his writings. An evening meal was shared with friends, and breakfast was served the following morning by Katharina in her new domain, the Black Cloister. Wine was sent as a gift from the Wittenberg town council. Two weeks later, following the custom, the union was celebrated with a larger feast with the university folk of Wittenberg, after a procession to the church for blessing, and more beer and wine as gifts.

Along with those who rejoiced for the couple there were also those to whom the union was simply scandalous (as spiritual cosmic pathology; Lindberg 2000, 134, 134–8) and a prescription for ill fortunes – such as the birth of an Anti-Christ, as Erasmus of Rotterdam predicted. The Luthers themselves rather looked forward to the birth of their first child! (See Brecht 1999, 198–9; Kroker 1906, 67–72; Beste 1843, 44–7.) The scandal surrounding their wedding was fueled by the prominence of the groom, to be sure, but also reflected the generally negative attitudes towards the first clergy marriages. It took a long time for the public to accept pastors' wives as legitimate. These women may have felt the heat under the lens through which their marriages were viewed, but the focus of attention had little to do with their persons and more with the principles debated. (See Mager 1999a, 122; Wahl 1999, 179.)

For Katharina, marriage with Luther meant a step into fame for better and for worse – and a step down in social scale. The eyes of the world, so to speak, were on them, and some of the "tabloid press" intended to hurt. (See Smith 1999, 754–8 for examples on the polemics occasioned by the Luthers' marriage from the sixteenth century and later, including the opinions of Johannes Cochlaeus, Hieronymus Emser, Simon Lemnius, and Johann Hasenberg.) "As we have seen, as a living symbol of her husband's beliefs, Katharina Luther endured much public ridicule and vilification during her lifetime. However, it is just this calumny that eventually motivated a closer look at her life by her defenders" (Smith 1999, 758). In a turbulent period of history – particularly so with the erupting Peasants' revolts – their marriage was not shaken, and, however it may have started off, the wedding was the foundation for a compassionate and loving matrimony. Luther's letters to his "Käthe," and to his friends about her, indicate how soon and powerfully Katharina – and marital bliss – had swept him off his feet. His most beloved "carissima" and "Herzliebe" was worth more than anything else to him. (WABr 4:1032, 4:1043, 8:3253, 6:1908; Bainton 1971, 26; Thoma 1900, 186, 51–61.)

The letters from Luther to his wife (21 of which are extant) demonstrate an affectionate bond between two adults. Unlike other high-profile reformers, Luther broadcasted his devotion to his wife in his talks and letters. Luther called Katharina his "Morningstar of Wittenberg" ("Morgenstern von Wittenberg," WATr 2:650 Nr 2772), and he named his most beloved New Testament text, the Epistle to the Galatians, "his Käthe von Bora." The "old loved one," as he signed his letters, would not change his wife for France or Venice, nor would he take another wife though he was "offered a queen." (WABr 3:900, 4:1032, 8:3253; 3:428; 9:168; 11:276; Bainton 1971, 33, 26; Mühlhaupt 1986, 11–12; Kroker 1906, 273–4.) (See Stolt 1999, Ihlenfeld 1964; Pearson 1983; Mügge 1999 on Luther's letters to Katharina, written mostly in German, between October 4, 1529 and February 14, 1546.)

Luther's letters offer valuable insights into the dynamics between the two and into Katharina's personality. More accurately called "the lady of the house" than a "Hausfrau," Katharina received several honorary titles from Luther – the Virgin, Doctor, even Preacher (at least once, in July 1545), he even invested the ordinary titles "Wife" and "Frau" with an affectionate and teasing reverence as well as giving her descriptive titles: the brewer, gardener, pig farmer, and, in reference to their farm, lady of Zulsdorf. Luther's "friendly beloved Lord" and "housewife" ("Meiner freundlichen lieben Herrn" and "Hausfrau") was his anchor and an intimate conversation partner to whom he could safely reveal himself, his aches and pains, his worries and amusements. In his letters, full of humor and teasing and personal information, Luther kept his "most holy Mrs doctoress" ("Allerheiligest Frau Doctorin") up to date about the theological negotiations he was involved in, about the quantity and quality of the beer he drank, and the exciting news about his bowel movements. He remembered to check on the children, and, so as to show his involvement, remind Katharina of the duties around the house ("remember to turn the wine and pick the mulberries," etc.) and give her endearing advise (borrowed from Argula von Grumbach) on breastfeeding and weaning babies – as if Katharina had not figured that out already with the first child (WABr 11:4203, LW 322 quoted in Pearson 1983, 289). Luther gently tortured Katharina about her constant worries over her spouse's health and safety (with teasers such as "the rumour has arrived here that Dr. Martin has been kidnapped" [WA 11:4207, LW 324, quoted in Pearson 1983, 290]) and warned her that "I'm afraid that if you do not stop worrying, we shall be swallowed up by the earth. Is this what you learned from the Catechism? . . . Pray – and let God do the worrying!" He reminded his wife of the importance of reading the Scriptures and the catechism (WA 5:1582, LW 211, quoted in Pearson 1983, 288). (See Pearson 1983, 286–90; Stolt 1999, 28–31.)

The letters give a window on their affectionate relationship, shared topics of interest, and ongoing conversations. For instance, he liked to flatter his wife, for whose care he was grateful. (His flattery is evident in Luther's letter to Katharina from Dessau of July 29, 1534 [WABr 7 no. 2130, transl. in Karant-Nunn and Wiesner-Hanks 2003, 18]: "Yesterday I had a drink of bad beer and had to sing. When I do not drink well, I am sorry. I would so have enjoyed it. And I thought what good wine and beer I have at home, and in addition a beautiful lady, or should I say lord." He asked Katharina to quickly send a keg of beer to him, as if to make her feel better about his absence, which always worried her.) His letters also reveal some of their shared views, likes and dislikes.

For instance, the couple apparently shared an attitude towards the Jews that for a modern reader is, to say the least, problematic, made evident in his letter of 1545 from Eisleben (February 1, 1545; WABr 11 No 4195, pp. 275–6, transl. in Karant-Nunn and Wiesner-Hanks 2003, 193): "To my beloved housewife, Katherin Lutherin, Mrs. Doctor, resident of Zölsdorf and of the Sowmarket, and whatever else she can be, Grace and peace in Christ, and my old, poor love, and as Your Grace knows, impotent . . . But if you had been here, you would have said that it was the Jews' fault or the fault of their god . . ." Then he described how he had become ill when riding through a village where 50 Jews lived, and had felt a wind blowing back into the wagon through his head, making his brain ice cold and leaving him feeling dizzy. Implying that the Jews had made him sick, he evoked his wife's anger towards those particular Jews as well. He concluded the story by saying, "If the main issues were settled, I would have to devote myself to driving out the Jews. Count Albrecht is hostile to them and has already abandoned them." Clearly this was an area of agreed concern between the two. (With a disturbing ease Luther moved on to discuss beverages and bodily issues: "I am drinking Naumburger beer . . . It pleases me well and in the morning gives me probably three stools in three hours . . .") We do not have Katharina's letters to Luther, but Luther's correspondence indicates she found time to write him in the midst of a very busy life.

Katharina mothered a house full of children: six of her own biological offspring, six or seven nieces and nephews, and four orphans, along with the many others who came under her roof. The children came fast; between 1526 and 1534 Frau Luther survived pregnancy and labor six times: Johannes, "Hans," was born on June 7, 1526, and the world was happy to find him a normal child contrary to the predictions of a monstrous fruit from the ex-nun's womb. Hans was prominent in Luther's letters, and he bore the burden of trying to equal his father. Elisabeth was born 18 months later on December 10, 1527, Magdalena on May 4, 1529, Martin on November 9, 1531 (or November 7), and Paul on January 29, 1533 (he was conceived while Katharina was still breastfeeding, and was born either on his mother's birthday or a day earlier, on January 28), and, finally, Margarethe was born on December 17, 1534 (the foremother for future Luther generations). In 1540 a difficult miscarriage nearly killed her, as Luther wrote to Melanchthon. (Treu 1999c, 163; WABr 9:70.35; WATr 4:4885; 5:5407; WABr 9:68). Her spiritual and mental stamina was equaled by her physical strength. Luther's exaggerated testimony to that can be heard from his amazement that two days after Madgalena's birth Katharina was fine "as well as if she had never had a baby" (WABr 5:1417; Bainton 1971, 36, 34–7). (For more on the Luthers' children, Mehlhorn 1917, 11–13; Kroker 1906, 122–62; Treu 1999b, 15–20; Thoma 1900, 61–72.)

The children brought along joy and sorrow. Their baby Elisabeth died in infancy, not quite eight months after her birth, on August 3, 1528. An even greater shock for them was the death of their older daughter "Lenchen," Magdalena, at the age of 13, on October 20, 1542. These tragedies tested the couple's faith, which eventually carried them through the spiritual crisis. (Ozment 1993, 167–8). The father's grief, expressed in his letters, also revealed the anguish of the mother:

> My wife and I should only give thanks with joy for such a happy departure and blessed end, by which Magdalena has escaped the power of the flesh, the world, the Turk, and the devil; yet the force of our natural love is so great that we cannot do this without weeping

and grieving in our hearts or even without experiencing death ourselves . . . Even the death
of Christ . . . is unable totally to take this away, as it should. (WABr 10:3794, LW 299, quoted
in Pearson 1983, 292.)

Earlier, when grieving for Elisabeth, he cried out "It is amazing what a sick, almost
woman-like heart she has left to me, so much as grief for her overcome me . . . Never
before would I have believed that a father's heart could have such tender feelings for his
child." (WABr 4:1303, LW 185, quoted in Pearson 1983, 291). The *Table Talk* tells that
"Because his wife was very sad [and] cried and howled, Dr. Martin Luther said to her,
'Dear Käthe, think about where she is going! She comes to good!'" (WATr 5 no. 5490,
transl. in Karant-Nunn and Wiesner-Hanks 2003, 198–99). Luther appears to have been
trying to find words to comfort himself and his wife. After their loss, Katharina apparently "tried everything to keep her children in her own house." (Treu 1999c, 164.) (On
children and losses, see Thoma 1900, 134–6; Bainton 1971, 34, 36, 37; Treu 1999c, 163–5;
Luther's words, WABr 4:1303; 10:146–9, 156; WATr 5:5459–502; Lindberg 2000, 138.)

Many of Katharina's friends suffered similar tragedies and endured multiple, difficult
pregnancies and miscarriages. Nursing, caring for ill children, and burying them young
was a regular part of women's life, as were frequent pregnancies during their fertile
years. Katharina and the other reformers' wives, Katharina Melanchthon, Walburga
Bugenhagen, and Katharine Jonas, supported each other in the tragedies that affected
nearly every household. An especially close friendship developed between Katharina
and Bugenhagen's wife who stayed with the Luthers periodically; on one occasion the
two women were expecting and gave birth around the same time. (Kroker 1906, 121,
195–219; Nielsen 1999, 147.)

Katharina has been mostly remembered in her role as the practical head of the Luther
household, one of the most prominent of parsonages. Rather than "only" a parsonage
– as her husband's duties were different from those of a regular pastor – her household
was more accurately a professor's house. The Luthers themselves understood their house
as a parsonage, and set a model for other similar arrangements. Theirs and other comparable reformers' homes became rooting places and the models for other households
from which evangelical faith would be fostered, and the reformers' wives needed to carve
a unique place for themselves and for their mission. Of all the titles and offices associated with her, Katharina could be most accurately identified as a reformer's spousal
partner. (See newer studies on this "office," Nielsen 1999; Mager 1999a; Janowski 1984;
Oehmig 1999.)

In her role as a reformer's wife Katharina modeled the theological vocation of a wife
in general, and of a wife of a pastor – and a professor – in particular. This new clerical
spousal office was an option only for Protestant women. Understood within the priesthood of all believers, this calling had many dimensions to it, not the least in the area of
practical theology and the ministry of care: One dimension of Katharina's calling was
to be a mother and spouse. That vocation was presented to Protestant women as the
highest and the preferred call. The vocation had theological and biblical grounding, as
articulated by her husband. The more public dimension of the call, in Katharina's case,
consisted of her role as the matron of their parsonage and "domus academus": As a
pastor's/professor's spouse, Katharina ministered and "lectured" to her family (both
biological and extended), friends, and an endless stream of visitors, that is, her "congregation," by feeding, nursing, clothing, loving, teaching, and disciplining. As part of her

devotion to assist her "partner in calamities," she took care of many of the mundane chores, thus enabling Luther to do what Luther had to do; her participation this way in his ministry and the well-being of the church through this domestic work was important and set the model for other pastors' wives who similarly assisted their husbands to do their work, not least by being responsible for structuring the life in the parsonage that would serve as the cradle for the Protestant ministry. From that place, in many concrete ways the Protestant wives served in the larger mission of the church. (See Nielsen 1999, 128, 147–8; Gause 1999, 75, 91)

The wife of Martin Luther, the mother of their children, and the manager of the Black Cloister and its finances – or as Luther called her, the "theologian" and "doctor," "my dear wife, Katherine von Bora, preacher, brewer, gardener and whatsoever else she might be" – brought structure to Luther's household (WABr 11:4139, 4203, 9:3519; WABr 9:168, 518–519; 11:149; Gause 1999, 75). Katharina partnered in Luther's ministry of teaching by providing material sustenance, managing a house full of people, running a boarding school for theology students, a hostel for visitors, symposia for theological conversations centered around her husband, occasionally turning her house into a hospital, receiving refugees, providing meals and beds for all, and finding money to cover all the costs. She also made tasty beer. In the different dimensions of her daily life, combined with her husband's teaching on women's domestic vocation, Katharina offered (an ambitious and) multifaceted model for what to aspire for, and what not, as a pastor's and professor's wife: her spouse acknowledged her wisdom in practical matters and welcomed her leadership in that area, but he did not invite her to business outside the house. Even if he mischievously and tenderly addressed her as a doctor, preacher, and lord, Katharina did not exercise any authority as a theologian or a proclaimer of the Word outside her domestic domain – neither did Luther encourage his wife in such activity. (See Stolt 1999, 25–6; Oehmig 1999, 97–108, 114–16.)

Luther made no move to help his wife find a public voice for theological debate or hold a preaching office any more than he did any other woman, and she does not seem to have sought any such role (Treu 1999a, 18). Arguments about women's inability in that regard or the scriptural prohibition against women's public teaching put aside, it may well be that for Luther the exclusion of women from church politics (and theological debates and political territory in general) seemed logical given the actual power structures of the time and women's limited access to decision making. At the same time, Luther did not imply women would be unable to "become" theologians and think theologically because of their gender. The women who did emerge as theologians, such as Argula von Grumbach, he genuinely respected. There is no reason to assume that his own wife was incapable of theological reflection, even if Luther apparently did not encourage her to use her theological voice outside her home, and even if Katharina never attempted to assume a right to enter into church politics or public theological debate. Her dinner table was a different matter!

Unlike Katharina Schütz Zell, spouse of a high-profile pastor/reformer from Strasbourg, and regardless of all her clout and connections, Katharina von Bora Luther did not follow this route; perhaps she did not see it as her primary place of contribution, or perhaps she had enough of it at her table, a regular scene for theological conversation. She did not write treatises but letters, eight of which have survived, all addressing practical issues. One looks in vain for evidence of Katharina's explicitly theological activities or interests. She experienced her "theological existence" within the limits of Luther's idea of a married housewife (Treu 1999b, 17–20). On her own part, it is also clear that she was incredibly busy, with no free time to sit down, reflect, and write. It also appears that she was most concerned about "living" the faith, not writing about it. Unlike academically inclined women such as Olimpia Morata, she did not make study her priority, not after leaving the convent anyway. Luther teased his wife that he would give her a reward of 50 Gulden if she would read the Scriptures – which gives us as much of an indication of Katharina's priorities in her use of time, as does her reply: she said she had read enough, now she wished to live it! (WABr 7: 317, 322; Treu 1999b, 18.)

Regardless of what Katharina's own interests were, her husband associated her with the "matter" rather than the "spirit," applying in his own marriage an androcentric dichotomous view of humanity in which men are associated with the spiritual and rational, and women with the material. His quip that in household matters he was ruled by his wife, but in matters of Scripture and knowledge by the Holy Spirit could be interpreted as a positive indication of Katharina's authority in the marriage – but also as a rude juxtaposion of his wife with the Holy Spirit! The realm of the Spirit was not for Katharina, no matter how much Scripture she read. Katharina herself did not seem to make a distinction between spiritual and material dimensions of life; the praxis concerned her as her area of duty, and in that she lived out her spirituality. (Treu 1999b, 16, 18–19.)

Regardless of Katharina's own interests, one should not expect too much theological engagement from her (or any of the pastors' wives), given general expectations in regards to women's place in the church. Mothers with children were to be particularly preoccupied with the holy task of raising children. Every woman was subjected to the teaching of the male pastors. The exclusion of women from the public arena of theology applied to all women in all classes. Only women with a special ambition, favorable circumstances, and a supportive husband (and typically without children) would even try – and some did. This is not to belittle the contribution of Katharina and women like her in comparison to the "writing" women. Her work, like that of any mother, was theologically important, so was her role as Luther's partner and as a Protestant believer living out the new theology. If the Katharina Luthers had not done what they did with the gospel proclamation that transformed their lives, what good would the theories of the Martin Luthers have done anybody? (See Nielsen 1999, 129; Mager 1999a, 122.)

The "Black Cloister," an abandoned Augustinian monastery Katharina renovated (for instance, by having a well and a new entrance installed), was her seminary and her church. That was where she "ruled" the large "congregation" that regularly occupied all of her 40 rooms and where she hosted meals for 30–40 on a regular basis and often banquets for as many as 120 people. The Luthers' household was a popular gathering place and setting for parties (apparently only the Melanchthons were more notorious than the Luthers for their spending on other people). After their model, the parsonages would become cornerstones in Protestant culture as places for gatherings, entertainment, conversation, and spiritual formation. (See Wahl 1999; Nielsen 1999, 147; Thomas 1900 Thoma 1900, 126, 154–73; Oehmig 1999, 97–116; Janowski 1984, 83–107.)

Through financial creativity, with her own and a few hired hands Katharina managed to maintain their largely self-sustaining household – for which she raised vegetables and fruit, maintained orchards (harvesting apples, peaches, cherries, pears, nuts, grapes, mulberries, and figs), kept farm animals (pigs, cows, calves, chickens, pigeons, geese, and the beloved dog), planted, fished, baked bread, made butter and cheese, and brewed beer (with a permit). Furthermore, she increased their wealth by buying land. As an aristo-crat, Katharina understood the value of land and envisioned there the long-term solu-tion for their financial worries. She won Luther over with her tears and acquired two farms and two orchards. Her treasure was her family farm at Zulsdorf (two-days' ride from Wittenberg), purchased from the von Boras (an interesting interaction given the lack of other communication). Luther often teased "the rich lady at Zulsdorf, Frau Doktor Katherine Luther, who lives in the body at Wittenberg, in the spirit in Zulsdorf, meine Herzliebe," for the obsession that took time away from her Luther-care. (Letter 1540; WABr 10:3519, p. 205; transl. in Karant-Nunn and Wiesner-Hanks 2003, 192; Bainton 1971, 33.) (See Treu 1999c, 168–9; Thoma 1900, 84–5.)

Katharina, just like the other first pastors' wives, faced the challenge of division of duties and realms of authority. According to the reformers' interpretation of the Scrip-tures, and the ancient division of duties between "oeconomia" and "politeia," women were expected to rule the households, as warranted by practical necessities, and be sub-jected to the authority of male heads: the legal authority of their husbands (or fathers) and the spiritual authority of their male pastors. Katharina has been characterized as a domineering and difficult woman who took charge and did not hold her tongue. To be fair, any woman failing to assimilate to the expected role of an invisible, meek, obedient wife with no voice of her own would be vulnerable for criticism, given the time's gen-dered ideals for women. Her critics may have also failed to recognize her groomed self-awareness (and class-awareness) as a daughter of the nobility and an ex-monastic. (Ranft 1999, 72, 60–2, passim.) Because of her unusually public role, "Frau" Luther's autonomy and rulership in the house were already of particular interest in her own lifetime. While Luther did not deem her his partner in preaching and ministry out "in the world," he otherwise considered her as an equal partner and equal "in Christ." In particular he most deeply appreciated her call as a mother as a vocation on a par with that of the apostles and bishops. From all that is known of their relationship, it was unusually egalitarian and mutually respectful, even with the traditional division of duties. Katharina ruled second only to the Holy Spirit in Luther's life!

Katharina's respect and love for her spouse can be seen in her consistent way of addressing him as "Sir Doctor" and "You" ("Herr Doktor" and "Ihr"), both formal, even courtly, manners of address that complement Luther's more casual use of the informal "you" and his various terms of endearment and artificial titles for her, such as "Sir," "Doctoress" ("Herr," "Doktorin") and "most holy." It appears that the relationship dynamics worked, and that neither party was suppressed, that it was a relationship in which two strong personalities bonded through the years in a mature, respectful, and compassionate love. (See Stolt 1999, 23–8; Thoma 1900, 153, 171–94; Lindberg 2000, 138, 141, 142.)

Being married to such a high-maintenance spouse as Luther meant that Katharina had to take the lead and be organized and disciplined. She needed to do many things for Luther, and had to be especially proactive about money matters (or teach Luther to say "no"; Bainton 1971, 32–3). For instance, Luther was not used to collecting hono-rariums for his books until Katharina made sure he did. She (like other pastors' wives) had to work miracles to secure income for the family in the absence of fixed salaries. (See Wahl 1999, 179; Treu 1999c, 166, 169.) Luther benefited greatly from his wife's leadership and autonomy and effective overall "caring." (As an example of Luther's reli-ance on Katharina for everything, he asked her to find a souvenir for the children on his behalf: "I can't find any suitable presents for the children in this town, although it is the annual fair. See if you can dig up something at home for me to give them." WA Br 6:1908; Bainton 1971, 39.) She also took care of Luther's many ailments, which were her constant worry, and prepared meals and curative concoctions. In his penultimate letter to Katharina, one week before his death, Luther told her a story about how a stone had almost fallen on his head, but how angels had protected him. He also promised that if Katharina did not stop worrying, "we shall be swallowed up by the earth." The letter was, as was typical, signed by "Your Holiness's willing servant, Martin Luther." (WABr 11:4203 LW 322, quoted in Pearson 1983, 288; Ihlenfeld 1964, 133–4.)

Katharina's calling was full time. A lesser known dimension of her role was her participation in the famous table talks. She knew enough Latin and Scripture (from her cloister days) to join the table conversations at their house, to the annoyance of some dining at her table who thought such behavior inappropriate in a woman. Luther never made a real effort to silence her, quite the contrary. Katharina would have her voice at the table talks. (For instance, she once argued with Luther about whether God truly wanted Abraham to sacrifice his son; she also exchanged words with him about polygamy.) Dissenting from the portrayals of Katharina as a pious German housewife who was not remarkably learned (with irrelevant and unflattering comparisons to those of her Protestant contemporaries who were known for their powerful publications, Argula von Grumbach and Katharina Schütz Zell [Thoma 1900, 191–2, 138–54]), it is safe to assume that Katharina's cultivation in theological matters only matured during the "in house" learning with Luther and other reformers. Besides, she was eloquent, she had a way with words – to the extent that Luther once told his English guest Robert Barnes that his wife would make a good German-language teacher for him. (See Treu 1999c, 172; Bainton 1971, 37–8; WATr 4:4860, 5:5659, 1:1033, 2: 2754b, 2:1461.) Luther wrote to her mostly in German, with some Latin included, perhaps in the assumption that more complicated Latin would have to be translated for her; this may indeed indicate her comfort level with written Latin. Her exact level of education remains unclear; as with so many other convent ladies who relocated in marriage, her accumulated learning and wisdom became filtered down to be used mostly in child rearing and family affairs. (Mager 1999a, 122; Treu 1999a, 19; Stolt 1999, 26, 83; Kroker 1906, 275–7.)

Katharina's contemporaries knew, and detested, her influence on Luther. Some feared that she "ruled" the reformer to the same degree that she ruled their house. Portraits of her personality in that regard, both contemporary and those written after her lifetime, have been conflicting and not always flattering. On the one hand she has been described as a proud, strong-willed, sharp-tongued, overly frugal housewife, on the other hand she has been remembered as a lively, vivacious, energetic, joyful person with charm, wit, wisdom, and healthy self-assurance. As was typical of the period in its assessments of women, she was judged negatively over her beauty or lack of it, her self-confidence critically opposed to her lack of meekness. Which is no surprise: any sign of self-confidence – more to be expected in learned and noble ladies anyhow – was detested as pride in a woman. Moreover, her intimate bond with Luther and her strong personality concerned those fearful of her dominance.

What we see of Katharina, however, we have learned mostly from Luther's writings, seeing her through his eyes. From the time of Luther's death on February 18, 1546 less is known about her, except that her last years were filled with difficulty of different kinds, until her own death on December 20, 1552. A precious glimpse of her person comes from the letter the grieving widow wrote to her sister-in-law Christina:

> The grace and peace of God, the Father of our dear Lord Jesus Christ, be with you, my friendly and dear sister. That you have a heart-felt compassion for me and my poor children I do readily believe. For who would not be fittingly saddened and concerned for such a worthy man as my dear master was, who served so well not just a town or a single country but the whole world. I am in truth so very saddened that I cannot express my great heart-ache to any person and do not know how I am and feel. I can neither eat nor drink. Nor again sleep. If I had owned a principality or empire I would not have felt as bad had I lost it, as I did when our dear Lord God took from me – and not only from me but from the whole world – this dear and worthy man. If I think of this, then for woe and tears (as God well knows) I can neither speak nor have others write down my thoughts. As you, dear sister, may readily judge yourself. (Katharina von Bora Luther in Smith 1999, 771, appendix, letter C., transl. by Humphrey and Rundell. See Thoma 1900, 194–216)

Furthermore, her sorrow can be heard in her letter to Christian III of Denmark, dated February 9, 1547. The letter underscores her status as a widow and suggests a heavenly reward for those caring for God's widows, as much it reports of the bleak times in Wittenberg struggling with war and plague:

> May Your Royal Majesty be assured of my fervent prayer always and with great diligence to God the Lord for Your Royal Majesty and all Your good deeds and happy reign. Most gracious Lord! After I have had this year much great and sever sorrow and heartache when first my wretchedness and that of my children set in on the decease of my dear master (being, however, his blessed and joyous return home to Our Saviour, Jesus Christ), the anniversary of which is now approaching on 18 February; and thereafter also these perilous wars and the devastation of these areas of our dear native land followed and there is still no end of this misery and wretchedness in sight; it has been to me a great and lofty source of comfort that Your Royal Majesty has with a most gracious missive and the dispatch of the fifty thaler for the comfortable maintenance of me and my children and further Your Royal Majesty's most gracious honor of announcing Your most gracious feeling for me, a bereaved widow, and my poor orphans; for which and for many other most graciously demonstrated benefactions I do most submissively thank Your Royal Majesty; hoping that God the Father, who calls himself father to widows and orphans, will richly reward Your Royal Majesty for such, as I do daily ask Him to; into Whose gracious protection and defense I do herewith and always diligently commend Your Royal Majesty and Your spouse, my most gracious Lady Queen, and the entire young lords with Your lands and people.

Signed by "Your Royal Majesty's obedient Katharina Luther, bereaved widow of Doctor Martin Luther blessed be his memory." (Katharina von Bora Luther in Smith 1999, 773, appendix, letter F1.)

Katharina's voice was recorded also in a handful of other letters she wrote or dictated to Christian III of Denmark and Albrecht of Prussia. In her letter from October 6, 1550, she again petitioned financial help from her noble benefactors and friends, underscoring Luther's contributions as well as her own status as his widow and a mother of their orphans. She wrote, "Submissively I request Your Royal Highness to accept my epistle graciously, in consideration of the fact that I am a poor widow and that my dear master, Dr. Martin Luther, of blessed memory, was a true servant of Christianity and in particular earned the grace of Your Majesty." She mentions the "annual emolument of 50 thaler" and thanks the king for it.

> Given that I and my children, however, now enjoy less assistance, and that the troubles of these times bring many tribulations, I ask you, Your Royal Highness, to graciously grant me such assistance henceforth. For I do not doubt that Your Royal Highness has not forgotten the great burden borne by, and the great work achieved by my dear master. Thus Your Majesty is the only king on earth to whom we poor Christians can take refuge, and God will without doubt give particular gifts and blessings to Your Royal Highness on account of such benefactions as were shown to the poor Christian practitioners and their poor widows and orphans – blessings for which I will truly and earnestly implore. May Almighty God graciously preserve Your Royal Highness and Her Royal Highness the Queen and their young highnesses. Dated Wittenberg, the 6th day of October, Anno D. 1550. (Katharina von Bora in Smith 1999, 773–4, appendix, letter F2)

Two years later, on January 8, 1552, she wrote to the same king, humbling herself to beg the "Christian king" her husband had loved,

> May Your Royal Highness rest assured of my most submissive service and my poor prayers to God always. Most gracious King! Your Royal Highness will graciously recall that You gave my dear deceased husband as well as Mr. Philippus and Dr Pomeranus an annual grant, which they were to employ for their households and young children; . . . since, however, my blessed and dear master always loved your Royal highness and consider Him to be the Christian king, and since also Your Royal Highness bestowed such grace upon my dear master (for which I submissively thank Your Royal Highness), I am moved by urgent need to submissively beseech Your Royal Highness in my wretched plight in the hope that Your Royal Highness will look graciously upon my unworthy epistle, written by a poor widow now abandoned by all and sundry. And I would submissively herewith beg Your Royal Majesty that Your Royal Majesty would in His grace bestow such money upon me . . .

Describing the woes of the oppressed, other widows and orphans, she writes, "I am forced to submissively beseech your Royal Highness after everyone has behaved in such alien fashion to me and no one will take pity upon me. I trust that Your Royal Highness will look graciously on this my pleas and send down the reward from God, the Almighty, who wishes to be a father to widows and orphans." The letter was signed by "His Royal Majesty's constantly devoted Katharina Luther, bereaved widow of Dr. Martin." (Smith 1999, 774, appendix, letter F3.)

One can read her growing desperation in all of her letters. One can also read the sadness at the cold treatment she now received from former friends and supporters of her husband. On the one hand she humbled herself to beg, on the other hand she boldly reminded her royal benefactors of their Christian duties and personal bonds with the Luther family. She also deliberately identified herself as the venerable Luther's widow, with a not so subtle suggestion that God would expect people with wealth to care for widows in particular! In her struggle, she continued to demonstrate her survival instincts and practical, brave mindset. She was not about to give up. She boldly faced the reality that, with Luther gone, their guaranteed income was lost, other than the inheritance he had left for her; she could not count on "alms" but actively pleaded for the kindness of the few people who continued to care for her even when the initial sympathy for the reformer's widow withered. (The lack of a special widow's pension hurt many of the reformers' widows in a similar situation, and she was not the worst off.) (See Thoma 1900, 194–261; Mager 1999b, esp. 124–5.)

Luther had predicted these difficulties in his letter of July 28, 1545, addressed "To my friendly, dear housewife Catharina [sic] of Luther, von Bora, preacher, brewer, gardener, and whatever else she can be . . . " Luther had urged her to move to Zulsdorf while he was still alive because, he predicted, after his death "the four elements in Wittenberg will probably not tolerate you" (WABr 9: 4139, pp. 149–50; transl. in Karant-Nunn and Wiesner-Hanks 2003, 194). Fortunately Katharina did not lose all her friends. Melanchthon and von Amsdorf (who initially had not been her friends) and Bugenhagen and Jonas (who had been close to the family throughout the years and were her best allies when she was widowed) supported her petitions earnestly, just as her friend Christian III continued to provide for her. (Thoma 1900, 244–5; Kroker 1906, 245–7, 251; Mager 1999b, 128).

Predicting these difficulties, and as a token of the particular equality in their marriage, Luther had actually insisted that his wife would be the main beneficiary and become the head of their family. This was quite radical for the time, and, for all the practical purposes, Luther's strongly expressed wish to have his wife continue as an independent head of the household was impossible. The Saxon lawyers had a field day disputing the arrangement that stood against the laws and mores prevalent in their society. They were not about to allow their world to be disturbed just because Luther loved his wife (Treu 1999a, 17). Chancellor Bruck, the executor of the will, ruled in favour of an arrangement that would send the children away from Katharina, except her youngest daughter, and strip from her all autonomy, and seemingly most of the wealth she had accumulated in the household and land they owned.

What was she left with? In one estimate, Luther left behind 1,500 Gulden, a small house, a farm in Zulsdorf, and 1,000 Gulden for her disposition and children's care. According to other notes, the Black Cloister and the farms and orchards were sold, the former to the University of Wittenberg – all went for less money than they had originally been purchased for, except Zulsdorf, which alone was sold at a profit. The books and the household items were to remain untouched during Katharina's life time; after her death the boys would inherit the books whereas the linen and bedding and everything of that sort would go to their surviving daughter Margarethe. In all, she had capital about 3,000 gulden's worth, and gold and silver worth of thousands of gulden. (See Kroker 1906, 238–47; Thoma 1900, 217–40; Mager 1999b, 124–7).

While the assessments about the actual inheritance are somewhat inconsistent, it is clear that Luther did not leave an entirely impoverished widow – quite the contrary. The couple had accumulated considerable wealth through the years. The most serious issues seemed to be whether the widow would have an authority over the possessions, and their children – and how to finance life when the assets were gone. Katharina fought diplomatically but in desperation. She wrote to authorities, and lobbied for support, and eventually her wishes won over the decisions of the Chancellor. She managed to keep with her all but the oldest child (who had, anyway, left home to study). With the gentle Melanchthon as her guardian she could continue to arbitrate her own decisions about her life and possessions. Her conditions, however, were less than pleasant and only deteriorated as time went by. Because of that, and given her warm relationship with Christian III, it may be that she planned to relocate in Denmark at some point. (Kroker 1906, 247–8; Treu 1999b, 19.)

Notwithstanding her concerns over her financial future and the need to fight for her children, other difficulties made her last years hard as well. The recurrence of the plague (in 1527, 1535, 1539), for one thing, forced her to leave her home more than once; the epidemics caused much hardship to all in the area and were followed by the final battles of the Schmalkaldic War in 1547. Once again trying to escape from plague-ridden Wittenberg, this time in 1552, Katharina was injured when she fell from a wagon, it seems possible that she also caught pneumonia. She died of her injuries on December 20, 1552 in Torgau, and was buried there with her daughter Margarethe by her side. (See Thoma 1900, 241–7, 258–65; Mehlhorn 1917, 18–20.)

The widow's gravest worry had been the wellbeing and future of her children. Her son Johannes (1526–75), on whom so many expectations had been founded, became a lawyer, married Elisabeth Kreuziker, and had one daughter Katharina, but no grandchildren. Her son Martin (1531–65) became a theologian, and died as an alcoholic at the age of 34; he left a widow, Anna Heilinger, but no children. Her son Paul (born 1533) became a successful court and university doctor, married Anna von Barben, and had six children. Her youngest daughter Margarethe (1534–70) married a noble Prussian Georg von Kunhein (1555), she died young, at 36, but had lived a happy life; only three of the nine children she had born survived, but it is through her that the line of Martin and Katharina continued and joined the father of the Reformation with the modern era. (Thoma 1900, 234–7; Treu 1999b, 20.)

Katharina had been Luther's rock, and Luther had been her teacher, till the very end. Luther's last letter to Katharina, whose fretting had concerned him even far away, provides a telling insight: "Do you teach the catechism and the creed? Pray, and let God worry. You are not commanded to be anxious for me or for yourself." Signed by "Your Holiness' willing servant, M.L." (Eisleben, February 10, 1546; WABr 11:4203, p. 291; transl. in Karant-Nunn and Wiesner-Hanks 2003, 195–6). Her love for Martin Luther and their children meant that Katharina never did stop worrying.

Conclusion

Katharina was a busy, talented, forceful woman. The glimpses and indirect insights into her personality and theological outlook can be gathered from her actions and her marital relationship. Anecdotal information sheds light on her spirituality which could be characterized as practical, and naturally "Lutheran." Fed by the Gospels and the catechism, and spiritually nurtured by the theology of her husband and his colleagues, she wished to live and express her faith in daily life. Her response to Luther's challenge to read the entire Bible (again) for money reveals the nature of her spirituality: enough with the studying, and more doing and living. She apparently loved life, she was spirited and filled with energy from her commitment to support her spouse, the church, and the Reformation with which she was very much involved both as Luther's spouse and as a believer herself. On her deathbed, she proclaimed her Lutheran Christian faith with confidence: "I will stick to Christ as a burr to a top coat." (Bainton 1971, 42; Thoma 1900, 193; Treu 1999b, 31; WABr 7:2267, WATr 4:5008, 3:3835; Brecht 1999, 235.)

Did Katharina have any influence on Luther's theological work? That is an intriguing, and somewhat enigmatic question. In previous assessments her influence has been downplayed. For instance, her biographer Kroker (1906, 282–4) has argued that Luther's assessment of Katharina's limited theological acumen was reflected in the fact that only in a few of his letters did Luther refer to actual theological matters. He made a similar point about Luther's limited use of Latin with Katharina to argue that matters of substance were not discussed between the two. Kroker's interpretation (drawing on Thoma's earlier work) downplays any possibility of her theological influence, although it underscores Katharina's influence on Luther in "other" matters. There are indications of Katharina's general influence on Luther, however. His colleagues would occasionally mention it, as would Luther in his correspondence. (A colorful illustration of Katharina comes from correspondence between Johann Agricola and Keuziger who called Katharina the ruler of heaven and earth, and the spouse of the Jupiter who ruled her man.) Kroker concluded sympathetically that Katharina's influence in any event did not arise from her hunger for power but from their love and friendship, a well-known example of which was her role in inspiring Luther to respond to Erasmus's treatise on freedom of the will, *De Libero Arbitrio*. While denying Katharina's influence on Luther's theology, the twentieth-century biographer did acknowledge that in many ways Luther developed in the marriage where he remained Katharina's "lieber Herr Doktor." (Kroker 1906, 277–285; Treu 1999b, 19; Stolt 1999, 25.)

While Katharina certainly was under the spiritual and theological sway of her husband, it is reasonable to assume at least some mutual influence and shaping of perspectives. Katharina was a significant part of Luther's theological and real-life landscape, especially with regard to the reformer's fundamentally important notions of marriage, love, family, gender roles, and the understanding of divine love and of God as a parent that they shaped (as evidenced, for instance, in his comparison between God's motherly love and that of Katharina's). "His marriage influenced his theology of human relations, especially in terms of the mutuality and reciprocity of love, and contributed to new perspectives on the dignity and responsibility of women." Such views were fermented by Luther's own marriage as much as his biblical exegesis. (Lindberg 1997, 101–2; 2000, 134, 138, 141–2; Bainton 1971, 38, 42–3; WATr 1:189, Nr. 437; WATr 3:1237; 4:49104.)

The rare fragments of the couple's theological conversations available to us shed some light on Katharina's theological perspectives. For instance, Luther once asked Katharina if she believed she was holy, to which she asked, how could she, being a sinner. Instead of judging that Katharina "failed" to give the correct answer about justification by faith, one could see her counter-question as rhetorical. On another occasion Katharina criticized a pastor who was not preaching enough gospel, to which Luther responded he was preaching gospel all right, but not enough law – a conversation echoing the tension around the Protestants' debate about the gospel–law balance. Yet another time, the sources tell, Katharina, in the company of others, challenged Luther on the issue of whether God truly had wanted Abraham to sacrifice his son. Abhorred by the very notion, she also argued with Luther against the biblical arguments for polygamy. Typically, Katharina's answers have been belittled as examples of her lack of understanding, but they may actually demonstrate her ability to think for herself and draw from her own experiences. (See Treu 1999c, 172; Bainton 1971, 37–8; WATr 4:4860, 5:5659, 1:1033, 2: 2754b, 2:1461. Kroker 1906, 272, 276; Thoma 1900, 191–3, 182–3, 174–94, 138–54.)

Among many of the Reformation women, Protestants and Catholics, important networks and friendships developed and they often hosted meetings of reformation personalities. Katharina did not seek to establish contact with women out of town, nor did she mingle with royal women or write letters to them. One royal woman, however, came to her: a most high-profile visitor and a personal acquaintance, Elisabeth von Brandenburg. Elisabeth was the sister of King Christian III of Denmark, with whom Katharina had a warm relationship that was one of the cornerstones of her life, from youth until widowhood. Running away from her Catholic husband, she invited herself into the shelter at the Luthers' house, before returning home to implement the Reformation. Indirectly, Katharina contributed to Elisabeth's mission by nurturing her to (at least relative) health. It is not clear if she ever met Argula von Grumbach, a well known pamphleteer from Bavaria who came to Coburg to meet Luther and, through him, offered Katharina advice on breastfeeding. Likewise, it is not clear what Katharina knew of the other Katharina in Strasbourg, Katharina Schütz Zell, an active pastor's wife and a writer. The problem may have been simply the lack of time and opportunities to travel and correspond, or the other women's lack of interest in Luther's wife, who did not seem to share their passion of teaching the Word outside her home. She enjoyed close friendship with reformers' wives in Wittenberg – Katharina Melanchthon, Walburga Bugenhagen, Katharina Jonas – with whom she shared many of the difficulties and privileges of being spouses, mothers, and pioneering Protestant women.

The diverse sources from which we can draw our evidence, with their conflicting estimates of her character and contribution, portray an image of a strong, courageous, and independent woman who was loyal in her relationships, worked tirelessly, and demonstrated remarkable creativity, intelligence and practical knowledge in her duties as the matron of the Black Cloister. With a genuine appreciation and embrace of Lutheran theology and spirituality, she did not pursue theology as a separate interest from her daily life – she wished to live her theology. Knowledgeable about the church politics, confessional battles, and dangers coming from many directions, both imperial and papal, she exercised common sense in advising her husband, whom she trusted with issues pertaining to the "politeia"; to her "oikonomia" was sufficient. (See Kroker 1906, 273–8; Thoma 1900, 191–3.)

She was familiar with the language of theology and the burning issues of the day were discussed at her dinner table. She devoted her energy to the domestic arena, where she emerged as the leader and an example of an ambitious and efficient Protestant mother and spouse of a reformer. She modeled an office in a vocation in which she excelled in and apparently found satisfaction. She transformed herself from the medieval ideal of a Christian woman – that of a noble nun – to become a model for Protestant women in her role as wife and mother by the side of Luther. The Reformer's wife exemplified the domestic dimensions of the priesthood of all believers and the sacredness of all vocations, especially parenting, and manifested no ambition beyond the walls of their home. The church pulpit and the university lectern and public affairs belonged to her husband. Together they fulfilled the roles of the apostle, bishop, and priest to their children (as Luther would explain the calling of parents) by nurturing them, and each in their own ways exemplified how the Protestants could live out the gospel-guided life in their most intimate relations and in the mundane aspects of life. (See Lindberg 2000, 140–2, 145; LW 45:46; Gause 1999, 75.)

A Word about Sources and References

For the core biographical information, see Treu 1995a and 1999 and Kroker 1906, and the bibliography for other sources used and recommended.

For the most recent biographical introduction, see Treu 1995a and his articles from 1999, as well as Smith 1999, the latter especially valuable also for its English translations of Katharina's extant letters and extensive annotated bibliography. In addition to Bainton's 1971 essay, an assortment of essays in an anniversary collection of articles edited by Treu 1999a, and the Evangelisches Predigerseminar collections of essays, with forewords by Peter Freybe, *Mönschure und Morgenstern, Katharina von Bora, die Lutherin* (1999) and *Frauen mischen sie ein* (1997) offer important interpretations on Katharina's life and role in the Reformation. These works build on, and correct, the details chronicled by Thoma 1900 and Kroker 1906, as well as Walsh 1752 and 1754, Hansrath 1883, Beste 1843 and Jo. Frid. Mayeri 1698. For novel-like approaches, see MacCuish 1983, Sachau 1991, Winter 1990, and Markwald 2002. Valuable information comes from studies of Luther's letters and private relations by Stolt 1999, Pearson 1983, and Mühlhaupt 1986, and on the developing parsonage institution from Nielsen 1999, Mager 1999a, and Janowski 1984.

CHAPTER 6

Argula von Grumbach, 1492 to 1563/68? – A Bavarian Apologist and a Pamphleteer

Argula von Grumbach

Argula von Stauff von Grumbach 1492 (1490/1493) – 1568 (1554/1563)

PARENTS
- Katherina von Thering (otherwise Törring)
- Bernhardin von Stauff

UNCLE AND GUARDIAN
- Hieronymus von Stauff

SIBLINGS
- Seven children besides Argula, names unknown

SPOUSE [1] 1516–30
- Friedrich von Grumbach (died 1530)

CHILDREN
- George (died 1539)
- Hans Georg (died 1544)
- Gottfried
- Apollonia (1539)

SPOUSE [2] 1533–5
- Poppo von Schlick (died 1535)

Introduction

"I am called a follower of Luther, but I am not. I was baptized in the name of Christ; it is him I confess and not Luther. But I confess that Martin, too, as a faithful Christian, confesses him." So argued Argula von Stauff von Grumbach, a Bavarian noble woman, in her 1523 letter to her "dear lord and Cousin," Adam von Thering, the Count Palatine's Administrator in Neuburg (Argula von Grumbach in Matheson 1995, 145, from here on AvG/Matheson). Argula had risen to notoriety when defending a student accused of Lutheran "heresy" and publicly chastising the learned university men for persecuting innocent believers who, in her assessment, believed nothing against the scriptural truths. Labeled as one of the "Lutherans" and an associate of the reformers, Argula suffered persecution as she involved herself in the affairs of the church and broadcasted her views through her widely circulated published letters. Not interested in party labels, she was passionate about Christian faith and justice. Her concern for the gospel made her willing to take considerable risks:

> "I am prepared to lose everything – even life and limb. May God stand by me! Of myself I can do nothing but sin." Furthermore, she says, "I had intended to keep my writing private; now I see that God wishes to have it made public. That I am now abused for this is a good indication that it is of God. ("To the noble and honourable Adam von Thering, the Count Palatine's Administrator in Neuburg . . . an open letter from Argula von Grumbach, née von Stauf," in AvG/Matheson, 141–9 at 149.)

One of the most visible women in Germany to write on behalf of the Reformation, who liked to remind her readers of her noble birth into the von Stauff family, Argula was, like Marie Dentière in Geneva and Katharina Schütz Zell in Strasbourg, a Protestant lay pamphleteer who never doubted her prerogative to address theological issues. Argula internalized and applied in her life the reformers' two central principles: the priesthood of all believers and the primacy of the Scriptures as the sole authority. She drew her authority to interpret Scripture and speak publicly from the first principle.

Argula's letters, which all date from a period of one year between 1523 and 1524, were published and widely read. Her first epistle, from September 1523, to the University of Ingolstadt, went through 14 editions in two months (29 in twelve months, Halbach 1992, 187) and made her the most famous female Lutheran and a best-selling pamphleteer.

> If the estimate that some 29,000 copies of her pamphlets circulated on the eve of the Peasants' War is approximately correct, and there seems no reason to doubt it, she has to be taken with great seriousness as one of the major pamphleteers of the Reformation. The fourteen editions of her first writing were a quite remarkable achievement, ranking her without any doubt as a 'bestseller' of formidable proportions. (Matheson 1995, 53–4)

Her other extensive correspondence to friends, family, religious and political leaders, and preachers is lost; her letters were either destroyed or not considered sufficiently important to preserve. "Much of her life still remains unknown," and literature in

English around her is scanty, while "scholarly work on Argula von Grumbach is very much in transition" (Matheson 1995, 57, 3; Joldersma 1997, 90, 93). Had she been a man, the past centuries would have recognized her as one of the important personalities of the German Reformation. Her sex makes the difference, as noted by many who are familiar with her story. (See Wiesner 1989, 22; Wiesner 1988, 169.)

Argula's life story closely follows the publication of her eight surviving texts. Her letter to the University of Ingolstadt, from September 20, 1523 ("Wie ain Christliche Fraw des Adels . . .") started the controversy that would have a tremendous impact on her life. She followed that with a letter to Duke Wilhelm (IV), written the same day ("Ein Christennliche schrifft . . ."). On October 27 or 28, 1523 she sent a letter to the mayor and the city council of Ingolstadt ("An ain Ersamen Weysen Radt der stat Ingolstat . . ."). On December 1, 1523 she wrote a letter to Count Palatine Johann von Simmern ("Ermanung an den Durchleuchtigen . . .") and to Fredrick the Wise ("Dem Durchleuchtigsten Hochgebornen Fürsten . . ."). In the same month she wrote the open letter to Count Adam von Thering ("An den Edlen . . ."). Months later, on June 29, 1524, eager to precipitate action she wrote again, this time to the city of Regensburg ("Ein Sendbrieff . . ."), and the same summer she crafted a response to an anonymous misogynist attack against her ("Eyn Antwort . . ."). Her letters expressed her tenacious yet futile attempts to engage the university men in dialogue and to prove them guilty for persecuting an innocent Christian student. The letters became an occasion for her to state her Lutheran Christian beliefs, defend her (and other women's) Christian rights, and show her impressive knowledge of Scripture. (See Halbach 1992, 192, 102–84 about the texts.)

Argula as a Defender of Faith – A Valiant Christian, or a Devilish Woman?

Argula von Stauff von Grumbach was one of at least eight children born to the von Stauff family. There is much inconsistency about the dates of both her birth and her death, ranging from 1490, 1492 or 1493 for her birth year and 1554, 1563, or 1568 for the year of her death. Her family descended from the house of Hohenstaufen, independent Frankonian "free lords" ("Freiherren") accountable only to the emperor. Her mother Katherina came from a noble and distinguished family from Bavaria, the Therings (or Törrings). The family lost much of its wealth thanks to a dispute involving her father Bernhardin and her uncle Hieronymus, but later Argula's father's loyalty to the duke won him governance over Schoenberg, and with it some assets.

A child of privilege and of a cultured and religious family, she enjoyed private education and, simply, the availability of books to read. At 10, she received from her father a copy of the famous Koberger Bible, a 1483 German translation, which she, like her mother, continued to study all her life, gaining remarkable scriptural knowledge. Her religious education continued at the royal court in Munich where the 15- or 16-year old served as a maid-in-waiting to Kunigunde, the sister of the Emperor Maximillian and the mother of Duke Albrecht. There Argula met Johann von Staupitz, Luther's spiritual father, and became interested in Luther.

Like many of her contemporaries, Argula experienced the devastation of the plague that rampaged through Europe in her lifetime. In 1509, while still only a young woman, she lost both of her parents to the plague within five days of each other. Her uncle Hieronymous von Stauff, a prominent man at the court, became her guardian. Argula was bereaved again when her uncle was executed on April 8, 1516, accused of political plotting. Later that year Argula married a well-to-do man with honorable Frankonian family roots: Friedrich von Grumbach, a northern Bavarian landowner. The couple would have four children, George, Hans Georg, Gottfried, and Apollonia, who, under Argula's supervision, were nurtured in the Protestant faith, even though their father remained a Catholic.

Very little is known of Friedrich. A sickly man throughout his life, he died in 1530, never having been either very literate or in favor of Luther. After the couple moved to Lenting, near Ingolstadt (where the Grumbachs had property), he served as an administrator in Dietfurt in Altmühtal under Duke Ludwig. As Katharina did in the Luthers' family, Argula took charge of the finances as well as child rearing. What little is known of their marriage indicates simmering tensions (hinted at in a poem Argula wrote in 1524 in which she defended herself against accusations that she had neglected her domestic duties and said she prayed God to teach her how to act towards her man) that would develop into violence, as suggested in Argula's letter to Adam von Thering, in which she invoked the help of God and her friend the count because her husband was persecuting the "Christian in her" (Kolde 1905, 145, 147, 192; Matheson 1995, 8–9).

Nevertheless, even if this became a cause of marital tension, Argula did not hide her sympathy for the Reformation. She maintained a personal contact with the Reformers in Wittenberg throughout her adult life, especially with Melanchthon, Luther, and Spalatin (see Kolde 1905, 169–70, 64, 115, 62), and her arguments certainly echoed those of the Protestant reformers whose basic theology she shared. She was informed especially by the reformers teaching of the priesthood of all believers, which she would develop even further (Halbach 1992, 119, 218–24). On the basis of her accumulated first-hand knowledge and her conviction about the reformers' teachings, she could argue with the university-educated men: "What do Luther or Melanchthon teach you but the word of God? You condemn them without having refuted them . . . For my part, I have to confess, in the name of God and my soul's salvation, that if I were to deny Luther and Melanchthon's writing I would be denying God and his word" (see "The Account of a Christian woman of the Bavarian nobility whose open letter, with arguments based on divine Scripture, criticizes the University of Ingolstadt for compelling a young follower of the gospel to contradict the word of God," in AvG/Matheson, 71–91 at 76–7).

Argula's personal connections and location were important factors in her religious development. Her family was connected to both Protestants and Catholics, and her marriage brought her to Lenting, close to the University of Ingolstadt where the Catholic Johann Eck was prochancellor and where, from 1522, the same year in which Argula's brother appointed a Lutheran preacher, her brother Marcellus was to be a student. Three of her uncle Hieronymous's daughters left their nunneries because of their Protestant faith. One can imagine the theological conversations among family members. Early on, soon after meeting Spalatin at the court in Munich, Argula established a contact with Luther's collaborator in Nuremberg, a German reformer called Andreas Osiander who would become a dear friend and even, later, a chaperon for Argula's children during their studies in town. She also had contact with the radical reformers, for instance, Balthasar Hubmaier, a city preacher in Regensburg, and Sebastian Lotzer, whose writings resembled those of Argula. Luther's writings were available to her, at least from 1519 onwards, and by 1523 she declared she had read all that Luther had published in German!

Her first contacts with Luther and Wittenberg were through Spalatin and, even more importantly, Paul Speratus, a cathedral preacher at Würzburg from whom she had asked for recommendations for Protestant readings and whose correspondence fueled her interest in the Wittenberg theologians. Argula's correspondence with Osiander, Spalatin, and Luther, based on preserved letters from the men, indicates her impressive knowledge of Scripture as well as of the current debates. Unfortunately her letters to Luther have not been found. (See WA Br 2:559–562; Matheson 1995, 10–12.)

A child of privilege, Argula had the opportunity to be tutored privately. "Argula was not so much self-taught, then, as a particularly brilliant product of the new 'distance learning' now possible for women and lay people. It is clear that she intentionally set about studying Scripture, spurned on in part by the writings of Luther and others, and no doubt by innumerable conversations of which we have no record." She did not consider herself unique in this regard, quite the contrary: "If her references to groups of women sharing her views are correctly understood, she also saw herself as part of a new women's movements, which had its own ethos and specific bank of experience" (Matheson 1995, 27).

Argula's commitment to the Reformation, and particularly the principle of "sola scriptura," was rooted in her love for Scripture, whose independent study she had sustained since her childhood. That knowledge, later enhanced with Luther's texts, led her to her conclusions regarding the "truth." A telling quote comes from her letter to the University of Ingolstadt:

> I beseech you for the sake of God, and exhort you by God's judgment and righteousness, to tell me in writing which of the articles written by Martin or Melanchthon you consider heretical. In German not a single one seems heretical to me. And the fact is that a great deal has been published in German, and I've read it all . . . I have always wanted to find out the truth. Although of late I have not been reading any, for I have been occupied with the Bible, to which all of [Luther's] work is directed anyway – to bring us to read it [Scripture]. My dear lord and father insisted on me reading it, giving me it when I was ten years old. Unfortunately I did not obey him, being seduced by the afore-named clerics, especially the Observants who said that I would be led astray. Ah, but what a joy it is when the spirit of God teaches us and gives us understanding . . . I don't intend to bury my talent, if the Lord gives me grace. ("The Account," 1523, AvG/Matheson, 86–7. Also Classen 1989, 140.)

Argula's readings shaped her mind and gave her confidence, as did the Protestants' principle of Scripture's ultimate authority and (at least theoretical) empowerment of the laity towards spiritual equality (Halbach 1992, 118–19, 204–7, 212–26). From a Scripture-based emancipation, she was confident enough to critique the failures she saw in the spiritual leadership of the day and to offer her advice to those in power. She reminded Duke Wilhelm in her letter that "the word of God alone should – and must – rule all things. They call it Luther's word; yet the words are not Luther's but God's." "God grant that the princes and lords will no longer let themselves be led along like monkeys on a chain by these so-called spiritual rulers" (see "A Christian Writing by an honourable noblewoman in which she exhorts all Christian estates and authorities to remain true to the truth and to the word of God and to take most earnestly their Christian duty in this regard. Argula von Stauff AD 1523, in AvG/Matheson, 100–12 at 101 and 108).

A woman with no formal education would face credibility issues. Having no skills in Latin was a deficiency in academia, yet Argula refused to let that hold her back. What she lacked in scholarly languages she compensated for with her conviction and sense of

Christian duty, her admirable biblical knowledge, and her excellent reading and writing skills in her mother tongue. She would also purposefully flaunt her "von Stauff" position. Flagging St Paul's first letter to the Corinthians, chapter 3 in particular, she disregarded the folly of human wisdom and credentials: "I have no Latin; but you have German, being born and brought up in this tongue. What I have written to you is no woman's chit-chat, but the word of God; and (I write) as a member of the Christian Church, against which the gates of Hell cannot prevail" ("The Account," in AvG/Matheson 1995, 90, also 89).

Argula entered the Reformation scene with her letters in 1523 and gained notoriety during the following year. Her time in the limelight was during the most active period for lay pamphleteering, and in a context in which Protestant activities were forbidden: on March 5, 1523 the Bavarian Court at Munich had decreed it illegal to discuss or even own Protestant literature. The stimulus for her writing activity was the "Affair of Arsacius Seehofer." (On lay pamphleteering, see Russell 1986; Chrisman 1982; Jung 2002, 169–221.)

Arsacius was an 18-year-old student at the University of Ingolstadt. In 1521 he had arrived there with new ideas and pamphlets from Wittenberg, where he had studied with Melanchthon and Karlstadt (during Luther's enforced "rest" in Wartburg). His Lutheran tendencies were not well received by Professor Johann Eck, at the faculty in Ingoldstadt; the known archenemy of Luther had already publicly disputed the reformer's teachings at the 1519 Leipzig Debate. In December 1522 Arsacius received a warning, his house was searched, Protestant materials were found, and the boy was imprisoned (three times) and forced to renounce Luther's teachings. He was about to face the burning reserved for the heretics, but his father's intervention moved the case from the bishop's jurisdiction to that of the state, which was satisfied with a public recantation. A list of 17 erroneous articles, with links to the Wittenberg theologians, were presented to Arsacius, who on September 7 recanted with tears and promised to steer clear from the Lutheran doctrine, thanking the university for treating him with such leniency. He was incarcerated and sent to the cloister of Ettal. (See Kolde, 49–58 and Halbach 1992, 35–47.)

Nobody came to Arsacius' defense publicly like Argula. What was happening to Arcasius she considered unbiblical, unjust, and a manifest abuse of power. Outraged, Argula first consulted Andreas Osiander, who was serving as a tutor and preacher in Nuremberg – traveling there with her little children and reportedly impressing him with her scriptural acumen. On September 20, 1523 she summoned the university and its rector and council with a candid, yet carefully articulated, letter and challenged them to demonstrate to her (and the public) of exactly which heresy Arsacius was guilty. She reminded the gentlemen of the youth of the persecuted boy: "For you have forgotten one thing: that he is only eighteen years old, and still a child. Others won't forget." God will not forget, declared Argula, but "God will look merciful on Arsacius." Furthermore, she pointed out, "a disputation is easily won when one argues with force, not Scripture" ("The Account," in AvG/Matheson, 82–3, also 81–4).

Argula was compelled to action by God and by the injustice she witnessed. She founded her arguments on the primacy of the Scriptures, supporting her case with over 80 quotations and clever rhetoric. She may have been inspired by Luther's words (Vom Missbrauch der Messe, 1521) about the necessity for women to preach the gospel when men are silent. She boldly demanded that the university men should not only listen to but also respond to her personally. Neither her lay status nor her gender nor her lack of Latin skills posed any impediment for her. With a Scripture-based authority and Christian moral duty to intervene (quoting Ezekiel 33) when a publicly-funded university was culpable of misconduct, she was outraged: "How in God's name can you and your university expect to prevail, when you deploy such foolish violence against the word of God . . . I am compelled as a Christian to write to you" ("The Account," in AvG/Matheson, 75, 77).

In another bold gesture Argula took a stand in defense of Luther whose views were also on trial. To Argula, his translation of the Bible was evidence of his orthodoxy and holiness; she was among the first to laud the translation and appraise it as pure and superior.

> Are you not ashamed that [Seehofer] had to deny all the writings of Martin, who put the New Testament into German, simply following the text? That means that the holy Gospel and the Epistles and the story of the apostles and so on are all dismissed by you as heresy . . . God grant that I may speak with you in the presence of our three princes and of the whole community. ("The Account," in AvG/Matheson, 89)

In another letter, to Duke Thering, she wrote, "It was never Luther's intent, after all, that one should have faith in his books; they should serve simply as guidebooks to the word of God" ("Adam von Thering," 1523, in AvG/Matheson, 148). In light of all this, she demanded specificity about the claims that seemed unjust to her: "I beseech you for the sake of God, and exhort you by God's judgment and righteousness, to tell me in writing which of the articles written by Martin or Melanchthon you consider heretical. In German not a single one seems heretical to me" ("The Account," in AvG/Matheson, 86). She signed off with her birth name "von Stauff," enforcing the entitlement of her rank (Schöndorf 1983, 190). She reminded her contemporaries that Luther's work was about the word of God (Halbach 1992, 203–4).

The letter to the university from September 20, 1523, which was at first circulated in handwritten copies and then printed with a preface by Osiander (or Balthasar Hubmaier or Sebastian Lotzer), became a bestseller that went through 14 editions in two months (see "The Account," 1523, in AvG/Matheson, 71–91; Schöndorf 1983, 193–4; Bezzel 1987). (See Halbach 1992, 102–22 on the text.) Little did Argula know what would ensue from the publication (which was repeated in 1524 in Strasbourg). Would she have guessed that her fame and fate would become such that she would be listed in Ludwig Rabus's 1556 history of the martyrs?

On the same day as that first letter, September 20, 1523, Argula wrote another letter, this time to Duke Wilhelm, with whom her family had ties. This letter would serve as a cover letter to the university letter, and articulated "a programmatic call for reformation." (Kolde 1905, 70; Bainton 2001, 101.) Aware of the intricate connection between religious and secular authorities, Argula the reformer admonished the secular authority to ensure the preaching of the true gospel (and, among other things, to promote clerical marriage). The letter was printed and addressed to the Christian estates – akin to Luther's Appeal to the German Nobility from 1520. Soon after this, and without her approval, other pieces of her correspondence were published, this time letters she had written to Johann of Simmern and Frederick the Wise.

The accumulation of widely circulated letters reflects Argula's frustration over the university's stonewalling of her challenge. She never received an official reply to any of her letters nor managed to initiate a debate. Instead, she was dismissed by the university men as a "heretical bitch" and a woman "hag." Given the conventions of the time, a woman really could not expect a personal response, which she knew, as her pre-emptive words reveal:

> What I have written to you is no woman's chit-chat, but the word of God; and (I write) as a member of the Christian Church, against which the gates of Hell cannot prevail . . . God give us his grace, that we all may be saved, and may (God) rule us according to his will. Now may his grace carry the day. ("The Account", in AvG/Matheson, 90)

Her biblically based and well argued, confident defense of herself, of Lutheranism, and of Christians' calling as God's vessels, was courageous and provocative (Classen 1989, 142, 145; Bezzel 1986, 202). Her added demand for the inclusion of women's voices and experiences made her as radical as, if not even more radical than, Luther himself.

For a woman to challenge the learned men was one thing, but to defend a Lutheran in a territory where Lutheran views were condemned was even more dangerous. Given the situation in Bavaria, which was one in which discussing Luther's teachings was against the law and in which women were not supposed to debate in public, Argula committed a double transgression. The furious Ingolstadt theologians, while refusing to respond publicly to a woman, were determined to have "the silly bag tamed" and punish the "female devil" in indirect ways: through her husband. Duke Wilhelm, acting under Duke Ludwig's advice, relieved her husband, who was not at all sympathetic to the evangelicals, of his post as an administrator in 1524. This hardly helped the already strained marital relationship, or their financial situation. Argula's letters to the city council and the mayor of Ingolstadt, with a copy to the university, included a request for monetary assistance, after the princes had refused to help her. (See Kolde 1905, 97–8; Bezzel 1986, 202; Bainton 2001, 104–5.)

She implored the council to consider the Arsacius matter in the light of Scripture. She reiterated her right and duty as a woman to speak up and her readiness to die – a real possibility given the persecution to which she was subjected: "I hear that some are so angry with me that they do not know how best to speed my passage from life into death. But I know for sure that they cannot harm me unless the power to do so has been given them by God. He will keep me safe, for His name's sake." She wondered, "I would dearly like to know what they have to gain if they were to murder me right now." Then again, she saw an opportunity to witness in martyrdom: "I am persuaded, too, that if I am given grace to suffer death for his name, many hearts would be awakened" ("To the honourable, wise Council of the town of Ingolstadt, an open letter from Argula von Grumbach, née von Stauffen. To the honourable, prudent and wise Magistrates and Council of the town of Ingolstadt, my good friends," 1523, in AvG/Matheson, 117–22 at 119–20). Suffering for the sake of Christ in the end of times remained a main theme in her texts (Halbach 1992, 119, 226).

While she was acting alone, she did not feel she was alone. She drew empowerment from "a school of women", that is, other women who were ready to fight for the same cause: "Yes, and whereas I have written on my own, a hundred women would emerge to write against them. For there are many who are able and better read than I am; as a result they might well come to be called 'a school for women' . . . We have to confess publicly . . ." ("To the honourable," in AvG/Matheson, 120–1; Joldersma 1997, 93). Indeed, she did confess – even if the letter achieved nothing she had hoped for. Instead, Argula and her family were banned from Dietfurt.

Argula's letter provoked Professor Hauer to give "virulent" sermons. On December 8, 1523 he preached angrily about "daughters of Eve," "heretical bitches and desperate fools," such as Argula. (Kolde 1906, 101.) The venomous shower of epithets – "You female desperado," "You wretched and pathetic daughter of Eve," "You arrogant devil," "You arrogant fool," "You heretical bitch," "You shameless whore" – were apparently mostly intended for Argula. (Matheson 1995, 19–20.) Members in the academia joined the slandering and offered crass responses, they invoked their duke to "tame the hag" ("die Vettel zähne" or "eam vetulam compescat" in Kolde 1905, 97) and prohibit further publication of blaspheming letters such as Argula's. Persistent stories about the princes discussing the benefits of cutting her fingers off or strangling her to stop her from writing have not been proven true, but her husband's anger towards her (especially after being fired because of her) is evidenced in her letters. She refuted the rumors that her husband had locked her up, but complained that he did all he could to persecute the Christ in her. (See her 1523 "A Christian Writing" in AvG/Matheson, 100–22; Bainton 2001, 104–5; Matheson 1995, 18–19.)

During the turmoil she wrote to Luther, whose admiration she had won with her valiance. Among other things Argula recommended him to get married; in their later correspondence she would offer advice on how to wean a baby, information Luther happily forwarded to his wife Katharina. Other than that, theological issues were pressing in their conversations. Luther respected Argula's fight and was aware of her difficult home situation, which he addressed in his letter to Spalatin, whom he commissioned to meet her. "I am sending you the letters of Argula von Grumbach, Christ's disciple, that you may see how the angels rejoice over a sinful daughter of Adam, converted and made into a daughter of God." (WA Br 2:503; Bainton 2001, 106; Kolde 1905, 114–15.)

To Luther, the most pious woman, Argula, was a special instrument and a disciple of Christ. Luther wrote:

> The Duke of Bavaria rages above measure, killing, crushing and persecuting the gospel with all his might. That most noble woman, Argula von Stauffer, is there making a valiant fight with great spirit, boldness of speech and knowledge of Christ. She deserves that all pray for Christ's victory in her. She has attacked the University of Ingolstadt for forcing the recantation of a certain youth, Arsacius Seehofer. Her husband, who treats her tyrannically, has been deposed from his prefecture. What he will do you can imagine. She alone, among these monsters, carries on with firm faith, though, she admits, not without inner trembling. She is a singular instrument of Christ. I commend her to you, that Christ through this infirm vessel may confound the mighty and those who glory in their strength. (Bainton 2001, 106; WABr IV:706; II:509)

(See Matheson 1995, 18, 21, footnotes 48, 58; WABr III: 247/25–34, 235, IV:605.)

Argula and Luther met, upon her initiative, on June 2, 1530 in Coburg, prior to the Diet of Augsburg. They exchanged a series of letters over the time, but all originals have been lost. Based on Luther's letters, he showed respect and care towards Argula. When finally writing about the Seehofer case and the "Bavarian pigs" to the University of Ingolstadt, though, he refrained from mentioning Argula's name altogether. Does this mean that in Luther's view, "individually, she might be worthy of praise and deserving of encouragement, but she had no place, it would seem, in the serious business of theology" (Matheson 1995, 21, also 21–3), or would direct communication with and about a woman have been "licentious" for a man of such stature (Joldersma 1997, 90)? (On Luther and Argula, see Stupperich 1955, 221–3; Kolde 1905, 114, 169–70; Bainton 2001, 101, 106–9; WABr II:509; IV: 713, 800; V:1581–4.)

Thus, as much as Luther appreciated Argula as one of his fellow reformers, her sex did pose a problem. Whereas theologically and in her criticism of the corruptions in the church Argula was in agreement with Luther, her "unfeminine" behavior was out of the norm and considered to be possibly harmful to the Protestants' cause. The fact is that

> she does insist on her inalienable rights as a woman to discuss her religious views, to explain her beliefs in public, and to read the Bible in German, all of which, of course, goes against Saint Paul. She goes so far as to claim that she was entitled to her personal interpretations of the holy text, thus establishing a dangerous precedent for both the Protestant and Catholic churches.

Luther probably deemed it safer to refrain from public association with a controversial figure who not only defied the prevalent contemporary ideals and norms for women but also offered "on the basis of her own exegetical interpretation, a revolutionary basis for possible riots of the local peasantry . . ." (Classen 1989, 146–7.) Argula slipped out of the mold presented for Protestant women. In domestic relations she may have appeared submissive, but where her religious views were at stake, she was nobody's subject.

Argula's writings exhibited her specific identity as a woman and a prophet and a reformer (Halbach 1992, 216–18, 213). What is intriguing is that she did not see herself as unusual; she was assured of the belief that "a school for women" existed as active disciples of Christ ("To the Honourable," in AvG/Matheson, 120). She was well acquainted with the word of Paul that women should be silent in church (1 Tim 1:2) but, echoing stories of other prophetic female voices, circumstances transformed the gender boundaries: "Now that I cannot see any man who is up to it, who is either willing or able to speak, I am constrained by the saying: 'Whoever confesses me' . . . Isaiah 3: 'I will send children to be their princes; and women, or those who are womanish, shall rule over them" ("The Account", in AvG/Matheson, 79). Argula followed in the long tradition of female prophets in Christian history who felt compelled – by God, they claimed – to take spiritual leadership and use their theological voice in the face of an apocalyptic situation. In other words, they expressed Christian discipleship in ways dictated by the Scriptures, the situation, and divine intervention. Indeed, there has been a school of women through the Christian centuries; Argula was correct.

Argula's fresh first-hand reading of the Scriptures shaped her inclusive view of the Christian Church and her conviction about women's rights. Using a wide range of books in the Bible (and benefiting from Luther's translation), most interested in the Psalms and the gospels, and with a thorough memory of the whole, Argula stressed, with other reformers, that the "Word of God alone must prevail" and is "its own best interpreter." Like Luther, Argula did not seek proof-texts in Scripture, but employed a hermeneutical lens of dialectic to interpret her times with scriptural wisdom. Like Marie Dentière, she read the scriptural stories as relevant models or mirrors for her context, placing her trust and hope in God overseeing everything. Her "ongoing dialogue" between her own experiences and the stories in Scripture shaped her unique lay-woman's theological perspective. "As educator, moralist, confessor, and reformer, she drew her inspiration from Scripture" (Matheson 1995, 38–9, see 27–39, also 158, 132, 181. Also Halbach 1992, 195–202, 226).

On June 29, 1524 she sent her last published letter (in part discussed above), her "apocalyptic appeal to the city of Regensburg," and an admonishment for people in Regensburg to adhere to the right faith. The text, not included in the Strasbourg collections, seemed to have been written in haste and had a cryptic and confessional tone (Kolde 1905, 150–9, 164–5; Stupperich 1955, 224). (See "An open letter by the noble-woman, Argula von Stauff to the people of Regensburg. To the honourable, prudent, and wise magistrats and council of the city of Regensburg, my good friends," June 29, 1524, in AvG/Matheson, 154–9.) This almost marks the end of Argula's public protestations for some years as the pressure on her, especially on the domestic front, grew too intense. This did not mean she lost interest or connections in the religious scene, quite the contrary. In a climate of an increased censorship and with the number of published pamphlets declining, Argula continued to write to her friends, including the reformers who kept her in the loop.

As one of her last public attempts to advance the cause of the Reformation, Argula had attended official meetings, and her attendance at the diets in Nuremberg (from November 24, 1523 until April 18, 1524) and Regensburg (June 27, 1524) indicates her stature in the Reformation scene. She would end up being criticized for using the golden opportunity to try to sway the princes attending, but, later, she even called a meeting herself, hoping to bring Melancththon and Bucer together in Augsburg over the issue of the Lord's Supper. As one of the first Protestant women to do so, she lobbied actively, and wished to use her influence to benefit the poor and to empower the laity. "She used her theological experience to support her political and social demands and vice versa." (Matheson 1995, 124–5; Classen 1989, 145.)

In her role as a lobbyist, she had also written to Fredrick the Wise, as well as Johann von Simmern, on December 1, 1523, urging them to stay faithful and firm in their opposition to those ruining the gospel (see her letter to Fredrick, AvG/Matheson, 129–34, and to "the noble Prince and Lord Johann, Count Palatine of the Rhine, Duke of Bavaria, Count of Spanheim . . ." 1523, in AvG/Matheson, 125–8.) She left the diets disappointed, concluding the attending men were more interested in drinking than serious matters, as she complained in her letters to Adam von Thering (December 1523) and other princes. One of her last measures, her letter to the city of Regensburg, expressed her frustrated opposition to the measures the city had taken against the Protestant faith and the lack of leadership from men in positions to act.

The last scandal that involved Argula was the "Landshut controversy" of 1524. In the fall of that year Argula decided to publish a long poem in response to a satirical anonymous poem about her from the same year. The anti-Argula poem of 130 lines (four sheets in quarto format), anonymous but revealing the writer in the text, had commanded the woman to stop meddling with God's word and to return to spinning. It suggested a sexual basis for the appeal between Luther and Argula, who from the title page on was characterized as unwomanly in her tendency to disputation. Argula's feisty and long response (over 300 lines) to her only literary opponent was published with the original poem by Johann of Landshut. With an eschatological undertone, the text repeated a firm defense of women from Scripture, and ended with a promise of "more to come": "God willing, another [poem] will follow. A. V. G. née von Stauffen (see "An Answer in verse to a member of the University of Ingolstadt in response to a recent utterance of his which is printed below. The year of our Lord 1524," in AvG/Matheson, 173–95). (See Bezzel 1986, 204, 206–7; Becker-Cantarino 1987, 106–7.)

After 1524, Argula began to disappear from the public scene, until reappearing in 1530. Her low-profile existence after the turmoil of Ingolstadt may speak of her disappointment with the overall situation and the lack of a respectful response, of her conceived failure in her lobbying, of the turmoil of the Peasants' wars of 1525, of the reemerging of the "old" church in Ingolstadt and Bavaria, or, simply, of her deteriorating family situation. There were only a few prolific and widely read female protestant writers like Argula and her Strasbourg contemporary Katharina Schütz Zell (who had the longest publishing career), and only a few followed their suit after the tightening of censorship from 1524 and especially 1530 onwards. Argula and Katharina may have known of each other's writings. (Matheson 1995, 23, 44–7; Jung 2002, 180–90.)

Argula's name appeared again during the Diet of Augsburg of 1530. It was while at the Diet that she tried to arrange the meeting between Melanchthon and Bucer, with hopes that the Swiss and the Germans would come to an agreement on the Lord's Supper – the point of lasting disagreement between those following the teachings of Zwingli and Calvin as opposed to those of Luther and other Wittenberg-influenced theologians (not to mention internal disagreements on both fronts). She met Luther in Coburg (where the outlawed reformer stayed in safety during the diet) on June 2, 1530, and she associated herself with Luther's sacramental theology. After the diet, Argula's active public involvement with the Reformation seems to have ended, and she may have lived the rest of her life in Lenting near Ingolstadt in her family estate. Or maybe she did not. Exact information about her activities is missing.

According to some traditions (for instance, the "Zeilitzheim tradition") Argula assisted in founding new local churches and traveled around the region on a similar mission (in Gerolzhofen, Schallfeld, Krautheim, and Brünnstadt. Leonard von Eck suspected she was preaching to commoners in Dietfurt). The little we know of her after 1524 comes from occasional references to her in correspondence with her children and among those involved in the Reformation. The fact that she remarried in 1533 has been well established.

After Argula's first (anti-Protestant) husband Friedrich died in 1530, Argula married a man more sympathetic to the Reformation, Count Poppo von Schlick. The count died two years later, in 1535 (perhaps after a brief separation). Three of Argula's children died (George in 1539, Hans Georg in 1544, and Apollonia in 1539) before her own death in what was more or less obscurity. When exactly she died, and what activities she had been involved in up until the time of her death, have not been conclusively determined. A report from 1586 claimed Argula had died in 1554, and some argue that she was no longer actively involved in the Protestant propaganda in her later years. Another tradition, from 1563, gives report of a "stubborn" old woman of the von Stauff family again leading people astray by gathering them and teaching them Protestant theology and conducting funeral sessions (with the assistance of the members of the Grumbach family). At the same time, a 1563 letter from the Duke of Bavaria to the town's council talks about the imprisonment (for the second time) of "the old Staufferin" who had been invoking ordinary people to disobedience, circulating Protestant books, holding private house services, and officiating at gravesite funerals. The woman in question was released by the council, the given reason being that the old "the Staufferin" was too frail and better left alone in her stupidity and high age. A woman agitator inciting people to rebel against the Catholic church and on an active mission may sound more radical than the Argula of her letters, but she may have grown so with age and become less concerned about her own or her children's safety. There is really no reason to doubt that she could have lived until 1568, as some have suggested; she would, had she done so, have only been 71.

A review of all the gathered evidence can only determine that there is no certainty that she had died by 1563, but no reason to think she died in 1554 either. The ending of her life remains a mystery, of which it is a more plausible conjecture than not that her commitment to the Lutheran Christian faith, for which she had taken considerable risks in the prime of her life and as a mother of young children, did not stop overnight. The later dates seem more probable than the 1554 date (especially in light of the implicit and explicit efforts to erase her memory). Argula may have continued to work the rest of her long life in a private circle of likeminded believers as an evangelical confessor, concentrating on bringing up her children and reaching outside her family with her letters. She was a lay theologian and a female reformer whose Reformation manifesto became public in her letters. (See Becker-Cantarino 1987, 109–10.)

Conclusion

Argula has been portrayed as a rebellious trouble-maker, as a faithful confessor, and even as a martyr. To a degree, all evaluations ring true. She certainly rebelled against the patriarchal conventions regulating women's life in assuming a public writing and debating role. Her demand to have not just respect but also an official response, a public debate, and her offering her own scriptural interpretation to correct the learned university men were bold acts for any lay person and particularly for a woman, even if of noble birth. In these respects she disregarded both Protestant and Catholic conventions. Furthermore, she rebelled against the Catholic church in her defense of Lutheran views as authentically Christian and scriptural. She rebelled against her husband when exerting her role outside the home. A theologian, she was one of those who were self-learned, fueled by religious passion, and intrigued by theological questions. She was a theologian with a public voice.

Very much akin to the causes embraced by Katharina Schütz Zell, for Argula Christian theology promoted justice, not violence, which she condemned as anti-scriptural. She was a confessor – which, among the Protestants developing their own hagiographies was a form of martyrdom and sainthood – who dared to confess in public what she believed in, even if her confession was that of the minority, and one who felt compelled by her faith to defend also the rights of others' to their beliefs and confessions. She applied her Christian right to confess her faith as a shield against those who wanted to silence her. Argula's confidence in her confessing was rooted in her first-hand biblical knowledge and her own interpretation of it, and was enhanced by her grasp of the urgent political and religious situation that called for her theological vision for religious freedom. Like those few of her female contemporaries exercising a similarly public voice, Argula drew her authority – and her identity as a Christian woman – from the Scripture, and likewise, she was satisfied that her noble family status, and, last but not least, the theological principle of priesthood of all believers gave her licence to speak. As for Olimpia Morata, access to knowledge and Scripture was a vital means of empowerment for Argula. (This proves true the notion that "danger" is imbedded in education; it may lead to increased self-confidence and the questioning of existing norms and systems.)

Did Argula die as a martyr, though? There had been speculations about her suffering, even at the hands of her own husband, but exactly how much and in what ways remains veiled. Argula was mentioned in the Rabus's History of the Martyrs of 1572 and was called a "confessor" and the "Bavarian Judith," titles that honored valiant confessors of the Protestant faith in the early years of constant danger (Luther was added to this list as well). Regardless of this, Argula was soon forgotten, and allusions to her are rare. She was mentioned in a 1688 defense of Argula against Cochlaeus, Luther's enemy, also by Christian Salig in his *Historie der Augsburgischen Confession,* and her first biography, by Georg Rieger, dates from 1737. (See Matheson 1995, 26–28, 48, footnote 144.)

Regardless of Argula's letters and lobbying, Bavaria remained in the Catholic faith. The fact that much of her controversial public writing around the Arsacius affair became widely (even if briefly) published and that she enjoyed personal admiration of major reformers speaks of her success. Her statements about the supremacy of the Scriptures and the validity of the priesthood of all believers formed an important manifesto for the Protestant faith, an exceptional one coming from the mouth of a woman. She fought in word and in person for the same basic causes Luther did. She never admitted to being a Lutheran, though, but called herself – like Luther himself, whose stimulus in her life she freely admitted – a Christian. She broke apart from Luther in one important area: in her assessment of women's right to enter the world of theology and church politics. Luther never criticized Argula for her involvement: quite the contrary, she earned Luther's respect. Because she was a woman, even if she was welcomed in the inner circle of Luther's associates (broadly conceived), she has nevertheless remained somewhere between the insiders and the outsiders in the Reformation saga as it has been told. In the narratives of the Reformation she has only recently been duly recognized for her role in the web of central connections.

Argula was born at the right moment in history, in the window of opportunity for lay pamphlet writing, before such opportunities became more controlled. Argula, and Katharina Schütz Zell, represent what "could have been" for Protestant women in the sixteenth century and more generally. Her story also demonstrates the impediments women writers and teachers faced. She embodied the hopes of an emancipated lay person, and more specifically, of a lay woman. She embodied the zeal of the early evangelicals as she spoke out of conviction and confession, as a Christian, as a bible teacher, and as a defender of people's religious rights, offering a lens to Scripture that could have radical social as well as theological ramifications. Contained within her actions and her words were potential repercussions for the emancipation of women and the rebellion of the suppressed peoples, such as the peasants. (See Matheson 1995, 43–4, 55; Jung 2002, 221.)

After a brief surge of interest in her story at the turn of the twentieth century (Kolde 1905; Thoma 1900), recent scholarship has rediscovered Argula with delight and excitement. "The challenge before us now, therefore, is to let her voice be heard at long last, to integrate her social critique, her interpretation of Scripture, and her innovative lobbying and publishing, as well as her pioneering role for women, into the mainstream of Reformation scholarship" (Matheson 1995, 56). Including her writings in the theological canon and relevant discourse is an important step in the processes of expanding the pool of theological sources and perspectives and reformulating the "questions of importance."

A Word about Sources and References

For critical biographical information and Argula's texts in English, see Matheson 1995, the most recent full biographical work providing the core information and a bibliographical listing of the other main biographical sources, and Halbach's 1992 dissertation, both following Kolde's classic 1905 work.

For valuable earlier works with much detail, see Theobald 1936; Rieger 1737; Engelhardt 1860; Pistorius 1854. For foundational interpretations on Argula as a writer and a reformer, see Classen 1989, 1991a and 1991b; Stupperich 1955, 1956, 1984; Bainton 1971/2001; and Jung 2002. Important perspectives on Argula as a confessing reformer offer Heinsius 1951 and 1928; Bezzel 1986 and 1987; Becker-Cantarino 1987; and Joldersma 1997. For descriptions on Argula's texts and the existing literature on her, see Schöndorf 1983; Halbach 1992, 9–13 and passim on texts; and Matheson 1995, 3–4, 49. For a popular portrait see Heinen 1981, also a multi-authored "Festchrift" to honor the five-hundredth anniversary of her birth, *Argula von Grumbach: selbst ist die Frau, 1992.*

CHAPTER 7

Elisabeth von Brandenburg, 1485–1555, and Elisabeth von Braunschweig, 1510–1558 – Exiled Mothers, Reforming Rulers

Christina von Sachsen – presumed – mother of Elisabeth von Brandenburg. From *Saints Genevieve and Apollonia* by Lucas Cranach the Elder

Elisabeth von Brandenburg, 1485–1555

GRANDPARENTS (PATERNAL)

- Christian I Oldenburg (1426–81) and Dorothea von Hohenzollern (von Brandenburg) (1430–95)

GRANDPARENTS (MATERNAL)

- Ernst von Sachsen (1441–86) and Elisabeth von Obermeyer von Bayern (married 1461)

PARENTS

- Johann Friedrich, King of Denmark, Sweden and Norway (1455–1513)
- Christina von Sachsen (1461–1521)

UNCLES

- Friedrich Der Weise/the Wise, Johann Der Beständige/The Steadfast
- Wolfgang

- ◆ Albrecht
- ◆ Ernst, Archbishop of Magdeburg

AUNTS
- ◆ Christine
- ◆ Margarete

SIBLINGS
- ◆ Johann, Ernst, Christian II (1481–1559 married Isabella of Austria 1501–26, sister of the Emperor Charles V), Jacob, and Franz

SPOUSE (1502–35)
- ◆ Joachim I (1484–1535) Elector of Brandenburg

CHILDREN
- ◆ Joachim 1 (1505–71)
- ◆ Anna (1507–67)
- ◆ Elisabeth (1510–58)
- ◆ Margaretha (1511–77)
- ◆ Johann (1513–71)

Introduction

The two Elisabeths, a mother and a daughter, played an instrumental role in the spreading of the Lutheran faith in Northern German territories. The younger Elisabeth in particular was a major force in securing the Reformation in her duchy. Both embraced Protestant theology at great personal cost and, fueled by their conviction, used their position of influence to ensure the legalization of the Protestant faith in their territories of Brandenburg and Braunschweig. Their stories demonstrate how the Reformation's success depended both on individuals' risky choices and the decisions of those with authority, whether noble or civic. Both women were mothers, both were married to Catholic husbands, and both, with eventual success, became brave and resolute advocates and implementers of the Reformation. Unlike some other women in similar strategic places of authority, the two noblewomen did not let the bearings of their social status impede their personal faith commitments. Quite the opposite, they intentionally employed their status for the cause of the faith of their choice and made their personal religious convictions known with no apologies, and with an intentional mission to convert others as well. (By comparison, Renée de France and Marguerite de Navarre arbitrated for their religious sympathies more cautiously in light of the politics of their position and the well-being of their children.)

The two Elisabeths demonstrate the fundamental influence women could have in the spreading of the Protestant faith. Their stories remind us of the tragedies mothers could endure for the sake of their religion. In their defiance, and in the course of the events that temporarily distanced them from their own children, they assumed the role of a mother in a broader sense of the word. Their care for the people's spiritual wellbeing and their concern for all their "children" explain some of their bravery. They witnessed to the important role mothers had in implementing the faith with their choices, in public as well as in private. These mothers' actions, and words, have been recorded, particularly those of the younger Elisabeth, who made an impact also as a writer and a politically pertinent figure in the history of her dynasty.

Elisabeth von Brandenburg née Elisabeth of Denmark – A Reformer in Exile

A Danish princess, the only daughter of Frederik I, the king of Denmark, Sweden, and Norway, Elisabeth stirred the waters when in 1527 she received Communion in both forms from a Lutheran minister. Elisabeth's social standing and the violence of emotion the theological issues at stake provoked in her age made an act that might, in other times and for other people, have been a choice of only personal spiritual consequence, of much greater significance.

She was born Elisabeth Oldenburg in 1485 in Copenhagen, a descendant of the Danish royal house of her paternal grandfather, Christian I Oldenburg, and grandmother, Dorothea von Hohenzollern (also known as von Brandenburg; a politically influential woman married to two consecutive kings of Denmark, Christopher of Bavaria and Christian I). Her mother Christina von Sachsen (of Saxony), a daughter of Elisabeth von Obermeyer and Ernst von Sachsen, was the sister of the famous princes Friedrich III, known as *der Weise* (the Wise) and Johann Der Beständige (John the Steadfast), and Archbishop Ernst von Magdeburg. These family members, especially her brother Christian II, were instrumental in instilling Lutheranism in Denmark and Germany (Kirchner 1866, 215–17; Riedel 1865, 66–7).

At the age of 17 or 18, in April 1502, the young Elisabeth married a man close to her age, Joachim I (born 1484), the elector of Brandenburg. A brother of Albert von Hohenzollern, Archbishop of Mainz and Magdeburg (who had purchased his office under-aged and without clergy status and, to pay off his debt, welcomed extravagant indulgence sellers in his territory, which chain of events provoked Luther to nail his 95 theses to the door of Wittenberg castle church), Joachim vehemently opposed Luther and the reforms he proclaimed. Trouble could be predicted even from the start in a marriage formed on the eve of the Reformation between families with conflicting loyalties.

The first few years were peaceful and happy, though, and soon motherhood took over Elisabeth's time. Joachim was the first born (1505) and would succeed his father as the elector in 1535. Daughters, Anna (1507), Elisabeth (1510), and Margaretha (1511), followed. When her last child, Johann, was born in 1513, Elisabeth was only 28 years old. The children were to be raised in Catholic faith, the faith of their father and the territory. It was in this area that Elisabeth would most prominently assert her independence and authority as the years went by, once her children were grown. It would seem that the autonomy she was able to claim as a middle-aged woman was guaranteed in the arrangement set down in her wedding contract, by which, as the wife of Joachim, Elisabeth received the nearby castle of Spandau and authority over the village and lands around it (including the hunting rights); furthermore, she was to receive an allowance of 6,000 gulden a year should she outlive her husband. This important compact would prove extremely beneficial to her as she found herself opposing her husband publicly in the most burning issue of the day, the religious reforms.

The couple became seriously estranged when Elisabeth openly adopted Lutheranism: her public conversion placed her politically and religiously in the opposite camp to her powerful Catholic husband. This was a risky proposition even for a royal woman with significant authority and powerful friends and family home and abroad. Her stubbornness in defending her right to her faith and the margrave's heavy-handedness in trying to force her out of her "Lutheran heresy" caused an unbridgeable gap between the two. (Riedel 1865, 69–72; Kirchner 1866, 220–5.)

How did Elisabeth come to be involved with the Lutheran faith? Her major influences were her own brother, King Christian II and his wife Isabella (the Lutheran sister of the Catholic Emperor Charles V), who legalized the Reformation in Denmark after they acceded to the throne in 1513. While in exile after the violent rejection of his rule in Sweden by the Swedish nobility and having forced through his reforms, he visited Wittenberg, where he absorbed Luther's theology. He remained in personal contact with the reformer through the years, and Elisabeth, being close to Christian and Isabella, was influenced by their Lutheran theology. In addition to personal conversations, hymns and treatises and itinerant preachers also brought Lutheran theology to Elisabeth, who could read Luther's translation of the Bible and other of his widely circulating texts at first hand. Her privileged status and connections gave her access to an assortment of printed works, and her determination and curiosity made her break her husband's edict against singing, teaching, or reading Luther's works (or even printing Luther's Bible). Joachim must have observed Elisabeth's growing interest and the books she was reading, but he made no effort to control her until she made her new faith public. (See Kirchner 1866, 225–32; Bainton 2001, 113–15.)

Just before Easter 1527, while Joachim was traveling, Elisabeth chose to receive Communion in both forms from a Lutheran pastor. This act appears to have been premeditated. Certainly Elisabeth was aware of the significance, symbolic and actual, of her act of defiance against the explicit orders regarding religious practice of the man who, as her husband and her feudal overlord, had dominion over her. Given the ongoing debates over the nature and practice of Communion in Protestant circles alone (for instance, the disagreement between Luther and Zwingli over whether the presence of Christ in the Lord's Supper was real or spiritual), not to mention the decisiveness of this issue between the Catholics and the Protestants, this personal act of faith would have inevitable political repercussions. (See Riedel 1865, 68–9; Kirchner 1866, 235–44; Baur 1873, 528–30.)

A persistent legend implicates her young daughter Elisabeth as the source of the "leak" that informed Joachim about his wife's actions. There is nothing to prove that, however. Elisabeth was already living apart from her husband, in Spandau, and there is no evidence of hostility between the mother and the daughter who, when she herself had married, often visited and corresponded with her mother against her father's wishes. Whether her daughter witnessed Elisabeth receiving Communion or not, such an act would not go unnoticed. It is quite plausible that Elisabeth intentionally proclaimed herself Lutheran in this way and did not wish to hide her decision. Aware of her mother's involvement with the Lutheran faith, the younger Elisabeth acquainted herself with Luther's works as well. In 1538 she would follow in her mother's footsteps, both in converting and staging a domestic rebellion. (See Becker-Cantarino 1983; Wiesner-Hanks 2000, 41–2.)

Outraged, Joachim consulted a team of learned men (bishops and doctors), who entertained different punishment options from imprisonment or drowning to exile or divorce. Joachim took a moderate road and demanded that Elisabeth return to the old faith within six months or be subjected to the discipline of the church. She was expected to attend Mass on All Saints' Day, November 1, 1527. When that date passed, Easter 1528 was set as the new deadline. There is no proof of Joachim mishandling his wife, but certainly of his threats of "surrender, or . . .!" The one thing she was asked for as a guarantee of avoiding maltreatment – to refrain from receiving communion in both kinds – she could not agree to. Her persistent resistance may have surprised Joachim: Elisabeth fighting for her religion was a different woman from the young bride he had married. She, in turn, must have known how futile it was to expect Joachim change his mind either. Yet she tried to bring him to do so, explaining her theological and spiritual reasoning in her letters. Elisabeth wrote to her husband (on October 15 of the year she left him) about why she could not disobey the will of God or the word of God, but would rather give up her life and all that she loved for it. (See Riedel 1865, 69–72, 80; Kirchner 1866, 235–45.)

Joachim would not bend. Elisabeth received support from Erich von Braunschweig and Albert of Mecklenberg, her sons-in-law, through letters from her brother Christian (October 1527) and from her uncle Johann Der Beständige (February 1528) who sternly opposed Joachim's demands and his treatment of his niece. Elisabeth eventually took refuge in the protection of her uncle Johann and brother Christian (now in Berlin), who advised her to flee. Her flight was the outcome of a conspiracy of a circle of high-powered men. During the night of March 24–5, 1528, while Joachim was in Brunswick visiting their daughter, Elisabeth left her castle in Saxony. With her lady-in-waiting Ursula von Zedtwitz, and with her portable treasures, she was transported first by wagon and then by boat to Torgau. Joachim learned the news immediately and was furious. (See Berbig 1911, 380–94; Bainton 2001, 115.)

On the very next day, March 26, 1528, Elisabeth pleaded in writing to the elector of Saxony. Joachim responded on March 30 with a demand to have her sent back without any conditions. She wrote several other letters, among them one to Cardinal Albrecht on April 1. Two years later, in 1530, Joachim complained to the Emperor Charles V at Augsburg that the Danish king should return his sister without conditions. In her defense, several reasons were given for Elisabeth's departure: her new insights into Scripture and religious differences between the spouses were the primary reasons, enhanced by the intolerable situation in which the margrave's demand that she receive communion in one kind only would force the margravine to "sin" against her conscience. She demonstrated passion for her faith on a personal level, but also acted upon her sense of responsibility for the good of her people. Although her flight angered numerous people, even Protestant leaders (such as Philip von Hessen), who did not appreciate such disobedience in a woman, she did not consider her womanhood either an obstacle or an issue. Deserted and humiliated, Joachim insisted that Johann force his wife to return – but to no effect. Johann disapproved of Joachim's use of force and his demands on Elisabeth with regard to her Communion practice. That kind of a theological principle was too important to be handled solely as a domestic issue! Another serious, more private reason that Elisabeth could cite for her continued absence, however, was Joachim's affairs with other women.

Joachim's infidelity played a role in both Elisabeth's decision to leave and her negotiations regarding her return. For at least two years Joachim had been sharing his bed with other women, married and single. In response to his requests for Elisabeth to return, Elisabeth made counter-requests: she demanded guaranteed safety for herself and her possessions, a right to call her own pastor and receive the Sacrament as often and as she understood proper from Christ's teaching, and she expected a return to marital relations. The last request is of interest: though the early modern Europeans had a negative opinion of divorce, it was regarded as warrantable if the sexual dimension in a marriage was lacking. Neither Joachim nor Elisabeth wanted a divorce. Joachim wanted his wife to return to the Catholic faith, Elisabeth wanted her husband to return to her bed. (Bainton 2001, 117–18; Berbig 1911, 381–94; Kirchner 1866, 235–352.)

Elisabeth's reasoning for her requests were complex. She could forgive adultery but she could not compromise on the issue of religion. She wanted her husband back, but not at the expense of her new faith. Joachim's return to her bed would seal his approval of her religious choice – and, in a way, his approval of Lutheranism in his region. She expressed unwavering commitment to her new faith, aware of the implications of her choices as a public figure, a position she saw as an asset rather than a liability. She demonstrated passion for her faith on a personal level, but also acted upon her sense of responsibility for the good of her people. She did not consider her womanhood an obstacle or a factor.

Ignoring requests for her return, Elisabeth remained in exile for several years. Either she never imagined her exile would last that long, or she considered that there was no price too high to pay for her faith. She was forced to get by with outrageously little in comparison with what her royal blood and marital status would normally have afforded her. Her sons secretly provided her with goods and financial assistance, but she was chronically lacking in money and incurred sizeable debts. Her travels took her from Torgau to Wittenberg to Weimar. She lived in a small apartment, suffering from hunger and illnesses, such as loss of teeth, cramps, arthritis, and gout (being particularly seriously ill between 1532 and 1533). Her mental health deteriorated as well. There are indications of severe mental stress, which manifested in erratic behavior.

Elisabeth was a high-maintenance houseguest, as the Luthers could testify, after taking care of her for about four months in 1537. She occupied more than her share of the already limited space and resources, and they did not appreciate her long stay, her moods, or her daughter Elisabeth moving in with her for several weeks after disregarding their polite refusal of her unsolicited invitation to move in to care for her mother. Just exactly how difficult a guest Elisabeth was can be read in Luther's letters where he complains about her childish, unruly, and erratic behavior and spendthrift ways (WA Br 3:3188, November 16, 1537) and argues that he is unable and unwilling to host her any longer. (Bainton 2001, 120; WABr 7:2160, 2164, December 11, 1547.) Luther's letter campaign – he wrote, for instance to Elector Johann – finally paid off and an alternative arrangement was made by Elector Johann Friedrich for Elisabeth to move to the castle of Lichtenberg. Luther visited her there, concerned about her wellbeing, and wrote about her sad situation to Justus Jonas. Difficult though she may have been as a houseguest, he felt pity for "a woman of such noble birth and character so grievously afflicted" (WATr 3: 3644, 4: 4647f. Bainton 2001, 118).

The tide changed for Elisabeth when Joachim died on August 16, 1532. At this point it would have been possible for the widow to have returned to Brandenburg, and her sons immediately began to work towards that goal and pleaded to her good sense to do so. She, in return, expected her sons to return to the evangelical faith, contrary to the promises they had made to honor their dying father's wishes. They promised her a secure place in Spandau and 6,000 gulden a year from her wedding contract, but she would not accept the offer until the issue of religion was resolved. Her condition for return was that the whole of Brandenburg should accept Lutheran theology in the form of the Augsburg Confession. It was not enough for her sons to obey, she expected the lords and the estates in Brandenburg to make the Lutheran faith official, "for the sake of the divine realization of the holy gospel." In her letter to her sons dated August 8, 1535, she demanded a Lutheran pastor, the preaching of the gospel, and the acceptance of the Augsburg Confession throughout Saxony. Elisabeth pleaded to her son (Kirchner 1866, 260),

> What we have in our motherly and faithful love done, most exalted prince, most friendly and dearest son: After your honorable and highly educated Martin (Luther), the Doctor of the Holy Scriptures, we have asked for us a good Lutheran Preacher, to perform religious ceremonies . . . We have discussed this with the above mentioned Doctor, and have spoken with him in person . . . This is our friendly and motherly request. (translation Stjerna)

The sons were in an impossible position, both because of their promise to their dying father to not introduce new faith in their region and because Joachim II had married Hedwig, the Catholic daughter of the king of Poland. Further, Ferdinand of Austria had warned him against harboring sympathies towards the reformers as inappropriate for men within the Halle alliance of Catholic rulers.

In another letter Elisabeth wrote again about the "truth" to her sons in a "motherly and friendly" spirit: she admonished them to take care of the reforming of godly ceremonies and wished that they would study the word of God. The letter that she had crafted out of love, of God's grace, and "in her own hand" concluded with a signature of the highborn Elisabeth, "born of the royal branch from Denmark, Margravine of Brandenburg, a widow." ("Von Gottes Gnaden Elisabeth geborne aus königlichem Stamm zu Dänemark etc, Markgräfinn zu Brandenburg, Wittwe etc. Elisabeth meyn hants, In Seiner Liebe eigenen Handen.") (Elisabeth von Brandenburg in Kirchner 1866, 260–1.)

Her younger son, Johann, had less to lose politically and warmed sooner than his brother to the idea of converting to the Lutheran faith; more under the influence of his mother, whom he wished to please, he became a friend of the Reformation. There was more at stake for Joachim, and even after he compromised he never did quite enough for his mother's liking; in her opinion, Joachim did not promote a "good Lutheran" reformation (Baur 1873, 535). In 1539, though, Joachim II had a change of heart and he took Communion in both kinds (repeating the act soon after in Berlin), but it still did not bring his mother home. Once he had made the decision to convert, Elisabeth urged Joachim to establish a church order for Brandenburg. She failed or refused to understand the pressures her son was under from many directions and insisted that the order he initially intended to adopt, which would have allowed the practice of some old ceremonies to continue, in agreement with Luther and Melanchthon, was too lenient.

When Luther was asked to mediate he presented a middle way: he wrote in a letter about the freedom in Christian life and the harmlessness of allowing people to maintain some of the old religious practices (even ones not allowed in Wittenberg). He reminded Elisabeth of the freedom of one's conscience and of the priorities of preaching the gospel purely and observing the sacraments correctly; as long as the Mass was abolished, and with that the invocation to saints, things were in good order. Elisabeth was not as tolerant as Luther (or, as Bainton says, Elisabeth was "not as broad as Luther. She was a precursor of the English Puritans who called the vestments of the clergy 'the rags of Antichrist.'" Bainton 2001, 122; WABr 7:3421, December 4/5, 1539.)

The margrave and his brother finally told their mother to do as she wished and asked her to let them do what they needed to in their lands – a blow softened with greetings from her loving sons, "we shall be bound to you as loving sons." (Bainton 2001, 121; Riedel 1865, 92–5; Kirchner 1866, 264, 268–9.)

Even her deteriorating health and an episode of grave illness (from 1540 until 1541) failed to mellow Elisabeth, as the debate over church orders shows. She was still unwilling to return and only did so a few years later (having spent about 18 years abroad, several of those years after her husband's death), in August 1545. Her son Johann came to retrieve his mother with 500 horses. More impressively, he agreed to her conditions and promised to pay her significant debts, secure her autonomy over Spandau where she would live, furnish her with an allowance, and give her the right to practice the religion of her preference with a pastor of her choice. Upon her return, she "conducted family devotions" in her household and remained active in religious affairs. She studied the Bible and the catechism. Her return to normal life was not easy though. Her will was strong "But her spirit was not healed." She dwelled on the past and was a "trifle querulous." (Bainton 2001, 122. See Jakobi 1989, 181–273; Kirchner 1866, 262–73; Baur 1873, 536–9.)

Ill physically and mentally, at the end of her life when she had reached the age of 70, she asked to be moved to Berlin. She returned there on June 1, 1555, to die just ten days later. She was ready for her death, as her few extant words reveal. She wrote to her son Johann,

> I cannot conceal from you out of motherly love that the dear God our heavenly Father, has laid upon me a heavy cross with sickness, poverty, misery, trouble, and terror, more than I can tell. I would not have believed that such trials could be on earth and would comfort myself with the words of Job, 'The Lord has given. The Lord has taken away. Blessed be the name of the Lord.' You should know how long I have lived in misery and great sickness and have had to suffer such shameful poverty in my old age as not to have a penny on earth, nor a bite of sausage in my mouth. If God in his special grace had not upheld me, it would have been no wonder if my heart had broken in two for sheer misery. (Bainton 2001, 122–3; Kirchner 1866, 279–83)

Revealing words follow: "Who is afraid of a 'clipse'? I believe in him who made the sun and the moon and all the stars and gave life to all creatures. He will uphold me. May he not tarry to fetch me. To him will I go. I am so weary of life." (Bainton 2001, 123; Kirchner 1866, 281.) The letter speaks of a powerful conviction of faith, of tenacity, and of a readiness to die. Elisabeth died as a confessor and believer, a holy mother of the land ("eine heilige Landesmutter"; Baur 1873, 538–9). She was buried, upon her request, next to her estranged husband Joachim. Their 27 years of strife had been over religion, more so than over infidelity or lack of affection. It seems fair to conclude that their marriage had been broken as much by Elisabeth's commitment to the Protestant faith as Joachim's sharing his affection with other women. At her death, after having won the religious dispute, in her eyes, she made peace with the husband of her youth. (See Riedel 1865, 98–100.)

Elisabeth's will was a telling testament to her faith (Riedel 1865, 99). Religion was central in her will. She began with her confession, stated her belief in the Trinity, and bade the estates to follow God's will, before turning to giving her advice to her children to do the right thing:

For the benefit of the salvation of their own souls, they should accept the holy and divine word and gospel of Jesus Christ, the only one who brings us salvation, as it comes to us by means of the Augsburg Confession and shines through God's special grace in this part of Germany, they should accept it in true and unfaltering faith, with their heart, and should keep it dear till the end. (translation Stjerna)

She underscored her expectation that the Word of God should be preached according to the Augsburg Confession in her land, and that her children should live and rule with justice and mercy, after she was gone. (See Baur 1873, 538; Kirchner 1866, 274–9.)

As a mother, she left a legacy in her children as well. Joachim (1505–71), her first born followed his father as the elector. In time, with his younger brother Johann I (1513–71), who had inherited the province of Küstrin – the Brandenburg lands to the east of the Oder – from his father, the elector implemented the Lutheran faith throughout the Brandenburg territories. Elisabeth's daughter Anna (1507–67) became the duchess of Mecklenburg, the youngest daughter Margaretha (1511–77) became the duchess of Anhalt, and the middle daughter, Elisabeth (1510–58) was married to the duke of Brunswick, Erich von Braunschweig–Calenberg. There the duchess conducted her own battle over the Protestant faith, enforcing a Protestant Church Order by 1542, very much influenced by her mother's example and encounters with Luther. Her children, Elisabeth von Brandenburg's grandchildren, Erich II, Anna Maria, and Elisabeth, continued to play important roles in the Reformation in their territories. The middle daughter, Elisabeth, provided an important chapter of her own in the Reformation history of Germany.

Elisabeth von Braunschweig-Lüneburg (Calenberg), 1510–1558

Elisabeth von Brandenburg, von Braunschweig–Lüneburg (Calenberg–Göttingen)

Elisabeth von Brandenburg, von Braunschweig–Lüneburg (Calenberg–Göttingen)

PARENTS
- Joachim I von Brandenburg (1484–1535) "Nestor"
- Elisabeth Oldenburg of Denmark (1485–1555)

SIBLINGS
- Anna, Margaretha, Johann, and Joachim

SPOUSE (1525–40)
- Erich I von Braunschweig–Calenberg (1470–1540)

CHILDREN
- Elisabeth (1526–66, married Ernst zu Henneberg 1543)
- Erich II von Braunschweig–Lüneburg (1528–84)
- Anna Maria (1532–68, married Albrecht von Preussen)
- Katharina (1534–59)

Like her mother Elisabeth von Brandenburg, the Duchess Elisabeth went into exile to enforce her territory's adoption of the Augsburg Confession. She has been characterized as one of the "more influential women in the politics of the Reformation . . . even more than her mother" ("who hurt her own influence by her exile"; Bainton 2001, 125. Also Stelzel 2003, 12.) As a ruler, as a politician, and the first writer in the Brandenburg and Braunschweig family, she was the embodiment of the new Renaissance ruler and was held in high regard by Lutheran reformers of the land, by Luther and Melanchthon. We still lack a conclusive biography in English, but the life and various contributions of

Elisabeth have been recorded in histories of the noble family. They record her birth into the noble family of "Kurfürst" on August 24, 1510, to the elector Joachim I (1484–1535) and Elisabeth Oldenburg of Denmark (1485–1555) as one of their five children.

By the time her mother converted to the Protestant faith in 1527, Elisabeth had already been married for two years to a man as firmly Catholic as her father. Her writings and command of language demonstrate her broad cultivation (which she owed to Fabian Frangk, a member of her father's court). Her education, made possible by the family resources and her parents' enlightened views, included reading, writing, religion, and geography, with limited instruction in the languages, for instance, in Latin. Her acumen in Latin is unclear. The lack of Latin books in her library could indicate either her insufficiency in the language or her dislike of it (Mengel 1952). Her instruction has been characterized as being of a more moral and practical nature than academic. (See Stelzel 2003, 13–15; Becker-Cantarino 1983, 204, 241, 239; Mengel 1954a, xx–xxi.)

At the age of 15, on July 7, 1525 (the summer of Luther and Katharina's marriage) Elisabeth was married to the 55-year-old Duke Erich von Braunschweig-Calenberg (1470–1540), whose territories included Lüneburg, Calenberg-Göttingen, Wolfenbüttel, and Grubenhagen. The wedding took place one year after the death of Erich's first wife, Katharina von Sachsen (the widow of Sigismund, the duke of Austria). Since Katharina's and Erich's only child had died early, it was hoped that Elisabeth would quickly produce heirs, which she did. She gave birth to four children: Elisabeth in 1526 (who married to Ernst zu Henneberg in 1543), Erich II von Braunschweig-Lüneburg in 1528, Anna Maria in 1532 (who married Albrecht von Preussen), and Katharina in 1534. Of all the children Erich, the heir, was the apple of his mother's eye. Her relationship with Anna Maria and her husband Albrecht, was close as well. She was particularly involved in the lives of these two children and in securing their happiness and status; for instance, she offered them unsolicited maternal advice, in print, on topics ranging from marital affairs to issues of regnancy and religion.

At first Elisabeth and Erich lived mostly in their castle at Münden. After the early years of happiness, trouble arose because of Erich's long-term lover, Anna Rumschottel, who had comforted Erich during his brief widowhood and with whom he resumed an intimate relationship during Elisabeth's long recovery from her labor with daughter Anna Maria and continued when she was well once more. His timing in returning to the arms of his lover was particularly painful to Elisabeth who was at that point "unequal to wifely relations." (Bainton 2001, 125. Elisabeth wrote angrily about this in her letter to Albrecht von Preussen in 1549. See Mengel 1954a, 52, Letter No. 35 from September 21, 1549.) Had Elisabeth had any illusions that the lover had "retired" with a handsome pension, or that she had died (as Erich claimed, going so far as to stage a mock funeral for her), the truth came out that Anna had given birth in a secluded castle. Elisabeth wanted the relationship terminated for good. Subjecting Anna to an inquisition, or, rather, a witch hunt, seemed like a reasonable course of action to her. Her husband disagreed, and his lover managed to escape, leaving Elisabeth to plead with her father to come to her defense. In the end she won a settlement that allowed her to separate from her husband for all practical purposes and rule the semi-independent territory of Göttingen and Münden. The latter became her residence and gave her an opportunity for hands-on experience in the governing office and skills she would need later in life.

At first both she and Erich had practiced the Catholic faith, but, starting in 1524 Elisabeth began to read Luther's writings and her views began to change the more she read. Her turning point can be timed from the visit made to her in 1538 by her mother and her brother Johann, who had recently turned to Lutheran faith. In the same year she corresponded with Luther and Philip von Hessen, a fellow-Protestant, who sent her on "loan" a preacher, Antonius Corvinus. Under the influence of Corvinus' preaching and other Lutheran contacts, Elisabeth proclaimed herself Lutheran in 1538. About ten years after her mother's escape to Berlin, she in the company of her court ladies received Communion in two kinds, according to the Lutheran rite (1535). (Her public conversion differed from her mother's initially private conversion. [Brenneke 1925, 153].) Erich chose to ignore his wife's conversion at first, but not for long. After a decade of marriage, religion would add to the pre-existing strife between the couple.

In contrast to the play of events in her mother's marriage, Elisabeth's husband at first agreed to a policy of mutual tolerance. In Erich's words, "My wife does not interfere with and molest us in our faith, and therefore we will leave her undisturbed and unmolested in hers." (Kurs 1891, 11; in Bainton 2001, 126–7.) Erich personally appreciated Luther, even sent him beer after the Diet of Worms, but nevertheless he wanted to die in his old faith, and had no interest in the "new" theology. Elisabeth, perhaps to Erich's surprise, wanted more than peace to practice her own faith: she would spearhead a daring, persistent mission to Lutheranize her entire land, starting during her Catholic husband's lifetime. The Emperor Charles V, whose authority in German lands was always questionable, aimed for a consolidation of his power through various diets and courts, through political and military pressure in religious as well as societal issues; he did not want the country to become Protestant. To balance the division caused by the Protestant Friedrich der Weise (the Wise) and his peers, it was crucial to him that Erich and Heinrich's neighboring duchies of Braunschweig-Calenberg and Braunschweig-Wolfenbüttel remained Catholic. Thus, what faith Elisabeth and her territory chose to condone was of significance in the larger scheme of things (as well as having financial consequences). Erich's original preference for neutrality proved impossible because of the tense political situation and his wife's active involvement with the Protestant side. Elisabeth's religious commitment put both Erich and his lands in an awkward position, and caused marital tension: The couple's agreement not to interfere in each other's religion ended when Elisabeth became fully involved in the confessional battle.

Erich was in an appallingly problematic situation. He could not support the Lutheran faith without upsetting the emperor, at the same time his wife actively and publicly associated with the Lutheran side. Nervous about his fate, and the simmering tensions, Erich crafted his will as early as February 4, 1536, delegating power in his lands in the event of his death. Upon his death in Hagenau (July 30, 1540), during a visit to the emperor, this will made his wife the actual regent for all practical purposes, and also gave her guardianship of their children (the latter responsibility to be shared with Philipp von Hessen and Elisabeth's brother, Joachim II von Brandenburg). Even if, customarily, women could not reign by themselves, Erich's will gave Elisabeth the right as his widow and as mother of their then 12-year-old son, the heir, to take charge, and, though not without considerable difficulty, she did so as a "Landesmutter" (Stelzel 2003, 18).

The will arranged for the appointment of guardians from the opposing religious sides, which was a complicating factor. Even if all virtual authority belonged to Elisabeth, with regard to the children she was accountable to Philip von Hessen, Elisabeth's brother Joachim, the elector of Brandenburg, and Heinrich von Wolfenbüttel, Erich's nephew and an enemy of the Protestants. Tensions also arose because Heinrich coveted for his uncle's lands, the inheritance of which had slipped further away from his hands with every new child Elisabeth had delivered. (Aschoff 1984, 30–4, 56.) The battle between Elisabeth and Heinrich came to a head as soon as Elisabeth began to take the lead in the affairs of her duchy to pursue her goals: to make herself and her land independent and self-sustained; to maintain Braunschweig-Calenberg intact and secure for her son Erich II; and to reform the religion in the spirit of Luther. The other guardian, Philip von Hessen, shared Elisabeth's Lutheran faith commitment and related to her as his partner. With his support and with the authority of the legal regent during her son's minority (1540–6), Elisabeth dived unwaveringly into the administration of her land and proceeded with several reforms in a land that was in poor financial situation. (Sprengler-Ruppenthal 1984, 30–8; Aschoff 1984, passim 28–31, 34, 37.)

Elisabeth took charge "energetically" (Goltz-Greifswald 1914, 153). She benefited from her earlier experience of ruling Münden and Göttingen, and from the financially independent position she had secured for herself – wisely so as a "deserted" wife, a widower, and a woman with the "wrong faith" with aspirations for political authority. She used the leverage of her widow's status to attain her goals. Introducing widespread reforms in the duchy in general, she participated in visitations and in writing cloister reform orders and, most importantly, the church orders, condoning them with her "widow's" signature. (Mager 1994, 212; Stelzel 2003, 16, 18; Becker-Cantarino 1983, 240.) Even so, she needed the collaboration of the pillars of authority in the society – the nobility, the clergy, the towns, and the city councils – as well as imperial approval. Through difficulties, Elisabeth succeeded in winning the approval of the estates for reforms that proved lasting and beneficial. (Stelzel 2003, 16–19, Brenneke 1928, 320–1; Brenneke 1924, 120–1.)

The unrelenting appropriative efforts of the problematic Duke Heinrich, who sought every opportunity to take control of Elisabeth's territories, which he persisted in claiming as his by right (even going so far as to solicit help from the emperor and vainly attempting to instigate an uprising among Elisabeth's subjects), came to an embarrassing end when his army was besieged by the Schmalkaldic League in the summer of 1542. Responding to Elisabeth's requests, Philip had Heinrich imprisoned (until 1547) for armed plotting against the Lutheran faith. Elisabeth's brother Joachim II replaced Heinrich as guardian, which allowed Elisabeth to reign for her son for five years. She took full advantage of the time. She took action as a reformer and with zeal led Lutheran reforms in her territory and crafted advisory texts to her children and subjects and the estates in her territory. A missionary zeal combined with maternal care characterized her actions. (See Becker-Cantarino 1987, 207–9; Wiesner 2000, 41; Stelzel 2003, 17–22; Brauch 1930; Havemann 1839, 49–51.)

With peace established, and with the help of pastor Antonius Corvinus, Elisabeth proceeded to implement Reformation in her land, where only four cities had already accepted the evangelical faith since 1530s. This was done through visitations, personal communications, and church orders. Her correspondence with Corvinus demonstrates her wisdom, care, and thoroughness in the process. Corvinus, who had been given the role of overseeing the affairs of the church, wrote the actual church order under Elisabeth's mandate and with her input. It was sent to all the estates, cloisters, and nobility in May 1542 followed by a mandate and a letter of exhortation from the duchess herself. (See Sprengler-Ruppenthal 1984, 36–52; Tschackert 1900.)

The four-part church order entailed provisions about education (including that of the clergy) and teaching the catechism, about administering Communion in both kinds, and adherence to the teachings of the Augsburg Confession, along with words of advice about preaching the Word. It included direction about the changes regarding the cloisters, showing exceptional sensitivity to the vulnerable status of women without protection, and the needs of the poor in the territory. It deliberated on the dynamics of the human rule and the godly will, the authority of the office, and the virtue of obedience. The order relied on Elisabeth's vision about her sovereign status with the rights to implement the changes proposed. The larger cities, to Elisabeth's dismay, did not receive the order favorably at first (but won the approval of the highest court by 1544). (See Sprengler-Ruppenthal 1984, 41, 47–52; Havemann 1839. 55–60, passim.)

An important piece of Elisabeth's writing was her "Sendbrief," her official letter to her subjects that she wrote in 1544 and that was printed in 1545. The relationship between the duchess and her subjects, especially the nobility, had its tensions, only intensified by the financial difficulties in the land and the newness of the reforms she spearheaded. She attempted to find mutual understanding with her subjects, and simultaneously foster their obedience. First part of the 72-page long "Sendbrief" contained a general exhortation for Christian life and betterment of life. The second part addressed different pertinent groups: the pastors, the cloister people, the nobility, the four big cities (Göttingen, Hannover, Northeim, and Hameln), and the smaller towns and farming villages. She urged all the parties to obey their duty in the name of God: priests to preach the importance of penance and the nobility to give up their sinful "Epicurean" ways, and the big cities their "usury" business. In general, she exhorted people to leave their sins and immoral behavior, especially chastising the interest mongers. Priests were ordered to marry their concubines. (See Becker-Cantarino 1987, 207; Tschackert 1899, 8–9, 13–14/Jahrbuch 52–7; Stelzel 2003, 30–3, 57; Sprengler-Ruppenthal 1984, 49–52; Havemann 1839, 59–60.) (See Elisabeth von Braunschweig-Lüneburg: *Der Durchleuchtigen Hochgebornen Fürstin und Frawen/Frawen Elisabeth geborne Marckgravin zu Brandenburg u. Hertzogin zu Braunschweig und Lueneburg beschlossem und verwilligtes Mandat inirem Fürstenthum Gottes Wort auffzurichten/Und irrige verfürte lerr außzurotten belangent* [Münden 1542]. Also *Ein Christlicher Sendebrieff der Durchleuchtigen Hochgebornen Fuerstinnen und Frawen F. Elisabeth geborne Marggraffinnen zu Brandenburg, etc. Hertzoginnen zu Braunschweig und Luneburg etc. Witwen/an alle irer F. G. und irer F. G. Hertzlichen Sons Erichs Untertanen geschrieben/ Christliche besserung und newes Gottseliges leben/ so in dieser letsten bösen zeit/ Die hohe nod fordert/ belangend.* [Hannover 1545].)

Elisabeth and Corvinus shared a vision about the reform: they understood that for it to be successful a firm legislated process was necessary. They also showed concern for the needs of the laity, and wished to enforce the teaching of the catechism. In addition, Corvinus wrote a hymnbook for Elisabeth, and the ordinance that mandated that the priests marry their concubines. In regards to the reform of the convents, which was articulated in the Cloister Order of 1542, Elisabeth showed particular sensitivity to the dilemma of the convent women: instead of rigid ruling and the use of force, she saw it wise to allow those who wished to stay in their convents to do so, while allowing individuals to leave at their own will. Her empathy is manifest in her later advice to her son about how to dissolve the convents without force but with understanding for the needs of the "homeless" women. (See Klettke-Mengel 1986a, 110; Havemann 1839, 58, 67, 78.)

Troubles continued. Namely, an anti-Schmalkaldic and thus anti-reformation group of nobility stirred in Calenberg-Göttingen, which made it impossible for Elisabeth to join the league, in spite of the support of her friend Philip von Hessen, a founding member. (To foster the alliance between these two, consideration was given to a marriage between Elisabeth's oldest son and Philip's daughter. The idea was dropped in the wake of the scandal that ensued when, upon Luther's advice, Philip bigamously remarried while his first wife still alive. Erich was married instead to Sidonia von Sachsen [1518–75], a young girl whose territory Elisabeth proceeded to Lutheranize after the death of her uncle Duke Georg von Sachsen, a known enemy of everything Protestant. Sidonia died in 1575, and Erich married Dorothée de France; he had no children.)

Marrying Erich to a Protestant family was important personally and politically. Erich, whose religious orientation was of interest to many competing for his loyalty, had his faith examined by Luther himself; on their visit to Wittenberg in 1554 Erich was declared soundly Lutheran. Elisabeth had succeeded in securing both Erich's reign and the Protestant formation of his territories, but, as it turned out, the battle was not yet over. Erich would not follow the path his mother had prepared for him. The ensuing years would bring Erich and his mother into painful strife.

Erich II began his rule over Calenberg-Göttingen on December 22, 1545, under the zealous wings of his (over)protective mother, who, as an expression of her motherly love – and in an effort to control him – wrote Erich a treatise about government. At the heart of the text resounded Elisabeth's exhortation to Erich to "obey God, the emperor and your mother." If Erich had only listened to his mother! (Bainton 2001, 133; Tschackert, 1899, 33, 10; Stelzel 2003, 21.)

But Erich did not obey his mother. Troubles began when the 18-year-old duke, fresh to his majority, traveled to the Regensburg Diet in 1546–7 and there joined the Catholic princes in the combat against the Protestants. This happened even after his mother had prepared him for his trip with Communion in the Protestant rite and strong maternal exhortation. Perhaps it is not really a surprise that Erich was transformed the first instant he was outside his mother's orbit and exposed to other influences. One of the first signs of the distance growing between mother and son had come earlier that year when Erich absented himself from his mother's wedding to Count Poppo von Henneberg-Schleusingen (1513–74). Erich stayed in Regensburg while in a wedding celebrated from late May to early June in Münden Elisabeth married a brother of her own son-in-law (two years her younger).

Two years later, during his 1548 trip to Spain, Erich returned to his father's Catholic faith. Furthermore, he accepted the emperor's Augsburg Interim, which gave mild compromises to the Protestants (such as the clergy's right to marry and the right of the laity to Communion in both kinds), but mainly sanctioned the return of Catholic practices, forcing those who could not compromise to leave. Elisabeth's devastation and anger showed in her letters to her son-in-law and confidant, Albrecht. While Philip von Hessen and others assembled to form a resistance, young Erich not only accepted the interim terms but even tried to persuade the senior Protestant princes to comply. He returned home from his travels bolstered with a zeal to restore Catholicism once and for all. For instance, in 1549 he wished to re-instate cloisters in the area and had Corvinus confined in seclusion in the castle of Calenberg. (See Stelzel 2003, 23, 57; Brenneke 1933, 163–4.)

Following the family tradition of disobedient Protestant wives, Erich's own wife, Sidonia, opposed him – and was "cast off." Elisabeth, somewhat helpless in the face of her grown-up son, who was now her lord, could not do much more than write reprimanding letters to him, pray for him, and seek for ways to strengthen the evangelical faith in her own territory of Calenberg-Göttingen. She wrote about her maternal agony:

> O Lord God, to whom have I given birth? Whom have I reared? To deny the plain truth is a sin which cannot be forgiven on earth or in heaven. To persecute, maltreat, and abuse the servants of the Word of God is to persecute, maltreat, and abuse Christ Jesus, our only Savior, mediator, and intercessor, who has borne our sins. My son has brought me to bed. If he keeps on, he will bring me to the grave. (Elisabeth von Braunschweig in Bainton 2001, 136, also 135, 138; Tschackert 1899, 127–9.)

What kind of a son would like to kill his own mother, metaphorically speaking? Who would dare to risk the wrath of God, as if the wrath of a mother was not enough?

> How have you fallen into such insane raving and raging against God, against his Word, his servants, his churches and against me, your dear mother, against the whole country and the poor oppressed subjects?. . . God have mercy on you. If you do not turn about, God will smite you . . . Woe, woe, woe, and again woe to you if you do not change. You have made me so sick and weak from weeping that I have not strength to write and have had to dictate. I must say this or my heart will break. If I do not speak the very stones will cry out.

After her raging, Elisabeth pleaded with tears: "I beg you as your mother that you desist from your godless abuses" (Elisabeth von Braunschweig in Bainton 2001, 136; see Tschackert 1900). Erich's response was negative. Her mother's involvement made him look bad. He reminded her of the hierarchy of authority: "I will act as answerable to Almighty God and the emperor." In other words, mothers do not rule over God and emperors. Erich also threatened to act, even if with pain, if her mother did not drop the subject. (As Bainton observes, Erich may have understood the ways of the world but was clueless as to a mother's pain: he had a sense of the reactions in the region but "Erich could not understand, because he had never been a mother. He did not grasp that he was the fruit of her womb. She had grounded him in the catechism . . . had glowed when Luther found him sound in the faith" (Elisabeth von Braunschweig in Bainton 2001, 137, also 138; see Koch 1905–6, No 50. See Goltz-Greisfwald 1914, 154–7.)

Relations between mother and son deteriorated until 1552 and the events leading to the Peace of Passau, when Duke Moritz von Sachsen – the scheming and arbitrating Lutheran who eventually played a significant role in securing Lutheran faith in Germany – ignored Erich and attempted to drive the Spanish out of German land. Alliances shifting politically, and power relations unstable, strange collaborations emerged: old enemies Heinrich von Wolfenbüttel – "the Wolf" and Philip von Hessen allied with Moritz for the reasons of national unity, whereas Elisabeth and Erich temporarily allied with Albrecht Alcibiades von Brandenburg-Kulmbach against Heinrich of Wolfenbüttel and his allies. Elisabeth mediated a significant bond between Erich and Albrecht von Preussen, her daughter Anna Maria's husband, in this politically precarious state of affairs. In a situation when the Braunschweig territory needed to take a stand, Erich made peace with his mother. He returned to the faith of his childhood. In a mandate of May 21, 1553, Erich confirmed the Protestant faith as the legal religion in his territory. Corvinus, who had suffered much whilst in forced isolation in the castle of Calenberg during the Augsburg Interim (of 1548), died soon after (in April 1553) without seeing the ensuing Peace of Augsburg in 1555 that guaranteed legal status for Lutherans in the land – a goal towards which he had greatly contributed in his work with Elisabeth. Although the Peace gave the Lutheran Protestants a legal status in the empire, it by no means ended the religious wars, which erupted again in the Thirty Years' War of 1618–1648. (Elisabeth and Albrecht, see Mengel 1953, 1954a, 1973.)

However, tensions arose once more between the mother and the son. After the devastating battle of Sievershausen on July 9, 1553, with Erich II and Albrecht defeated by the Catholic army and Moritz dead, Elisabeth had to accept the difficult terms for peace dictated by Heinrich: she and her daughter Katharina were to be expelled from her duchy to her husband's estate. In spite of her protests, she lost all her influence in the territory, and nearly all her possessions apart from her castle at Ilmenau. She became very ill, and it seems that there may have been marital discord, as her husband refused to go with her, perhaps because of an extra-marital relationship. (See Elisabeth's letter to Albrecht, Brief No. 205 from July 14, 1553, about the Sievershausen, in Mengel 1954a, 208.)

Steady comfort through the trying times came from Elisabeth's son-in-law, Albrecht (1490–1568) and daughter Anna Maria (1532–68). Forty years senior to Anna Maria (18), the 60-year-old Albrecht was closer in age to his friend Elisabeth with whom he shared Protestant convictions. (Notably, the age difference in Anna Maria's marriage was similar to that between her parents.) Elisabeth's and Albrecht's friendship seems to have preceded them becoming in-laws, a situation that greatly pleased Elisabeth who had been actively looking for a Protestant match for her young daughter. Soon after Albrecht's sick first spouse Dorothea died on April 11, 1547, a new marriage contract was in place by 1548, with the marriage being celebrated two years later. The costly wedding, on February 16, 1550, as well as the dowry, were paid for by Anna Maria's brother Johann, as Elisabeth was chronically nearly bankrupt.

As a bridal gift, just a few days after the wedding, Elisabeth wrote her daughter a treatise with advice on the marital relationship, upbringing of children, and gender relations. She reminded her daughter of the arrangement of different roles and power, and of the wife's duty to be obedient and "rule him by love and reason without bitterness." The 14-chapter-long treatise (136 leafs in octavo format) offered a Lutheran definition of marriage and an interpretation of the biological and moral role of a wife as a form of service to God, amidst general theological and ethical advice on the primacy of Scripture, the example of biblical women, etc. As in her other works, she named herself as the author. Her relationship with Anna Maria appears to have been good and less complicated than that with Erich. (See Tschackert 1899, 48, 62–4/Jahrbuch, 18–21, 18–65; Wiesner 2000, 44; Stelzel 2003, 36–8, 57; Becker-Cantarino 1987, 209.)

Ousted to Hannover, during her three-year-long exile with no income and dependent on the help of others, Elisabeth devoted her time to writing hymns and letters, including letters asking for money from her son-in-law, Albrecht von Preussen, and others with whom she was in favor. These writings have provided a precious source to Elisabeth's thinking, her faith, and her theological tendencies, as well as to the contemporary events as seen from her perspective. She wrote letters with her brother (1543–5), with Albrecht, with Corvinus, and with other reformers like Mörlin, Melanchthon, Luther, and others. Two letters from Luther to Elisabeth remain, one from September 4, 1538, thanking her for a gift, and one from January 29, 1540 (see Stelzel 2003, 42–7; copy in Havemann 1839, 53). Among her extant letters remain letters to her first husband, her brothers Joachim and Johann (11 letters between 1535 and 1555), daughter Anna Maria (1553), son-in-law Albrecht, her nephews, father-in-law, Philip von Hessen (four letters, 1540–55), and his wife Christine von Hesse (1544, 1546). (Stelzel 2003, 42–56; Havemann 1839, 105–110.) (On her relationship with Philip von Hessen, see Stelzel 2003, 56; Sprengler-Ruppenthal 1984, 37, 28–9.)

Another source of information on Elisabeth's faith is the collection of the emotion-filled songs she wrote between 1553 and 1555 (not printed). Lacking in artistic original-ity perhaps, they illustrate Elisabeth's sense of herself and her place in the world. If her letters were her "book of lamentations," her hymns would be her "book of psalms. Here breathe constancy, love and joy" (Bainton 2001, 141). For instance, she wrote, "Joyful will I be, and bless his holy name. He is my help and stay, and comfort in my name. Joyful will I be, if he is but near. The cross has overcome, and nothing need I fear" (Elisabeth von Braunschweig in Bainton 2001, 141). (See Wiesner-Hanks 2000, 145; Goltz-Greifswald 1914, 155; Becker-Cantarino 1987, 213–15.)

After three years in exile, she returned to Münden, with the help of Albrecht von Preussen and Joachim II. She was given a pension of 5,000 gulden a year, by the order of Erich II, but she was not granted her request (made on March 21, 1552) for the res-toration of her territory in Calenberg-Göttingen. Repeating the fate of her mother, Elisabeth's last years were sad. Her health and mental balance deteriorated and tensions intensified between her and her husband, especially from 1556. The last insult, which broke her spirit, occurred in 1557 with her youngest daughter's wedding: without her mother's consent, young Katharina, now in her early twenties, who had accompanied her mother through her exile and times of suffering was married off to a Catholic bur-grave Wilhelm von Rosenberg in Böhmen (1535–92). To add to the insult, Elisabeth was even made to miss the wedding. Given the wrong date (because of Erich's fear that she would interrupt the festivities), she arrived late.

During this difficult time late in her life, the duchess recovered sufficiently to compose another treatise, this time a book of consolation for widows: *Elisabeth of Braunschweig, Der Widwen Handbüchlein durcheine hocherleuchte fürstliche Widwe/vor vielen Jahren selbst beschrieben und verfasset/Jetzt aber wiederumb auff newe gedruckt/Allen Christli-chen Widwen/hohes und nieder Standes/zu besonderem Trost.* The book, written speedily between December 11 1555 and December 26, demonstrates her unbroken faith (Goltz-Greifswald 1914, 162). Designed as a wedding gift for her sister, she drew from the Scriptures words of consolation for widows who were vulnerable without the protection of a man. The manuscript was first published as early as 1556, and then again in 1598, and was widely disseminated in northern and middle Germany between 1571 and 1579, with five reprints taken by 1609. This text more than any other proved Elisabeth's caliber as a biblically knowledgeable lay theologian, the first of the kind in her family – and, more particularly, a theologian of the cross. (Mager 1994, 218, 223–4.)

Elisabeth's zeal and vision as a reformer became documented in the variety of works she penned: her mission letter "Sendbrief," her ruler's manual for her son – the "Regier-ungshandbuch" – her maternal advice on marriage for Anna Maria, her book for widows, her rich letters, and her hymns. Two of these have received most interest for their political, personal, and spiritual dimensions: the manuals she offered for her son and her daughter, both published posthumously (see *Unterrichtung und Ordnung für*

Herzog Erich d.J., in Fürstenspiegel aus dem 16. Jahrhundert in 1824, 57–130). (See Becker-Cantarino 1987, 216–17; Wiesner 1998, 146–7; Wiesner 2000, 40, 46–7; Tschackert 1899, 13–22/Jahrbuch 57–64.)

Elisabeth began to write her manual for her son in the spring of 1544, with the intention of offering him both religious and political advice as a mother and a ruler in her own right. By January 1, 1545, the treatise was ready. That it is her authorship is undeniable; Elisabeth identified herself in the preface and at the end, where she stated she was writing in her motherly duty and office. (Note: This text belonged in an expensive "Silberbibliothek," a collection of 20 reformatory writings all in "Silbereinband," or full silver binding, which were lost during the Second World War, 15 of them were recovered later.) The text was not printed during her lifetime; the first published edition dates to 1824 (Tschackert's 1899 work uses the original text). The handwritten text consisted of 46 chapters (over 195 sheets in quarto format), a foreword, an ending, and an appendix. The thoroughly Lutheran book covered issues of faith, religion, ethical deliberation, and political considerations. One third of the book dealt with religious issues and reflected on the gospel, the catechism, and Scripture in general, amid practical advice about how to rule the territory and the household (including guidance on marriage). Lutheran theology of sacraments, work of the law, faith, baptism, penance, the Lord's Supper, and the notion of Scripture were discussed as well. In a sense, the book was Elisabeth's "summa theologiae." (See Becker-Cantarino 1987, 207, 210; Stelzel 2003, 33–6; Wiesner 2000, 43–4; Tschackert 1899, 14–15/Jahrbuch 59–61, 68.)

Similar "mirrors" were written by other regent women who wished to give general religious and moral guidance, typically to their own children. Written by women, these mirrors combined practical and didactical elements and were shaped by their own experiences and situations, often including explanations of the reasons that lead the author to write in the first place. That they were writing for a presumably closed audience of family, friends, fellow reformers, and subjects, made their activity acceptable. Elisabeth, for instance, explained: "I have written this book for you myself with my own hand, from the beginning to the end . . . I have written this for your benefit, out of motherly love and good intentions . . . Do not scorn what I have said here, for to scorn your mother . . . is your own shame. (Elisabeth von Braunschweig in Wiesner 1998, 146–7. See Wiesner 2000, 43–4; Mengel 1954a, xxii–xxiii.)

It is worth noticing how openly Elisabeth used her name in writing (compared to, for instance, Marie Dentière, who decided at first to write anonymously and then used only her initials). Elisabeth's position in the social scale, her sense of her own authority and importance were certainly factors, as well as her passion for spreading the Lutheran faith with all the means available to her, including her family name and her widow's status. With so much to lose in the process – her children, her position and lands, her authority – she nevertheless gave religion priority, which made her a true "confessor." Her "confession" can be read in the "Sendbrief" that was sent with the church orders she had penned with Corvinus to convince the people in her land of the rightness of the Lutheran faith and the necessity of implementing it. Both as a writer and a ruler, Elisabeth acted as a woman of high nobility with a powerful family background, unusual depth of education, and different means of power at her disposal. She did not apologize for her actions, for her sex, or for her religious choice. She did not consider herself to be "just" a woman and accordingly assume a subordinate position. She acted as independently as the other main players in the Reformation, presenting a unique voice and the viewpoint of a mother of the land, "Landesmutter," and a mother who cared for all her children, confident of her rights and abilities. (See Wiesner 2000, 41; Becker-Cantarino 1987, 213–16.)

Elisabeth was openly Lutheran, and the Lutheran faith was the central motif in her actions and words. Her mission to introduce and instill the Reformation in her territory of Braunschweig-Calenberg all but consumed her interests (bordering on fanaticism, according to Mengel 1954a, xxii). In this her efforts were recognized by the male reformers, who actively supported her. She drew her deepest inspiration from the Luther Bible – especially the Psalms, the contents of which she knew very well. As a well-educated woman, thanks to her mother and the women in the court, she was comfortable in writing in High German. The remnants of her personal library, which may be taken to reveal at least a sample of what she read, contain plenty of Reformation literature, works from Luther, Bucer, Rhegius, etc., but nothing in Latin. (Mengel 1986a, 67–72, passim; Mengel 1954a, xxii; Klettke-Mengel 1986a, 68–71; Becker-Cantarino 1983, 206.) With her four books, two printed in her lifetime, and several songs and letters, she was the first author for two dynasties from the Brandenburg and Braunschweig houses. Among the earliest Protestant rulers, she was the first to write her own "Fürstenspiegel" for her son. (Becker-Cantarino 1983, 208–9; Tschackert 1899, 5, 49; Wiesner 2000, 40. See Klettke-Mengel's works.)

Elisabeth's sense of theological authority and biblical knowledge is demonstrated in, among other examples, the active role she took in the notorious Osiander controversy. Her reflections on Osiander's contested perspective that justification by faith implies the indwelling of the divine Christ can be read in her correspondence with her son-in-law Albrecht. (Klettke-Mengel 1986a, 75–81, also 1954). She sent two "Gutachten" (letters of advice) about Osiander to Preussia in 1551. Elisabeth's involvement in the controversy over Osiander's interpretation revealed the depth of her theological erudition and that she remained conversant with the theological issues of the time. Her position in the matter also gave insights into her Lutheranism and her main principles in that. For instance, in her defense of Osiander (who according to her reading had been misunderstood) she restated the basic Lutheran appreciation of the individuals' right to read and interpret Scripture for themselves. (She wrote on June 16, 1551 in defense of Osiander; on August 10, 1551 she wrote about issue of righteousness. Some of her 1551 letters were responses to Osiander's written confession and disputation about the justification doctrine given earlier that year on October 24, 1551; Klettke-Mengel Mengel 1986a 1986b, 75–81.)

Elisabeth died at the age of 48 on May 25, 1558 at the castle of Ilmenau. At the time of her death the fate of the Lutheran faith in Braunschweig territory had not been solved. Her body was laid to rest in the family burial site of the Hennebergs, later to be moved to St Johan's church in Schleusingen. Her success both as a mother and as a reformer was evidenced after her death: Without the unresolved antagonism with Elisabeth even Heinrich agreed to negotiate with the bordering duchies, and the soil was prepared for Lutheranism. In Braunschweig, the Lutheran Augsburg Confession of 1530 became widely accepted, a goal for which Elisabeth had laid the groundwork with pastor Corvinus (in a typical "working relationship" between a female ruler and a male pastor). The success of the Reformation in Braunschweig was due not only to a specific mandate "from above" but was also a result of the brave confessions and persistent conviction of the first Protestant believers, pastors and parents alike. The Duchess Elisabeth set the bar high with her own example.

Conclusion

Elisabeth's actions and convictions in securing the evangelical faith in her land proved her a bona fide reformer, in the private and the public realm. Both a woman and a lay person who turned Protestant in her personal religious life, she also became an active public instigator of the Reformation in her territory and took all legal steps possible and necessary, in addition to forcefully steering her children in the same faith. The remarkable sense of authority and the courage Elisabeth demonstrated as a female reformer could be explained from her noble status and its related "clout" and her empowerment through education. Even more than this, her fire for the reforms was kindled, first and foremost, by her reading of the Scriptures and the reformers' texts – and thus-formed Lutheran faith – and second, her motherly calling and instincts. Her acts as a reformer can be interpreted as acts of a mother safeguarding the spiritual wellbeing of all her children, biological or subject. She did not conceive of herself as a teacher, preacher, or prophet, but as a mother with a duty to the children in her family and her duchy. She can be honored with a title "mother-reformer" or a church mother (like Katharine Schütz Zell). Her internal self-authorization as an educated, firmly Lutheran, Christian mother made her a highly effective mother of the land, or "Landes-mutter," and joined her in the company of the powerful, successful female rulers who fought the religious cause. (See Wiesner 2000, 47–48; Becker-Cantarino 1987, 213–14). As a proof of her success, the Reformation continued after Erich's death on the very foundations she had laid in her lifetime.

Like her mother, Elisabeth von Braunschweig stands out in history with her story of personal courage and religious conviction, because of which she was willing to endure poverty, separation from her children, public humiliation, and other forms of punishment. Her story depicts the sometimes tragic turns of events, when private matters become public, and when political concerns and religious convictions clash. The two Elisabeths both demonstrate the difficulty of a situation when wives' religious convictions differed from those of their husbands, and how difficult were the power struggles fought in domestic and political realms. Both Elisabeths acted consciously within the possibilities they had as women in positions of authority and took full advantage of the means they had at their disposal. They also efficiently relied on the networks among Protestants in exile or in strategic places; they were connected with both the center and the margins in terms of power. They both were inspired by Luther and both continued his work, with his personal involvement in their lives. In concrete ways they prepared the way to first introduce and then secure the Lutheran faith in strategically important northern German principalities. They acted upon a religious calling, without the official authorization of their church or their constituency, unhindered by their sex, and fueled by their Scriptural knowledge and personal faith conviction. Their stories offer a personal, female face and both a domestic and a political perspective to the Reformation's complicated progress in German ducal territories.

A Word about Sources and References

Biographical information is gathered from a variety of sources, in the absence of authorita-tive biographies; among the more recent works, most important have been Klettke-Mengel 1986a, Wiesner 2000, and Becker-Cantarino 1983, in addition to Bainton's 1971/2001 essays on both Elisabeths which are valuable sources in English.

Groundbreaking earlier studies and profiles on Elisabeth von Brandenburg as a reformer come from Kirchner 1866, and also from Riedel 1865; Berbig 1911; Jakobi 1909; Baur 1873. On Elisabeth von Braunschweig, the standard nineteenth-century work comes from Tschackert 1899, followed by important portraits of her as a confessing reformer by Brenneke 1933, 1924, 1925, and Brauch 1930. The foundational studies by Mengel (later Klettke-Mengel) on Elisabeth's life, texts, relations, and correspondence from 1952, 1953, 1954, 1958, 1959, and 1973 (many of which are reproduced in the 1986 collection) have prepared the way for more recent examinations of her contributions as a mother, as a reformer with important connections, and as a religious writer by Stelzel 2003; Spengler-Ruppenthal 1984; Mager 1994; Becker-Cantarino 1983 and 1987; and Wiesner 1998.

CHAPTER 8

Katharina Schütz Zell, 1498–1562 – A Publishing Church Mother in Strasbourg

Woman giving birth, anonymous woodcut, Augsburg, 1540

© AKG-IMAGES

Katharina Schütz Zell, 1497/98–1562

PARENTS
- ◆ Elisabeth Gester (died 1525)
- ◆ Jacob Schütz (born 1543)

SIBLINGS
- ◆ Five children besides Argula, names unknown

SPOUSE (1523–48)
- ◆ Matthias/Mathaus Zell (1477–1548)

CHILDREN
- ◆ None survived

Introduction

Katharina called herself a church mother ("Kirchenmutter"). She saw herself as being called by God to care for the church and its people. The most published female lay theologian of the time, she cared for a heterogeneous flock of Christian men and women. She presented an option to Protestant women that most of them did not strive for or manage to achieve: having a public office and a voice. Not satisfied to support the Reformation only in the domestic front in the noble calling of a pastor's spouse, like Katharina von Bora Luther, Wibrandis Rosenblatt, and others, she was closer in spirit to Argula von Grumbach and Marie Dentière, fellow pamphleteers from Bavaria and Geneva. Furthermore, she developed her wifehood into a theologically meaningful calling that involved action and leadership outside the parsonage. She gave a broad interpretation of what being a Christian spouse ("Ehefrau") could mean (Becker-Cantarino 1987, 101).

Katharina was an extraordinary sixteenth-century woman, deemed as the "most interesting" Reformation woman in many accounts (Jung 2002, 231). For one thing, she explicitly presented herself as her husband's equal helpmate and partner in ministry, and extended that role outside their household. She expanded the reformers' vision of women as domestic partners in their capacities as spouses, mothers, and household managers to include a call to "speak out" and act in church and society for the sake of the gospel and the wellbeing of her neighbors. (See McKee 1992.) She understood her role as a church mother as an office ("Amt") that came with responsibilities and authority. A woman who buried her own infants young and fostered others' children, Katharina's motherhood consisted of active partnering with her pastor-husband for the well-being of the people in Strasbourg, particularly in the area of pastoral care and hospitality. Unflappably ecumenical and an advocate for religious tolerance – in a time when religion had little to do with tolerance – she embraced the needs of all the people she encountered or who sought for her counsel, regardless of their theological views. She loved all her "children" and accepted no obstacles in her mission of care, while she did not approve of all her children's "errors" in views. She did not hesitate to intervene in the affairs of the church and the city and to proclaim the gospel through writing, speaking, personal interaction, and caring acts. Her call as a church mother, which she creatively placed within the priesthood of all believers and the vocational theology offered for women, had its foundation in her Christ-centered theology, which, in return, was shaped by her maternal visions.

Drawing from her first-hand reading of the Scriptures, her life experiences, and interactions with different reformers, Katharina enforced the Reformation ecumenically and charitably. In her diverse writings, she addressed real life situations and issues theologically. She was respected for her good deeds by her contemporaries – whom she could also alienate with her tongue and determination. As an outspoken woman, as a Protestant clergy-spouse, and as a tolerant influence in an increasingly rigid confessional climate, she lived a life shadowed by one controversy or one conflict after another. Her contributions as a theologian and as a proponent of religious tolerance have yet to be fully appreciated.

A Church Mother, a Pastoral Care Provider, a Writer, Even a Preacher

Katharina's context was the free city of Strasbourg with its historic bishop's seat and visible presence of clergy, monastics, and other religious. The city had a reputation of tolerance in religious affairs that attracted a diverse group of preachers and believers, before it rejected all but Lutheran forms of Protestantism in favor of the Augsburg Confession. The largest city in Alsace (with a population of 20,000), it enjoyed many privileges as an independent political unit (for instance in taxing, defense, and foreign policy), which undoubtedly provided soil for religious freedom as well. The merchant and artisan families (Katharina's class) were the backbone of its society, even if political power belonged to the landed aristocrats and canons. Citizenship, which was coveted, could be purchased or gained by marriage, which may be one reason for the rumblings of discontent the first clergy marriages caused. Importantly, Strasbourg was a hub of publishing in the early 1520s, providing population with pamphlets and books, mostly in German, from a variety of authors, many of whom were not considered orthodox by the mainstream. (See Chrisman 1982, xxii–xxix; McKee 2006a [the edited translation of Katharina's writings by Elsie McKee, hereafter KSZ/McKee], 4–14.)

Katharina was born on July 15, 1497, or early in 1498, to the well-to-do and well connected artisan family of Schüsters and Taylors. One of the six surviving children of Elisabeth Gester (died 1525) and Jacob Shutz (born 1453), a woodworker, she was named after the fourteenth-century Italian saint, Caterina da Siena. Devout and intelligent Katharina benefited from her religious upbringing at home and her vernacular education in a girls' school in town. Her early schooling did not include Latin, but she would learn the basics in practice, conversation, and worship. She read and wrote fluently in German and became quite knowledgeable in the area of Christian history and texts. Her lack of formal higher education did not hold her back, quite the contrary: she continued her independent learning throughout her life. She studied the lectionary and Luther's 1522 New Testament translation (which replaced the earlier German Bible dating from 1485) and other of Luther's works. Her correspondence with major reformers, such as Bucer, Capito, Hedio, Calvin, and Luther, served as an important form of "distance learning." Her marital years would become the essential period for her theological formation and the time in which she found her own voice as a theologian. In that regard, her husband's role would be vital in welcoming and supporting Katharina's ambitions and initiatives with apparently no "ifs and buts."

Katharina's conversion to the Protestant faith happened around 1521 or 1522, after she had read Luther's works and listened to Protestant sermons. To Katharina, having a spiritual and religious calling did not exclude responsibilities in the society, rather the opposite. She learned the craft of tapestry weaving from her guild, something that set her apart from many of the other prominent reformers' wives, who, typically, did not have a trade of their own outside their homes (and a fact that reminds us of the many women, nameless to us, who served in different trades). With no initial intention to marry, or to join a convent or a group of religious lay women like the Beguines, she planned to support herself in tapestry business. When marriage and the Reformation changed the direction of her life, they also offered her another vocational path to create for herself. Like many of the medieval female mystics, she dated her budding inclination to a religious life from the tender age of 10, when she dedicated herself to the church and the proclamation of God's good news. She would become a church mother. "Since I was ten years old I have been a church mother (7), a nurturer of the pulpit and school" (KSZ/McKee, 226 [see below for McKee's full enumeration of Katharina's self-designations]).

Katharina's early spirituality was influenced by her contemporaries' deeply felt insecurity about salvation and their anxiety over the omnipresence of death in their society. Luther's theology about the gift-nature of salvation allowed her to change focus and reappropriate gospel into her life; she shifted from worrying about her own salvation to becoming a "fisher of people" and assuring others' of their salvation and God's grace. Her spiritual maturation evolved as she found herself a vocation in the church, first in her craft, and then as a pastor's wife and partner in ecumenical ministry and charity, that is, as a church mother. (See KSZ/McKee, 15–16; Jung 2002, 126–7, 252–3, 163–265; McKee 1999a, 11–29; Moeller 2005, 46–7.)

Even in her youth Katharina had a reputation as a devout person who pursued a godly life and her advice was sought after by women in particular. She never proclaimed herself to be a church leader or a member of the clergy but cherished her identity and religiosity as a lay person. At the same time, she wished to raise the level of women's active involvement in the life of the church. Katharina clearly came to understand herself as a reformer, as a main player, so to speak, not only a recipient of the reforms preached by others. She took to heart the Protestant principle of the priesthood of all believers and lived it out in her calling as a pastor's spouse and in the encouragement she gave to other women to find a similarly satisfying calling. She spoke and wrote with a confidence that was rooted in biblical knowledge and her sense of the equality and shared concerns of the Christian community. She evolved as a Protestant reformer on her own, with her own particular interpretation about what the gospel called for. In the circle of the reform-oriented theologians and their wives in Strasbourg (including the Bucers, Capitos, and Hedios), Katharina was one of the very few women who published her thoughts. She also stood out as a theologian who showed originality in how she combined pastoral care and ecclesial concerns in her vision for the reform. (See Jancke-Pirna 1997, 56–69; Mager 1999a, 88–9; KSZ/McKee, 15–17.)

Katharina came to know her husband first as a parishioner. She appreciated his sermons about the gospel of liberation. Matthias Zell had come to Strasbourg in 1518 as the new priest of the large cathedral parish of St Lorenz and the bishop's penitentiary. Without calling himself a Lutheran, he was among the town's leading preachers (with Wolfgang Capito and Kaspar Hedio) to articulate public criticism of the current Catholic theology and corruption in some of the central practices in the church. As elsewhere in Europe, in Strasbourg clerical marriage would mark one of the most visible changes brought about by the Reformation. Once the clergy began to marry, Katharina was the first respectable citizen to enter such marriage. It is worth noticing that she married before Martin Luther did, being influenced by his teaching on the matter, and that she married for a vocational reason. "Katharina Schütz was convinced that she was called to marry Matthias Zell as an expression of her faith in God and her love for others." (McKee 1999a, 48, also 49.) Their partnership was founded on shared religious zeal and confession, and Katharina became Matthias's equal partner.

Matthias and Katharina were married by the reformer Martin Bucer on Thursday December 3, 1523, bright and early at 6:00 A.M. (probably to avoid the public eye) and with select friends present. The wedding vows were exchanged at the door of the cathedral, where Katharina received a golden ring, before the party continued into the church for early morning Mass. She confessed to her Protestant faith by, first of all, marrying a Protestant clergyman, and secondly, by receiving Communion in both kinds

("Katharina was receiving the cup for the first time in her life!" McKee 1999a, 49). This did not go unnoticed in the community and added to the stir caused by her marriage in the first place: not everybody understood why a respectable religious person such as Katharina would want to marry at all, and to a clergy person of all men! (Her friend Agnes Roettel married Matthias's associate Capito with much less controversy.) The introduction of the clergy marriage in general caused scandal in town; much of the initial criticism seemed to culminate in reaction against the Zell's marriage in particular. The young wife's public defense of her own marriage and those of others, on theological grounds, added fuel to the fire, as did the direction in which she took her new role as a pastor's wife. (See Chrisman 1972, 151–4 on the first clergy marriages in town and idem. 156–8 on Katharina's unique position among the new pastors' wives.) It is fair to say that the cloud of controversy would remain a constant part of a life consumed by her efforts to fulfill her calling to be a church mother.

Katharina's marriage provided her with the soil for continued theological cultivation and maturation. With a supportive husband – and, to be sure, she would not have married a non-supportive man – Katharina continued to learn not only from books but also from personal relationships with the leading figures from the different sides of the Reformation, such as Martin Bucer, Kaspar Hedio, and Wolfgang Capito, Johannes Oecolampadius, Kaspar Schwenckfeld, and others. On her travels with Matthias she visited Luther in Wittenberg (1538) and also met Philipp Melanchthon and Nicolaus von Amsdorf (1538), Urbanus Rhegius, and (after Matthias's death) Conrad Pellicanus, a known German humanist and theologian. She hosted Ulrich Zwingli and Jean Calvin in her house and carried on active correspondence with various of the reformers (Calvin, Sebastian Franck, Urbanus Rhegius, Paul Fagius, Conrad Pellicanus, Johannes Zwick, Johannes Brenz, Otto Brunfels, Sébastien Castellion, Johannes Bugenhagen, Desiderius Erasmus, Johannes Agricola, and Johann Marbach). (Katharina as an ecumenical correspondent, see McKee 2007, 90–101.)

Unlike many other women in correspondence with religious leaders, Katharina was not "only" on the receiving end seeking spiritual counsel for herself. She offered pastoral care and advice to others in her letters. She wrote about issues she was well informed of due to her personal interactions and constant reading (for instance, she knew of Castellion's writings on tolerance and Melanchthon's *Loci Communes*, quoted Augustine and Girolamo Savonarola, used Ludwig Rabus' history of saints and the Marburg Articles, mentioned Kaspar Schwenckfeld, Johann von Staupitz and Flacius Illyricus, and associated with the mainstream reformers as well as Anabaptists and spiritualists). Her written comments on the conflict around the Lord's Supper revealed her familiarity with the arguments from different sides. The range of her readings and the varied conversations, in person and in letters, fertilized her theological mind and shaped her ecumenical horizons early on. (See Jung 2002, 134, 152–8,165; KSZ in McKee 1999b, 94–153; McKee 2007.)

Katharina was thus influenced by a rich assortment of reformation personalities – from Luther to Zwingli to Bucer to Schwenckfeld. She remained throughout her life particularly devoted to Luther's theology, even if her role in Strasbourg and some aspects of her theology associated her with the "reformed" or the Swiss protestants ("KSZ has only praise for 'the dear Luther', even when she mentions disagreements on the sacraments. Luther was the reformer par excellence, with Matthew Zell close behind. Wolfgang Capito ranked next after Luther and her husband for KSZ but she also speaks highly of Kaspar Hedio and Martin Bucer" [McKee 1992, 252]). She knew of Luther's early works, had read his writings on the two sacraments and was particularly fond of his interpretation of the Psalms (for instance, Psalm 118). Katharina was mentioned by Luther in his introduction to his 1530 printed sermon on Psalm 110 and the second article of faith. She dared to disagree with and even advise him. For instance, in a letter about the Lord's Supper she wished to downplay the differences in the interpretations of the Lord's Supper, either because she failed to grasp the nuances or, more probably, because of her commitment to unity. She was one of the few theologians of the time who truly could be called ecumenical. (KSZ/McKee, 69–71; Moeller 2005, 47–9.) It is quite possible that she had sent her works to Luther, who may have (indirectly) responded to her writings, and definitely wrote to her in December 1524 soon after the publication of Katharina's Apology. (Some of her booklets have been bound and published with writings from Luther and other reformers.)

If Luther stood at one pole of her theological landscape, at the other pole stood theologians who did not all have his approval, those with more spiritualist tendencies, such as Kaspar Schwenckfeld and Sebastian Franck. She built her Protestant theology on the foundation laid by Luther, but expanded it into a more inclusive theology as a result of her conversations with people about issues that mattered to them individually, such as the sacraments. Given the location of her ministry in the free city of Strasbourg where dissidents and the persecuted were a common presence, and her own interpreta-tion of Scripture as a lay woman conscious of the effects of narrow interpretations of the gospel, a certain degree of ecumenical sensitivity and tolerance could be expected. There was pressure on her from the different directions, and the perspective that arose from her experience of being in the "middle" in many ways – surrounded on either side by lay versus career theologians, Lutheran versus spiritualist theology, first versus second generation reformers – may have been the stimulus for her constant search for a joint understanding and conversation with different parties. Compassion and what she saw as a Christian mission were of the utmost importance to her. (Conrad 1998, 130, 126; Mager 1999b, 88.)

The Zells lived out a shared calling and a passion to serve God, gospel, the church, and their neighbors. To Katharina, to be a wife of a reformer meant to be his helper ("Gehilfin") in ministry. The vocation of motherhood so extolled by the reformers was not tied to the household, in her view, but evolved in her understanding into a broader motherhood of the church, into an office in itself. Her husband wholeheartedly approved: "Matthias also commissioned Katharina to be a 'mother to the poor and refugees.'" Katharina's office as a church mother was interwoven with the office of her spouse, whom she set out to serve as a way of serving the gospel – with the understanding that the service of the Word was most central. (See McKee 1999a, 39, 48–50; Jancke-Pirna 1997, 62–7.) The stimulus and the justification for her work came from the gospel, which would override all other hierarchies or priorities.

In her marriage to a reformer Katharina carved herself a theological place and a spiritual vocation that benefited her neighbors and her husband's congregation. She provided an important dimension to the Reformation ministry in Strasbourg with her gifts and her empathy for her fellow human beings' needs. An important – and the most socially acceptable – dimension of her work was the diaconal service and pastoral care ("Seelsorge") she practiced in and out of her house. She was inspired by the early church's diaconate and the strong female figures in the Scriptures. In her multidimen-sional call, she embraced the identity of an apostle, a deacon, and even a prophet in the time of change when women and children were being called to join the work of the kingdom. (Moeller 2005, 61; Jancke-Pirna 1997.)

Throughout the Christian centuries, while the preaching office was an exclusively male office ordered by the church, Christian women engaged in public teaching and preaching by claiming the calling of prophecy, especially at times when the "end" loomed near signaling the dissolution of the existing structures and order. The mainstream Reformation women rarely identified themselves as prophets, but Katharina did identify with them as a woman irresistibly called by God to work for the gospel. Her interest was in the present, however, and in working in the present for the future, rather than in foretelling the future (see Jancke-Pirna 1997, 71–2). Her main concern was the actual service of other people in deeds as well as words. In this light her prophetic function seemed less alarming and her actions more fitting to a woman, given the options even theoretically available for women in the church. With her well-rounded knowledge, many gifts, natural understanding of human life, her empathy, and her desire to make a difference in the lives of others, she made an essential contribution to the life of her congregation and the evolution of the Reformation in Strasbourg in general. Her childlessness proved a tragic blessing in that regard. (Becker-Cantarino 1987, 102.)

The tragic loss of both of her infant children (one in 1527, another after 1534) caused life-long sorrow to Katharina. Her publishing and ecumenical work may have helped in some little way to compensate for the loss. Whether or not she consciously focused on extra-domestic activities as a spiritual mother to compensate for her private empty nest, the fact is that, without children, she did have much more time in her hands than somebody like Wibrandis Rosenblatt who raised a large family with four different husbands, or Katharina Luther, who cared for an extended family of biological and adopted children and, it seems, the entire populus of Wittenberg. The childless Katharina (like Margaretha Blarer, who, unmarried, was also childless) stands out as a woman exceptionally involved in theological conversation and writing. She was thus a "different" pastor's wife. (Nielsen 1999, 129; Becker-Cantarino 1987, 9, 102.) (Chrisman [1972, 156] characterizes Katharina as "unique" among all the pastors' wives because of "her self-assurance, her conscious commitment and dedication to the reform – her being childless being a factor in her self-appointed role" as Matthias' helper.)

The Zells set an example in Strasbourg, like the Luthers in Wittenberg, for a Protestant parsonage. The Zells provided the model for a parsonage with an open-door policy and endless hospitality, in the spirit of the Luthers: they opened their house to everybody, ready to feed and offer shelter and, on the side, "argue cordially with those who had not yet come to understand the absoluteness of Christ and faith alone." (McKee 1999a, 50.) Their parsonage was open for theologians on the road (including Calvin at one point) as well as refugees (Bucer, Flacius, Capito, and Schwenckfeld), and those suffering from poverty or illness; at one time they played host to a large group of soldiers trapped in the city. Their house would be as much the center for their activity as was their parish of St Lorenz, and their ministries reached out. Their house of theology and refuge became famous for the indiscriminate hospitality, humanitarian care, and peaceful mediating over theological disputes to be found within its walls. The Zells's ecumenical and charitable spirit enabled them to host, entertain, debate with, and care for a colorful mix of personalities. Katharina showed "unstinted kindness to anyone who sought her help. Some people thought KSZ was indiscriminate, if not downright heretical, in both her religious views and her charity" (McKee 1992, 246). (Katharina's initiative in this can be read from contemporary observations, such as Buzer's "Matthias lagged because Katherine dragged" [Bainton 2001, 66].)

"Understanding herself as a reformer, partner with her husband, colleague with his colleagues in the gospel (both in Strasbourg and abroad), KSZ was respected and loved by the many people she helped, and feared by those whom her strength, determination, and sometimes sharp tongue irritated" (McKee 1992, 246, see also 245, 258–61). Her mission was theological and visionary, but she was human, with no pretense at being anything else. While she would argue fiercely on principles, her actions with people showed kindness and acceptance. While she accepted people regardless of their faith or status or gender, she did not hesitate to voice her disagreement on theological grounds, and ended up ruffling many feathers. Her tolerance had its limits. She did believe false doctrines should be "verbally combatted" (McKee 2007, 104). Like many of her contemporaries, Katharina was guilty of xenophobia and passing judgment on the Jews in particular. She did not condone persecution or coercion, however, and her condemnation was not "personal" but about principles of faith. She believed a distinction should be made between people and creeds, the care for the former outweighing disagreements on the latter. She did not advocate fellowship without discernment about the boundaries; in charity and Christian love, however, there were no boundaries. She practiced what she preached. She refused help to no one as no particular theological confession could overrule the most compelling confession of all: the gospel and its call to love one's neighbor. (See McKee 1992, 245–61; Jung 2002, 144–9.)

While Matthias busied himself preaching, Katharina was active in her visitation ministry, continuing there the early church's office of the deaconate. Her vision of the calling of a "pastor's wife" and church mother was inclusive and expansive and involved risk-taking: instead of remaining limited within her own household, in her pastoral ministry all the children of God were her flock, especially those in need (including children), the imprisoned, the sick, and the refugees. She fought the authorities for her right to visit the sick and the imprisoned without restrictions. She had a particular concern for Kaspar Schwenckfeld, who caused turmoil with his views about the Eucharist and the independent work of the Spirit, and was "misunderstood," in the opinion of Katharina, who offered him shelter at their house (1531–3). She did not shun those who were feared or despised for any reason. For instance, she cared for numerous plague victims during the outbreaks, and, again, in 1558 when one of the chief magistrates of Strasbourg, Felix Ambrosiaster, fell ill with leprosy, Katharina was there to visit and comfort him, as well as his nephew who was suffering from syphilis. These visits occasioned a theologically important text from Katharina, her expositions of the Psalms, the Scriptural text that had been of comfort to herself during the difficult time of her children's death.

The church mother was so revered in her role of pastoral caregiver that, for instance, Kaspar Hedio specifically requested that Katharina attend him on his deathbed. She had a practical mind and natural tendency to take charge of a situation that is evidenced in the directions she gave to correct the appalling conditions of the hospital she visited, demanding pastoral care and decent nourishment, among other things. Concerned about the spiritual needs of her fellow citizens, she argued for an organized chaplaincy for the poor and sick in general. She was listened to, even if some of her recommendations were difficult to realize. She took active leadership in other areas, too, where there was a vacuum in care giving, or where the realization of the gospel was at risk. Her proposals for changes were theologically grounded. To her, social and diaconal work was a natural dimension of theology and preaching. Her involvement in town affairs continued the original vision of the reformers about the urgency of welfare and care of the sick and needy as a continuation of right worship and proclamation of the gospel. She did, somewhat frustrated, what she expected from the pastors, and practiced an expanded version of women's historic ministry in the diaconate, for the good of the gospel. (See Jung 2002, 133, 145–8; Moeller 2005, 61, 50.)

In addition to participating in Matthias's ministry and having her own flock to care for, and developing her own ministry of pastoral care, her service-oriented ministry included writing, an expression of her most far-reaching and lasting "care." She developed a distinctive voice as a lay theologian and as a female pamphlet writer with a practical twofold interest: the care of those in need and ecumenical bridge-building. These tasks she took upon herself as a church mother when others failed to do so. Katharina, with Argula von Grumbach and Marie Dentière, was one of the few Protestant female theologians who published; all of them were harassed for it, but unlike the others, Katharina was protected by her husband. A lay theologian with no formal training, without explicitly identifying herself as a theologian or a pastor, she interpreted Scripture in light of her experiences, in an office she created for herself. Her husband seems to have approved of her actions and welcomed her collaboration; to others she was highly irritating. (See KSZ/McKee, 17–20; Jung 2002, 159–64, 128–33; Conrad 1998, 130–31; Jancke-Pirna 1997, 56–61.)

Katharina's texts, most of them written during a controversy of one kind or another, are available in critical edition in both German and English (produced by McKee 1999b and KSZ/McKee.) Unlike most lay writers who wrote during the burst of lay pamphleteering in 1521–5, Katharina continued to publish after the big watershed of 1530s (when lay pamphleteering significantly slowed down) until her death. It is interesting that Katharina continued to use her father's name Schütz, or Schützin, in her publications; from 1530s she used also her husband's name, in its feminine form, Zellin.

Like most women writers, she did not write explicit summas of theology in the formats of "school theology." Rather, she wrote distinct texts relevant to particular situations, in all of which particularly rich theology unfolds. Three categories can be seen in the writing she produced for a public purpose: her works are roughly polemical, catechetical, and pastoral, the latter dominating her writing. (A prime example of her pastoral instincts as a writer is her consolation to the women of Kentzingen and to Felix Armbruster discussed below [Moeller 2005, 58].) Well aware of the limitations her gender imposed on her as a theological writer, Katharina still produced materials that could and did function as sermons, public speeches, and theological and biblical treatises; in other words, she breeched the exclusively male domains. (Wiesthaus 1993, 126.) Even her more private reflections and correspondence were to be published when Katharina had a message to convey to a larger public. More often she wrote for others, explicitly so, than for private purposes. (For instance, at the time when the laity's education about new religious ideas and practices happened mostly through sermons and catechisms, educational media were desperately needed, and Katharina used her pen to provide a hymnbook, thus supplying the call for new catechetical material.) Her multidimensional writing had many ingredients and tones: she left behind private and public letters; apologetic and polemical works as well as treatises for pastoral counsel; homiletical, biblical, catechetical, and devotional pieces; personal meditations, historical and autobiographical themes, and even sermons. (See McKee 1999b, vii–ix; Conrad 1998, 125–6.)

Katharina wrote her first two booklets during the first two years of her marriage, one for the pastoral consolation of women whose husbands were trapped in Strasbourg after losing to their Catholic opponent, and another as a feisty defense of clerical marriage in general and her own in particular.

The first treatise, *Entschuldigung Katharina Schützinn/für M. Matthes Zellen/jren Eegemahel/ der ein Pfarrher und dyener ist im wort Gottes zu Straßburg. Von wegen grosser lügen uff jn erdiecht* (1524) (KSZ in McKee 1999b, 15–47), that is, "Katharina Schütz's Apologia for Master Matthias Zell, her Husband," was an animated apology for Matthias and for their marriage (KSZ/McKee, 56–82). It opens a window to the firestorm that followed the first clerical marriages in Strasbourg. This was a difficult development in all Reformation contexts, but in Strasbourg, regardless of the town's support, clergy still could be punished for marrying as late as 1524. The treatise also gives insights into the private story of Katharina's married life, starting, as it did, in the midst of controversy. The marriage of the first daughter of a citizen of the town to marry a priest had received exceptional attention.

> With God's help I was also the first woman in Strasbourg who opened the way for clerical marriage . . . since I saw the great fear and furious opposition to clerical marriage, and also the great harlotry of the clergy, I myself married a priest with the intention of encouraging and making a way for all Christians . . . many people have been greatly amazed by my marriage. (KSZ/McKee, 77)

In late January 1525 Katharina wrote a letter to the bishop, William von Honstein and presented her biblical arguments for the marriage of clergy. Katharina's letter "admittedly 'smoked'" (Bainton 2001, 57, 55–7). The bishop in his furious response called Katharina a priest's illegal concubine for whom Matthias had not yet paid a tax (as was the punitive arrangement for the illegal partners and offspring of the clergy)! It was not a charge that would sit too well with Katharina.

In her forceful apology for her own marriage Katharina also spoke on behalf of clerical marriage in general, on the basis of what constituted a good pastor, what the Scriptures said about marriage, and what justification by faith was all about. Her own marriage, for instance, was nothing less than a means of saving souls. She defended her right both to marry and to speak up from her interpretation of the scriptural passage concerning the equality of men and women in Christ. Scripture, according to her reading, invited women to take part in the life of the church. Her "outrageous" and "creative" apology thus both defended Protestant teaching in general and argued for the laity's right of speech. She also took an opportunity to name the cause for "evil" of many kinds in bad teaching! "Indeed an evil teaching is more dangerous than a wicked life." (KSZ/McKee, 69.) She concluded that wrong teaching and "falsehood" causes unnecessary suffering – while suffering for the sake of truth, and Christ, was to be expected. The fiery letter was at first circulated (in 1524) in an anonymous publication. The city council asked Matthias to keep his wife quiet – the situation was messy enough without having a woman involved. She did not see eye to eye on the matter with the council: this was her business, she knew the "truth." (KSZ/McKee, 56–62, 77–82; 1999b, 15–20; Jung 2002, 129, 152–3.)

Katharina had been careful to explain that she was writing on her own without Matthias's knowledge. She did not write under her husband's name, nor did she wish him to be harmed by her actions. She argued that silence on matters of importance was wrong and un-Christian:

> Thus I cannot excuse myself and persuade my conscience that I should be silent about these very great devilish lies that have been said and published about me, as I have been silent until now. Yes, just as the commandment to love my neighbor does not allow me to excuse myself from acting, so also I cannot excuse myself for the following reason. That is, it is proper to (and part of) being a Christian to suffer, but it is not at all proper for him to be silent, for that silence is half a confession that the lies are true. (KSZ/McKee, 64)

The call of a Christian superseded any other orders and rules. She wished to remind her readers of the ultimate priorities in life. In the same treatise Katharina also articulated a defense of Martin Luther and his teaching against his known enemy Johannes Cochlaeus and others. Her bottom line concern was the grace and forgiveness she wished to model in her own life, even in the midst of an acrimonious situation: "I forgive all people as I believe God also forgives me" (ibid. 69–71, 82).

In addition to clerical marriage, other important Reformation milestones involved changes in worship life and sacramental practice, as well as in the use of the vernacular in liturgy and prayers: the Mass was offered in German, "saint-talk" and sacrificial language were eliminated as much as possible, Communion was offered in both kinds, and it was no longer obligatory to confess in order to receive Communion. The changes were quite radical from the perspective of the laity, but, of them all, it was the issue of clerical marriage that remained hotly debated. To set an example, Wolfgang Capito, Kaspar Hedio, and Martin Bucer decided to marry as well.

The marriage of another reformer provides an interesting footnote to Katharina's own story. When Martin Bucer's wife Margaretha was dying she begged Katharina to play the important role of matchmaker and arrange a new marriage for her husband with Wibrandis Rosenblatt, who had, herself, been widowed three times. Her first husband was the humanist Ludwig Keller, with whom she had had one child; after his death she had married Johannes Oecolampadius, and they had had three children together. He, too, died, and she remarried, this time to the widower of Katharina's dear friend Agnes Roettel, Wolfgang Capito, who was the father of her fifth child. Left alone again by her third husband's death, Wibrandis benefited from Katharina's matchmaking and did indeed marry Bucer with whom she had two more children, a little Martin and a little Elisabeth. (On Wibrandis, see Mager 1999a, 128–9, 147; Bainton 2001, 79–95; Chrisman 1972, 154–6.) Obviously, the model she presents for the life of the wife of a reformer and pastor is very different to that of Katharina, but one can see why Katharina valued Wibrandis' contribution!

Another example of Katharina's lifelong care for women is her comforting letter to the women of Kentzingen, the second earliest of her published texts, titled *Den leyden-den Christglaubigen weyberen der gmein zu Kentzigen minen mitschwestern in Christo Jesus zu handen* (Strasbourg, 1524) (KSZ in McKee 1999b , 1–13), that is, "Letter to the Suffering Women of the Community of Kentzingen" (KSZ/McKee, 47–56). As was typical, Katharina's writing stemmed out of a troubling situation, this time war.

In the middle of 1524 the Catholic bishop began to reenforce the 1521 Edict of Worms, and 200 evangelicals were expelled from Kentzingen on June 24, 1524 as the Catholic soldiers took over. As a result, the Protestant men involved in the war could not return home but fled to Strasbourg, where Katharina provided shelter and food for nearly 100 of them for three weeks. Concerned for the women at home in Kentzingen, Katharina wrote a letter of pastoral care to the men's wives. In her letter, dated July 8, 1524, she expressed her sympathy for the women and suggested that her "sisters" in Kentzingen consider their ordeal a proof of their being God's children and growing in faith. She reminded them that there was no true faith without "Anfechtung" (strife) and that God's love would protect and help them through their suffering. In all their suffering, the women in Kentzingen should stand as examples of the faith of Abraham, who also had suffered under God's command to kill his own son.

She wrote to the "dear Christian women" and "dear sisters,"

> So I beg you, loyal believing women, also to do this: take on you the manly, Abraham-like courage while you too are in distress and while you are abused with all kinds of insult and suffering . . . When your husbands and you yourselves may be killed, meditate then on strong Abraham, father of us all [cf. Rm 4:16]; struggle after him as a good child should follow his father in a faith like the father's. (KSZ/McKee, 51)

She reminded her "sisters" that the Scriptures needed to be fulfilled and that there was, of necessity, suffering in following Christ, and told them to rejoice in that privilege and "calling":

> So you also, if you want to be Christians and to enter into His glory with Him, you must also suffer with Him, and for this you encounter abuse. Yes, even if you are put in chains for Christ's sake, how happy you are [cf. Matt. 5;11]. Would that God would regard me with such grace and favor, and favor me with such great honor so that I should have gifts unlike yet also like yours, to suffer such things with His dearest Christ and with you. Then I would be more happy, proud, and glad than all the nobles at Strasbourg . . . Yes, I would be happier in that suffering than if I were the wife of the Holy Roman Emperor . . . For I know and am certain, that such things [as persecution] are only signs of His fatherly love, and (indeed) the most trustworthy signs. (ibid., pp. 52 and 53)

Furthermore, she assured the women of God's involvement in their ordeal: "Therefore, dear Christian women, consider these words are not mine but are from the Spirit of God, and be thankful and welcome such gifts of God," (p. 54) and later, "He will not abandon you, nor forget you. He also says in the prophet: 'As little as a mother may forget her suckling child, so little may I forget you; and if she does forget her child, still I will not forget you' [Isa. 49:15]," (pp. 54–5) and, "So, dear Christian women, I cannot comfort and exhort you more and better now than to counsel you to accept such suffering with right patience and spiritual joy, for these are fruits of the Spirit . . . He Himself wants to be your Comforter, trusted Guardian, and Protector [cf. John 14:16]. Amen" (p. 56). The letter was published twice in 1524 (first in Strasbourg, then in Augsburg).

On other instances as well Katharina opened her house to be a home for refugees and locus for theological negotiations. In 1529 Philip von Hessen brought a group of Germans and Swiss together to Marburg (a meeting that resulted the 1529 Marburg Articles expressing an agreement on 14 theological points but not on the issue of Christ's real presence in the Lord's Supper). On their way to Marburg, Zwingli and Oecolampadius stayed in Strasbourg – and where else but at the Zells? As Katharina cooked for them for two weeks, one can be certain that theology was discussed at the dinner table with the hostess eagerly participating. A similar occasion came in 1538 when they hosted Jean Calvin. These were occasions for her to offer the ministry of hospitality and to learn from the table talks.

Katharina was concerned not just to receive but also to pass on education, and, realizing the lay demand for educational material beyond sermons and catechisms, rose to the occasion and produced one of her most influential and most widely used texts – the hymnbook she edited from an earlier Bohemian Brethren's Hymnbook: *Von Christo Jesus unserem saligmacher/ seiner Menschwerdung/ Geburt/ Beschneidung/ etc. etlich Christliche und trostliche Lobgsang/auß einem vast herrlichen Gsangbuch gezogen/Von welchem inn der Vorred weiter anzeygt würdt* (Strasbourg: J. Froelich, 1534–6), that is, "Some Christian and Comforting Songs of Praise about Jesus Christ Our Savior" (KSZ/ McKee, 82–96; KSZ in McKee 1999b, 55–64).

Katharina had been concerned about how ordinary Christians could be nurtured in their faith, given the lack of adequate sources of devotional and educational works. People should be able to "learn and know the faith" for themselves (McKee 2007, 85). Making an intelligent use of the material available to her, she displaced unacceptable songs with biblical songs and with lyrics resonating with Protestant theology. Her hymns would both educate and empower the laity in their holy vocations and inspire them to proclaim the gospel. The inexpensive hymnbook would nurture lay spirituality from the cradle, would lend itself for use at home, and it would enhance people's involvement in worship. She prepared the hymnal between 1536 and 1539, and it was published in four smaller books, consisting of 159 songs (85 with annotation) that originated from Michael Weisse's 1531 Bohemian Brethren's hymns. (This edition became the first edition of the Bohemian Brethren's hymnbook to be published in German, and the only one to appear in Strasbourg.) She wrote, "I found such an understanding of the work of God in this songbook that I want all people to understand it. Indeed, I ought much rather to call it a teaching, prayer, and praise book than a songbook. However, the little word 'song' is well and properly spoken, for the greatest praise of God is expressed in song" (KSZ/McKee, 93, see 82–96). (See McKee 1994, 17–21, 26–37.) Katharina's objectives as a church mother and her "feminist undercurrent" became clear in some of her strikingly feminine imagery. In her editing, Katharina showed concern for women's issues, for instance, the feelings of a mother who had lost a child, an experience she knew at first-hand. (See McKee 1999b, 55–7; 1994, 39–40, 61–2.)

The hymnbook was a

fascinating monument to a strong, talented, astute, and convinced lay reformer: a woman who stood on the boundary between clergy and laity, working on the continuum between liturgy and popular piety, understanding and sharing many concerns of ordinary Christians, and acting with all the resources at her command to encourage and cajole, argue and persuade her beloved fellow citizens to sing their way into the religious renewal of the whole of their lives. (McKee 1994, 63. See Conrad 1998, 130)

The hymnbook more than any other work, perhaps, shows the many dimensions of Katharina's contributions as a reformer, as a theologian, as a catechetical teacher, as a pastoral caregiver, and as an empowerer of the laity. First, her hymnbook presented a nuanced, biblically based, praxis-oriented theological vision, addressing the spiritual needs of the laity. The material of the hymns was Scripture as well as life experiences, which meant that the theology was grounded in reality as it was known to people. Secondly, she gave people a concrete tool to reform and deepen their spiritualities, to learn, and to have a voice – through hymns. Singing "her" hymns, people in Strasbourg would be singing theology, her theology. Third, the hymns offered a medium for healing the soul and for bringing unity to the congregation. (Moeller 2005, 50, 55–7, 59.)

Much of Katharina's theologizing happened through her vast correspondence, which demonstrates her connections and wide-ranging interests. Of all the correspondence, the most intriguing, and most traumatic to her, was that with Ludwig Rabus. In the course of this particular correspondence, the otherwise so compassionate "Seelsorgerin" (pastoral care provider) loses her patience as she feistily defends her own accomplishments as a church mother and the first generation reformers against a personal attack. The letters offer important autobiographical reflection as well as shed light on the confessional battles of the day. (See Wiesner-Hanks 1998, 144–5.)

Ludwig Rabus (1524–92), who, following Matthias's death was the new cathedral pastor, represented the kind of rigid confessionalism Katharina had fought against throughout her whole career. The tense relationship between the two illustrates the increase in confessionalism and the theological disagreements between different Protestants in Strasbourg as well as elsewhere. For instance, Ludwig voiced loud criticism of all others than the adherents to the 1530 Augsburg Confession. He had no sympathy for the fact that this confessional document served only Lutherans and did not apply to other Protestant groups, such as the Zwinglians and Calvinists and Anabaptists. Now Matthias's successor turned against Katharina in particular and criticized the Zells' tolerant approach to religious and confessional differences in general. Rabus attacked the widow who had nurtured him as her "son," accusing her of causing disturbance, leaning towards heresy, and supporting heretics, such as the Schwenckfelders. Katharina rose to oppose Ludwig's rigid confessionalism and to defend the early reformers' legacy and the gospel itself, as she saw it. To say that the relationship between Katharina and Rabus became estranged is an understatement.

When, in 1556–7, Rabus left abruptly and without the city's permission to become superintendent of the church in the city of Ulm, Katharina wrote and asked for his reasons. Rabus sent her letter back unopened, with an accusation that she was a heretic, Zwinglian, Schwenckfelder, devilish, stinking liar, pharisaic, a false witness, a rumormonger, inspired by the devil, poisonous, pagan, and a fool who caused trouble at the church and was about to receive God's wrath. He told her to stop meddling in affairs that were not her business anyway. Katharina defended herself and her rights with support from Galatians 3:28 and Joel 3:1. Referring to her call as a church mother since childhood, she reminded her readers that "I have loved all the clergy, visited many, and had conversations with them . . . about the kingdom of God. Therefore also my father, mother, friends, and fellow citizens, and also many clergy (whom I have much questioned in order to learn) have held me in great love, honor, and fear" (KSZ/McKee, 226).

She wished to remind her city of Strasbourg of all her service and ministry:

> Since then the Lord drew me from my mother's womb and taught me from my youth, I have diligently busied myself with His church and its household affairs, working gladly and constantly. I have dealt faithfully according to the measure of my understanding and the graces given to me, without deception . . . So, constantly, joyously, and strongly, with all

good will have I given my body, strength, honor, and goods for you, dear Strasbourg; I have made them a footstool for you . . . My devout husband too was very heartily glad to allow this; and he also loved me very much for it . . . And I also have loved and served you, Strasbourg, from my youth, as I still also do in my old age and almost sixty years. (KSZ/McKee, 224–5)

In a letter of defense against the confessional "hothead", she recalled how, first of all, people had always sought for her advise (not the other way round), especially in their anxiety over the issue of salvation and grace, and secondly, how Luther's texts had led her to a revelation on the matter:

Then God had mercy on us and many people. He awakened and sent out by tongue and writings the dear and now blessed Dr. Martin Luther, who described the Lord Jesus Christ for me and others in such a lovely way that I thought I had been drawn up out of the depths of the earth, yes, out of grim bitter hell, into the sweet lovely kingdom of heaven. (KSZ/McKee, 226)

She reminisced about her marriage to Matthias, her work at his side, her pastoral care service, and her fond relations and collaborations with many of the older reformers, whom she considered her partners and teachers: "I heard their sayings and sermons, read their books, received their letters with joy, and they received mine with joy." "In summary, I am writing all this because I must show how in my younger days I was so dear to the fine old learned men and architects of the church of Christ (5) . . . They never withheld from me their conversation about holy matters and they gladly (from the heart) heard mine [cf. Heb 4:10]" (ibid., 227, 228). Statements like this alone bolstered Katharina's authority.

In addition to her defense of the reformers' theology, her response to Rabus also presented her persistent vision for religious tolerance. She also tried to put young, ignorant Rabus in his place, acting as a firm mother with a disobedient child. She considered this letter her testament and confession of faith. Titled *Ein Brieff an die gantze Burgershafft der Statt Straßburg/ von Katherina Zellin/ dessen jetz saligen Matthei Zellen/ deß alten und ersten Predigers des Evangelij diser Statt/nachgelassne Ehefraw/Betreffend Herr Ludwigen Rabus / jetz ein Prediger der Statt Ulm/ sampt zweyen brieffen jr und sein/ die mag mengklich lessen und urtheilen on gunst und haß/ sonder allein der war heit warnemen. Dabey auch ein sanffte antwort/ auff jeden Artickel/ seines briffs* (Strasbourg, December 1557) (KSZ in McKee 1999b, 155–303), that is "A Letter to the Whole Citizenship of the City of Strasbourg from Katharina Zell . . . concerning Mr Ludwig Rabus" (KSZ/McKee, 215–31) addressed to the whole city of Strasbourg, it consisted of several letters, including Rabus's letters to her, and a letter to the city of Strasbourg. (The first letter, from December 1555, followed by a shorter piece in February 1556, was sent to Rabus when he was still in Strasbourg. The third letter, dating from March 1557, was sent to Rabus in Ulm. Rabus's reply was dated April 19, 1557, and was followed by Katharina's letter to the city of Strasbourg in December 1557.)

One could speculate over the reasons for Katharina corresponding with Rabus in the first place and for doing so in such a negative tone. The most apparent reason, the one she gives herself, was her desire to speak the "truth." She defended all the "maligned" and "accused" for the sake of "truth." (McKee 1992, 251–7; KSZ/McKee, 23;

Wiesner-Hanks 1998, 145–6.) She "knew", unlike Rabus who had actually not known personally the very people he accused.

Of the accused heretics, closest to her personally was Schwenckfeld. He and the Zells had been friends for years and she perhaps shared his theology more than was admitted. (She was often associated with the "Schwenckfelders," in both critical and positive terms, despite her objections. [KSZ/McKee, 23].) Zwingli and Oecolampadius she knew from their works and from their two-week stay at her house in 1529. In her defense of the men she knew, versus Rabus's ignorance of them, she turned her attention to the basics of faith and the limits of tolerance. Personal and generational issues were at stake, as were theological principles. Making references to the notorious *De heretics* by Sébastian Castellion (1554) she argued for religious tolerance by reminding her reader(s) of the "chief point," the principle of faith: that Christ the savior was true God and true human. Furthermore, faith, as a spiritual issue, was not something the magistrate should try to control. She reminded the city and its council of its long history of theological tolerance! She even appealed to Rabus himself as his former "mother." All was in vain. Anyway, as poignant as her statements against violence in religious matters were, a woman's arguments would not be employed in the continuing toil towards religious toleration. (See Wiesner-Hanks 1995, 252, 245–7, 254–61; McKee 1992, 251–2.)

In addition to the issue of tolerance and personal tensions, she also discussed the sacraments. Leaning towards a more "Zwinglian" interpretation of the Lord's Supper – the most divisive issue for Lutherans, Zwinglians, and Calvinists – she emphasized the spiritual presence of Christ in the holy ritual, digressing from both Luther's teaching of the "real" presence of Christ and from the Catholic doctrine of transubstantiation in regards the change of the substance of the elements. On baptism she adopted, likewise, a more Zwinglian perspective, considering it to be a sign without the power of imparting grace, though affecting a rebirth in the person. (Also her notion of the role of the law in Christian life has "a Reformed flavor" [KSZ/McKee, 127].) Katharina's experience of any mother's greatest fear shows as she seeks for comfort and assurance about the fate of dead unbaptized children. Her perspective on the sacraments put her in a difficult position after the town embraced the Lutherans' Augsburg Confession as normative (following the Wittenberg Concord of 1536). She did not live to see the banning of the Calvinist services in 1557.

In this writing we find an insight into how Katharina balanced her sense of self and the time's restrictions for women. In her writing, Katharina "fashions a female self and locates it in the spectrum of feminine roles available at her time." She described herself "as unlike any other woman she knew." She applied an autobiographical topos employed by medieval women saints and mystics before her – one of, being singled out by God since childhood. This model she then fused with the reformers' ideal of chaste, male-defined femininity: she delineated her life according to the three phases of women's lives defined by their relationships with men – as a daughter, wife, and widow. Yet she felt herself to be different. "Katharina's distinctive sense of separation from other women is complemented by an unwavering loyalty to the 'glorious' and 'very beloved' male reformers." (Wiethaus 1993, 127, 128.) After all, she stressed her role as a wife, as a piece of Matthias's rib. Her identity and authority as a reformer were tied to her marital relation. In retrospect, her defense of her marriage was ultimately a defense of herself. Furthermore, it was exactly in the marital partnership that Katharine developed her self-understanding as a reformer. (See KSZ/McKee, 224–8; Wiesner-Hanks 1995, 249–52.)

McKee (KSZ/McKee, 220) provides a list of Katharine's self-designations: she understood and presented herself as (1) Matthias's "wedded companion," (2) "faithful help in his office," (3) "mother of the poor and exiled," (4) "Matthew's rib," (5) "fellow worker," (6) "fisher of people," (7) "church mother," and (8) "widow" (or identification with widows).

Knowing well the traditional interpretation of the words in 1 Tim. 2:12 about women's silence in church, she was "deeply convinced of the authority of Scripture to reject the Pauline limits placed on a 'regular' preaching ministry for women." She interpreted such prohibitions "narrowly." Never attempting to hide her gender, she did not underscore it either. (McKee 1999a, xvi–xvii; Wiesner-Hanks 1995, 252.) Her focus was on the work that needed to be done. In that she identified herself with the women and men of the Scriptures (Job, David, Judith Anna, Daniel, Abigail), not wishing to be remembered as a woman, but for her acts of love and service to the city.

Katharina wrote several treatises during her 35-year-long career. Her voice as a female theologian and writer, as well as her gifts as a pastoral care provider, was demonstrated particularly clearly in her last publication, Meditations on Psalms and the Lord's Prayer (305–66). Titled *Den Psalmen Miserere/mit dem Khünig David bedacht/ gebettet/ und paraphrasirt von Katharina Zellin M. Matthei Zellen seligen nachgelassne Ehefraw/ sampt dem Vatter unser mit seiner erklarung/ zugeschickt dem Christlichen mann Juncker Felix Armbruster/zum trost in seiner kranckheit/ und andern angefochtenen hertzen und Concientzen/ der sünd halben betrubt &c. in truck lassen kommen* (KSZ in McKee 1999b, 305–66), that is, "The Miserere Psalm Meditated, Prayed Over, and Paraphrased with King David by Katharina Zell . . . Sent to the Christian Man Sir Felix Armbruster" (KSZ/McKee, 123–73).

The work, consisting of a collection of devotional and didactic texts, was divided into three parts: after a letter of dedication to Sir Felix Armbruster came her meditations on Psalms 51 and 130, and, last, her exposition of the Lord's Prayer. Whereas Katharina's visits to Felix took place in 1558, her original meditations on the Psalms can be dated to the 1540s and earlier: the Psalms had been of special importance for Katharina at the time of her children's deaths, and were again during the last years of her life, which were shadowed by difficulties, especially after Matthias's death in January 1548. This substantive work was published in Strasbourg in 1558 (at first without the original explanation of the Lord's Prayer from 1536, which was included later). (McKee 1999b, 305–9.)

As her theologically richest work, this treatise was occasioned by her tireless visitation ministry, and her particular concern for a suffering friend. One of the chief magistrates of Strasbourg, Felix Ambrosiaster, had fallen ill with leprosy and Katharina began to visit him, and wrote a word of consolation, a Meditation on the Lord's Prayer. This treatise marked her "personal development as a woman of faith and spiritual mother or friend." It was not coincidental that the treatise spoke of the maternal character of the divine and the grace of God in Christ and left an excellent example of her work as a "Seelsorgerin." The treatise also offers a model of a woman employed in pastoral care through letters. (McKee 1999b, 305–6. Also KSZ/McKee, 44–6; Moeller 2005, 53, 56–8.) Intentionally presenting "Sir Felix as a model of the way a faithful Christian should deal with affliction," Katharina also addressed two specific issues: the human and divine roles in consolation – the former subordinate to the latter, the Holy Spirit as the ultimate comforter – and her own experiences of suffering and God's consolation.

She wrote, "The Spirit's visiting is above all human visiting, conversation, and comfort . . . it pierces the heart so that the person willingly entrusts his body in obedience to Christ on the cross." "And yet," she says,

> we ought to exercise and practice toward each other our office (commanded to us by God), the office of care and love . . . For, just as much suffering comes upon us because of Christ, so also much comfort comes to us through Christ. Yes, the whole Holy Scripture teaches us to love and serve our neighbors as the members of one body help each other bear evil . . . So also the Spirit of God must come to help our speaking, praying, comforting, and everything, to give force, breath, and life, if our actions are to serve and be useful to people. (KSZ/McKee, 131–2)

She argues in her writing, and in her actions, that "the lay pastor has biblical authority for this duty of love," that is, to console the suffering with the Word of God. Unlike in her youth, when she readily acknowledged her lack of knowledge and experience, now she confidently relied on her knowledge and her "existential justification as a fellow sufferer" to speak out. (KSZ/McKee, 124–5.) Telling of the many weeping people who had been seeking her out, she explains her reasons for writing from her own dark experiences and desire to comfort others:

> This same Miserere psalm . . . I also meditated on once alone before God, when I was in great affliction and distress. I prayed and paraphrased this psalm when my heart and conscience were tortured, together with Psalm 130, the De Profundis, when I was torn apart inside between the wrath and the grace of God . . . Since I have experienced so many afflictions in myself and in others, and also God has given me again much comfort . . . I wanted to share these two psalms with you in writing. (KSZ/McKee, 133–4)

This treatise is both theological and personal. In the second part of the book, Katharina "invites Sir Felix and other readers into Katharina's most private place of prayer. In effect, to comfort her friends, Matthias's widow took out the booklets in which she had prayed, wept, and lamented her way though the book of Psalms at a time of deepest desolation, probably the months following Zell's death" (Ibid., 127). Interestingly enough, in the third part of the book, her explanation of the Lord's Prayer, Katharina concludes that "the basic source of consolation for sick souls is true teaching; that Christians are made right with God solely by Christ's grace" (ibid., 128). Drawing from her own experiences of suffering, she gives her treatise a feminine face. Reading it one is struck by the "feminine language for Christ. Here Katharina the mother, probably only recently bereaved of her own babies at the time she composed this text, reflects vividly on the maternal work of Christ in the salvation of those who are His children as well as His brothers" (ibid., 128–9). She wrote,

> A woman who has never had a child, never experienced or felt the pain of birth and the love of feeding a nursling, cannot understand. Who could love, treat kindly, and have compassion for helpless children as the true mother can and does? So also God . . . But the grace of God through Jesus Christ is the true mother, that Christ who is in God and God in Him.

As Christ embraced humanity in incarnation and knows human life and suffering at first-hand, Christ knows and loves humans with an experience similar to that of a birthing mother. At the same time, as Christ has delivered humans in his suffering, and nurtured them with the drink of his breast, Christians have become the children and heirs of God the father. (KSZ/McKee, 152–4.)

This treatise manifested Katharina's love for the Word and the principles of her theology. (See Jung 2002, 135–7, 140–7.) She was extremely Word-focused and, as was typical for women writers of the time and for the reformers, she used the Bible as the foundation in all her argumentation and as the norm for discerning the truth and for finding comfort. Last but not least, she employed Scripture as the principal source for empowering herself as a woman, as well as empowering other women. With what could be called a feminist intent, she wished to apply the wisdom she gathered from biblical passages about women to her situation as a woman in Strasbourg. For instance, she identified herself with Mary Magdalene in her eulogy at Matthias's burial, as well as with Mary, the mother of Christ, and with Martha. She also identified herself with the prophet Anna, with Hanna, and with Sara and Rebecca as a woman who was childless against her will. At the same time, she saw no problem in doing the same with male characters in the Bible.

The treatise portrayed Jesus at the center of Katharina's faith and confession. Drawing particularly from the Gospel of John she held on to Christ's humanity (John 2:19–22 and 10:17ff.). She offered comfort from her trust in the work of God's spirit over death and suffering – central themes to her personally and theologically – and her Christology gave her the necessary foundation for her pastoral care. Her central consolation came from the conviction that Christians are made right with God, whom she understood through maternal images, by grace alone, and that right teaching will help us face the evil and dangers in life. (KSZ/McKee, 126–9; Jung 2002, 135–7, 140–7.)

Of all of Katharina's writings, her exposition on the Lord's Prayer and her foreword in particular stand out for their feminist theological value and for demonstrating the uniqueness of this lay theologian. Katharine offered her explanation of the traditional prayer in response to a request for pastoral care from two women from the city of Speyer. A "catechetical-cum-devotional" treatise "it presents careful, conscious thought by a Protestant lay theologian, a mother writing as a pastor for women and children, inviting her hearers to think about the central biblical prayer and the God whom it addresses with trust and confidence, and using a combination of scriptural wisdom and homely images to teach and pray with her readers." As McKee's analysis demonstrates, "The most distinctive aspect of Schütz Zells' foreword to the Prayer is the vivid maternal imagery used for the work of Christ, which even spills over occasionally onto God the Father." In her treatment of the Lord's Prayer, "the extent and character of her maternal language about the Christ who labors with children in great travail on the cross and bears, nourishes, and cares for them as a mother does her nursling, is particularly notable." Her point in all this is the message of the gospel she wishes to proclaim: "Practical and Protestant as she was, the lay theologian puts the principal emphasis on God with us, for us." With strikingly "maternal metaphors" for the "redemptive work of Christ," whose passion can be read as "the birth pangs of a woman in labor," she wishes to assure her readers of how "this Father loves us and will never forget us even should a mother forget her nursling, this Christ brought us to birth as new creatures, and the power of this Holy Spirit teaches us to live rightly and holds us in the family of God as His beloved children." (McKee 1999c, 240–7.)

The theology in Katharina's works relied on the central Protestant principles of Christ and the work of Christ, the gift nature of faith, the compassion commanded by the gospel, and the work of Christ's spirit, to which she gave her own emphasis. Her theological exposition drew on the Scriptures. She interpreted what was her most accessible source and form of empowerment as a lay theologian (McKee 2007, 86) in the light of the life she lived, experienced, and witnessed, and with the understanding that had been shaped by the sermons she listened to, the treatises she read, and the conversations she had. She repeatedly brought forth arguments about issues she considered to be of ultimate importance, and did so with scriptural "ammunition": the care of the laity, the poor, the needy and the suffering; the proper and real proclamation of the gospel in words and deeds; the values of tolerance and compassion were some of the principles she constantly preached and theologized about. (See Jung 2002, 205, 135–150, 194–7, 158–68.)

Katharina's entire theology was shaped by the perspective of compassion and care. For instance (as Natalie Zemon Davis characterizes her thinking, referring to McKee), her meditation on the Lord's Supper and her impulse to "ethical action" – the prayer that Christ "may abide in us and we may abide in him and not die" – according to Katharina, should lead believers to perform charitable actions as nourished spiritually by the communion bread, the body of Christ, because "the command to love the neighbor was as important as the cardinal doctrines of Protestant faith" (Davis 2000, 125–6). The Christian command to love one's neighbor was the compelling reason for all Christians to speak up, out of concern for others and for justice. (See McKee 1992, 1997. Also Wiesner-Hanks 1995.)

Envisioning God's love as that of a mother, Katharina did not express interest in developing a particularly womanly theology or spirituality. She identified with the biblical women but held the "manly faith of Abraham" that rests hope and trust in God as a positive ideal to all – men and women, learned and laity, first generation and second generation reformers, Lutherans and spiritualists, all groups between whom Katharina operated as a theologian. In that "between" place she developed a characteristically Christocentric theology, affirming the Spirit's work in the individuals' calling, sanctification of all believers, and a spiritual notion of the Church. (Conrad 1998, 130; Jung 2002, 194–6.) Going beyond personal spiritual reflection or piety, Katharina employed central Protestant principles and scriptural examples to provide theology that was designed to speak to praxis and that helped make sense of and better the lives and ease the suffering of people around her. She applied her Protestant principles of faith and her first-hand interpretation of the Scriptures in particularly difficult situations, often under the clout of controversy, and without the status or a training of a "school theologian," thus comparisons with other theologians of the time seem hardly fair. Her theological writing exhibits certain characteristics unique to her: employing biblical authority, Katharina presents uncompromised authorial confidence; it is existential as well as practical, with an essentially religious nature. She writes for the public, but with a certain degree of autobiographical introspection. (KSZ/McKee, 25–9.)

The Zells' marriage had been a lifelong partnership in ministry. Apart from their work in Strasbourg, the couple had traveled together to Wittenberg to meet Luther and Melanchthon, Nicolaus von Amsdorf and others. Their long trip took them through Switzerland, Swabia, Nuremburg, and the Palatinate, and they met many learned individuals. They had hosted a large company of major participants in the Reformation (including Capito, Bucer, Hedio, Calvin, and Zwingli), and they negotiated changes with the city officials and the Catholic party. In every respect, Katharina had been in the thick of things with the Reformation in Strasbourg and connected with people across the confessional divides. She had contributed from a position of partnership with Matthias, as wife and helper on a radically equal footing. In theory she had acted as a "helper," but in actuality she emerged as a leader with a vision of her own. That remained possible as long as she was married, and at least theoretically subjected to her husband. With her husband gone, the reality was quite different.

Without Matthias, Katharina was heartbroken and alone. Regardless of all her labor and achievements, the Zell widow would end up without status or sufficient support. As with Katharina von Bora Luther, loyal friends naturally did what they could in soliciting support for her. Still, her joy and livelihood were gone with Matthias. Without Matthias she received more opposition toward her involvement, opposition she faced alone, quite fearlessly and forcefully. During her last years the general political situation became tenuous too. The 1540s were a dangerous time, as tensions grew between the Catholics and the Protestants and the imperial forces occupied south German cities, approaching dangerously close Strasbourg. Amid all the uncertainty, Katharina continued her ministry and her defense of the first generation reformers.

Matthias died on January 10, 1548. The next day, in front of a large audience at his burial in Kurbau, Katharina gave an impromptu sermon. The frail widow gave a speech after Bucer's sermon, and talked about her husband's beautiful death and his ministry and care, as well as about her own role as the helper of her husband for 24 years. A handwritten text of this speech, which matches Katharina's style, was not published until the next century. Her words for Matthias's burial were later published, without any doubts about the author, under the title *Klag red und ermahnung Catharina Zellin zum volk bey dem grab m: Matheus Zellen pfarer zum münster zu Straßburg/ deß frommen mannß/ bey und über seinen todten leib* (January 11, 1548) (KSZ/McKee 1999b, 65–94), that is, "Lament and Exhortation of Katharina Zell to the People at the Grave of Master Matthias Zell" (KSZ/McKee, 96–123.)

Her participation at the graveyard service was witnessed by, for instance, humanist Abraham Löscher and others, but it is improbable that she would have read the entire printed text on that cold winter morning. It is quite possible that she spoke freely at the graveside and later wrote the text for publication. (Regardless of the alterations and additions to the text during its elaboration and future publications, according to McKee [KSZ/McKee, 99, footnote 68] "the present text can be regarded as faithful to what Schütz Zell wrote." See KSZ/McKee, 98–9.) In any event, this was a highly unusual act for a woman, even someone as self-assured and well-positioned as Katharina. (Rumors say Argula von Grumbach, her German contemporary, engaged in similar activity, but there is no documentary evidence of this. It is not a coincidence that both women were vehemently attacked and ridiculed.)

After her speech, the eyewitnesses tell how the widow collapsed and was moved to a friendly house for care. Bucer wrote to her hosts: "Her zeal is incredible for Christ's lowliest and afflicted. She knows and searches the mysteries of Christ . . ." (Bainton 2001, 67, 66.) She lived through interims when the Reformation changes came to a halt and the Catholic rites and the Mass were returned with the ultimate goal of extinguishing reformation. She endured the recurrence of plague in town (1553, 1553, and 1541) and remained in contact with other reformers (she sheltered Bucer and Fagius for four weeks, for instance). The 1555 Peace of Augsburg brought an apparent peace as its principle "whose land, whose faith," allowed Catholic and Protestant princes and cities to choose between the two faith traditions, and let respective territories coexist without mutual interference. This political agreement did not speak of religious tolerance in the true sense of the word, but at least it stopped the mutual killing of Protestants and Catholics, until religious strife erupted again in 1618 with the beginning of the Thirty Years War.

Katharina continued her ministry of care and visitations, teaching and consoling, until the end of her life. What was perhaps her most radical act was yet to come. Out of pastoral concern, she took on a priestly role – an outrageous act for a woman – and performed the funeral of a known Schwenckfelder, Elisabeth Häckleren, the wife of a noted physician. She committed the "transgression" faithful to her calling to spread the gospel and to give pastoral care: as there were no other pastors willing to perform the burial she had to do it! Namely, as a condition for an official burial, the local pastor had demanded that the wife be declared as having fallen away from true faith. The widower refused and invited Katharina instead to perform the clandestine 6:00 A.M. service. Katharina, already too weak to walk, had to be carried to the grave, where she did conduct the service, fully aware of the repercussions. She would have been penalized gravely, according to the city officials, once she got better, but she died in the same year on September 6. By then Katharina had been charged with another crime. She had preached at another burial, that of her friend and associate Kaspar Hedio, who had called Katharina to his deathbed a little earlier. Controversy followed her to her grave. Deemed a Schwenckfelder because of her personal associations, it was only as a result of her friends' and supporters' forceful assembly that she herself was buried in a church ceremony at the church graveyard.

Katharina's memory dimmed, and her full contribution as a reformer has been acknowledged only recently, along with that of Argula von Grumbach, Olimpia Morata, and Marie Dentière, the other writing Reformation-era women. She had broken the rules against women speaking in the Church because of her commitment to the Christian faith and gospel. Katharina's motto throughout her life had been that Christians could not be silent, that their duty and call was to work for justice and speak for justice. Christian love would call believers to break silence, at all cost, and that is what Katharina did.

Conclusion

Of all the Reformation women, Katharina Schütz Zell stands out as extraordinary. Thriving in her role as her pastor-husband's "helper," she developed her own calling as a church mother with duties fitting to her personality, learning, and passion. Her vocation was shaped by her gender, to a degree, and by her context: she responded as a woman to the needs of the people in her town. Indiscriminate in her Christian compassion and willingness to care pastorally for those in need, she was a mediating voice between disagreeing theological voices, seeking for unity and peace for the sake of the gospel. Her charitable and ecumenical actions and her defense of the first generation reformers speak loudly about her commitment to the gospel and the Protestant faith. Her writings prove her a gifted and effective theologian who was not only able to translate theological principles into counsel that brought comfort, guidance, and meaning to every day life, especially for those who were suffering, but was committed to doing so. Her activities in her town and in the reformation circle in Strasbourg (and beyond) speak about the broadness of her calling and the holistic nature of her theology – the world was her church, and all the people she encountered were welcomed to her household, her "congregation."

Katharina's gender awareness and the influence of her gender in her theology has been evaluated with different emphases. Whether or not one could see in Katharina a fusion of a specific calling and a male-defined femininity (Wiethaus 1993, 127) and a disinterest in developing a specifically womanly theology or spirituality, is not that easy to assess. Similarly, to what degree and effect she had internalized a negative image of women (Conrad 1998, 130) cannot be deducted from her holding up a "manly faith of Abraham" as a positive model for women as well. How she applied a woman's perspective in her theology – for instance, in her understanding of God's motherly love (Mager 1999b, 88) – needs to be evaluated in the light of the patriarchal setting in which she grew without the existence of actual contemporary models for emancipated women or building blocks for feminist theological perspectives. That she saw herself in a spiritual office on a par with the ministry of Word and sacrament, a role reserved for men, can be gathered from her actions.

Unique in her boldness as a woman and a lay writer, Katharina differed from, for instance, the medieval female teachers in the justification she gave for her writing. Not relying on supernatural or mystical experiences, she drew her authority from Scripture and the sense of a calling (something she experienced as a child, akin to the medieval visionaries who were often similarly called). Her Protestant theology underscored the primacy of the Word and the responsibilities it brought for everyone. Although her own vocation was particular to her, she saw everybody called to do likewise! In the face of the call to proclaim the gospel in deed as well as word, existing gender norms proved irrelevant to her, unbiblical even. She provided the model for how things could have been for women in general as a result of the Reformation's initial vision, yet she stands in a league of her own, in terms of her actions, the way she used her voice, her influence, her sense of herself and her calling, and her explicit arguments for her rights as a woman and as a Christian.

A Word about Sources and References

For the core biographical information, and for critical German and English editions of Katharina's works, see McKee's foundational works from 2006 and 1999, as well as the bibliography in this volume for other sources.

Elsie McKee's ground-breaking works from 1992, 1994, 1995, 1997, 1999, 2006, and 2007 provide substantial biographical study and critical editions and analysis of Katharina's writings. Valuable articles and chapters interpreting Katharina's life and calling come from Bainton 1971/2001; Becker-Cantarino 1987; Conrad 1998; Jancke-Pirna 1997; Wiesner-Hanks 1995; and Douglass 1985. Her role as a writer, reformer, and theologian has been evaluated by Jung 2002, as the spouse of a reformer and pastor by Mager 1999b and Nielsen 1999, and as a pastoral caregiver by Moeller 2005. Older sources – Meyer 1960, Heinsius 1951, and Stupperich 1954 – offer important insights as well. More popular works such as by Haase 2002 shows that interest in Katharina is both current and continuing.

CHAPTER 9

Marie Dentière, 1495–1561 – A Genevan Reformer and Writer

HEVER CASTLE LTD, KENT, UK/THE BRIDGEMAN ART LIBRARY

Anne Boleyn (1507–36) by Holbein, Hans the Younger – in the absence of images of Marie Dentière, a French reformer known for her "Defense of Women", this portrait is used of the mother of Elizabeth I, both important defenders of Protestant lives, and Anne dying a martyr's death, for reasons Marie would have deemed misogynist and unjust.

Marie Dentière, 1495–1561

PARENTS
- Jérome d'Ennetières/Dentière
- Mother, name unknown

SPOUSE [1] (1528–33)
- Simon Robert (died 1533)
- Children
- five, names unknown

SPOUSE [2] (1533)
- Antoine Froment (1508–1581)

Introduction

"Not only for you, my Lady, did I wish to write this letter, but also to give courage to other women detained in captivity, so as they might not fear being expelled from their homelands, away from their relatives and friends, as I was, for the word of God." So wrote Marie Dentière to the famous queen consort Marguerite de Navarre, who had implored information from her about the situation in Geneva. Even if the words imply that the author expected an audience of women, the letter was not meant to remain private and "only" for women. With a broader readership in mind, and making clever employment of the literary conventions, the author articulated a strong defense of women's public teaching voice. (See Marie Dentière in McKinley 2004, 53, also 56, from here on MD/McKinley).

Marie could be described as an early feminist. She was unabashedly and openly Protestant, once she had left her monastic life and married a fellow reformer. Her confidence as a writer and her feminist and Protestant convictions are evident in her address to Queen Marguerite, the older sister of the French king and a known supporter of the humanists and evangelicals. Writing in the midst of the turmoil of the Genevan reformation, the expulsions and returns of Jean Calvin and Guillaume Farel, and the initial implementation in the city of the Reformed beliefs and practices, she called a female audience to action with her eyewitness account and her female-centric interpretation of Scripture. Like so many women before her, she argued from the point of emergency: turbulent circumstances made it necessary for the benefit of the Christian faith for women to transgress the artificial boundaries set up by humankind.

She wrote,

> For what God has given you and revealed to us women, no more than men should we hide it and bury it in the earth. And even though we are not permitted to preach in public in congregations and churches, we are not forbidden to write and admonish one another in all charity. Not only for you, my Lady, did I wish to write this letter, but also to give courage to other women detained in captivity, so that they might not fear being expelled from their homelands, away from their relatives and friends, as I was, for the word of God. And principally for the poor little women [femmelettes] wanting to know and understand the truth, who do not know what path, what way to take, in order that from now on they be not internally tormented and afflicted, but rather that they be joyful, consoled, and led to follow the truth, which is the Gospel of Jesus Christ.

And further,

> For until now scripture has been so hidden from them. No one dared to say a word about it, and it seemed that women should not read or hear anything in the holy scriptures. That is the main reason, my Lady, that has moved me to write to you, hoping in God that henceforth women will not be so scorned as in the past. (MD/McKinley, 53–4; also Douglass 1985, 103–104; Herminjard 1965–6, *Epistre* 5:297–8).

Marie Dentière wished to negate misogynist interpretations of women's place in Christian history and absolve women from unnecessary guilt for the ills in the Church. She wished to demonstrate from the Scriptures the Christian responsibility falling on women in particular and articulated a startlingly feminist call with a biblical foundation for women's emancipation.

> Even though in all women there has been imperfection, men have not been exempt from it. Why is it necessary to criticize women so much, seeing that no woman ever sold or betrayed Jesus, but a man named Judas? Who are they, I pray you, who have invented and

contrived so many ceremonies, heresies, and false doctrines on earth if not men? And the poor women have been seduced by them. Never was a woman found to be a false prophet, but women have been misled by them . . . Therefore, if God has given grace to some good women, revealing to them by his holy scriptures something holy and good, should they hesitate to write, speak, and declare it to one another because of the defamers of truth? Ah, it would be too bold to try to stop them, and it would be too foolish for us to hide the talent that God has given us, God who will give us the grace to persevere to the end. Amen. (MD/McKinley 55–6.)

Marie chose not to hide her talent (any more than Argula von Grumbach did in Bavaria). She offered a unique perspective – and a chapter of her own – to the Genevan Reformation. She also articulated a particular theological vision and utilized a biblical hermeneutical lens that drew from her experience as a woman.

Marie Dentière – A Feminist Reformer and Biblical Interpreteter

The words "perseverance" and "boldness" well characterize this nun-turned-reformer-and-historian who spoke with a forceful voice, self-confidence and conviction. Her feminist theological voice and her defense of women's right to speak, combined with her unapologetic criticism of corruption in church affairs, violence, and hypocrisy in religious matters, exposed her to harsh criticism herself. Her story was one of defiance and survival. Her role in the reforms in Geneva, especially as a leader among women, and her interpretation of the events as a female eyewitness cannot be overestimated. Yet she has only recently attracted scholarly attention.

Very little is known of Marie's life, with no certainty even about her birthday. She was born around 1495 in Tournai, France, to the noble family of Jérome d'Ennetières and died around 1561. Even the spelling of her family name in documents has been irregular, d'Ennetières and Dentière being the most frequent spellings while d'Entiere is also relatively commonly used. In 1521 she joined an Augustinian convent at Tournai, where some sources suggest she may have held a superior office. She left after she became attracted to Luther's writings and converted to the Protestant faith (sometime around 1524). Her footsteps can be tracked from her move to Geneva through Strasbourg, which happened after 1526 (as she indicated in her writings), the year in which she was "chased out" from her home and her church because of her religious views. By 1528 she was married to a fellow Protestant, a former priest from Tournai, Simon Robert (who had been associating with the French reformers since 1525).

The city of Strasbourg was an important stop in Marie's journey. The tolerant independent city offered refuge to many persecuted Protestants and provided a setting for formal and informal contacts with major reformers, such as Martin Bucer and Jean Calvin, and other remarkable personalities in the local scene, most prominent of whom were the local pastor Matthias Zell and his "helper" and wife Katharina Schütz Zell. Marie and Katharina, also a writer, reformer, and activist, may have known about each other, but they never developed a friendship. It is not unthinkable that Marie was inspired by Katharina's example, however. Marie and Simon Robert left Strasbourg in 1528 to follow Calvin's colleague Farel's mission in Valais – from the April of which year the wife, "uxor," is mentioned in Bucer's letters to Farel. "They were the first French married couple to accept a pastoral assignment for the Reformed Church." Simon served as a pastor of the church at Bex in 1528 until the couple moved to Aigle, a nearby city, maintaining contact with Farel and his follower Antoine Froment. After Robert died in 1533, Marie, a widow with five little children, married Froment, and the family moved to Geneva in 1535.

During the second stage of the Reformation, after it had been declared Protestant in 1536, Geneva became Jean Calvin's center of operations upon his return from the exile that was the result of his quarrels with the city council about authority in worship and other Church matters. Under Calvin's leadership Geneva became a center for the Protestant mission in Europe. The position of women in the town has received mixed reviews for the simple reason that Calvin's own position on the matter was ambiguous.

Studies on women's social situation in Geneva from 1550 to 1800 have led to the conclusion that "the consistory in Calvin's years, though generally strict, was on the whole quite egalitarian, treating men and women alike. In fact, their fairness caused many complaints from the men, who were no longer benefiting from the traditional double standard." At the same time, "the education available for girls, though probably improving basic literacy to some degree, did not permit women in the coming years to play a significant role in cultural life." After Marie Dentière and her contemporary nun Jeanne de Jussie no other female authors rose to fame. As in other contexts, it seems that "the women lost out to the tightening up of institutions as the Reformation was firmly established. Special roles for women were permissible during an 'emergency' situation but no longer tolerated when the new order was instituted" (Douglass 1985, 105). On the whole, whereas a continued qualified but definite subordination of women is a recognizable feature of the Genevan reformed church (Head 1987, 266; Thompson 1992, 187–226), at the same time, their situation appears to have been unusually egalitarian, with a long history of women preachers from before the time of Calvin, who may have initially approved of it (see Douglass 1985, 104–5, 83–107; also Monter 1980; Davis 1975, 65–95).

Marie Dentière connects with two storylines having to do with women and Geneva: the Genevan nuns' fierce opposition to the Reformation, on the one hand, and the relationships between Calvin and women sponsoring the Reformation, on the other.

Marie was actively engaged in a mission to persuade nuns to leave their convents and embrace new lives in accordance with the Reformation teachings. This led to a tempestuous relationship with another female religious leader in town, Jeanne de Jussie, who with an equal force fought for the opposite cause. Another thorn in Marie's flesh was no less a figure than Calvin himself. Even if Marie was a visible and vocal figure in the same town and working for the same cause, and even if Calvin showed much interest in Protestant women in leadership positions outside Geneva (such as Renée de France and Jeanne d'Albret), Calvin never developed a close relationship with Marie. The man whom Marie defended personally against the city council seemed irritated by her: "Forced as a woman to find non-institutional ways to promote reform through writing and public preaching in taverns and on street corners, she incurred the wrath of Calvin, who publicly discredited her by calling her a heretic" (Blaisdell 1999, 154). (Farel's 1540 letter to Calvin and his comments about Marie corrupting her husband are telling [Rilliet, 333].) (See Bothe 1993, 18; Skenazi 1997, 13–15.)

Regardless of what Calvin thought of her, Marie was one of the rare published female theological voices in the Reformation scene in general and among the French-speaking women in particular. She may have been the first Protestant writer to give an eyewitness account of the events in Geneva, and she was among the first women (if not the first) to articulate and defend Reformed theology in French (Åkerlund 2003, 111; McKinley 2004, 2). Her report of the events in Geneva was published, but not necessarily well received, due to her gender and her straightforward criticism of the male leadership in town. She showed no sense of inferiority when taking it upon herself to tell the story, highlighting, among other things, the war between the convent women and the town's women. The arguments she put forward for her right to speak theologically and in public were based on her interpretation of Scripture. "It seems she has so internalized the Reformed teaching of the freedom of the Christian and has so situated herself in the biblical view of God's liberating work in history that she feels called to write and speak, knowing full well that these roles are neither ecclesiastically nor culturally approved for women" (Douglass 1985, 103).

Marie's time in Geneva coincided with the turbulent events with Jean Calvin and Guillaume Farel (whom she had known since 1526). She witnessed at first-hand the city's revolt against the Catholic clergy and the evolution of the Protestant Reformation and Calvin's leadership there. As everywhere, the issues of clerical marriage, the use of the vernacular in worship, and the changes in sacramental practices caused much turmoil. Marie was there to witness and report. The earliest work attributed to Marie is the history of the Protestant reformers in Geneva: *La guerre et déslivrance de la ville de Genesve fidèlement faicte et composée par un Marchand demourant en icelle*, or "The War for and Deliverance of the City of Geneva, Faithfully Prepared and Written Down by a Merchant Living in That City" offered a colorful history of the events of 1532–6, the formative years of the Genevan reform. No known copies have survived of the original 1536 publication.

Beginning with the series of events caused by the arrival of Farel in Geneva in 1532, the treatise, which was written between February and May 1536, comments on the years between 1504 and 1536 and draws comparisons between the situation in Geneva and biblical narratives. Marie was less concerned with chronology and factual detail than with the interpretation of the events; the treatise emphasized, in metaphorical language, what had been said rather than what had happened. For her the turmoil of the Reformation had been "the shouting war, rather than the shooting war" fought in the hearts and souls of the people (Head 1987, 261). Marie interpreted the events in Geneva as religious warfare, and she herself took up arms in the war of words.

It was brave and outrageous of Marie to describe the tyrannical leadership as she saw it and name real people as culprits. "It is striking" as Jane Dempsey Douglass has demonstrated, "that the deliverance by God which Dentière describes is almost exclusively corporate." "In view of the sixteenth-century context, it is also striking that the enemies God is battling in Dentière's account are very concrete, historical enemies." The devil was not the culprit in their suffering but the people themselves (Douglass 1991, 231). At the same time, her goal was to offer a comforting message: she wished to give her theological interpretation of the overall situation with a prediction of the upcoming triumph of God's justice and deliverance. Drawing from the Protestant principle of *sola gratia*, she interpreted the Hebrew Scripture's promise to the suffering Genevans. She offered the image of the suffering children of Israel as a model for those suffering in Geneva as a fortification to their faith in the ongoing battle between good and evil. (As Douglass points out, Marie draws from the stories in Exodus 1–2 and Acts 7 and even her manuscript illustration included a picture of Moses with the tables of the law on the left and the Israelites worshipping the golden calf on the right [Douglass 1991, 233].) She looked in the book of Exodus for clues as to how God intervenes in the world, including her world, and in how God is present in the ongoing battle between good and evil, between service of God and idolatry. She boldly argued that the people's suffering had its origins in false preaching (as proven by the suffering of her fellow Genevans who were listening to false proclamations). She also predicted that any attempts to destroy the gospel and its proper proclamation would only have the counter effect of making the people yearn for more. In other words, good preaching was a necessity that could not be suppressed; there was a need for it among people and it would eventually cause changes and end the suffering in Geneva – just as had happened to the Israelites in the story of Exodus. She remained an optimist because God was the source of hope for the people of Geneva as much as god had been for the Israelites. Her emphasis on "hope against all hope" was, then, an emphasis characteristic of her – as was her application of the Hebrew Scripture with the principle of *sola scriptura* and the way she rooted her words to real places and persons. God was the God of hope, in reality, for Marie and her contemporaries. (Douglass 1991, 231–7, 228.)

The treatise was used as propaganda by the Protestants in Geneva. Soon after its publication, however, the work all but disappeared. No copies of the original print are extant, and the treatise was not considered to be Dentière's until the nineteenth century. The issue of her authorship has been raised again in recent scholarship (see Head 1987, 262; also Backus 1996, 474; McKinley 2004, 7). (It may be that her personality and her clash with the town's leadership were factors in this disappearance and maybe, too, the all too common lack of care in preserving women's writing. What is more, the accurate attribution of material from an age and tradition in which valuable texts were not expected from women and where women themselves chose to hide their true identity behind a pseudonym is not without challenges.) The work itself does not give many indications of the sex of the author, or display an interest on the part of the author in gender issues. Only artificial apologies are given for the author's lack of literary refinement (while apologies were to be expected from most women writers of the time). What is more, the text portrays biblical women as "passive victims" without a role in "heroic accounts," which is not what might be expected from a female writer (such, for instance, as Katharina Schütz Zell). Furthermore, "the authorial first-person voice speaks only once and identifies itself as a man." Marie's contemporaries speculated that it was perhaps her husband Froment who had authored the work. After all, the text says "it is impossible for a merchant such as I am to be able to write about it adequately" (McKinley 2004, 7).

Scholars disagree on the authorship. Some (Douglass 1985, 103 and Åkerlund 2003, 111) value *La guerre* as coming from Marie, and highlight its significance as a rare contemporary female view of the events and as one of the first Protestant treatises published in Geneva at the time. In support of this view, it is noticeable that both *La guerre* and Marie's later work *Epistre* have the same foreword, "Read and then judge," among other similarities (Rilliet contributes both works to Marie) (Åkerlund 2003, 111; McKinley 1997, 87). Today some remain skeptical about Marie's authorship (McKinley 2004, 6, footnote 16; 1997, 87), while others (Denomme) suggest the possibility of a collaboration between Marie and Froment, a suspicion that was already in the minds of Marie's contemporary opponents (see McKinley 2004, 25, footnote 50 and 15–16).

Whether Froment collaborated with his wife, which would not have been unheard of among French reformers, the suppression of Marie's identity as the author or even of her involvement with the text has to do with "the early modern climate that refused women a public voice" (as McKinley 2004, 15). Finding the truth in the matter at this point is complicated. This said, while waiting for further study on her work, it is assumed here that the work originates indeed from Marie's pen, with or without collaborators. (Bothe 1993, 16; Douglass 1991, 228, 230; Rilliet 1881 [*La guerre*], 339, 343; Backus 1991, 181.)

If the first treatise attributable to Marie caused a stir, her second, three years later, in 1539, caused a plain scandal. This treatise, signed with the author's own initials left, no doubt about her identity, sex, or feminist concerns, or about her alliance with the reformers in town. Titled *Epistre tres utile faicte et composée par une femme Chrestienne de Tornay, Envoyée à la Royne de Navarre seur du Roy de France, Contre Les Turcz, Iuifz, Infideles, Faulx chrestiens, Anabaptistes, et Lutheriens,* that is, *A Most Beneficial Letter, Prepared and Written Down by a Christian Woman of Tournai, and Sent to the Queen of Navarre, Sister of the King of France, Against the Turks, the Jews, the Infidels, the False Christians, Anabaptists and the Lutherans,* the text included a radical piece called "Defense of Women." Addressed to Marguerite of Navarre, it explicitly defended not only the evangelical theology but also women's place in theology.

The queen, who was godmother to Marie's daughter by Simon Robert, had made inquiries of Marie about the situation in Geneva. She wished to know why preachers had been expelled and what the disagreements were about (1538). Marie desired to proclaim the "truth" and set the record straight. The title page urged the reader to "read and then judge." She described the difficult situation to the queen (whom she had met and corresponded with earlier) and asked for her help – even appealing to her brother the king (whose tolerance had already run out after the Affair of the Placards, in October 1534, when Protestants put up posters attacking the Catholic Mass around Paris and even at the royal court). While the letter overtly solicited Queen Marguerite's personal support, the words were clearly intended for a larger audience. Only two copies of this work have survived. The other copies were destroyed, seized from the shop of the printer Jean Girard, probably on account of the author's sex.

Typical to Marie, she did not mince her words even if her conversation partner was a queen, who, in Marie's view, needed admonishment as well:

> However, my most honored Lady, I wanted to write you, not to teach you, but so that you might take pains with the King your brother, to obviate all these divisions which reign in the places and among the people over whom God commissioned him to rule and govern. And also over your people, whom God gave you to provide for and to keep in order. For what God has given you and revealed to us women, no more than men should we hide it and bury it in the earth. (MD/McKinley, 52–3)

She knew of Marguerite's care for other women and her protective work with them and with persecuted Christians and seized the opportunity to plea for her help. In addition, she offered a word of admonishment and encouragement for the queen so that she not loose her courage but use her position responsibly:

> Be therefore vigilant and ready in tribulation, for you will certainly be hated by all because of me, led before kings, princes, and lords because you give witness to truth in my

name . . . As they have persecuted me, so they will persecute you. The servant is not greater than his lord . . . Be on your guard and vigilant . . . And you, unless you are totally out of your mind, shouldn't you keep watch even more . . .? (MD/McKinley, 57)

The issue of the author's sex is of importance. Whereas the earlier work that presumably came from Marie's pen was written under a pseudonym – by "a merchant living in that city," according to the title page – the 1539 text, as has been pointed out, she signed with her initials "M.D." This use of her initials speaks of her increased confidence and her maturation as a writer and a reformer who had become comfortable enough to write under her own name. She may also have been disillusioned by this stage about the possibility that people, and the council, would be receptive to her writings if they did realize they came from a woman; it no longer mattered to her to have a cover. She no longer wished to hide behind a male pseudonym but stated on the very first page that the author was a Christian woman from Tournay. Furthermore, the cover letter explicitly justified her writing as a woman. She argued that all the lovers of truth needed counsel in the dangerous times of rampant heresy. She had two major concerns: upholding women's right to preach and speak in public, and criticizing the current leaders as culpable in Calvin's exile. The tone was argumentative, preachy, and aggressive even from the title page, where she condemned the Lutherans and the Anabaptists as well as the Catholics and non-Christians. (See McKinley 2004, 49, 10–21; Head 1987, 264; Douglass 1991, 240, 228–9.)

The *Epistre* revealed Marie's familiarity with the misogyny imbedded in theology and the Church. It also revealed her Protestant reliance on Scripture. (See Denommé 2004, 186–8.) Her "Defense" argued from Scripture for women's right to a public voice in religious matters. Marie ruffled many feathers with her piercing words and authoritative, critical tone, as well as the theological interpretation she had to offer: "This conviction of Dentière that God is now giving women grace to write about theology and preach the gospel and that they are under obligation now to use that talent and gift of grace is an essential part of her vision of God's present activity in the world. This vision was offensive to the Genevan pastors." Douglass 1991, 243. (Three months before Dentière's second book, during their exile, Farel wrote to Calvin in 1539 that even women were taking it upon themselves to discuss "these very things" and to accuse ministers; it seems, then, that at the time other women may have been similarly practicing their Christian freedom [Douglass 1991, 243].) It is of interest that Calvin's *Institutes of the Christian Religion* was published in March 1536 (the year that the Genevan men voted for reform), and Marie finished her treatise between Easter and Pentecost of the same year, without either one of them acknowledging each other's work.

In her *Epistre* Marie developed remarkable arguments for women's right to write and act as ministers: even if women were not permitted to preach in assemblies and churches (following the order presented in the First Letter to Timothy 2:11–12) they – or "we" as Marie said – were not prohibited from writing and giving advice in the spirit of love. In the beginning of the "Defense of Women," and of her entire *Epistre*, Marie issued "a strikingly feminist message, defending the right of women to interpret Scripture and to teach that interpretation to one another privately even if they were prohibited from preaching publicly." She explicitly and intentionally refuted misogynist principles and practices in the church that had excluded women from the pulpit and from interpreting Scripture for themselves; she also wished to correct misogynist reading of Scripture by re-interpreting women in Old and New Testaments. (See also Head 1987, 264, McKee 2004, 24–5, Denommé 2004, 195–6.)

(Interestingly, the "Defense of Women" was excluded from Herminjard's nineteenth-century edition, which made no reference to it. A later edition by Rilliet did include the "Defense" as an appendix to *La guerre*, but with no comments. After Herminjard and Rilliet, Marie's works were not edited for about hundred years. This "sudden ellipsis" of Marie's text, to borrow McKinley's words, speaks of the radicality of Marie's words, and of the impact of censorial editing. See McKinley 1997, 86; Rilliet, 337–80.)

In her arguments, Marie acknowledged the long tradition of women serving as pastoral care givers in the Church. She evoked the memory of strong biblical women (mostly from the Old Testament) as an inspiration for all women and as a proof against claims about women's weakness. The central Reformation principle of the priesthood of all believers had, in Marie's view, to include women as well as men. Knowingly or not, she contributed to the long-lasting debate about women's nature and rights with a feminist viewpoint. (Head 1987, 263–4; Bothe 1993, 15–16; Skenazi 1997, 8–13.)

Marie acknowledged that such words coming from a woman would offend some:

> Some might be upset because this is said by a woman, believing that this is not appropriate for her, since woman is made for pleasure. But I pray you to be not offended; you must not think that I do this from hatred or from rancor. I do this only to edify my neighbor, seeing him in such great, horrible darkness, more palpable than the darkness of Egypt.
>
> No man could be able to expose it enough. How, therefore, will a woman do it? In spite of that, be diligent in examining carefully the texts and the consequence of what they say, and you will see that I speak the truth. (MD/McKinley, 76–7)

She had the word of "truth"; thus she could even assume the authority of a preacher. In using the words "prescher" and "prescheresse" about herself she was "conveying conviction that women should not simply teach doctrine to other women in private but should preach to both men and women, 'openly before every one'" (McKinley 2004, 25).

Not satisfied with spiritual equality "just" in private, and deeply concerned about issues of liberty and justice and women's theological roles, Marie argued from the basis of her Christology (Gal. 3: 26–8) and the examples of biblical women for women's right to use their public voice, to interpret Scripture as theologians, and to preach (see Skenazi 1997, 3, 5, 11–12, 16, 26–8; Backus 1991, 182–5; Bothe 1993, 17–18). She offered powerful cases in support of her point: "What a woman was a greater preacher than the Samaritan woman, who was not ashamed to preach Jesus and his word, confessing him openly before everyone, as soon as she heard Jesus say that we must adore God in spirit and truth? Who can boast of having had the first manifestation of the great mystery of the resurrection of Jesus, if not Mary Magdalene, from whom he had thrown out seven devils, and the other women, to whom, rather than to men, he had earlier declared himself through his angel and commanded them to tell, preach, and declare it to others?" (MD/McKinley, 55) As other examples she cited Moses' mother, who had defied the pharaoh's edict in order to save her son, and the women at the tomb of the resurrected Jesus. Her defiant arguments declared women innocent and men guilty of the gravest of crimes: no woman, according to her reading of the Scriptures, had betrayed Jesus or developed heresies or false prophecies; men, on the other hand, had. (MD/McKinley, 56; *Epistre*, Rilliet 378–80; Douglass 1991, 243.)

The reaction of religious leaders and townspeople alike to being publicly humiliated by a woman was as negative as might be expected. Her steaming criticism of the town's clergy in combination with her feminist arguments and, simply, her sex, brought down their wrath on her head: the publisher, Jean Girard, was arrested, books were confiscated, and the preexisting censorship was tightened. The ploy to mislead the authorities by listing on the title page "Martin L'Empereur" from Antwerp ("Anvers, chez Martin Lempereur") as the printer was discovered and the real printer, Jean Girard, was arrested and the books confiscated. Of the original 1,500 printed copies apparently 450 were sent to safety in Thonon, where Marie's husband served as a pastor. Jean Girard was later released but the books were not, and no permission for a reprint was granted to Froment, who continued to lobby for it (while denying his participation in the book's production). While most of the remaining copies were deliberately destroyed and the circulation of the book thus seriously interrupted, some copies did survive (see Head 1987, 265 and McKinley 2004, 14–15). It seems safe to conclude that Marie's publication contributed to the ensuing tightening of printing regulations in Geneva (where nothing was to be published from that point on without a prior official authorization) and that her gender was at the heart of the matter. It is revealing that "Froment later remarked that the greatest regret of the council members about the work was that they had been so 'wounded, piqued and dishonored by a woman'" (Head 1987, 265, footnote 28).

Marie's husband Froment stayed with her throughout the tribulations, at first consistently denying his part in any of her work. Girard, the publisher, defended Marie's work as not being Lutheran but Christian. Two years after publication of Marie's *Epistre*, in September 1541, Calvin returned from his exile (without Farel), without expressing any appreciation for the defense Marie had offered for him. Marie and her husband were no longer in Farel's list of favorites either. To the contrary, Farel denounced Antoine for "complicity" in his "domineering" wife's actions, and blamed Marie for leading her husband into "moral turbitude." The Genevan pastors and leaders, who had less than amicable relations with the couple to begin with, chastised not only Marie but also found ways to ridicule and penalize her husband. Froment was criticized for his involvement in the business of selling oil and wine while also serving in a pastoral role, and for his apparent inability to curb his wife's tongue and get her under control. It is not surprising that the marriage suffered from this negative attention. While we do not know the exact dynamics of the relationship, it appears that Marie was the stronger, perhaps the more intelligent and definitely the more outspoken party. The assessments of her character as a woman and as a spouse from her enemies are hardly reliable or fair. It is evident that Antoine later remarried, but whether this was after Marie's death or following a separation it is impossible to say. (See Head 1987, 265–6, Farel's letters from 1538 and 1540; McKinley 2004, 16–19, 21.)

When one assesses Marie's role in the overall scheme of things, "there is no doubt, however, that Marie Dentière played an active role in the events of those years, becoming an outspoken participant in the reform movement, preaching her opposition to religious celibacy, and advocating women's pastoral role in the new church" (McKinley 2004, 8; see also Bothe 1993, 15–16). In addition to reporting on events and soliciting support for the reform, she deemed it necessary to actively advocate Reformation theology, especially among women: she proclaimed the good news about marriage and preached mightily against celibacy and the monastic life. While she proselytized to all women, urging them to find emancipated roles in the church, nuns were the particular subject of her mission. Eyewitness records of her endeavors come from her arch-opponent Jeanne de Jussie, the leader of the nuns who resisted Protestant reform ideas regarding their religious calling and lifestyle.

As Marie, along with other reformers, preached about the harms of celibate and monastic life in comparison to the virtues and pleasures of marital life, the Poor Clares – the sisters in the St Klarakloster – and Sister Jeanne de Jussie of their order were her special target. The Protestants had paid visits to the convent to make sure nobody was held there by force. Marie Dentière, with Farel, was among the main "invaders" in 1535. She could not understand why women would not be rushing leaping with joy out of their convents – because she had: "Ah, poor creatures, if only you knew how good it was to be next to a handsome husband, and how God thinks it pleasing. I was for a long time in that darkness and hypocrisy where you are, but God alone made me recognize the abuse of my wretched life, and I came to the true light of truth." She had taken 500 ducats with her and was proud to say that "I left that unhappiness, and, thanks to God alone, I have five beautiful children, and I live a salutary life." (MD/McKinley, 94–5.) What Marie interpreted as the gospel of liberation was considered to be just the opposite by the nuns who saw "a new constraint" being offered in the form of marriage. They responded by spitting, shouting, and closing their doors (Douglass 1985, 100–1; Head 1987, 263; also Skenazi 1997, 13, 12).

The battle between Marie and Jeanne de Jussie in particular became personal and heated. Both women wrote down frustrated notes about the encounter. Jeanne's portrayal of Marie was not flattering: "In that company was one false abbess, wrinkled and of diabolical language, possessing a husband and child, named Marie d'Entiere of Picardy, who mixed herself up in preaching and in perverting the people from devotion" (see Jeanne de Jussie, *Le levain du calvinisme, ou commencement de l'heresie de Geneve*, Chambery, 1661, repr. 1853 Geneva; McKinley 1997, 94, also 95; see idem 2004, 8–9). (See Åkerlund 2003, especially 106–110, 117–119; Lazard 1985.)

Marie and Jeanne, the last two women to publish in Geneva for a long time, disagreed on two issues in particular: ideas about chastity and virtue, and women's right to preach. (Head 1987, 264.) Jeanne defended women's right to choose the monastic celibate life and spoke equally strongly against their public teaching and speaking role (justifying thereby her own refusal to debate in public). To Jeanne, marriage did not promise religious freedom and opportunities, nor did Reformation theology in itself suggest significant improvements to her theology or lifestyle. To her "Lutheranism" meant negative changes, such as "contempt for the Sacrament, iconoclasm, and this new lauding of marriage" (Douglass 1985, 100, see 98–101). Marie, on the other hand, judged the celibate lifestyle as lazy and harmful, and she explicitly argued for women's calling to speak in public. The disagreement between the two women demonstrates the complexity of the Reformation's "good news" and women's mixed responses to that.

Jussie's portrait of Marie echoed a similarly negative appraisal from another contemporary, Jean Calvin. In his 1546 record of meeting Marie (1546), Calvin ridiculed her as an "unruly" woman who was alienated from the people she wished to support and thus deserved only contempt (McKinley 2004, 19). Not appreciating Marie's public role – or her relatively recent public support of him – he joined those who scorned her:

I'm going to tell you a funny story. Froment's wife came here recently; in all the inns, at almost all the street corners, she began to harangue against long garments. When she knew that it had gotten back to me, she excused herself, laughing, and said that either we were dressed indecently, with great offense to the church, or that you taught in error when you said that false prophets could be recognized by their long garments . . .

. . . Feeling pressured, she complained about our tyranny, that it was no longer permitted for just anyone to chatter on about anything at all. I treated the woman as I should have. (McKinley 2004, 19, also 16–18)

It is perhaps odd piece that evidence of Marie's powerful personality and ability to ruffle feathers big and small should come in this unexpected, distant alliance between two persons in opposite religious camps, Jeanne de Jussie and Calvin, but if in nothing else, they were united in their contempt of Marie; desiring to keep women in their place they were agreed in their negative assessment of Marie as an outspoken, disruptive woman. The reasons for their criticism were different, however: Jeanne de Jussie confronted Marie primarily on the basis of a different vision for what constitutes a godly call for a woman, and only secondarily with arguments against women employing a public voice. Calvin's grounds for defaming her were not necessarily theological but arose from his irritation with her forceful personality and her disobedience as a woman; he was impatient with Marie's theological ambitions and her open criticism of the male clerical leadership in "his" town. (See McKinley 2004, 10, 19; 1997, 94–5.)

Given the cool relations between Calvin and Marie, who would have guessed that in 1561 he would ask her to write a preface to his sermon on female apparel or that Marie would accept the invitation! The content of what she wrote was as surprising as the fact that she wrote at all. She spoke in her preface about "womanly vices," pointing to excessive fineries as manifestations of women's covetousness and vulnerability to the manifest work of the devil. She claimed that extravagant clothing was against the order of God and that makeup erased God's image (for this she relied on the wisdom of the Church fathers!). Her arguments emphasized the priority of God's will and the harm of coveting temporal things. There is a certain dissonance between the words and vision regarding women in this brief work and Marie's earlier publications, in particular the "Defense of Women." Bearing her initials, "M.D.," the text was published in 1561 with Calvin's sermons on Paul's epistles to Timothy in a volume titled *The Behavior and Virtues Required of a Faithful Woman and Good Housekeeper: Contained in chapter XXI of the Proverbs of Solomon. Rendered in the form of a song by Théodore de Bèze. Plus a sermon on the modesty of Women in their Dress, by Monsieur John Calvin. In addition, several spiritual songs with music. M.D. LXI* (see McKinley 2004, 89). (See McKinley 1997, 91–4, 98; MD/McKinley, 89.)

Some general observations can be made about Marie's writing and perspective on the Bible. First of all, Marie's texts demonstrate the profound depth of her biblical knowledge and her theological grasp of her materials. She developed her own, feminist interpretation on the theology of the texts she used, and she wrote bluntly and boldly in uninhibited prose that was "colored with biblical allusions and fervent moral indignation" – for instance, she called the Genevan religious rulers "cockroaches". Developing a style of her own, "Dentière emerged as a fine rhetorician, preaching a sermon brimming with both biblical and popular allusions." (Head 1987, 262, 264–5.) She was familiar with the effective use of sermon style as well as propaganda, indeed, in some of her writing there is "an energy and rhythm that often suggest oral delivery" and had characteristics associated with polemical works printed in secrecy and haste (for instance, the original text had no paragraphs). (See McKinley 2004, 38–9; Bothe 1993, 17–18). In this light, comparisons between her works and conventional chronologies or theological treatises would hardly be fair. Marie stood in a category of her own as a Protestant female author.

The depth of the authority with which she could use biblical material is evidenced in her interesting connection with a specific group of reforming women of the time. The correspondence of several reforming noblewomen revealed their shared interest in the Hebrew language; Hebrew language and grammar books were discussed in letters from one woman to another (for instance, Marguerite de Navarre used the letter "mem" and posed language-related questions in her letters). At the time, several small grammars were published (often bilingual, Hebrew–Latin) including some for children's use, and these copies circulated between friends. Marie was one of the women interested in Hebrew and perhaps had at least rudimentary understanding of it. In her correspondence with Marguerite, Marie mentioned a little book on Hebrew grammar her daughter Jeanne had written for girls to use that Marie wished to send to Marguerite's daughter Jeanne. Her first husband Simon Robert had collaborated between 1525 and 1528 on a translation of the Old Testament, and she herself was apparently knowledgeable of the language and had studied the Hebrew Scripture. (Kemp and Desrosiers-Bonin 1998, 126–7, 129–34; McKinley 2004, 23–4, 53, 71.)

In terms of her theology, Marie was a full-blown Protestant, and, while not necessarily a follower of Calvin, more in line with the Swiss reformers. She called herself an evangelical and a Christian. Holding an inclusive view of the gospel (with which she defended the exiled and persecuted reformers), she did not want to label herself as belonging to any party any more than Argula von Grumbach and Katharina Schütz Zell did. The Scriptures were the source of Christian identity for all of them, and for Marie the Word of God was the center of her theology, her source of inspiration, guidance, and authority. (See Head 1987, 264–5; Skenazi 1997, 11.)

Using Scripture and inspired by it, she continued to "speak with a discomforting prophetic voice, pressing the newly reformed church to continuing reformation" (Douglass 1991, 244, 243; see Denommé, 192–4). Her book *La guerre*, rather than being a simple chronicle of events, presented a theological interpretation of what had happened in Geneva and conveyed a hope of liberation. "The power of the 'pure Word of God' to liberate the oppressed is a central theme of the theology of history of Marie Dentière" (Douglass 1991, 227, also 228). The Bible, for Marie, was not a book of law but "a story of God's unmerited saving activity," in which light she interpreted her time. Starting from the perspectives of justification being granted through faith by grace alone and of the predestination being an expression of God's love and care, Marie saw the preaching of the Word of God as the only proper way of ruling the world and bringing hope to those in despair and need. She believed in the liberating power of the Word, especially for women, whom she saw as among those most oppressed and in need of that Word (Kemp and Desrosiers-Bonin 1998). (See Backus 1991, 177–89, 192–5 and Denommé 2004, 184–92 about her theology.)

After much visibility and notoriety, as a woman who had stepped on to the central stage in Geneva and stood apart as one of the first and the longest writing women in Geneva, Marie disappeared from the scene towards the end of her life. Even the date of her death is uncertain. Her memory was suppressed. The antipathy towards Marie was such that in Aimé-Louis Herminjard's *Correspondance*, the important nineteenth-century work on the Reformation in the French-speaking countries, Marie is barely mentioned; in what little is said the pejorative description "dogmatizer" is used and no reference made to her "Defense of Women." That said, seven years after Herminjard's work was published, Albert Rilliet did include the "Defense," in his edition of her works with no negative comments about the author. (McKinley 2004, 34–5; McKinley 1997, 97.) It seems reasonable to explain the "severe treatment of Dentière" by past scholars (Herminjard) as misogyny: "she was a woman who persisted in forcefully expressing her convictions without caring about others' reactions, that she used colorful, even crude language to voice her anger, and that she was an outspoken activist, even an extremist, in the struggles of the Geneva Reformation." (McKinley 1997, 96; also 2004, 37. Also Åkerlund 2003, 112–15.) As a woman, she was criticized for achievements and fortitude for which a man would have been praised.

Conclusion

"Ironically Dentière's success as a polemicist has caused her omission from the literary canon. . . . [she] and her suppressed works have been almost forgotten." This was not an accident: "Marie Dentière fought not only for the causes of the evangelical reform in her adopted city, but also for the place of women in that movement." Both causes came with risks. It was especially troubling to the authorities that she articulated the "aspirations of women to preach and interpret that Gospel message for themselves." Especially as the Reformation became instilled and institutionalized, women's rights in particular were firmly narrowed. (Head 1987, 266.) Women like Marie were "forgotten" and their writings suppressed, as if to erase the effect that they had had. Denying the contributions of women like Marie has been part of the distortion of the collective memory of a particular history, and has deprived later theological traditions of feminist examples and stimuli. (McKinley's use of the term "ellipsis" to describe the disappearance and resurrection of Marie's works is most apt.) Today, centuries after her death, because of her preserved writings, Marie offers a powerful lay perspective and a critical woman's voice with which to interpret the Genevan Reformation and the Protestant theology that was preached on its bedrock.

Marie's life was shaped by her response to the Reformation: responding positively to Luther's call, she left her celibate monastic life, married, gave birth to both children and books, and became an active voice for the Reformation in Calvin's orbit. Through her personal example and written word, she made a contribution to the implementation and dissemination of the reformed faith in her locale. In an oddly distant relationship with Jean Calvin (which may prove just exactly what were the limits of Calvin's appreciation of women's role in religious affairs), she for all practical purposes acted as his associate and disciple, albeit without his recognition or approval – unless his use of Marie's preface in his sermon about "women's issues" could be seen as a minor nod in that direction. Never acknowledged as a teacher or a preacher, because of her sex, she nevertheless became one, taking to heart the reformers' principles of *sola scriptura* and the priesthood of all believers. She expressed a calling to interpret Scripture to her fellow Christians and to preach the stories from the Scriptures with a relevance to the life situation of those she addressed. She did that explicitly as a woman. She gave a laywoman's perspective to the history of Reformation in Geneva with a chronicle that consisted of eyewitness reportage and feminist Scriptural interpretation. As a Christian Protestant woman her passion was to "tell the truth" at all costs and to persuade others as well with the power of her word, both written and proclaimed. For her the truth was to be found in Scripture, and it was for her, as well as for other women, to interpret, which she did with perseverance and passion, on a par with the most prominent of the reformers. In 2002, Marie's name was finally added to the Wall of Reformers in Geneva.

A Word about Sources and References

See McKinley 2004, the most recent full biographical work, for the core information, and the bibliography in this volume for description of the other main sources.

Important surveys on Marie's life and studies on her theology come from McKinley 1997, Douglass 1991, Head 1987, and Bothe 1993. For a feminist interpretation on Marie's work and role, see Backus 1991, Skenazi 1997, Kemp and Desrosiers-Bonin 1998, and also Wengler's 1999 dissertation. See Åkerlund 2003, Lazard 1985, and Douglass 1985 for Marie's relationship with Jeanne de Jussie, and Thompson 1992 (40–5, 187–226), Douglass 1985, and McKinley 2004 on Marie's relationship with Calvin. A foundational source in French with primary texts was published in 1866–97 by A.-L. Herminjard and reprinted in1965.

CHAPTER 10

Marguerite de Navarre, 1492–1549, and Jeanne d'Albret, 1528–1572 – The Protectors of the French Reformers

Marguerite de Navarre

Marguerite d'Angoulême/de Navarre 1492–1549

PARENTS
- Louise de Savoy (Savoie, 1476–1531)
- Charles d'Orleans, Charles d'Angoulême (1459–96, cousin of Louis XII)

SIBLINGS
- François d'Angoulême (1494–1547)

SPOUSE [1] (1509–25)
- Charles Duke of Alençon (1489–1525)

SPOUSE [2] (1527–49)
- Henri d'Albret (1503–55)

CHILDREN
- Jeanne (1528–72)
- Jean (born and died 1530)

Introduction

In a visible place as the sister of the king of France, Marguerite de Navarre carved her own place in the European scene as a diplomat, a writer, and a patroness of arts, literature, and religious reforms. She provided crucial protection and stimulus during the early years of the Reformation in France, without ever publicly claiming herself to be either a Lutheran or a Calvinist. She gave birth to a daughter, Jeanne d'Albret, who would openly engage herself with the Protestant faith and fight on the side of the French Reformers. Well connected with influential and reform-oriented men and women (for instance Renée de France, Anne de Bretagne, Elizabeth of England, and Marie Dentière), the mother and the daughter, although they had different strategies, both became leaders in religious affairs to whom those persecuted for their faith would know to go to. Both women (with Renée de France and a small group of other noblewomen) held positions that were key to the Protestant mission in the French-speaking world and Jean Calvin worked hard to recruit them. Marguerite paved the way for the expansive work of Jeanne, whose contributions as a bona fide Protestant religious leader and an exceptional Reformation woman have been overshadowed by the accomplishments of her mother, husband, and son. Here, however, the interest will focus on Jeanne.

Unlike her mother, Jeanne grew up thoroughly Protestant and openly confessed her faith leaving no doubt about her religious affiliation. Not only did she offer asylum to persecuted fellow believers (as her mother had done), she joined the Huguenots and their army, and implemented the Reformation through legislation that condoned (unusually at the time) religious tolerance and freedom in the expression of faith: Even if her life was a continuous battle against "enemies" – as a woman, as a Protestant, as a queen – she was a rare monarch in her era for not wishing anyone to be killed or martyred for his or her faith. (Bainton 2001, 43; King 1991, 141.) Instead, she led exemplary religious as well as social reforms in her sovereign territories of Béarn and Navarre through legal ordinances, she established a Protestant academy, and with her personal support made possible Protestant preaching, worship, and welfare practice.

The hopes of the Huguenots in France were at their greatest during the peak years of Jeanne's authority. She was, after all, the "highest ranking Frenchwoman ever to become a Calvinist" (related by blood to the throne and a mother of the future king of France) and wielded considerable influence both at the royal court (especially in 1561 and 1568–70) and in her own land. On her death, at only 44, after a short life full of adversity and drama, Agrippa d'Aubigne gave chauvinist praise: "So died this queen who was a woman only insofar as concerns her gender, but a man in spirit, invincible to adversity." Her life story exemplified the complexity of the gender factor and the intertwinement of political and religious issues. She navigated successfully in dangerous waters, but her merits have been largely ignored because of her sex. (See Roelker 1972a, 180, 183.)

Marguerite d'Angoulême/de Navarre, 1492–1549 – The Illustrious Queen, Writer and Spiritual Mother

Marguerite d'Angoulême, the duchess of Alençon and the Queen of Navarre was born on April 11, 1492 to Louise de Savoie (1476–1531) and Charles d'Orleans (1477–98), the Count d'Angoulême. She and her brother François (1494–1547), younger by two years, were educated with the best of teachers, especially in preparation for François to take the throne, which happened after Louis XII's death in 1515.

Marguerite had "two great passions, love for God and love for her brother." (Bainton 2001, 13.) She also loved France. Out of her royal (and sibling) loyalties, she remained outwardly in conformity with the Catholic faith. At the same time, her actions on behalf of the French Reformation proved that her private and public choices were not always in harmony. Her contribution to the Protestant cause was undeniable and vital.

As her brother's confidant and helper (especially after their mother's death in 1531), Marguerite mingled in top politics from the 1510s to the 1540s, with remarkable charisma and authority of her own. Once François had made her his own vassal by creating her duchess of Berry in 1517 and elevated the title to a ducal peerage she moved to her brother's side and, as one of the few women ever to become a peer of France, exercised unprecedented authority for a woman. The siblings remained close through the years regardless of their religious differences, during which time Marguerite put her diplomatic skills at her brother's service. For instance, in 1525 she negotiated François' release from captivity in Spain (in exchange for his sons) after he was captured fighting against the Emperor Charles V at the Battle of Pavia in 1525. Her husband, Charles duc d'Alençon, to whom she had been unhappily married since their union in 1509 when she was 17, died of pleurisy two months after the battle. Soon after, in 1527, Marguerite married Henri d'Albret, 11 years her younger (engaged the previous year). The marriage benefited both parties in terms of the protection and expansion of their territories. Neither of her husbands shared her interest in religion and reform. From her two marriages only one child survived, her daughter Jeanne, born in 1528. Her son Jean died on Christmas Day 1530, and several miscarriages and stillbirths followed as she yearned for more children. (On her marriage and years as Queen of Navarre, Cholakian 2006, 171–206, 207–41.)

Marguerite held a central place at her brother's court, where François, Louise, and Marguerite formed "the trinity" of power (Blaisdell 1972, 199). While the king headed the political front, the charismatic Marguerite hosted intellectuals and artists at the court and provided the "queenly leadership" her constantly pregnant, frail sister-in-law, Claude, could not. She intervened on behalf of persecuted reformers and personally provided a group of intellectuals envisioning a church reform with hospitality and at times protection, and assisted in the publication and dissemination of their work (the Circle of Meaux). Her birth, personal charisma and ambition, and the respect in which her brother held her gave Marguerite exceptional leverage at the court. Besides, she was not just "a woman subservient to the king, Marguerite had a unique status as an 'honorary' male, and was one of very few female peers of the realm in France" (Stephenson 2004, 3). "Her political position, while dependent on the king, and her force of personality combined to make her a woman who was taken seriously not only by scholars but by the king and his advisors" (ibid.).

Respected sister of the king, confidant and advisor to him, in matters pertaining to Navarre Queen Marguerite stood as his brother's peer. It appears her gender posed no actual obstacle for her – other than keeping her from the throne of France. "Once Marguerite was recognized as a prince capétien, she became an 'honorary male,' and so entitled to the peer status and appanage that accompanied that rank. Marguerite was able to take on male status and therefore a male role, without denying her gender" (Stephenson 2004, 111). (See Stephenson 2004, 8–9, 113–47; Jourda 1930, 43–59.)

A genuine Renaissance woman, Marguerite had received extensive education, thanks to her mother and privileged birth. She also knew Latin, Spanish, Hebrew, French, and English, and some Italian and German, in addition to having studied Scripture and classical philosophy. Her writings reveal her erudition as well as her gifts. A lifelong scholar with a bright mind and intellectual curiosity, she read Luther as well as Plato and Dante, she corresponded with Calvin, and wrote her own poetry and treatises. (On her education, see Cholakian 2006, 8–39.)

In addition to writing letters (for instance with Briçonnet), she was already writing religious texts in 1520s, even if she published them only later. She did not publish her poetry until after the deaths of her son in 1530 and her mother shortly thereafter. Her first published poem, The *Mirror of the Sinful Soul* ("Miroir de l'âme pécheresse," 1531), was her "contribution to the literature of évangélisme" (Roelker 1972a, 173). It was translated into English in 1544 by an eleven-year-old from England, the future Elizabeth I, whose mother Anne Boleyn had been the owner of the original French manuscript. (Anne had served as a lady-in-waiting in Marguerite's court, a time of profound transformation for Anne, who would later die as the second wife of Henry VIII.) The Sorbonne condemned the poem in 1533, regardless of the author's rank, which is a clear indication of the scandalous content and its weight as a theological treatise. Thanks to the king's intervention, its publication continued, however. As early as the period of 1523–4 the University of Paris was alarmed by the presence of evangelicals and "heretics" in the court and were targeting Marguerite as a front figure for them. She survived the accusations and disciplinary actions by the intervention of her brother the king. Well aware of the risks, she nevertheless continued her involvement with the issues of theology and religion that were dear to her. Particularly drawn to mysticism, she envisioned Church reform to unfold from the spiritual renewal of individuals.

From 1521 Luther's writings had found their way to France and some had been translated into French, more often than not with Marguerite's involvement. She herself translated into French his Meditation on the Lord's Prayer and was intrigued by his *On the Babylonian Captivity of the Church* (1520). As early on in the history of the Reformation as 1521 on Marguerite was corresponding and associating with reform-minded humanists, especially Guillaume Briçonnet, Bishop of Meaux, Jacques Lefèvre d'Etaples, Giullaume Bedé, and her favorite preachers Arnauld Broussio and Michel d'Arande, an ex-Augustinian who was to be brought before the Inquisition to be examined for heresy while under Marguerite's personal protection. She was also friends with her chaplain Gérard Roussel, Pierre Caroli, Guillaume Farel, and François Vatable. She sponsored the so-called Circle of Meaux, led by Guillaume Briçonnet, which included some of the France's brightest Christian humanists and religious leaders in favor of reforms and "evangelical" theology. Their vision of "reform within" the church and the deliberation on the doctrine of justification by faith coincided with Martin Luther's revolutionary re-reading of the Scripture and the resulting religious reforms in Wittenberg. Regardless of the risks, Marguerite supported the dissemination of Briçonnet's ideas, which opposed the selling of indulgences and the exhibition of saints' relics in French territory, and saved Jacques Lefèvre, the translator into French of the New Testament from execution after his condemnation by the Sorbonne. When the French court became too dangerous for them to remain under her care any longer, Marguerite directed many of the persecuted reformers to Ferrara, to the care of the one-time Renée de France, now Renata di Ferrara. (Her extant correspondence with Briçonnet in particular – correspondence in which she learned to use the written word as not only "a source of knowledge and spiritual solace but as a means of self-expression" – gives some insights into her internal development and involvement with the reformist movement [Cholakian 2006, 103].)

The Reformation in France sparked from the famous All Saints' Day Sermon by the new rector of the Sorbonne, Nicolas Cop in 1533; in its aftermath, Cop and Calvin, among others, sought Marguerite's protection. After leaving her court, Calvin corresponded with Marguerite, as did others, both Calvinist and Lutheran, who placed their hopes in Marguerite for their own safety and for the success of the Reformation in France. After the king lost his initial guarded interest in the evangelicals, the situation changed and they were dispersed. This occurred after the notorious Affair of the Placards when, in October 1534, posters blaspheming the Catholic Mass appeared at the royal court, appalling even those in favor of the Protestants' call for reform. The outrage even led Marguerite to leave the court temporarily.

She returned in 1535 and continued her mediating work between the opposing religious factions. The situation demanded her skills in arbitration and necessitated that she should not to take sides, which disappointed the Protestants who had been expecting a more militant leadership on their behalf. Calvin, among others, worried, or angered rather, over Marguerite's "indecisiveness." "Our greatest hope is in the Queen of Navarre but we cannot place on her too great reliance" (Bainton 2001, 29). (On her role in politics and religion between 1534–9, see Cholakian 2006, 171–206.) It worried Calvin that, under the persecutions, some of the French Huguenots (especially those at the court) had begun to conform and compromise in regards to Catholic forms of piety, and that the court hosted what were in his view "suspicious" libertines drawn to mysticism and anti-authoritarianism (Quintin du Hainault, Antoine Pocquet, Claude Perceval). Marguerite rejected Calvin's denouncement and continued to outwardly observe Catholic religious practices, to Calvin's dismay. Some of her writings may be seen as her written response to him. (See Stephenson 2004, 178–9; Blaisdell 1982, 75–6.) (Concerning their letters, Marguerite to Calvin, July 25, 1540, CO, XII, col. 64–8, no. 634; Calvin to Marguerite, April 28, 1545, CO, XII, col. 64–8, no 634; Blaisdell 1982, 76.)

Calvin's criticism of Marguerite seems harsh. After all, Marguerite had taken enormous risks while carefully calculating her leverage and options. She supported the reform because she believed in the cause for genuine religious reasons. Calvin failed to see that

> because of the indistinct line between orthodoxy and heresy, because of her refusal to be pinned down to one confessional allegiance, and because she crossed gender and political boundaries, Marguerite was able to serve as a bridge between the orthodox, humanist, and reformist networks operating in the first half of the sixteenth century to further her own goals of bringing religious reform to France. (Stephenson 2004, 183)

(See also Bainton 2001, 183.)

As disillusioned as her Protestant protégées may have been, so was Marguerite herself in terms of her hopes for ending the religious persecution. Her brother had stopped listening to her. The circle of Meaux was dispersed. People close to her were executed.

She left the court for Navarre, where she opened her home to Protestant refugees (Clement Marot, Michel d'Arande, Lefèvre d'Etaples, and others). She began to worship with the Protestant chaplain Gérard Roussel whose sermons had been condemned as heretical. She founded hospitals, engaged in charity, and visited her territories (akin to the German "visitations" of the local towns and congregations in preparation for the reforms). She was concerned about the abuses in the Church and invested in providing written materials in vernacular, and addressed the pastoral, catechetical, and liturgical needs of local churches. The queen, in many ways, acted as a reformer in her territory, and remained available for individuals.

Marguerite's extant correspondence of 886 letters has provided information about the extensity of her relationships in many directions. Many a letter addressed to the "The Most Illustrious and Most Christian Prince the Lady Marguerite Queen of Navarre" remains and reveals her networking, as well as her continued concerns for religious reform and her own role in the process. While 186 of these letters were exchanged with her brother, she also corresponded with Protestant towns (Geneva and Bern), individual humanists and reformers, men and women (Calvin, Melanchthon, Farel, Bucer, Luther; Vittoria Colonna, Marie Dentière, and Renée de France), and several popes (Leo X, Adrian VI, Clement VII, Paul III, in all 36 letters). (See Stephenson 2004, 149–83, 15–43; Jourda 1930, 247–9.)

A politically powerful and well-connected figure, Marguerite also espoused the role of spiritual mother, as evidenced in the links she forged and maintained and in her correspondence. Women in particular looked upon her for guidance and support, and she developed several close long-distance friendships with her peers (she was godmother to one of Marie Dentière's daughters [McKinley 2004, 402]), as well as caring for women below her rank. Her posthumously published *Heptaméron* (with 72 novellas) included detailed narratives of women abused by members of the clergy. Her work joined the simmering criticism of corrupt clerics and demonstrated her concern for women's wellbeing. She used her authority to record the stories as a means towards putting a stop to the abuse. In this she seemed to have been driven by her sense of a "calling" as a Christian and a fellow woman. (The Heptaméron, particularly its tenth novella can be interpreted autobiographically about her relationship to her mother; Cholakian 2006, 21, 37–8.)

Marguerite's *Heptaméron* "related chilling accounts of women who were raped, threatened, and harassed by priests." More than accounts, "Marguerite's stories offer an insightful look at the victims' pain, as well as strategies for the prevention of such violence." She "not only gave voice to victim's experiences, but she also challenged her society's assumptions about the victim's complicity in sexual crimes." She argued that it was necessary for the Church to address sexual violence in the clergy and drew from Scripture as a source for the pastoral care for the victims. "She also believed that the Holy Spirit would empower both women and men to work toward moral reform and other needed changes in the church." (Schroeder 1993, 171.) In light of the reformers' emphasis on justification by grace, Marguerite argued that "rape has no power to destroy the value or honor of a woman for whom Christ died" (ibid., 175). Furthermore, in this book, Marguerite expressed her view for the Church she wished to see reformed: "The church envisioned by Marguerite was a community in which women and men, inspired by Scripture and the Holy Spirit, could tell the truth about their lives and about the grace of God" (Schroeder 1993, 187). (See Jourda 1930, 661–76.)

Marguerite's religious, devotional writings had a certain Neoplatonic and Calvinist tone to them, and some of them resonated with those of the medieval mystics. A mystical writer of the new era, a closet-evangelical, she was intrigued by the perspective of justification by faith – a topic much discussed in her theological circles. She wished to understand sanctification and election in Christians' lives. Several themes central to the reformation theologies could be seen in Marguerite's *The Pearls of the Pearl of Princesses*, in which she reflects on the primacy of Scripture, the notion of justification by faith, and the issue of election. (Bainton 2001, 21, 25. See also Cholakian 2006, 279–314)

> While there is a great deal of consistency in Marguerite's religious poetry, there is also a clear progression from a spirituality based upon *imitatio* to one governed by solafideism, and, within the latter, movement from exegetical commentary and definition to representation of mystical themes – divine immanence and transcendence, inner voices, rapture. Marguerite's growing interest in mysticism and mystical stages inevitably influences both her appreciation of poetry and her perception of her role as writer. (Sommers 1989, 102)

As many of the Catholic women invested in the reform of the Church without converting to Luther's or Calvin's or Anabaptists' theology, Marguerite saw the reform of the Church beginning from the reform of the individual. Respecting the tradition of mystical knowledge, she believed in the power of spiritual advancement. The mystical aspect or inclination in Marguerite's spirituality, and writing, was manifested particularly in her language about her personal connection with Christ. "Marguerite describes mystic union with Christ in terms of sensory experience" and her "poetry described her intense longing for mystic union with God." (Schroeder 1993, 174.) In *Mirror*, for instance, she uses mystical language about the union and being made "divine" and "godded" as Christ's brother, sister, mother, and wife. Marguerite's interest in mysticism did not draw her to asceticism, however. Theology intrigued her intellectually without drawing her to any particular spiritual praxis. Furthermore, she was visionary in her appreciation of the holiness and integrity of the human body, an area in which her emphasis resonates with modern feminist theology's concerns (for instance, the holiness of the body and the soul; understanding the union with God from the experience of love and friendship). (See Schroeder 1993, 174–5; Bainton 2001, 25–6; Lerner 1993, 148–9; Jourda 1930, 887–912.)

Marguerite's mystical, and at times devotional, tone also comes across in her letters. For instance, in the following excerpt from her letter to her cousin Vittoria Colonna – who was also interested in the reform of the Church through the spiritual transformation of individuals' – Marguerite writes,

> As to the flesh, I believe you died long ago, and that your Adam with all his desires died and was crucified in our Lord Jesus Christ, with Whom and for Whom you died and rose again, living in the new flesh of the Lamb – who died before the Creation of the world, by Whom you have been renewed in the Spirit – walking on a new earth, contemplating the new heavens, considering that the old external order of things has passed away, because what is exterior will come to an end, and nothing will last except that which is interior, so much so that no mortal thing is worthy of desire by those who have their heart set on the Eternal God and the enjoyment of his eternity. (Collett 2000, Appendix B)

In another letter to Vittoria from 1545 she stated her view that institutional reform needed to start from an individual: "If the ministers of the church would follow in word and behavior those of whom they claim to be successors, the Christian rulers and people would amend their own mistakes, and the criticism of those who despise and accuse them would be silenced" (Collett 2000, Appendix B).

Marguerite can be considered to be a mystical writer. Furthermore, "Marguerite's texts are allegories of the Christian's search for the Word" and "Marguerite's poems are also allegories of the Word's operation in human language." Scripture was her focal point, while she combined the centrality of Scripture with the centrality of the Spirit. Her poetry was based on the mystical tradition that cultivated the contemplative life; her poems were "signed" to God. In the company of those mystics who displayed an extroverted impulse and social concern, Marguerite's mysticism included a political dimension and a vision for a transformed reality. "Seeking to recover Silence, that is to say, the primal metaphor that antedates the signifying chain of narrative time, each of Marguerite's texts is a discourse whose structurality, or metaphoricity, holds out the promise of a final – though perpetually deferred – return to the 'Absolute Perfection' of the Word." (See Cotrell 1986, 312 and Thysell 2000, 124.)

At the same time, there is a particular "social dimension" in Marguerite's thought and her "contribution to the religious and political debates of her period." As Carol Thysell concludes, "from early characterizations of her essentially 'quietistic' spirituality to more recent claims that the omission of the communal aspect of Christianity is indicative of her individualistic piety" a conclusion can be made about the way her theology bridges the spiritual and political, the allegorical and social.

> For Marguerite de Navarre, allegorical rhetoric allows this basically theological but also political aspect of her response to Calvin to be couched in a work that does not announce a political position only for the moment but encourages the perennial project of "bridging" both spiritual and political dimensions of a community through a bond that is deeper than any of their individual convictions. (Thysell 2000, 124)

In her mystical writing, the anguish and experiences of Marguerite's own life found literary expression. For instance,

> she had lived through the burnings at the Place Maubert, the massacre at Merindol, flights of exiles and returns and flights again, stately processions, sumptuous repasts and shrieks of burning men, prisons, tortures and the stake and all for the love of Jesus and of God. Her longest and her greatest poem, entitled *Prisons*, is a recital of the vanities of earth's delights, truly delights, but prisons in the end, tarnished by greed, lust, ambition and the love of self. (Bainton 2001, 36–7)

As another example, after Marguerite's beloved brother died in 1547, and his heir succeeded to the throne as Henri II, the events surrounding her personal devastation stimulated Marguerite to write her *Comedy on the Passing of the King* in 1548. A year later, on December 21, 1549, Marguerite herself died reaching the "gentle sleep" she had desired. Her work continued with her daughter, Jeanne d'Albret. (Blaisdell 1982, 76; Jourda 1930, 80–2; Roelker 1968, 11.)

According to Jeanne, her mother died in the Catholic faith, in conformity with the external rites that she considered "inconsequential to her inner, spiritual beliefs." Nevertheless, the question remains unanswered, was she really a Calvinist or perhaps a Lutheran in her heart? Looking at her associations and at the respect with which she was held among Protestants, as well as the suspicion she aroused in Catholics, it would appear that though she never confessed to it, she had crossed the line. Her writings indicated that theologically she was closer to Calvin in sacramental theology, while Luther's justification by faith (an idea that had also been introduced by Jacques Lefèvre d'Etaples at the French court) had shaped Marguerite's faith radically. In her mysticism she drew from the Catholic tradition and her experiences as a woman, all of which distinguished her from some of her reformer associates. For instance, "she agreed with Calvin on some points of theology but obviously disagreed with him on others. But the truth that she understood though mystical illumination was larger than Calvin's immediate, prophetic message" (Thysell 2000, 123). She was actually closer than has been recognized to Luther, whose theology entailed a central mystical dimension (especially in his envisioning of the reality of the union between Christ and human and the real presence of Christ in the Word and the sacrament).

Because of the genres Marguerite chose, and her sex, her role as a theological writer has not been duly recognized until recently. She did not write a theological *summa*. The issue of gender does not fully explain why we have no "systematic theology" – understood in a narrow sense – from Marguerite or other contemporary women (a poignant question posed by Roland Bainton decades ago; Thysell 2000, 125). She was certainly not unaware of what society expected of her sex, but this external pressure did not hamper her, it may even have shaped her theological thinking as much as her own visions and experiences did. It appears, ultimately, that she did not allow her sex to limit her, but knew how to make the most of her options and found ways for self-expression and influence in what were typically considered to be male realms. An intelligent, educated, privileged, and gifted woman, she possessed the skills for writing theological treatises in the conventional style of male academics; she knew the genres very well. She also knew the obstacles and the hazards involved for a woman (and particularly a Protestant) endeavoring to produce such writing. It is quite feasible, therefore, that she intentionally did not write primarily for school theologians, but that she wished to remain cryptic in her intent. She chose to write as a layperson, in forms that appealed to her personally and with a potentially large audience. Her typically allegorical styles allowed her to mask her theological intent cleverly and creatively. In her letters, poems, and novels she wrote as a theologian with a style of her own. Men in the Sorbonne recognized her theological weight: "Her poetry was clearly understood to be theological, or it would not have been censured by the Sorbonne" (Thysell 2000, 125, also 94–5, notes 34, 35, 37).

Her impressive résumé and the rich texts drawn from her life experiences, accumulated wisdom, and perspectives shaped by the mystical tradition as well as both Protestant theologies and humanist ideals, ensure that Queen Marguerite stands out in the front line of women who have challenged the criteria for theological reflection and argumentation. Her voice is among those calling for an expansion of the theological canon and method. She also needs to be recognized among one of the most important sponsors of the Reformation not only in France but elsewhere in Europe.

Jeanne d'Albret, a Protestant Queen and a Huguenot leader, 1528–1572

Jeanne d'Albret, Reine de Navarre by François Clouet

Jeanne d'Albret 1528–72

PARENTS
- Marguerite d'Angoulême de Navarre (1492–1549)
- Henri d'Albret (1503–55)

SIBLINGS
- Jean (born and died 1530)

SPOUSE [1] (1541–5; MARRIAGE ANNULLED)
- William, Duke of Cleves (1516–92)

SPOUSE [2] (1548–62)
- Antoine de Bourbon de Vendôme (1518–62)

CHILDREN
- Henri (1551–53)
- King Henri IV of France (1553–1610)
- Louis Charles (1555–7)
- Madeleine (1556)
- Catherine de Navarre (1559–1604) (married Henri I, Duke of Lorraine)

Jeanne was born in Pau on November 16, 1528, the only daughter of Henri d'Albret, King of Navarre, and Marguerite d'Angoulême, the sister of the King of France. The Kingdom of Navarre, though small, was coveted for its strategic position on the slopes of the Pyrenees, facing both France and Spain. Her younger brother Jean died only few months after his birth in 1530, and her mother's ensuing miscarriages left Jeanne as the only, ever so precious heir. As the daughter of a powerful family line, and as niece to the French king who was engaged in a power struggle with the Emperor Charles V – the Spanish king – Henry VIII of England, and the pope, she occupied a strategic position in the royal bridal market. Jeanne's marriage prospects were of consequence and were effected by the ongoing factional fighting in France – much colored by the worsening religious division – and the ever-changing international alliances, as well as her own father's ambition to conquer back the lands lost to Spain in 1512.

"The issue of Jeanne's marriage became one of royal dominance" (Stephenson 2004, 107). Both her father and the king realized her value as a marital pawn. When, after the death of the duchess d'Angoulême, Marguerite and Henri contemplated leaving the royal court to return to their territory at Pau and Béarn with their daughter, the king seized the plans and refused to allow Jeanne's departure from the court, let alone France. In his desire to control Henri and build beneficial alliances for himself, François interposed in Henri's dreams of marrying Jeanne off, perhaps to Charles V, once he could claim authority over the child. Well aware of his sister's maternal aspirations and heartache (she continued to have phantom pregnancies even in her late fifties), François exercised his prerogative in relation to his vassals, and Jeanne became a marital hostage to fortune in the hands first of François, and later of his son. As political authority overruled parental authority, even as the most powerful woman in court, Marguerite, had to surrender. For her part, Marguerite was wise to the ways of the court and knew how far the entitlements of rank and sibling privilege went. Before she could be betrothed, the princess's upbringing needed to be properly overseen. As a nod to his sister, the king chose as Jeanne's governess, Aimée de la Fayette (or Aymée de Lafayette), one of his Marguerite's friends.

Even before the king made the arrangements to move the 10-year old to Plessis-les-Tours, the daughter of the time's most famous "career" woman (Roelker 1968) had lived apart from her parents from infancy. Not unusual for children of her rank, she rarely saw either one of her parents, what time she did spend with them was mostly spent with her mother. She visited her uncle frequently, becoming the darling of the court, "La Mignonne de Deux Roi," which does not necessarily indicate an affectionate relationship. Acclaimed for her beauty, the delicate princess was prone to sickness. She may have lived her childhood emotionally neglected and have alienated people around her with her moods, crying fits, and plain stubbornness, but materially speaking she lived a life of pampered opulence.

For starters, Jeanne had her own tutor, Nicolas de Bourbon, attendees for all her needs – including a pastry-maker – exotic pets, and first-class entertainment. La Mignonne de Deux Roi enjoyed quality education with private tutors, many of them representatives of the Reformed faith, especially during her early years when studying under her educated mother's supervision. (This can be certainly assumed, even if concrete evidence is lacking. Cholakian 2006, 152–3.) Exactly what she studied is less known, but for a young lady in her position studies in Latin and in the literature of her own country and of the Ancient world were to be expected. It is not clear how much she studied Greek or Italian or Hebrew even, but Spanish she was well familiar with, and she was tutored in theology and religious matters. Under her mother's influence she was exposed to the thoughts of humanists and reformers and their works from early on, and also observed how dangerous association with the Protestants could be. As a child she had lived through the notorious Affair of the Placards in 1534 and the resulting persecutions of the Huguenots. She never attained her mother's elegance in writing (poetry), but her quick mind and forceful, independent spirit have been well evidenced, most poignantly so in her belligerent resistance to her first wedding.

In search for the best match, François (as well as Jeanne's father) had briefly entertained the thought of marrying Jeanne to the family of the France's enemy, Charles V. The king's son Henri's name was also mentioned, but eventually the king settled for a German Protestant, Duke Wilhelm of Cleves, "a thorn in Charles V's side." (Wilhelm's sister Anne was married to England's Henry VIII, whose marriage suit had been rejected by both Jeanne's mother and Renée de France out of loyalty to Katherine of Aragon, Henry's first wife.) Jeanne's parents both initially rejected the match that to all intents and purposes meant a declaration of war with Spain, but, as the king's vassals, the members of the house of d'Albret could do little but surrender: in noble marriage contracts, feudal obligations superseded sibling loyalties. Resistance was also futile from the representatives of Henri's sovereign lands, Navarre and Béarn, who initially refuted the notion that a foreign ruler who could determine who would be the future heir to the throne in Navarre.

Marguerite was awkwardly placed between her husband and her brother over her daughter's fate; Marguerite, Henri, and Jeanne were caught in the middle of the delicate international strife between François I and Charles V. Marguerite found it wise to obey her king in public, while conducting a personal letter campaign on Jeanne's behalf (Stephenson 2004, 132, 108, footnotes 140–2; de Ruble 1877, 80–119). Young Jeanne herself fought in words, in writing, and by physically refusing to walk down the aisle. She persisted in her public resistance, placing on record the fact that she did not recognize the validity of a forced marriage. She would repeat her protest and later swear on it. Her threats to go to monastery or to kill herself infuriated her king, but she was relentless. He responded to her letter with a threat of execution, at which point Marguerite intervened with a letter of apology on behalf of her daughter. Reminding her brother of her family's service to him, she acknowledged his right as king to do as he wished, but humbly cautioned against the wisdom of this marriage plan.

Jeanne wrote, witnessed by her physician and members of the court,

I, Jeanne de Navarre, persisting in the protestations I have already made, do hereby again affirm and protest, by these present, that the marriage which it is desired to contract between the duke of Cleves and myself, is against my will; that I have never consented to it, nor will consent; and that all I may say and do hereafter, by which it may be attempted to prove that I have given my consent, will be forcibly extorted against my wish and desire, from my dread of the king, of the king my father, and of the queen my mother, who has threatened to have me whipped by the bailif of Caen, my governess. By command of the queen my mother, my said governess has also several times declared, that if I do not all in regard to this marriage which the king wishes, and if I do not give my consent, I shall be punished so severely as to occasion my death; and that by refusing I may be the cause of the ruin and destruction of my father, my mother, and of their house; the which threat has inspired me with such fear and dread, even to be the cause of the ruin of my said father and mother, that I known not to whom to have recourse, excepting to God, seeing that my father and my mother abandon me, who both well know what I have said to them – that never can I love the duke of Cleves, and that I will not have him. Therefore, I protest beforehand, if it happens that I am affianced, or married to the said duke of Cleves in any way or manner, it will be against my heart, and in defiance of my will; and that he shall never become my husband, nor will I ever hold and regard him as such, and that any marriage shall be reputed null and void; in testimony of which I appeal to God and yourselves as witnesses . . . admonishing each of you to remember the compulsion, violence, and constraint employed against me, upon the matter of this said marriage" (Jeanne d'Albret in Freer 1855, 20–1; also Roelker 1968, 54.)

Whether Marguerite ever did try to beat her daughter to obey is not proven. Her writing was to no avail. The betrothal took place as planned. She crafted a second letter.

I, Jeanne de Navarre . . . signed the protestation which I before presented . . . perceive that I am compelled and obliged by the queen my mother and by my governess, to submit to the marriage demanded by the duke of Cleves between himself and me; and that it is intended, against my will, to proceed to the solemnities of a marriage between us; I take you all again to witness that I persevere in the protest I made before you, on the day of the pretended betrothal between myself and the said duke of Cleves, and in all and every protestation that I may at any time have made by word of mouth, or under my hand; moreover, I declare that the said solemnity of marriage, and every other thing ordained relative to it, is done against my will, and that all shall hereafter be regarded as null and void, as having been done, and consented to by me, under violence and restraint: in testimony of which I call you all to witness, requesting you to sign the present, with myself, in the hope that by God's help it will one day avail me. Signed by Jeanne de Navarre. (Jeanne d'Albret in Freer 1855, 21–2)

The wedding took place in an extravagant ceremony on July 15, 1540 at Châtellerault. The bride, dressed in a golden robe heavy with jewels, an ermine cloak, and wearing a golden crown on her head, stalled as if unable to walk under the weight of her ornaments. The annoyed king ordered General Master Anne de Montmorency to carry the squirming bride down the aisle – a cause of humiliation to both of them (and especially damaging to Montmorency). The grand party and following eight days of expensive celebration was not enjoyed by the bride who rather avoided her groom. She continued to make it known that the forced marriage was not valid in her eyes.

The marriage was indeed not valid as it would never be consummated. The groom merely placed his foot on the wedding bed, and Jeanne's parents had won an agreement that no intercourse would take place before their daughter was menstruating. Given the fact that one of the most compelling reasons for a marriage to be annulled was that it had not been consummated, it shows clever planning on Marguerite's part that Jeanne stayed with her after the wedding. This, and her continuous, calculating letter-writing campaign pressing for the annulment reveal her personal opposition to the marriage. At the same time, following good protocol, Marguerite wrote kind letters to her new son-in-law, who had returned home in June 1541. In letter after letter she gave excuses for her daughter's illnesses that kept her from traveling, hoping to placate the duke. (Stephenson 2004, 68–9.)

Jeanne wrote to her husband as well, first kindly and with gifts, describing her illnesses and reiterating her hope of seeing him soon, sending greetings to his mother, and signing her letters somewhat humorously, or cunningly, as "your very humble and obedient wife" (Roelker 1968, 60–1, footnote 36). Just two years later her tone was drastically different, as she rekindled her original resistance to the forced marriage, to which she was "abandoned" by her parents and her king, and which led her to turn to God as her only "recourse":

> I cannot deny the ceremonies which took place and the honor which the King conferred on [the duke] at Châtellerault. Even less can I deny [that it was done] by the said King and by the King and Queen of Navarre, my father and mother. But, seeing that the King had determined to give me to him without being willing to listen to me, and that when I tried to speak of it to the King and Queen of Navarre they were even less willing to hear me, using the strangest pressures in the world against me, because of my opinion, which was against their will, and feeling myself abandoned by the King and my father and mother, I decided to turn to God – my only recourse. (Jeanne d'Albret in Roelker 1968, 63)

This time her letter was perceived more warmly by the king who no longer benefited from the marriage. (de Ruble 1877, ch. 3, 139–204.)

By 1543, when this letter was written, François was no longer interested in alliance with the Cleves and Germany. In September of that year Wilhelm had returned to the Catholic faith and obedience to the emperor, and had signed a treaty accordingly. He was no longer France's ally. In a letter of April 1545 Jeanne repeated her protest from 1541; this time her application for the annulment was heard and she would never have to leave for Germany. Back in the king's favor, she wrote,

> Monseigneur le cardinal, and you, my lords the bishop here assembled, in your presence, and in that of the notaries here in this place, I declare that I have before written and signed with my own hand two protests . . . and intend to maintain it now, and for the future – to wit, that I never had the will, nor am I so inclined at the present moment, to bind myself under the law of marriage to that said sieur de Cleves, nor to accept him for my husband . . . I, therefore, demand judicial testimony of this my declaration made before you my lords, the cardinal and bishops here assembled, from the notaries present for that purpose. (Jeanne d'Albret in Freer 1855, 31–2.)

Just weeks later, on October 12, 1545, the pope granted annulment on the grounds that the marriage had been forced by violence and was never consummated.

The story of Jeanne's marriage demonstrates the delicate situations many a noble-woman found herself in. Her mother, even though the beloved sister of the king, had to surrender as his vassal in the matter of her own daughter's marriage. Jeanne herself, like other brides in her situation, was quite powerless and groomed for heartache in a forced marriage, which could be suddenly annulled in favor of a new alliance because of changes in political considerations. While the bride's desires were usually of no concern, Jeanne was exceptional in her firm belief in her rights to resist an undesirable marriage – this speaks of the strong character she had already formed at young age. One is forced to wonder how the dramatic circumstances surrounding her first marriage shaped Jeanne as a person: she evolved into a sovereign who abhorred the use of force and violence, in religious as well as political matters, and who became a proponent of tolerance and peace in her own dominions!

The marriage ordeal, furthermore, sheds light on the complexities of mother–daughter relationship: whether Jeanne ever understood her mother's tactics or forgave her (whether in regards to this or her ways of dealing with the Protestants), one can sympathize with Marguerite whose divided loyalties in both matters made them into hard dilemmas. The complex mother–daughter-relationship vacillated between luke-warm and cool to warmer towards the end of Marguerite's life, the time when she needed her daughter more. (Roelker 1968, 67–9, 81–8, 105.) During her unfortunate marriage to the duke of Cleves, Jeanne had enjoyed a brief time at her mother's court, first in Nerac then in Pau, in Béarn, during which time she benefited from first-hand contact with the reformers. Influenced by their Protestant doctrine, Jeanne studied Scripture under the leadership of Bishop Gérard Roussel, the queen's almoner. She befriended Théodore de Bèze who became her mentor and a lifelong friend. After the king's death, her life took a new direction.

With the accession of the new king, Henri II (who, although married to Catherine de Médicis, remained in a long-term relationship with Diane de Poitiers), Marguerite withdrew from the court, and Jeanne was married again, which interrupted her studies. This time she approved of the groom, even if her parents or the estates of Navarre did not. Interested in uniting the southern and northern parts of France, King Henri married Jeanne to Antoine de Bourbon, Duc de Vendôme (1518–62). (Before him, both Philip of Spain and François de Guise were considered, who would have made interesting matches given the difference in their different religious loyalties and Jeanne's.) Antoine was handsome, even if vain, unreliable, and capricious when it came to politics, while charming and possessed of many appealing characteristics. As a First Prince of the Blood, he was in line for the throne after the four Valois princes; he would later be made Lieutenant General in exchange for renouncing the right to the regency that this standing gave him. The marriage was celebrated with relatively modest festivities on October 20, 1548.

The Huguenots were happy about the union as Antoine was known as a friend of the Protestants. While the bride's parents were hardly able to hide their unhappiness, the bride herself was giddily happy. The couple were infatuated with one another, for the time being anyway. Jeanne and Antoine together presented a powerful combination: their heirs would have some of the most legitimate claims on the French throne. After the death of their first child in infancy, two of the five children Jeanne gave birth to survived: her son Henri (born December 14, 1553) and her daughter Catherine (February 7, 1559) became both important players in France's religious history, the latter as a committed Protestant, the former as the future King Henri IV of France, who would exchange his Protestant faith for the throne and for the political unity of his country. (Henri, in his time, would continue the d'Angoulême tradition and exploit his sister for political gains.)

The couple were happy at first, as evidenced by their correspondence. Two issues would pull the couple apart, however: Antoine's infidelity and their different religious (and political) commitments. Jeanne "stuck" with both the spouse and the religion she had given her heart to, Antoine remained undependable in both matters (see Cazaux 1973, 171–85 on Antoine). In addition to his loyalty to the French throne, Antoine had a special interest in the benefits of his own duchy. The situation changed when Jeanne's father, Henri d'Albret died, on May 29, 1555 and Jeanne and Antoine ascended to the throne as the queen and king of Navarre. Jeanne's responsibilities and authority now expanded, while Antoine struggled for respect and even approval in face of the resentment of the Estates. The couple swore to make no administrative changes.

The new king and queen of Navarre gave hope to the persecuted Protestants, at first. They offered an asylum and were personally involved in the movement. Up until this point, Antoine's religious associations had been more visibly with Protestantism than Catholicism, and especially so as the new king when he took part in a religious service on February 4, 1558. The level of Jeanne's involvement went somewhat unnoticed until on Christmas Day 1560 she declared herself a Calvinist by participating in Protestant worship at the Cathedral at Pau and receiving Holy Communion in both forms. The timing of this public conversion, which signaled the beginning of the new reign, is interesting. It is unclear whether she had waited for an opportune moment in terms of her father's death, her spouse's mood, or the Guises's decreasing power in France. (According to Bryson 2004, 503–4, Jeanne had been Protestant secretly before her husband's involvement with the Huguenots.) In her brave decision to declare her Protestantism she made herself the enemy of the pope, the Guises, and Philip of Spain, even more so as she proceeded to actively root out the faith in her land. For instance, she donated monasteries to the Protestants to be converted into church buildings and later would give the monastery of the Cordeliers to be turned into a college.

Jeanne's conversion had not happened overnight. Her strong conviction had matured over time – through interaction with reformers (especially Théodore de Bèze, her mentor) and in reading their works – and it would remain uncompromised through the rest of her life. The early influences in her mother's company had prepared her theologically and spiritually to take the decisive step in her adulthood from which she never vacillated. Interestingly, her religiosity developed in a different direction from that of her mother. "Jeanne's religion was never marked by the complexities and ambiguities of her mother's. There were no flights of Neoplatonic rhapsody. When Jeanne came to embrace the Reform it was Calvinism undiluted" (Bainton 2001, 43, 45). Calvin's theology and spirituality seemed to fit Jeanne's personality very well. (Roelker 1968, 152, and 106–54.) From a practical perspective, mystical experiences would not have been the primary concern of a woman using her public office to fight for the survival of the Protestants in her land. At the same time, her determination during the Wars of Religion sprang from her a conviction in her faith that was personally meaningful.

Her letter of August 1555 to the Vicomte de Gourdon offers limited insights into Jeanne's religious evolvement and personal history:

> I am writing to tell you that up to now I have followed in the footsteps of the deceased Queen, my most honored mother – whom God forgive – in the matter of hesitation between the two religions. The said Queen [was] warned by her late brother the King, François I of good and glorious memory, my much honored uncle, not to get new doctrines in her head . . . Besides, I well remember how long ago, the late King, my most honored father . . . surprised the said Queen when she was praying in her rooms with ministers Roussel and Farel, and how with great annoyance he slapped her right cheek and forbade her sharply to meddle in matters of doctrine. He shook a stick at me which cost me many bitter tears and has kept me fearful and compliant until after they had both died. Now that I am freed by the death of my said father two months ago . . . a reform seems so right and so necessary that, for my part, I consider that it would be disloyalty and cowardice to God, to my conscience and to my people to remain any longer in a state of suspense and indecision. (Written in Pau, August 22, 1555, signed by Jeanne, the Queen [in Roelker 1968], 124, 105].)

Protestant faith had been preached and practiced in France since the 1530s, very much under the wings of Jeanne's mother Marguerite who had sponsored the Circle of Meaux and personally protected several leaders of the movement. For instance, among others of the persecuted Protestants who had pleaded to her for help, Jean Calvin had sought asylum with her. She had been instrumental in allowing Protestant materials and teaching into the royal court, as well as rescuing individuals from execution as heretics. Her daughter continued her legacy: Jeanne's castle too became a safe haven for French Protestants. Her time of influence coincided with the peak of Huguenot influence in France, in particular the period from September 1561 until January 1562. After her departure from the royal court more restrictions were issued on the Huguenots' lives and religious practices. Jeanne's influence, however, continued outside the court. From the moment she declared herself a Calvinist she became the front and leader of the Huguenot party, a role that culminated in the period of 1568–71 when she resided at La Rochelle. There she headed the so-called Queen's council, which included the fore-most Huguenot princes to revolt and with them prince of Condé, the most prominent among them. Jeanne herself remained the highest ranking French noble to confess the Protestant faith and proved the most influential in the long run, on a par with Calvin's associate and biographer, Théodore de Bèze. (On her "entourage" in La Rochelle, see Rambeaud 2004.)

Jeanne's bravery and religious commitment in this precarious context was quite remarkable, admired even by her enemies who wished her ill. After all, she chose to confess the Protestant faith in a poisonous context in which feuding noble families were willing to end each others' lives for the sake of religious faith and political differences. The houses of the Valois, Guise, Châtillon, and Bourbon were all intertwined in the battle. Jeanne, herself a Valois, was married to a Bourbon, allied with the Châtillons and fought the Guise. She lived through the famous Colloquy of Poissy of September 1561 when hopes for religious unity slipped away with de Bèze's ill-chosen words about the spiritual meaning of the Lord's Supper, a highly contested and divisive theological issue. She was a proponent for the edict of the equality of confessions in that same colloquy, and for the 1562 Edict of Tolerance, which, however, did not prevent the massacre of Vassy in 1562 and the ensuing civil wars. Jeanne herself was excommunicated for her Protestant heresy in 1563, and violence over religion continued regardless of her valiant efforts. A condemned heretic spearheading a desperate congregation of noble religious rebels, Jeanne eventually resorted to armed resistance, after years of striving for peace through negotiations and peaceful means. She was instrumental in reaching the Peace of St-Germain-en-Laye in August 1570, with Coligny, and in winning the king's permission to organize the first Protestant synod in La Rochelle, from April 2 to April 11, 1571, which was led by de Bèze. By 1571, after all the bloodshed, reform efforts finally seemed to take root, at least in her own land of Navarre.

Jeanne was especially busy during her last five years, in which time she proceeded to solidify her reforms in religion, administration, and economic and judicial systems, while mothering two of her own children and filling that role for several others in loco parentis – in addition to personally heading the Huguenot party with an army. She was busy. Through the varied turmoil and drama of the French Reformation, Jeanne's position remained solid, even after her excommunication from the Catholic church. Calvin remained in close contact by letter. He recognized Jeanne's key position and influence in the larger mission of the reformed. Likewise, her Catholic enemies knew that they had to take her seriously into account, and continued to wish for her downfall. As a matter of fact, when she died on June 9, 1572, "ultra-Catholics all over Europe rejoiced because they recognized her as the real leader of the party." In the words of the papal nuncio reporting to the pope, "God has snatched . . . an important enemy of Mother

Church . . . This death . . . has caused universal rejoicing among Catholics." (Roelker 1972a, 188–9, footnote 42; Roelker 1968, 154, 395. See Bainton 2001, 46–7.)

Jeanne's time as the queen of Navarre can be appraised from many angles: as a story of the causes she undertook, or as a story of her evolution as a woman and as a Protestant leader and believer, or as a story of her skilled leadership in her administration as the queen. (See *Jeanne d'Albret et sa cour*, 2004.) In general, she was successful on all accounts. What is most striking in assessing her contribution to the Reformation is the particular effort she put into instilling the Reformation in her lands through legislation and institutional changes, as much as through sponsoring theological work. Her goals were ambitious: The "queen of Navarre, played a leading role in an attempt, at first by peaceful and then by military means in the years between 1555–1572, to establish a Protestant homeland" (Bryson 1999, 1–2). Jeanne emerged as both a religious and a military leader during her residence at La Rochelle in 1568–71. The extent of her role in Navarre, and in particular in Reformation history, has been under-appreciated in comparison to the interest her husband and son have drawn.

The evolution of Jeanne's involvement in the Reformation can be read in her letters. Of particular interest are her words in the *Mémoires et poésies de Jeanne d'Albret*, "a political manifesto justifying her joining Condé's rebellion," written in September 1568, and published in 1570. Written in first person (probably with an amanueunsis), it constitutes an apology or defense of her life (see Kuperty-Tsur 2004). Other letters from Jeanne remain as well, 300 in all. About two thirds of her letters have been published, most from 1571 (80), and some (15) from the time before she became queen (Roelker 1968, 454, note 13; see also Pascal 2004). (A rare collection of Jeanne's letters, the "Portefeuilles Vallant" of 15 volumes, comes from an abbey collection of Dr Jean Vallant in 1686. While scholars debate the authenticity of these texts, Jourda and Roelker accept at least in part the letters that Ritter and Cazaux consider a forgery [see Vallant/ Dubrowski quoted in Bryson 1999, 12–13; 1999a; see also Bryson 2004, 501–2].) Glimpses of Jeanne can also be gained from the correspondence of Jean Calvin and Théodore de Bèze. (See also the letters of 1577 between Antoine and Jeanne in de Ruble, 1877.)

A most significant window on Jeanne's theology and church politics is afforded by her church order, *Ordonnances ecclesiastiques* of Pau (given in 1561, renewed 1566, and published on November 26, 1571) and from the Ecclesiastical Discipline of La Rochelle, also known as the Confession of La Rochelle, which she sponsored (April 6– April 12, 1571). Both documents were instrumental in her reforms, very much as the reform of Braunschweig was under the leadership of her contemporary Elisabeth von Braunschweig-Calenberg. (On sources, see Bryson 1999, 8–9, 12; Roelker 1968, 340–432; Dartigue-Peyrou 1934. On Jeanne's Ordinances and collaboration with a group of theologians, see Roussel 2004, esp. 22–31.)

The reformation in Jeanne's Béarn was intertwined with the bloody religious wars in France, religious factionalism, and civil wars. Yet Béarn's story was different, because of Jeanne's leadership. Under Jeanne's rule, Béarn was made into a liberal, tolerant territory that welcomed open preaching and the sale of religious books. She strengthened her authority by disengaging herself from the different factions and aiming for general neutrality. She proceeded as did reformers elsewhere, forbidding images and processions, as well as the Mass, instituting Protestant worship, building a theological academy for training new pastors, establishing a synod, and providing confessional texts. Had Jeanne's spouse (a legitimate heir to the throne of France and its Lieutenant General) stayed with the Protestants, who knows how victorious the Huguenots might have been, especially during the time when the king and his mother were sympathetic to the cause. Once he joined the Catholic side, however, Jeanne had to face an enemy within her own marriage too; Antoine did all in his power to force his wife to participate in the Mass.

Much of their public marital strife over religion took place at the royal court in Paris. There, taking considerable risks, Jeanne actively continued to promote the Protestant faith, even after most of her peers had disappeared underground. Against the preferences of the queen regent and the king, she held Protestant services in her apartments. Fighting physical illness at the time (probably tuberculosis), she resisted her husband's threats of divorce and expulsion. She reportedly swore to the queen regent that she would rather lose her son and her kingdom than ever again attend the Catholic Mass. After Antoine forced her to participate in the Mass, and after he himself worshipped with the Guises on Palm Sunday in 1562, Jeanne made her young son swear never to do so, and left the court on March 6, 1562, for Vendôme.

It took only few months before Jeanne's son surrendered under much pressure and Catholic tuition. (For a time he had been in the care of Renée de France while recovering from illness [Roelker 1968, 202–3, 399].) In 1562, while Jeanne was still traveling through her duchy of Vendôme, undaunted by threats of kidnap and witnessing Huguenots engaging in iconoclasm (for which she presented them with a receipt), the first civil war broke out between the Huguenots, led by Prince de Condé and Gaspar de Coligny, and the Catholics, led by the Guises. Her husband died in this battle, reportedly adhering to the Augsburg Confession; before Jeanne could rush to his side, his mistress had found her way there. Widowed, Jeanne officially joined Condé and the Huguenot army, to Calvin's delight. Unlike suggested in two contemporary records, Jeanne never married again, publicly or in secret (Roelker 1968, 433–4).

Calvin had been paying close attention to all the drama in Jeanne's life. He recognized her key position as a woman able and willing to support the Protestant mission even more openly than her mother had and from a more powerful position than Renée de France. His first contact with Jeanne in 1561 had been occasioned by her public confession of the Protestant faith in December 1560. Through the years his letters reminded her of her duty, and the support of his right-hand man and successor, her own lifelong friend, Théodore de Bèze, along with other ministers sent from Geneva to strengthen her. His harsh tone with Jeanne is reminiscent of his correspondence with Renée de France. For instance, in his letter from December 1561, he had barked at Jeanne that her husband needed to take a stand for the Protestant faith and expressed concerns about the influence of Jeanne's liberal consorts on her son's education. (As with Renée, also with Jeanne, Calvin's primary concern appears to have been the success of his mission rather than pastoral care for Jeanne.) After Antoine had left the Protestants, more hopes had been attached to Jeanne. In March 1562 Calvin expressed his sympathies for her after her husband, having given up his efforts to force her into religious cooperation, had tried to drive her away from the court. When her husband's death freed her to reign on her own, Calvin wrote to Jeanne again, in January 1563, and quickly sent new ministers to her side (Jean-Raymond Merlin and Jacques Spifame). (See *Calvin à la Reine de Navarre*, January 1561, CO XVIII, col. 313–14, no. 3315; December 1561, CO, XIX, col. 196–8, no. 3662; March 22, 1562, Co, XIX, col. 347–9, no. 3748; January 1563, CO, XIX, col. 643–8, no. 3904. See Bainton 2001, 45.)

We must suppose that Calvin was pleased with the edict Jeanne issued in June 1563 that abolished the Catholic Mass and papal authority in Béarn. In another edict she redirected funds from Catholic institutions towards Protestant churches. Jeanne made an effort to communicate peacefully between Queen Catherine de Médicis and Condé and his troops, and put her energies into reforming administration in her land with a reorganized judicial system and economic structures, with the foundation of models that would remain in place until eighteenth century. Taking advantage of the new freedoms gained in her widowhood, Jeanne carried on with her primary mission of rectifying religious practices – continuing to abolish Catholic celebrations, images, and forms of worship. Her religious reforms touched on civil issues as well, with ordinances regarding baptisms, marriages, patronage, jurisdiction, etc. Given the scope of the reforms she initiated, it would be unrealistic to expect that Jeanne would have managed to avoid rebellion and resistance in her territory. She was especially vulnerable to criticism as a queen regnant with no male overseer, and as a Protestant who, in a predominantly Catholic context, boldly declared herself Calvinist and stated her intent to make her faith the faith of the region. Church leaders in Rome and Spain tried to threaten her – with excommunication, for instance, with plots for kidnapping, and by sending in the Inquisition. Her brisk rejections of an unsolicited marriage proposal and a papal delegate provoked especially furious responses.

Philip II of Spain made the most audacious proposal: he hoped Jeanne would marry one of his sons. One has to wonder what he was thinking, whether he realized how unacceptable such a union would have been for Jeanne for religious reasons alone. Furthermore, as for Elizabeth I of England, marriage would have meant yoking herself to a man who would take over her realm, and who would probably try to control her religion as well. Marriage to a foreigner and a Catholic would have been extremely ill-advised – even if it could have rescinded her father's dreams of an alliance between Spain and Navarre. During the proposal negotiations (which she endured, to be sure, pro forma), she met demands to give up her religion and change her religious policies. Jeanne was outraged: "Although I am just a little Princess, God has given me the government of this country so I may rule it according to his Gospel and teach it his Laws. I rely on God, who is more powerful than the King of Spain." Philip's response brought negotiations to an end: "This is quite too much of a woman to have as a daughter in law. I would much prefer to destroy her and treat her as such an evil woman deserves" (Jeanne d'Albret in Roelker 1968, 216, see 214–17, 192–5).

On August 18, 1563 Pius IV wrote to Jeanne with a warning of excommunication, and a delegate tried to speak sense to her, as much as to scare her. Cardinal d'Armagnac, someone Jeanne had known virtually all her life, spearheaded the papal attack, pleading with her "as an old friend and a legate of the pope" (See Roelker 1968, 217). The tense correspondence, with much at stake in both ends, was so weighty that it was published as a pamphlet (Roelker 1968, 217, 221). Jeanne told him to save his tears, and reminded him that Béarn was not under the pope's authority. (Letters with d'Armagnac, Freer 1855, 211–15.)

> Mon cousin . . . The reformation in religion which I have commenced at Pau, and at Lescar – I am very earnestly resolved, by the grace of God, to continue such reformation throughout my sovereignty of Béarn. I have learned to do so from my Bible (which I read more than the works of your doctors) . . . I am not yet so forsaken by God and my friends, as not to have still some worthy persons near me – persons who not only wear the semblance of religion, but practice its precepts: for, such as the head is, so are the members. Neither

have I undertaken, as you assert, to plant a new religion, but only to build up again the ruins of our ancient faith, in which design I feel certain of a fortunate issue . . . The said states have tendered me obedience in religious matters . . . I do nothing by compulsion: I condemn no one to death, or to imprisonment, which penalties are the nerves and sinews of a system of terror. (Jeanne d'Albret in Roelker, 1968, 219)

She reiterated that she was a sovereign in her territory – with God as her source of determination and guidance – and that unlike other rulers she was not guilty as charged for using force in religious matters.

If the Spirit of God did not lead me to this conclusion, my common sense would teach me the lesson by infinity of examples . . . I blush for you, and feel shame, when you falsely state that so many atrocities have been perpetrated by those of our religion. Pull the mote from your own eye, then shall you see clearly to cast out the beam in your neighbor's eye! Purge the earth first from the blood of so many just men shed by you and yours; take in witness of which the facts that you are well aware.

Considering persecution as pollution of faith, she wished to correct her opponents' misconceptions about the actual numbers of the Protestants and about her competence and sources:

You are pleased to assure me that the number of our people is small. I, on the contrary, inform you that our faithful increase daily. As to what you remark respecting the books of the ancient fathers of the church, I hear them constantly quoted by our ministers, and approve them. Nevertheless, I own that I am not learned as I ought to be in this matter; but neither do I believe that you are more competent than myself . . . . We unite in opinion, as you state, on the necessity of studying the Holy Scriptures; but we care not to look beyond. (Jeanne d'Albret in Freer 1855, 211–13)

Jeanne also addressed the issue of the Holy Supper and defended Calvin's interpretation of the words "this is my body" at the Lord's table: "an error of the kind, nevertheless, would be excusable in a woman, such as myself; but, certes, mon cousin, to see an old cardinal like yourself so ignorant, kindles shame." In form of a confession she stated, "We have one God, one faith, one law; and the Holy Ghost has promised to be with His Church to the end of time, to bless and to maintain this faith." She also exerted her sovereignty over that of the pope: "In Béarn I recognize only God, to whom I must account for the rule he has given me over His people." (Jeanne d'Abret in Freer 1855, 211–15.)

Very soon after, a synod took place at Pau, and no less than a month later, on September 28, Pius IV issued a bull concerning Jeanne's heresy and ordered her to present herself in front of the Inquisition in six months' time ("this is called *monitoire*, being put on notice" Roelker 1968, 221). Forced to fight for her sovereignty against outside threats and amid scandals, Jeanne joined the Huguenot princes, in the face of her opponents the pope himself, her powerful neighbor in Spain, and her Catholic enemies in France. The Pope's threats had gone too far even in the eyes of Philip of Spain and Catherine de Médicis, and the French government, however, and Jeanne actually benefited from the discord among her opponents over her fate and carried on her reforms.

By an Edict of February 2, 1564, Jeanne permitted Mass to be celebrated in places where it was currently authorized, but not where it had been suppressed. The movable wealth . . . of the church and the religious orders was liquidated and the money distributed to the poor by secular authorities. Calvinists might hold services wherever they were presently permitted and in others the Queen chose to add. All crimes committed under the pretext of religion were pardoned unless lese majesty was involved. Dartigue notes that this was the first official proclamation of religious toleration within a single kingdom in European history. (Roelker 1968, 224–5). Furthermore, Huguenot marriages were to be considered valid, and no force was to be used against any subjects, or children, in an effort to make them worship against their will. In other words, she gave an official proclamation of religious tolerance. The example she had given remained rare, with only the Peace of Augsburg in Germany and the Act of Uniformity in England providing contemporary comparison or even coming close to what she achieved. The former in particular was a political peace that gave the right to practice their faith only to Catholics and those who signed the Augsburg Confession. Her proclamation pointed the way for the future Edict of Nantes in France. The path was not easy, however.

From December 1565 until March 1566 Jeanne was back in Paris, where she was reunited with her son, but the political climate at the court changed once more for her when the Catherine withdrew her support. In 1567 Jeanne returned to Béarn, this time with her son. In 1568 the third civil war broke out, and she faced the dilemma of whether to stay with her son or flee to La Rochelle and join the Huguenot princes there. Furthermore, up until now, she had promoted tolerance and peaceful means of religious reform. Different measures were needed in desperate times, and, at the time of the height of her power, she gave all she had to resolve the situation. She used military suppression as well as legal actions and political pressure, followed by a pardon for all. "Her procedure was to suppress an insurrection and then issue a general amnesty" (Bainton 2001, 62–3). (See Roelker 1968, 287–9, 278.) (According to Bryson 2004, 506, she may have been aware of and accepted occasional other forms of violence.)

The years leading to the peace of 1570 were difficult and she needed to suppress three revolts against her edicts. The stakes were high, for her personally and for the Huguenots in general.

> For Queen Jeanne, the war was "in my guts," a conflict between her personal faith and identity with what she had come to accept as the "true religion" on the one hand, and, on the other, the external demands of the exercise of political and military power for "the general cause" of the Reformed party, the preservation of her dynasty, her sovereign realm of Béarn and Navarre, and the territory of Guyenne under her family's government. (Bryson 1999, 3)

(See Freer 1855, 291–326.)

In other words, the war in her "bowels" had to do with her maternal feelings, dynastic responsibilities, and her personal faith commitment: "her responsibility to Henry was not merely that of a mother, but also that of a queen, the guardian of the prince of the blood." How could she stay and let others die for the faith to which she was committed? Putting her trust in God, as she said, she traveled to La Rochelle, arriving there in September 28, 1568. (See Cocula 2004.) The trip occasioned her *Memoires*, her apology, which, with her letters, revealed her internal conflict. She reiterated three points over and over again: her loyalty to God, to the king, and to the blood of the Bourbon house.

She also defended the Huguenots, presenting them as fighting for the king and the queen mother.

Defending her choices, she wrote also to her friend Elizabeth I (who had congratulated her on her conversion to Calvinism):

> I address you as one of the royal nurses of our church . . . I would be ashamed if I did not join myself to the princes and lords, who all as I and I as they are resolved under the Lord God of hosts to spare neither blood, life nor goods to resist this horror . . . My son and I are opposing those who . . . have violated the Edict of Pacification and plunged us into a pitiless war . . . There has been a plot to kidnap my son. We are not guilty of lese majeste. We are faithful to our king and our God. (Jeanne d'Albret in Bainton 2001, 65.)

(On Jeanne and Elizabeth, see Freer 1855, 391–2, chs. ix, xii.)

During her three years in La Rochelle (1568–71), the time was "momentous for French Protestantism" (Bainton 2001, 66). Whether she could be called the "minister of propaganda" (as in Roelker 1968, 312), while at Rochelle she definitely "exercised the functions of a queen (Bainton 2001, 66) and wrote manifestos and letters for financial support of the Huguenot cause. In addition to lending her personal support and presence to the Protestant resistance, she was in charge of the finances, personally giving her wealth, including her jewels, to secure the foreign loans needed for assistance. She used her position and charisma as the queen to strengthen the troops. She sponsored a seminary established at La Rochelle and personally paid the salaries of the reformers who taught there; the academy prepared men for ministry and was led by intellectuals drafted in by Jeanne. She had various translations made, including a version of the New Testament in Basque dialect. She also had the Genevan Catechism and the new Liturgy translated. Involved at all levels, she even traveled through the defense lines and accompanied Coligny. Her goal was to establish a Protestant homeland in Guyenne, using arms if needed to. (Bryson 1999, ch. 6; Roelker 1968, 324–5, 301, 312.)

In 1571 she was back at home, and in November issued an ordinance according to the terms of which she expected everybody in her lands to be free to adhere to the confession of La Rochelle (Dartique-Peyrou 1934, 430–1, 154–4). Practices in both Catholic and Huguenot traditions were to be allowed – and, furthermore, Church attendance was strongly urged by the Queen. A university was established, as was poor relief. Poverty was to be eradicated. (At the Synod of Pau she had declared that "God's wealth" had to go to the poor, the schools, and evangelical ministry.) Her ordinances resembled Elizabeth I's 1559 Act of Uniformity and demonstrated how Jeanne relied on her sovereign status. She understood herself to bear a special Christian responsibility, as a ruler, to ensure that the "right" Christian faith be practiced in her lands:

> There is no monarch alive who is not obligated to use his full powers to place his subjects under the rule of Jesus Christ, since the Eternal Father has given Him all power in Heaven and earth and commanded all His creatures to seek Him above all things . . . In order, therefore, to obey the Lord's commandment, to fulfill the obligations of a Christian, to respond to the vocation given us by God, to procure the salvation of our subjects, to assure the unity of our administration and of the public peace, to follow the example of good princes and kings, to avoid the terrible wrath of God's judgment, and to comply with the request of the latest Estates of Béarn, the sovereign country bound to obey us . . . in which they begged us, of their own free will, to banish all false services, idolatries, and superstitions and to declare the pure word of God and to administer the baptism and Holy communion according [to his word] . . . it is our will that all subjects of the said country,

of whatever quality, condition, sex, or estate, shall profess publicly the Confession of Faith that we here publish by our authority as surely founded on the doctrine and writings of the Prophets and of the Apostles. (Formulated in April 1571, Jeanne d'Albret in Roelker, 1968, 430–1, 275–7; Dartigue-Peyrou 1934.)

Furthermore it was declared that "every power granted to the Béarnais church is ultimately checked or controlled by the sovereign's authority, and every religious duty of Jeanne's subjects is decreed by her and is to be enforced by the secular arm" (Roelker 1968, 432).

In the same year the Huguenots had won certain rights elsewhere in France too: in August of 1570 the Peace of St Germain had been signed by Charles IX, with significant input from Jeanne. The Huguenots were granted freedom to worship anywhere outside the city of Paris or the court and were allowed to hold public offices; four cities were to be under Huguenot rule. These concessions did not please the Catholics in France or bring peace. While Charles considered a war with Spain to restore unity in France, the queen mother, Catherine, deemed an "inter-faith" marriage more likely to be fruitful: the marriage of Henri de Navarre, the son of Protestant Jeanne, and Catherine's own Catholic daughter Marguerite would ally the Bourbon and Valois families. Jeanne feared more for the future of France than the possibility of her son's conversion and corruption through his new relations and thus agreed, with some conditions: Cardinal Bourbon should perform the marriage as a prince rather than a priest, and the ceremony should take place outside the church building. Catherine agreed, and the wedding, intended to be grand, was planned for 1572. Prior to the wedding Jeanne wrote to her son (and Queen Elizabeth) about her fears, and urged him strongly to heed her maternal advice and leave the court as soon as possible. In this she acted very similarly to Elisabeth von Braunschweig who, like various other literate parents in comparable positions, wrote a "mirror" for her son. (See Desplat 2004.)

Jeanne missed the wedding. She died just two months beforehand, on June 9, 1572, of tuberculosis, after collapsing a few days earlier on June 4. (Poisoning was ruled out in an autopsy.) Her ministers had read Psalm 31 and John 14–18 to her, as she had requested, and prayed with her, "O God, my Father, deliver me from this body of death and from the miseries of this life, that I may commit no further offenses against Thee and that I may enjoy the felicity Thou hast promised me." She had her will prepared, leaving a mission for her children and people. She was buried next to her husband. Her immature death saved her from the terrible St Bartholomew's Day massacre, which was everything Jeanne had fought against. Six days after the wedding of August 18, 1572, a cold-blooded massacre of Huguenots took place within the closed gates of the city. Fingers pointed at Catherine de Médicis as the most probable suspect, but without proof. In the week-long massacre thousands of Huguenots were killed, including Coligny and many of the leaders. A civil war ensued, La Rochelle, like other Huguenot towns was put under siege, and violence continued until the Peace of La Rochelle was signed on July 6, 1573.

One of Jeanne's dreams had come true, while others were lost, as becomes evident from the story of her son Henri, the embodiment of her legacy as the future king (see Bryson 2004, 509). After Henri III was assassinated in the War of the Three Henris, Jeanne's son succeeded to the throne. In the early years of his reign he associated with the Protestants, but eventually publicly embraced the Catholic faith, for the sake of uniting France, which was seriously split between religious factions. His conclusion that

"Paris is worth a Mass" illustrates his motives. He would follow his father's pattern of prioritizing political gains over religious issues. A Catholic for public purposes, he made sure the Huguenots' cause would not be lost: in the famous Edict of Nantes in 1598 he at last fulfilled his mother's dreams of legislated religious tolerance.

Compared to her father, husband, and son, Jeanne presented a different backbone and endured admirably in her religious commitment, even during the most trying of circumstances. She had been willing to stake all she had and take enormous risks, not for her personal gain but for the sake of the Reformed faith, which speaks of her character as well as her commitment to her faith. Compared to her mother, as well, she distinguished herself in her religious "hands on" leadership role. Mother and daughter expressed their religious calling in different ways, Marguerite through interpersonal support and lobbying, and in writing, Jeanne by more aggressively defending and instilling the new faith in the lives of the people she "reigned" and cared for as queen. She did not write about her spiritual life or concerns. We can read her theology in her actions and in her legislations, in addition to her letters and memoirs. Her religious interests were not introspective or introverted, her passion was for the reform of the Church through institutional changes rather than individual renewal. What she valued important as a person, she implemented in legislation, firmly believing in her authority and duty to do so as a Christian queen. After her death, Béarn remained Protestant, and the structures set in her time continued to be employed by future generations. The history of the Reformation in France thus very much peaked in Jeanne's story. The years between 1559 and 1572, the time of her most active involvement, marked the highpoint of the Protestant faith in France.

Conclusion

The history of the French Reformation would read very differently without the involvement of Marguerite de Navarre and Jeanne d'Albret. The two most famous French queens to be involved in the Reformation were among the most visible and powerful supporters of the reform in French-speaking context, and thus of great interest and value to the French reformer Calvin. Their connection with Renée de France and Marie Dentière suggests the important networks women established for supporting each other in the new faith – whether it was in protecting the persecuted or sharing Hebrew grammars and other written materials. They both had to negotiate between their private beliefs and public position. Each in turn was compelled to marry a man not of their choosing, and both lost a child to death. They both exerted authority as rulers, and their right to authority as women rulers in particular, both aware of but ignoring the existing gender norms and boundaries set for their sex. The way they did this and coped with the obstacles and attitudes they found in their way, makes them as not just as women but as people, quite special. Without these women, it is difficult to imagine the Protestant faith having gained any foothold in France. Without them, the death toll of Protestant martyrs would have been even greater than it was. Their stories in that regard need to be told together: as the mother protected the sowing of the seed by the early reformers, so the daughter fostered the rooting and evolution of the new church by those who had embraced the emerging theology. They both performed vital, albeit distinct, roles as religious leaders. Each fought for the success of Protestant theology that appealed to them as a theology offering hopes and meanings worth fighting for.

A Word about Sources and References

For core biographical information, see Jourda 1930 and Roelker 1968, and other works listed in the bibliography.

Roelker's 1968 and Freer's 1855 rare English biographies, both of which owe a debt to the foundational works of Mlle Vauvilliers (1818) and (the detailed if incomplete works of) le Baron de Ruble (1877, 1881–86, 1897) give detailed biographical information on Jeanne. Articles and chapters interpreting Jeanne's role in the Reformation and as a religious and political leader come from Bainton 1971/2001, Bryson 1999, and a collection of essays edited by Berriot-Salvadore 2004, and the 2004 edition of Colloquy (2001) papers, "Jeanne d'Albret et sa cour"; Blaisdell's 1972 and 1982 studies about Calvin and the French noble ladies are most illuminating. Cazaux's 1973 critical biography has been followed by Kermina's 1998 popular narrative. Stephenson's 2004 work on Marguerite's political patronage offers an important interpretation of Jeanne and the mother–daughter dynamics. Concerning Marguerite, there is no lack of sources (see Clive's 1983 bibliography) or critical editions of her works (see for example, Salminen's works). The still standard biography and analysis of her letters is Jourda 1930, 1932, and Cholakian 2006 is an important source of information on her life. Interpretations of her texts and theology, as well as her political and religious roles come from Collett 2000, Thysell 2000, Bainton 1973/2001, Sckommodau 1954, Schroeder 1999, and Reynolds-Cornell's 1995 collection of essays.

CHAPTER 11

Renée de France, 1510–1575 – A Friend of the Huguenots

© PHOTO RMN – © RENÉ-GABRIEL OJÉDA

Renée de France

Renée de France, 1510–75

PARENTS

♦ King Louis XII of France (1462–1515) (following Anne of Brittany's death married to Mary Tudor, 1514, sister of Henry VIII of England)

♦ Anne, Duchess of Brittany (1477–1514) (previously married first to Maximilian of Habsburg, by proxy, in 1490 [Queen of the Romans], next to King Charles VIII of France 1491; no children survived)

SIBLINGS

♦ Claude (1499–1524) married François d'Angoulême (1494–1547), king of France 1515–47, brother of Marguerite d'Angoulême (1492–1549), future queen of Navarre. Children: François, Henri (future King Henri II, 1519–59, married Catherine de Médicis, 1519–1601), Charles, Madeleine, Marguerite, Charlotte and Louise. [Following Claude's death François married Eleanor of Austria 1498–1558 from 1530–47]

SPOUSE (1528–59)

♦ Ercole d'Este, duke of Ferrara (1508–59) (son of Alfonso I d'Este, duke of Ferrara, Modena and Reggio, and Lucrezia Borgia, daughter of Pope Alexander VI)

CHILDREN

♦ Anna (1531–1607) (married first to François de Lorraine, duke of Guise [1519–63] from 1548–63, and to Jacques de Savoie, duke of Nemours [1531–85] from 1566–1607. Children: Henri [1550–88], Catarina [1552–96], Charles, and Louis [1555–88, archbishop of Rheims, Cardinal de Guise])

♦ Alfonso II (1533–97) the last duke of Ferrara (married Lucrezia di Cosimo de' Medici, Barbara of Austria [daughter of Emperor Ferdinand I], and Margherita Gonzaga)

♦ Lucrezia (1535–98) (married Francesco Maria della Rovere)

♦ Leonora/Eleonore (1537–81)

♦ Luigi (1538–86)

Introduction

Had she been a man, Renée de France would have succeeded her father King Louis XII to the French throne. Instead, the petite princess, born under the most promising stars, was married off to a distant corner of northern Italy. There, as Renata di Ferrara, the duchess grew into her prominent role in the house of the d'Este in Ferrara, a known sponsor of the Renaissance art and music in Italy. Influenced by the early evangelicals in France, and later the persecuted Huguenots in Ferrara, she became the protector of Protestants and other "dissidents," including the Jews. What she achieved was not done without personal sacrifices. Renée's fate was to balance between the papal Inquisition, her Catholic opponents, her personal faith commitment, Jean Calvin's high expectations, and the well-being of her children and her persecuted friends, the Huguenots. Her story involved other women invested in reforming the Church (such as Marguerite de Navarre, Jeanne d'Albret, Anne d'Este, Olimpia Morata, and Vittoria Colonna), as well as high-profile men involved in the Reformation (for instance, Bernardino Ochino, Fulvio Morato, Jacques Lefèvre d'Etaples, Clément Marot, and Jean Calvin).

The Catholic sources have stressed Renée's piety and her, at least apparent, fidelity to the Catholic church, whereas the Protestants, frustrated by her evasiveness and the lack of documents about her faith, have tended to highlight her personal connection with Calvin and her faithful protection of persecuted evangelicals. Because she carefully avoided explicitly revealing her religious loyalties and convictions in faith, it has remained a subject of debate whether or not she died as a Huguenot. (Similarly conflicting assessments have been made about her looks, level of literacy, and intellectual gifts.) Renée's story proved complex, tragic, and triumphant, regardless of the simple expectations laid on her: all that was expected from Renée was for her to be a willing pawn in successful dynastic politics and to produce heirs. She had very little say in her fate, except when it came to her personal religion.

Given her family and political situation, it is peculiar that she would evolve into an enduring protector of the "dissidents" of two predominantly Catholic contexts, Ferrara first, and later France. She carved herself an area of independence in her religion. She is an example of a woman whose identity and values were radically transformed by her encounter with Protestant theology and who found a vocation and a public role in protecting those persecuted for their faith, and in preparing the way for religious tolerance. Her story has important connections to Marguerite de Navarre and her daughter Jeanne d'Albret in particular.

The duchess' life story can be gathered from scattered sources, including some of her letters, while she did not leave any formal theological treatises, written church orders, public manifestos or texts of that sort. What she left most importantly was the impact of her actions on the lives of the individuals she saved and, in the broader context, her role in the survival of the evangelical faith in Italy and France. Her theological and spiritual preferences – and her identity as a reformer – were manifested in her choices and actions as a princess and a duchess, a daughter, a spouse and a mother, a friend of the Huguenots, and a Christian who (atypically among the crowned heads) resisted the use of violence or the abuse of power in handling the dilemma of religious difference.

Renée – A French Protector of Huguenots in Italy and France

Renée's life story begins with her high-profile parents, King Louis XII (1462–1515) of France and Anne of Brittany (1477–1514). Anne, a strong personality known for her piety and well educated ladies of her court, had married two kings of France. With no sons, she raised two daughters, Claude (1499–1524) and Renée, who became heirs of her lands in Brittany as well as pawns in dynastic marital politics to fortify the throne.

Born on October 25, 1510, in the Château de Blois, France, Renée was the youngest (by 11 years) of the two daughters born to Louis XII and Anne. Her sex was a disappointment to her parents who were eagerly anticipating a male heir to secure their dynasty. A royal infant's birth was celebrated with a lavish baptism attended by members of nobility. Renée was born with physical problems and did not meet the standards for beauty of her time. Many enough biographers have apologized for her less than ravishing looks, if not called her plain ugly. (For instance, her future husband supposedly complained after their first meeting "But madame Renée is not beautiful" [translation Stjerna] Ryley 1907, 251, 254–8.) Like her mother and her sister she suffered some physical irregularity, but in her it was more marked. One of her legs was shorter than the other and her stance made her shoulder "protrude." It has been suggested that to balance her physical unattractiveness, she learned to rely on her wit and knowledge rather than her looks. Whereas in some assessments Renée has been complimented for her cultivated intelligence and vivacious spirit, others have belittled her lack of refinement, how bright and intelligent she was and even her character. These mixed appraisals demonstrate not just the conflicting impressions of Renée but also the shallowness of some of the factors used to value a woman of her time. (See Puaux 1997, 98; Blaisdell 1972, 202, 219; Valeria 1969, 58–61; Barton 1989, viii–ix, 10–13; Rodocanachi 1896, 14–17.)

Renée lost her mother in January 1514 at the age of four. Her father's cousin, Louise de Savoie (Savoy), came to care for the children, bringing with her many ambitions for François (1494–1547), her son by Charles d'Angoulême, who was the closest male heir to the throne. Through his marriage to his cousin Claude, François was to become the new king after Louis died in 1515. For many years, the new king's power was checked by the two women on his side, his mother and his charismatic older sister. Especially before the year 1534, the liberal influence and advise of Marguerite d'Angoulême (1492–1549), who was later to be Marguerite de Navarre, balanced the conservative voices whispering in the young king's ear on many affairs, including religion. Renée's childhood at the royal castle of Blois coincided with these "liberal years" of François' rule and Marguerite's influence. (Blaisdell 1972, 199.)

Renée's childhood years at Blois after her parents' deaths where pampered but lonely: she had five women of honor, two chambermaids, two valets, a chaplain, an apothecary, and a staffed kitchen to tend to her needs but often felt neglected, especially so after her companion Madame de Soubise (Saubonne), a Huguenot, was fired by Louise (who wished to rid her court of such strong personalities). The reserved girl with perhaps less than dazzling looks did not naturally draw that much attention to herself, while her birth status made her a player in the long-term politics of the court, especially in the matchmaking game. It has been surmised that her childhood experiences taught her to stand tall in the status of her royal birth, as well as the values of generosity and compassion. What shaped her personality and religious interests essentially were her studies and her relationship with Marguerite.

A "voracious reader" (Barton 1989, 12), the princess enjoyed a privileged education, including studies in sciences, philosophy, classical authors, ancient history, Latin, Greek, and perhaps Hebrew, Arabic astronomical texts and "newer" works such as those of Erasmus of Rotterdam. Her learning made her a versatile conversationalist, but she left no evidence of literary eloquence. Quite the contrary, her letters reveal her struggle with language, even with the structure and the style of her native tongue. Comparisons to someone who was as charismatic a writer as Marguerite d'Angoulême have not been favorable to Renée; more important is the respect and affection between the two. (See Blaisdell 1972, 200–1; Rodocanachi 1896/1970, 6–14; Puaux 1997, 42–54.)

The king's sister Marguerite had a fundamental influence on Renée and her education as if she were her second (spiritual) mother, who showed the child the affection she so craved, and who exposed her to the new currents in religion. Under Marguerite's wings, she could absorb influences from such reform-minded men as Charles d'Orléans, Jean Meschinot, and Clément Marot. The latter was particularly known for voicing criticism against the corruption in the Church and had a significant influence on both Marguerite's religiosity (and her turn towards mysticism) and also on Renée's curiosity about theology. When Marot finally fled France, Marguerite advised him to find shelter with his lifelong friend Renée in Ferrara. Under Marguerite's wings Renée had benefited from the mentoring and textual work of the humanist Jacques Lefèvre d'Etaples, the librarian at Blois, who translated the New Testament into French and wrote about the central reformatory principle of "justification by faith" even before Luther articulated his vision for salvation based on faith and grace. Like Marot, he would later find himself at Renée's court, as a refugee hired to be a tutor for her children.

It was very much under the protection of Marguerite that Lefèvre and the famous circle of Meaux (Guillaume Briçonnet, Gérard Roussel, Guillaume Farel, François Vatable, and Michel d'Arande) ignited the Reformation in France. After the theologians of the Sorbonne condemned Luther as a heretic, the group was dissolved; Briçonnet was whipped in front of his church; Farel and Calvin left France for good. Renée was there to witness both the early excitement with the reforms and the violent dispersion of the "radicals" after François' initial tolerance changed in 1534 with the Affair of the Placards, when posters appeared in the palace blaspheming the Mass and the doctrine of transubstantiation.

In the aftermath of the dramatic Affair of the Placards and in the eve of the bloody religious wars in France, it is interesting to see the various roles and networks the different reforming women took in France. The hugely important Marguerite, especially known for her support among Protestant women, never openly confessed her Protestant faith but courageously interceded on behalf of many, vitally sponsored Protestant works, and continued to be centrally involved in the Huguenots' resistance network. She raised a thoroughly Protestant daughter, Jeanne d'Albret who in her turn would rise as frontwoman for the Huguenots and become in more explicit ways involved with the reformers in France. Somewhere between these two stands Renée, who, after Marguerite's model, would seek to protect the Huguenots, and, like Jeanne, became recognized as a frontline person in the eyes of both pro- and anti-Protestant camps.

In saving Protestant lives, Renée tangibly contributed to the Reformation. Her contribution in this has been vastly underappreciated, and grossly misrepresented. While some have deemed Renée a devout Catholic who was attracted to dogmatic debates and issues, others have rated her piety over her aptitude for theological discernment. In both evaluations, her ability to think for herself theologically has been downplayed, and her public vagueness about her faith has been interpreted to negate her importance as a committed protector of the Protestants. It is clear, nevertheless, that her appreciation of the Protestant faith matured over the years through study, reflection, observation, and personal contacts. The path on which she started in her childhood, in no small regard thanks to Marguerite, led her to protect the faith that was considered the enemy of the Catholic French throne she loved. Renée had much to lose and her royal "buffer" alone would not protect her in the religious wars where much (also noble) blood was shed. The story of her religious maturation and the conflict of loyalties she faced between her religion and her royal and family obligations cannot be told apart from her marriage.

Religion and marriage were the two intertwined factors that determined Renée's life and the choices she had. In both realms she "disobeyed," regardless of her apparent surrender to the will of her king, her husband, and the papal-led church. Under the most repressive circumstances she carved herself freedom of choice in matters of faith and fought for that right for others as well. Perhaps to everybody's surprise, the initially obedient, quiet bride, willing servant of her king and country evolved in her marriage into an independent, courageous woman who would not allow her marital or dynastic bonds to dictate her decisions in issues of greater moment, such as religious freedom.

Before she was married, and before the completion of the engagement negotiations with its many twists and turns, Renée enjoyed some of the most carefree periods of her life, spending time with her frequently pregnant sister and going on a pilgrimage. As an infant Renée had been engaged to her cousin Gaston de Foix, but after his death, Charles of Austria, the future emperor of the Holy Roman Empire, emerged as fiancé in an arrangement by which he would surrender all his claims to Brittany in exchange for a handsome dowry – until François' own daughter was married to him. Plans for her marriage to Charles' brother Ferdinand also fell through. After a change in political

alliances, a new candidate for the hand of 12-year-old Renée emerged from the elector-
ate of Brandenburg, this time in exchange for François' vote in the upcoming imperial
elections. When it was clear that her former fiancé Charles would take the imperial
throne, as the Charles V (1519), this alliance was no longer beneficial for François,
whereas her betrothal to the king of Portugal just might be! Another competing candidate for the, by then, 13-year-old Renée was the widowed duke of Bourbon, one of
the most powerful princes in François' home territory. Complicated legal proceedings
over the possessions of the Bourbon lands after the death of the duke's wife Suzanne
made this union lose its appeal. In 1527, when Henry VIII of England announced his
wish to annul his marriage to Catherine of Aragon, Cardinal Wolsey again favored Renée
as his new bride, but Henry was intent on marrying Anne Boleyn. (The proposition was
rejected by the king's sister Marguerite out of loyalty to Henry's first wife, Catherine
of Aragon.) (See Puaux 1997, 17–19, 21–3, 37–9, 42–3, 63–7; Barton 1989, 11–12;
Rodocanachi 1896, 18–27.) After all these prominent candidates, the final choice was a
surprising letdown.

The ultimate decision may have been influenced by the accumulating difficulties and
public humiliation of the king. After the child-birth-exhausted Queen Claude died of
an infectious disease on July 26, 1524, François' adventures led him to be imprisoned
not once but twice, in Italy and in Spain. His release was negotiated by his mother Louise
and his sister Marguerite, who rescued the comatose king from Spain in 1525 (in
exchange for his two young sons). Back in the saddle, the king arranged a pleasing
remarriage of his widowed, 35-year-old sister Marguerite to Henri d'Albret (1503–55),
king of Navarre since 1517. She would offer continued protection for the Huguenots
from her new residence at the castle of Nerac, where among others Lefèvre d'Etaples
visited her.

Renée's bridegroom came from Italy: a Renaissance prince, Ercole d'Este, "il duca di
Ferrara," duke of Ferrara (1508–59) was the least impressive of all the candidates, but a
man whose alliance would keep the Italian duchy closer to the French throne (and
strengthen the Valois' claim to the duchies of Milan and Naples), bolster the French
position against both the Holy Roman Empire and England, and perhaps assist in deal-
ings with the pope. Renée, by her birthright, was a great "catch" for Ercole, while the
union must have been disappointing to the daughter of one king and sister-in-law of
another king – notwithstanding her husband's looks and charm. Moreover, in her marriage Renée would surrender her claims for her mother's territory of Brittany; from
far-away Ferrara she could hardly press claims on it.

The wedding was celebrated one month after the engagement in Paris, on June 28,
1528, with festivities lasting for weeks, before the couple traveled to Ferrara. The people
of Ferrara welcomed the new bride with cheer, but the duchess arrived in the plague-
stricken town in tears. (Similarly difficult journeys were made by other noble ladies who
were sent to foreign, even hostile lands. Warnicke 2000, 4, 7, 1–11.) She accepted her
"exile" as a mission from her king, but continued to subtly resist by surrounding herself
with all things and persons French and by refusing to even try to learn the language of
her new land.

According to her biographers, the match proved problematic on many accounts. The
20-year-old Ercole, a son of the beautiful, flamboyant, and irreverent Lucrezia Borgia
(1480–1519, daughter of Rodrigo Borja, later Pope Alexander VI) and Duke Alfonso of
Ferrara (1476–1534), a handsome, playful, and self-indulgent man, was cultivated in the

Renaissance spirit, and fancied himself a patron of the arts and literature. Renée, at eighteen, was frail and plain, with a serious streak to her that her husband, who was of very different moral character and upbringing, seemed to lack. Renée was interested in theology, Ercole in politics. Her keen mind and generous spirit, however, as well as her royal heritage eventually "captivated the initially unwilling Ercole". (Barton 1989, 12–13; Puaux 1997, 67–70.)

The couple's differences in appearance and interests did not bring them closer in the politically arranged marriage. Their religious differences in particular were to become the cause of major friction, as were their different political loyalties. Ercole's family was loyal to the pope (whom he had met at the age of 15) and invested in the welfare of their Italian duchy, whereas Renée remained French at heart and was intrigued by the new theology that disapproved of the papacy and the current papal-led church – and, thus, much of what Ferrara represented. Homesick from the start, Renée brought along as much of France as she could in her entourage and precious possessions. The duchess's "foreign" values and religious interests were not welcomed in her new home, least of all by her husband, who was especially annoyed by her French Protestant companion and counselor, Madame de Soubise.

The duchess took with her from France a book that had been commissioned for her religious education probably by her mother: The *Little Book of Prayer*, or the Flower Prayer Book, which consisted of 26 pages and 12 stories with illustrations, five of them featuring Renée, included the words for the Our Father, the Ave Maria, the Creed, and other standard prayers and devotions. The paintings were probably the work of a court painter, and the work may have been presented to the princess after her parents passed away, as revealed in the words of a prayer written for her: "My God, lean your ears to our voice: we beg You to welcome, with mercy, into your kingdom of peace and light the soul of your servants; King Louis, my father, and Queen Anne, my mother."

That Renée's clung to her French heritage, even to the point of not going so far as to try to learn the language of her new subjects, could be interpreted as an expression of defiance, unless, of course, she was simply unable to learn it (or, as Parker 2003, 8 says, she "loathed" Italy). She had surrendered to the circumstances of her foreign marriage with dignity but she remained French and chose to speak French. The lack of a common language maintained a gulf between the duchess and her husband and the people in Ferrara, as did her preferred association with mostly French-speaking and reform-minded people, both "alien" to the Catholic Italians of Ferrara. With her indiscriminate generosity and interest in alleviating human suffering, however, she won the affection of many in any event. She became known as a protector of those persecuted for the sake of religion, especially her compatriots and Protestants, but also others, including the Jewish community in Ferrara. Her Catholic husband was less than thrilled with this, or with Renée's spending. Under his watchful eyes and those of his papal friends, Renée created a safe haven for the Protestants in the court that was known as early as 1536. She espoused a role similar to that of Marguerite de Navarre and her daughter Jeanne d'Albret, who also "networked" and referred refugees and materials to each other; Marguerite guided several French reformers to Ferrara.

As with other ladies in prominent positions, Renée was expected to produce male heirs. After her first child miscarried in 1529, to everybody's relief, she gave birth, on November 16, 1531, to a healthy girl by the name of Anne (1531–1607), whose subsequent marriages, first to the ultra-Catholic family of the Guises in France and, later, to a French Protestant, kept her personally involved in the religious wars in France. She remained close to her mother, even if for a period of time her marriage to the Catholic Guise family placed her in the opposite camp to her mother who continued to involve herself with the Huguenots. Correspondence between the two retains important insights into the lives of the individuals as well as the religious scene in France. Two years after Anne's birth, on November 22, 1533, Renée gave birth to a son, Alfonso (1533–97), who would become the last of the dukes of Ferrara, Duke Alfonso II, godson of King François I. Another daughter, Leonora (Eleonore) (1537–81) was born on June 19,1537, a frail and delicate woman whose life intersected with that of the famous poet Torguato Tasso who immortalized her in his poems, she reigned for her brother Alfonso in his occasional absence. On Christmas Day, 1538 Renée gave birth to another son, Luigi (1538–86), who received baptismal gifts from the pope himself and would be invested as a cardinal at a young age. Some years later, in 1571, she gave birth to her last child, Lucrezia, who suffered an unhappy marriage with Francesco Maria, last duke of Urbino, was known for her intellectual power, and established an asylum for women separated from their husbands. Given that Renée gave birth to five live children who all survived to adulthood, she may have been less "frail" than has been assumed. (See Rodocanachi 1896, 88–91, 108–14; Barton 1989, 14–15.)

Renée fostered her children's education early on with the best (even if irreverent) of teachers. Over the years her court hosted an assembly of humanists, reformers, writers, artists, and other noteworthy individuals. Clément Marot (who translated the Psalms into French), was the most long-term refugee to seek sanctuary with her; the known critic of the pope and the Church arrived after the affair of the placards and remained with Renée as her secretary. But other well-known figures were also grateful for her hospitality, even if they did not stay so long. For instance, there was Bernardo Tasso, John Calvin, Vittoria Colonna the Marchesa di Pescara, Lavinia della Rovere (the grandniece of the pope Julius II), Bernardino Ochino (Capuchin leader and preacher), Fulvio Peregrino Morato (an acclaimed teacher), and his learned daughter, Olimpia Morata. Throughout this time, the duke fostered relations with the pope and welcomed members of the Inquisition to the palace, which became a scene for the battle between the Huguenots and the Jesuits.

Renée's associations with those who in the eyes of Rome were dissidents, and in the eyes of the Ferrarans foreigners, did not help in the affairs of the duchy where the d'Estes had a history of tense relationships with the papacy. After Duke Alfonso died, in October of 1534, Ercole took over the reins of government and needed to bargain (like his father before him) for papal confirmation of his authority. Meanwhile, as the duchy and his own position consumed Ercole's interests, his wife's persistent association with antipapal dissidents and her flaunted preference for "everything French" became both politically and maritally unacceptable. Ercole started to purge his court of its French, beginning with the expulsion of Madame de Soubise, the thorn in his flesh, on whom he blamed Renée's wanderings with the "wrong crowd," especially the Protestants. Madame de Soubise left, shamed and falsely accused for rumor mongering, but not without trying to arrange for Renée to join her at the king's temporary court in Lyon. Ercole's refusal to allow her to go, backed up with poor excuses about Renée's poor health, postpartum weakness, the inclement weather, etc., infuriated both the king and Renée, who was made a prisoner in her own castle. The situation so inflamed François that he sent his men to town, Marguerite of Navarre sent her bishop, and Jean Calvin himself arrived.

Throughout what were occasionally precarious times and tense marital and political situations, Renée managed, while putting on a good public face with her husband about the state of their marriage, to continue to host the impressive mix of personalities in her court. Among them, one of the most intriguing figures was Olimpia Morata. Olimpia, who would become one of the most literate and accomplished female writers of the time, was employed by Renée as a study companion to her daughter Anne. She honed her skills in the court, developing under Renée's wings into a skilled writer and translator. Unlike Renée, Olimpia soon came to profess her adherence to the Protestant faith in public, and in writing. After the situation changed in Ferrara with the arrival of the Inquisition (which had its special court in Ferrara from 1545), and Olimpia's and Renée's relationship cooled, Olimpia found her destiny in Germany, the homeland of her new husband. She stayed in contact with Anne, however.

It was not only on Renée's invitation or to seek sanctuary with her that all those who were notable for their part in the reform movement arrived at the Ferraran court. It was upon Ercole's invitation that another significant female guest, Vittoria Colonna (1490–1547), the female poet visited Ferrara from 1537 until 1538 (in time to assist Renée in the birth of her daughter Leonora in 1537). Vittoria was also passionate for a reform of the Catholic ways of observing faith and her associations with learned men sponsoring the reform of the Church made her suspect to the Inquisition as well. (See Puaux 1997, 158–62; Bainton 2001, 201–18; King 1991, 128–34, 143–4.) Interested in mysticism, she had become close to the Valdensians in Naples, a group quite Lutheran in doctrine but that envisioned reform from within the Catholic church. It was during Vittoria's visit that Bernardino Ochino and Ignatios Loyola, the founder of the Jesuit order, arrived. Vittoria wished to build a place of retreat in Ferrara for the Capucins, and at her instigation the charismatic Ochino actually preached with great success at Renée's court during Advent, echoing the views of Luther as he addressed the issue of the morality of the monks and emphasized the authority of Scripture and the laity's right to read it for themselves.

Other female associates and contemporaries of Vittoria, Caterina Cibo (a granddaughter of Innocent VIII), Giulia Gonzaga (a Valdensian), and Isabella Manriquez, had similar concerns to her own. (See King 1991, 153–44; Bainton 2001, 171–98.) They recognized some of the abuses in the Church needing to be addressed (for instance, the abuse of the indulgences and the theology of merit). Like Renée, Vittoria chose to shelter in her court those guilty of reformist agendas, without taking an active role herself. Like Marguerite de Navarre, and unlike the more dogmatically oriented Renée, Vittoria was interested in individual reform and the mystical aspects of faith. Age and other differences put aside (Renée was 27 and Vittoria 48), the ladies may have become friends during the visit filled with conversations about religious matters, though after Vittoria departed following her 10-month visit, there is no evidence of continued communications.

Days before Vittoria's departure, Ercole's aunt Isabella, the dowager marchioness of Mantua, paid a visit to Ercole's delight. (These happy times were followed for Renée by the birth of their son Luigi the following Christmas [1538].) Despite his good mood, Ercole denied his aunt's request to let Renée visit her in Mantua. The duchess was for all practical purposes a prisoner in the castle of Ferrara. In her growing isolation, she drew comfort from her friendship with Madame de Soubise's daughter Anne de Parthenay and her husband Antoine de Pons, both Protestants and fellow French. The potentially scandalously intimate friendship between Monsieur de Pons and Renée has been adjudged "the one wholly tender circumstance in Renée's life" (Ryley 1907, 282–3). (See Barton 1989, 32–6; Puaux 1997, 165–7, 181–3; Rodocanachi 1896, 98–103, 138–52; Valeria 1969, 7–8.) ("Monsieur Pons represents the solitary scandal of Renée's existence. Some writers do not like M. Pons" writes Ryley 1907, 282.) Letters between the duchess and Monsieur Pons reveal her special care for her friend and "cousin," and even suggest certain intimacy. And yet, "was their relationship more than platonic? Probably not." (Barton 1989, 34–6, 73; also Ryley 1907, 282–91.) Many of the letters were exchanged secretly during Monsieur Pons' stay in France – until the letters were confiscated by the suspicious duke who himself had suggested to the king of France to call the de Pons back home. When in Paris, Monsieur de Pons found himself in disfavor at court; his duchess was missing him. He returned to Ferrara and the duchess celebrated, but his wife had fled to Venice, after false accusations were circulated that she was spreading rumors about the duke's plans to harm the duchess. Inevitably, by 1543, Monsieur de Pons also had to leave, and they never met again.

The exiling of the de Pons signals increasing hardship in the duchess's life and the pressure that was being mounted on her by her husband. (For instance, for a period during the de Pons' absence she had enjoyed the company of Madame de la Roche, a French companion sent by Marguerite de Navarre herself. Once the new arrival's Protestant faith became apparent, however, she was sent back. "There would be no more French companions for the Duchess.") The duchess was increasingly isolated from her French and Protestant connections. Furthermore, in September 1541, she was sent to a castle in Consandolo about 15 miles away (an estate that, ironically, had been donated to her by the duke on July 8, 1541 as a sign of marital affection). The duchess' return to Ferrara would be prompted by the visit of Pope Paul III to the d'Este court in the spring of 1543.

In Consandolo the duchess devoted her time to study, her children's education, and correspondence, most of all with Calvin (from whom she repeatedly asked for Protestant female companions). Against her husband's orders, she never stopped collaborating with the Protestants. For instance, with her neighbor Galeatto Pico della Mirandola, she assisted the underground network that smuggled heretics to safety (including Ochino and Celio Curione in 1542). Her court in exile became a center for refuge and "secret Protestant preaching." The use and origins of a secret chapel have been debated in light of new excavations on the site, but its very existence and "plain appearance" (before the frescoes added in the nineteenth century) could provide important proof of Renée's Protestant faith. (See Roffi 1984, 264–7, passim.)

Ironically, the duchess' exile ended because of the visit of the new pope (from 1534), a friend of Ercole's father. Paul III's visit to Ferrara prompted the duke to call Renée back to entertain the pontiff's large entourage at the castle. The pope made it clear he wished the couple's separation to end, and gave Renée a golden rose and a ring as tokens of his friendship. (The warm relations between the d'Este family and the papal court are also indicated in the pope's proposal, albeit futile, that Renée's daughter Anne should marry his nephew.) In addition, he issued a letter guaranteeing that in all faith-related issues Renée would belong under the jurisdiction of the papal Inquisition rather than the local bishops. This privilege would turn out to be a double-edged sword as the duchess herself would become a suspect of the Inquisition that the new pope, Julius III, would wield heavily to eradicate heresy in the church.

There were further changes for Renée. In France the religious situation altered after François died in 1547 (followed by Marguerite in 1549) and his heir Henri II (1519–59) ascended to the throne. Renée became involved with the French scene more personally as Ercole, to her horror, betrothed their daughter Anne to the notoriously famous François de Lorraine, duke of Guise (1519–63). The wedding took place in December 1548.

During one of his visits to Venice, Ercole had made himself a patron of the Society of Jesus, whose members, in the aftermath of the Council of Trent (1545–63), had become the right arm of the pope and the "orthodox" Catholic faith; as a mobile spiritual army they were instrumental in the Inquisition procedures in many contexts including reenforcing Catholic theology and spirituality. Now, having secured an ultra-Catholic son-in-law, he called in the Jesuits (1548). Meanwhile, the duchess corresponded with Calvin in Geneva. With the duke and the duchess politically and religiously opposed, and their personal support lobbied by both sides, the battle between the Catholics and the Protestants came to a climax in Ferrara.

The duchess was under pressure from both Loyola and Calvin, and their respective followers. Both men saw it as imperative to their mission to ally with strategically positioned royal women, and both were extremely interested in the Duchess of Ferrara (see Blaisdell 1992, esp. 239). Neither man seemed to appreciate the delicacy of her public, and personal, position or the wisdom of her disinclination to commit to either side publicly. Her religious tolerance and indiscriminate help for the persecuted made both Loyola's and Calvin's blood boil, and they each blamed her for a lack of commitment. She did not care. "Although Calvin criticized her for her reticence and demanded that she make open profession of her faith, Renée firmly maintained the position of a crypto-Calvinist and apologetically recoiled from the demands that he made of her. Her reticence remained an issue between them, always". "In fact, Renée's ambivalence infuriated Calvin." (Blaisdell 1982, 79.) Furthermore, "Renée developed a less defined and more tolerant attitude toward religion, more akin to that of the French reformers of the earlier generation whom she had known in her youth, while her friend and mentor in Geneva became increasingly austere, intolerant and committed to an organization and a doctrine. Renée never openly embraced Protestantism" (Blaisdell 1972, 206–7).

Renée's persistence was remarkable, considering the pressure from the Inquisition and especially from her mentor and friend Calvin. She had met the reformer at least once, in 1536, the year of the publication of the *Institutes of the Christian Religion,* when he visited Ferrara under the pseudonym of Charles d'Espeville. The two of them corresponded through the years, and Calvin had great hopes that Renée would use her position to bolster the cause of reform. He had developed similarly close, personal long-distance relations with other noblewomen in strategic positions of authority, his mindset always on the successful completion of his mission to spread the Reformation in French-speaking regions. Aristocratic women such as Jeanne d'Albret, her mother Marguerite de Navarre, and Renée received his personal attention – and verbal whipping at times – along with the support of ministers he also sent to them from Geneva. The correspondence between Renée and Calvin was especially long and frequent; although some of the letters have been lost the attention he paid to her is clear in those that remain. As important as his mentorship was to her, though, in the end, Calvin may have needed Renée more for his mission than she needed him.

More than any other person, Calvin became Renée's personal connection with the Reformation, and she became a key individual in the objectives of his French policy. It is very significant that she seems to have thought of Calvin as her religious mentor and that they remained friends up until the time of his death in 1564. This is as much a testimony to Calvin's dynamism as to Renée's personal preference for the French Reform movement, even during her stay in Ferrara as Duchess. (Blaisdell 1982, 79. Also ibid., 68–81)

(See Blaisdell 1992, 236–7, 245, 248.)

Her long-term relationship with Calvin can be considered as weighty evidence of Renée's reformed faith. The status he gave to her in his mission – and the admonitory style he adopted in his pastoral care of women – are demonstrated in a statement he made in a letter to her: "Considering the rank and preeminence which God has given you [Renée], it appears that all of us whom the Lord in His goodness has called to be ministers of the Holy Word ought to be especially diligent in concerning ourselves with you because, far more than persons of private rank, you are able to promote the Kingdom of God." (Blaisdell 1982, 40; Calvin à la Duchesse de Ferrare n.d. CO XI, col 325–6, 1541.) Renée would receive reproachful reminders about her responsibilities for the kingdom of God throughout the 20 years or so of their correspondence (Barton 1989; Blaisdell 1972). (On Calvin and Renée, see Puaux 1997, 145–51, 279–82; Rodocanachi 1896, 103–27; Valeria 1969, 8–9; Bates 1872, 64–84; Barton 1989.)

Many sparks flew between Renée and Calvin during the years when she suffered under the Inquisition and, in Calvin's view, failed the Protestant cause and gave the Catholic observers reason to rejoice over her apparent, forced return to the faith of the papal church. What exactly happened is an intriguing story that gives insights into Renée's character and to the ways the Protestant faith could survive in a predominantly Catholic context, often at great personal cost.

Given the visibility of Renée's protective work with the Huguenots, on the one hand, and the court's ties with the Jesuits and the pope, on the other, it is not surprising that Ferrara became a scene of the Inquisition and religious persecution, or that the duchess in particular, over whose intellectual and religious life Ercole seemed to have no authority, and whose royal blood made it difficult for anyone to discipline her, was the main target of the examinations and purges of the court. She was attacked twice, first relatively inconspicuously in 1536, and for the second time in 1554 in a systematically executed plot by the papal theologians with the full support of her own husband. To a French princess the very notion of being scrutinized or judged in public was horrifying (although she had had a forewarning of what could happen when she witnessed the trial of Marguerite de Navarre in her youth). During the interrogations that targeted her, her staff and associates, and her children, Renée's commitment and sincerity were sorely tested, and her course of action left observers ambivalent and confused.

Even as early as 1536, when the first persecution of Protestants in the court of Ferrara took place, the Inquisition was involved: in his desire to take over the control in his court and rid his household of the significant Lutheran and Calvinist presence for good, Ercole had needed their help. An opportunity had arisen on Good Friday, 1536, when, after a performance at the court, one of the singers from Renée's household, Chonnet de Bouchefort, shouted out blasphemies about the Mass and the Lord's Supper. This was embarrassing to all, but especially to the duke. Letters were sent to Rome, Lyon, and Navarre from both sides, as the machinery of French and Italian diplomacy started to react to the possibly grave complications of the incident. The king of France was called on to intervene, but he reminded Ercole of who it was to whom he was married. Under torture the singer, named Zanetto (whose shady past included encounters with the law), implicated loyal members of the duchess' court as his accomplices. Instead of sending the prisoners to the pope's court, Ercole stalled and had them all, including Renée's confidant and long-term treasurer Jean Cornillau, interrogated in Ferrara. Renée insisted on her own innocence and that of her court. Regardless of the support of her "own" bishops sent from France to stand by her, she faced the wrath of her husband and the Inquisition. She proceeded to elicit help from the queen of Navarre and "her" cardinals and the papal nuncio. Meanwhile Ercole was cold shouldered by both Rome and Paris and told to handle the issue with the dissidents "domestically" with his spouse.

As if things were not complicated enough, one of the prisoners escaped, perhaps with the help of the duchess. The facts about who escaped and with whom are far from clear, even Calvin and Marot have been indicated. What is known for sure is that an accused heretic escaped with the help of someone sympathetic to the Huguenot cause. Ercole, temporarily reconciled with his wife following the birth of their daughter Leonora in 1537, was willing to settle, or even drop the case, but the Inquisition was not. Renée remained under suspicion and surveillance, along with the others, as the Inquisition maintained a watching brief at the court. (The years 1539 and 1540 saw an increase in censorship in Ferrara, extending to the Jewish community as well; Blaisdell [1972, 209–10.]) She was not allowed to leave the duchy even to attend the wedding of François I's daughter. Nevertheless, it seems that until 1548 Renée and Ercole maintained a fragile agreement about each other's religious liberty, dependent on Renée not openly renouncing the faith of the d'Estes. This arrangement frustrated both her spiritual mentor, Calvin, and her husband who had to tolerate the continuous presence of the dissidents in his court and in close contact with his wife. The situation changed, however, after the deaths of François I and Marguerite de Navarre.

With Henri II's accession to the throne of France in 1547 the era of the Inquisition truly began. In Ferrara the early symptoms of this included the ousting of the openly Protestant Olimpia Morata. Duke Ercole initiated a systematic persecution of those favoring the reformed religion. The first martyr was Fanino Fanini da Faenza, also known as Camillo Fannio, who had studied the Scriptures in Italian translation and come to Ferrara to preach "heresy." Released from the prison after his recantation, he resumed preaching and was imprisoned again. Renée interceded on his behalf with Rome, but to no avail. Fanino was tortured and executed on August 22, 1550. His body was burned and the ashes thrown into the river as a warning to others. Further martyrs would follow.

The second persecution took place quite soon after this tragedy. By May 1551 Ercole was boasting to the pope that his court was free from Protestant heresy. Mathew Ory, a Dominican Inquisitor, had been sent to the court to address the embarrassing situation of the king's aunt, the duchess. For the same reason a Jesuit named Pelletier had arrived earlier with a mission to become the duke's confidant, isolate the duchess, and rid the court of heretics. Ercole's words were premature, however, not least because of the depth of the duchess's involvement, the extensiveness of which he may have been in denial about, until he was presented with an undeniable proof: on January 16, 1554, Renée refused the last rites to her servant Ippolito Putti, and at Easter that year she forbade her daughters from making a confession. These were bold acts, and striking from the mother of a new bishop: Luigi d'Este had been made the bishop of Ferrara in December 1553. To Ercole, it was the last straw, which led him to banish all the reformed from his court on March 18, 1554 – although the order was never fully executed. He also asked for help from the king of France (on March 27, 1554).

Signing his letter "Your humble and obedient servant, Ercole d'Este, Duke of Ferrara," Ercole wrote to Henri II on March 27, 1554 grieving over his wife's involvement with the Lutheran preachers. After reflecting on Renée's actions with Putti and their daughters, he stated,

> Seeing her so obstinately determined to act against the honor of God and bringing constant infamy upon my house, I begged her thousands and thousands of times that for the love of God and for the reputation of our posterity, she would renounce her fantastic heresy, not bothering her head anymore with what she heard from her ribald preachers . . . that she ought to follow the religion of her father and mother, and that of her sister, Your Majesty's mother . . .
>
> I resolved to say to Madam in all kindness that I wished absolutely for my daughters to hear mass regularly, confess and communicate at Easter; . . . The upshot of that was that she said the mass is idolatry, with other words I am too ashamed to repeat, exhorting my daughters in my presence not to obey me. (In Barton 1989, 84–7; from Archivo storico italiano 13:417–20. Biblioteque Nationale, fonds française 3126, fols 56–60)

Ercole asked the king to send a French theologian to Ferrara to draw his French wife back from "her enormous heresy." He also wished the king to be forceful: "Do not refrain from using very brusque words in your letter to her. I have found in her such incredible obstinacy and hardness of heart that I doubt if the Lord should put out his holy hand, she would return from her heresy" (ibid.). What more convincing proof could there be of Renée's Protestant commitment and her fortitude than these words from her own husband!

In 1554 the situation became more heated as the duke made increasing attempts to control the duchess and her activities in the religious field. Renée was pressured to attend Mass in public, and she became more and more isolated under the watchful eyes of her husband and his priests. One can appreciate Ercole's point: "To have so prominent a protectress of the heterodox in so prominent a court as Ferrara was intolerable in the inquisitorial climate that prevailed on the eve of the Council of Trent" and it became necessary to send French inquisitors "whose special mission was to harness the runaway princess" (King 1991, 141–2). Similarly Calvin saw it as urgent that he should send preachers from Geneva to "inspire her" in a battle that could have led to martyrdom, had she not been of royal blood and the subject of the French king (Blaisdell 1972, 210).

In June and August of 1554 Renée was interrogated (as Anne had warned her she would inevitably be if she remained resistant); she was resistant to the inquisitors and the first interviews were unsuccessful. On September 7 she was condemned to imprisonment as a heretic. On September 13 Loyola received reports that there was no hope for the duchess' conversion; she had been refusing the confessors who were sent for her. She was kept under house arrest, isolated in a neighboring castle, where she was cut off from the world and her children, her two young daughters having been sent to a convent. She had no books and only two attendants, who had orders to "touch the person of the lady" if necessary. By mid-September there were rumors that the duchess was surrendering. Hopeful reports for the Catholics that she was receiving Mass were countered with affirmations of her resistance. Help had been dispatched to Renée from France. Lyon Jamet, her friend arrived from Geneva with a letter, as did François de Morel, providing yet more proof of Renée's importance to Calvin who had sent him. In 1555 yet another man, Antonio Caracciolo, was sent by Calvin to meet Renée in secret, with a letter of encouragement. Calvin wanted to fortify the duchess as well as to prepare her for martyrdom as she was brought to the cardinal's palace and from there to the palace of justice for interrogation and to be forced to listen to Ory's sermons. If Ercole had at first wanted only outward conformity, he now demanded Renée's full return to the Catholic faith if she wished to keep her children.

The ordeal was an unimaginable blow to the princess's ego, and whilst enduring it she had many considerations weighing upon her. "It appears that only when imprisonment and separation from her children became unbearable for Renée did she capitulate to the demands of the Duke and Pelletier" (Blaisdell 1972, 217–18). Yet she was also concerned to protect her subjects. Calvin's chastising letters were of little help. On September 21 the duchess asked for a priest and to make confession. Her daughters were returned to her. In Calvin's eyes (as he wrote in a letter of November 1, 1554) the duchess had "fallen." For her part, Renée was glad to have her children returned to her and resume her position in the court.

Her decision can be appreciated with sympathy: "by giving in to the demands of orthodox conformity she gained her freedom and the chance to resume her life at court in Ferrara, whereas by remaining intransigent she would risk compromising her royal dignity and everything she held most dear" (King 1991, 218). Or, seen another way, "her 'conversion' to Catholic orthodoxy was surely a superficial accommodation to events." We do not know what her state of mind was for sure, but it would be unreasonable to assume that she had a complete change of heart and mind in a matter of days – especially given her life-long association with the Protestant faith. According to the Jesuit records, during the period in which she was under scrutiny, hundreds of letters and vernacular books (in German and Italian) of suspicious nature had been found from her rooms and burned immediately (Blaisdell 1972, 216–17). The most convincing extant evidence of her Reformed faith comes from her later correspondence with Calvin, fragments of her letters surviving (see below, her letter from March 1564).

In some assessments of Renée's commitment to Calvin's theology, and in light of her public surrender, doubts have been raised about her ability to understand the depth of theological issues and argumentation, doubts based mainly on observations on her mediocre letter-writing skills. (Valeria 1969, 58–61.) At the same time, whatever limits there were to her nuanced understanding of Calvin's teachings, Renée embraced and sponsored the Protestant faith in her rescue mission for decades even though she cannot have failed to be aware of the dangers involved. From all the evidence, she was Calvin's disciple and associate, who saw it wise to confirm to the rituals of the Catholic faith outwardly, assuming the freedom to practice the faith of her heart in private. ("She remained at heart a Calvinist, but attended mass and in other ways conformed to the rites and ceremonies of the Church of Rome" [Fawcett 1905, 271].) She was theologically cultivated and informed enough to discern theological differences, while she was also sincerely religious with an exceptional openness about spiritual practices. She was also stubborn, willful and politically shrewd. She could smell manipulation, and she could manipulate the situation herself as well. As her enduring principle we can name her unprejudiced protection of the religious freedom of others as well as herself.

Whether or not Renée had been hypocritical in her recantation "is a moot question. She had done the only thing possible under the circumstances" (Barton 1989, 110). Instead of reading her action as sign of weakness, we might complement her for her clever handling of the precarious situation and her clear-headed strategy for her own survival and that of others. Her royal status and her character must also be taken into account in analyzing her actions. "Renée was not as a rule a dissimulator." Furthermore, she liked to "justify herself in the name of her royal standing." Losing the support of the French king would have been unfathomable to her. She had to surrender for the sake of appearances, even if she did not surrender in her heart (Blaisdell 1972, 219).

Her last years in Ferrara were less eventful. She continued to spend money on the extravagances of court life and correspond with Calvin who still had big hopes for her. In his letter of February 2, 1555, signed under his pseudonym Charles d'Espeville, he scolded Renée and urged her to persevere, trusting that God, who was testing her, would listen to her groans (Barton 1989, 273, 101–3, 114–15, 132–3), and he adopted a similar tone in his fifth extant letter, dated July 29, 1558. At the end of her life, Renée would become involved in the bloody events that shaped the future of Catholics and Protestants in France. In 1559, the year in which Henri II died, Ercole also passed away, and his son Alfonso II (1533–97) succeeded to the throne. Alfonso gave his mother an ultimatum: she could either abandon the reformed faith or leave Ferrara. Renée left Ferrara in September 1560, after 32 years. The decision was not a matter of course. She knew that her departure would deprive those persecuted for their faith from her protection. Calvin's advice to her was ambiguous (1559): "Jesus Christ certainly deserves that you should forget both France and Ferrara for him" (Barton 1989, 151–3, see also 150).

She settled in a castle in Montargis where she governed as "la Dame de Montargis" and created another fortress for both persecuted Huguenots and Catholics. In 1561 she asked for a pastor from Geneva, and François de Morel was sent. "Morel's mission must be considered one of the most significant pieces of available evidence of Renée's religious position at that time" (Blaisdell 1972, 215). The two would clash at times, over noble-women's rights to participate in politics and church affairs, for instance, over religious organization at Montargis, and over her household's conduct in general. Calvin got to hear both sides: Renée complained to Calvin about de Morel's lack of respect for her, and de Morel expressed his outrage over Renée's desire to attend synods and involve herself in the affairs of the church: "if we let females mix in our affairs, we will become the laughing stock of Anabaptists and papists alike" he cried! Renée defended herself, reminding Calvin that she had never expected special treatment (even if she could have expected it) and that she had even left her children to follow God's path, daring at the same time to wonder why only men could serve in the Consistory (Barton 1989, 214–17, 200–1, 247). (For Renée's time in France, see Audibert 1972, 38–43; Puaux 1997, 232–7, 254–60; Rodocanachi 1896, 401–22, 319–37.)

Renée's overall position in France was difficult. Related by blood to the crown, and affiliated through her daughter Anne's marriage to the Catholic de Guises, her personal religious commitment was with the "heretics." "She always felt the strong pull of family loyalty, and her Calvinist sympathies frequently competed and interfered with her loyalties to the royal family and her children." To add to the pressure, "Calvin gave her no peace on the subject of her loyalty to her son-in-law" (Blaisdell 1982, 82). Her son-in-law's instrumental role in the beginning of the religious wars in France was a scandalous problem (see her letter of March 1564 below).

When, in 1562, the Colloquy of Poissy was followed by an edict of toleration that promised the Huguenots minimal rights and brought a period free from persecution, Renée hurried back to Montargis to further build up the Protestant city she had established there. Only 40 days after the Colloquy, however, her son-in-law the duke of Guise went hunting and murdered a barn-full of worshipping Huguenots at Vassy 1562. The religious war was on. Determined to stop the violence and bring order to her town, Renée closed the gates of Montargis, hanged a group of men found guilty of plotting a massacre, and established an order for freedom of worship for both Huguenots and Catholics whom she welcomed to the town. Montargis became known as a place of refuge, and she for a heroism and generous charity that inspired reformers to dedicate works to her, such as, for instance, Théodore de Bèze's edition of Calvin's works (Blaisdell 1972, 206).

Montargis was not immune to the violence of the religious wars, however, neither internally nor externally. In an effort to appease the internal situation in the castle, Renée stopped worshipping with the Huguenots. She forbade assembly for any reason and asked the Huguenot princes for support troops. Her daughter Anne paid a visit, urging her to send the Huguenots away and return to the Catholic faith (or be sent to a convent). She was followed by the young king himself, Charles IX, and by the duke of Guise. As chaos and destruction ensued, the duchess used all her royal authority and even threatened to throw herself first to the slaughter rather than let the Huguenots be murdered in her castle. "She maintained that in France she was subject to no one but the King." She also "obtained a proclamation from the king ordering, under penalty of death, that no one should be interfered with in the practice of either religion" (Fawcett 1905, 287–90; Barton 1989, 178–82).

Her position of tolerance in religious matters was evidenced when her dreaded son-in-law was assassinated. She rushed to the deathbed of a man Calvin had already envisioned in the flames of hell. The duchess of Guise, Anne d'Este, who had been raised as a Protestant, experienced a temporary change of heart: instead of continuing to be a moderating influence between different parties, she became a leader among the Catholic ladies as she thirsted for revenge for her Catholic husband's death. Along with her son Henri she wanted to hurt the very people her mother wished to protect. Even Renée had to defend herself against accusations of being involved in the murder of the duke of Guise, in which her good friend and leader of the Huguenots, Coligny was implicated and found guilty.

Calvin tried to comfort her:

> I know, Madame, how God has strengthened you during the rudest assaults and how by God's grace you have courageously resisted all temptations, not being shamed to bear the opprobrium of Jesus Christ . . . I know also that you have been, as it were, a nursing mother to those poor, persecuted brothers and sisters who did not know where to go. I know that a princess, considering only the things of the world, would have been ashamed and taken it almost as an insult that her castle should have been called God's hostelry. But I cannot pay you a higher compliment than in expressing myself thus, to recognize and commend the humanity you have exercised toward the children of God who found refuge with you. (Barton 1989, 190–2)

Calvin's last letter to Renée, dictated on his death bed, reminded her of her influence, once again, and in it he uttered his last command: "I am confident that you will do your whole duty according to your zeal for having God served and honored more" (April 4, 1564, in Barton 1989, 222). Calvin died less than two months later, in late May 1564.

The final words of a rare surviving letter from the duchess to the reformer, sent shortly before his death on March 1564, indicate the volume of letters exchanged between the two over the years, and may explain why the bulk of her letters did not survive:

> Monsieur Calvin, all these concerns have caused me to be prolix in this letter and in others which I have written you from time to time, and which I have begged you to burn, as I now do with this one. And I beg you to continue to write to me freely whatever seems good to you, which I shall always receive gladly. (Barton 1989, 218; see p. 242, note 2)

The long letter – "a paraphrase," "reconstructed from a number of sources" (Barton 1989, 213–18) – reveals her independent spirit and sense of authority in her own territory, while she also expresses her trust in Calvin's continuing guidance, which she would "take or leave" as seemed fit in her precarious situation. As she wrote:

> Monsieur Calvin, I was not able to answer your letters of 8 and 24 January immediately because I was preparing to return to the court at Fontaine-bleau to finish some necessary business . . .
>
> The reason I left there before the king was my being forbidden to have preaching there, as I had for several days. It was refused me not only in the house of the king but also in one I had bought in the village and had lent to be used for assemblies when I was not at court. What particularly hurt me was that this happened at the solicitation of a husband and wife who are communicants and who have ministers . . .
>
> As to the present and the New Year's gift you sent me, I received it with much pleasure . . .
>
> Now I must tell you, first, that I read your advice in regard to my subjects and my household. As to my subjects, I began the work long ago and am striving to complete it, if it pleases God. As to the matter of administering justice and to the daily subsistence to the poor . . . and the providing against vice and scandals generally, you will hear all about this . . . Those matters will be settled by whatever means you advice and by a good arrangement which you will suggest for the future. (Barton 1989, 214)

> I wish you could be here to see and understand what goes on better than I can describe it. I realize that the remonstrances you send me are necessary in order to maintain the church, and I wish that my judgment and intelligence were greater; but according to the qualities God has given me and the advice you have sent me through messengers and letters, it seems to me that so many ministers and people coming here, each one shouting his opinion, are unnecessary. (Barton 1989, 215)

The letter gives insights into her battles as a female ruler who was excluded from consistory meetings. It also reveals her admiration of other female rulers protecting the reformed faith, and speaks of her own difficulty in balancing her religious commitment, her political responsibilities, and her maternal duties and affections. She complains about her treatment at the hands of de Colognes, a man sent by Calvin who had forbidden her to attend consistory meetings, among other things.

> Then he told me it was unnecessary for women to attend, not even me (although I knew that the queen of Navarre, Madame the admiral's wife, and Madame de Roye took their places in the consistories, and I felt that the prerogatives of my house should be observed.)

I did not insist . . .

As to the members of my household, most of them are of the religion and are communicants. Some few are not yet Reformed, but I hope God will draw them to himself. (Barton 1989, 214.)

Interestingly, she mentions Jeanne d'Albret, in great admiration:

the lady is so zealous and has such sound judgment on most things that I admire her. As the late queen of Navarre [Marguerite] her mother was the first princess of the kingdom to favor the gospel, it may be that the present queen of Navarre will complete the work by establishing it in her kingdom. She is well equal to that task. I love her with a mother's love and praise the graces God has bestowed upon her. (Barton 1989, 216)

The fate of her son-in-law and Calvin's judgment of him gave the duchess an opportunity to address suspicions about her "maternal affections" and suggest her view of divine damnation and grace. She would rather err on the side of grace than judgment:

As to my late son-in-law, it seems to me that there is more than enough evidence to judge whether I gave up my beliefs on his account in any way. It was he who yielded, to protect those of the religion here . . . There are other extenuating facts which other people do not want known and which I say before God that I know to be the truth. (Barton 1989, 215)

I know that my son-in-law did persecute, but I do not know nor do I believe (to express myself freely to you) that he was a reprobate by divine judgment. For he gave signs to the contrary before he died, but people do not want that to be spoken of . . .

I know I have been hated and held in abomination by many because he was my son-in-law . . .

If they say that my outlook is distorted because of my affection for my late son-in-law, I can answer that I was never so passionately devoted to him or to my own children. Perhaps my accusers have not considered that I left my children to follow the path on which God has led me. (ibid., 216, 217)

The letter reveals her commitment to the Protestant faith and the integrity with which she fought her battles and defended others. She assumed no special privileges, nor did she think she could judge others or God's will with others. She was committed to following God's will, as she discerned it, in her own life, as much as she was committed to avoiding bloodshed and martyrdom. She wrote,

As for thinking that I or anyone in my household should be considered privileged, I assure you that I have never required or wished for special treatment, and that I have had so few privileges among the faithful that whatever affects me is ignored or disregarded. My ladies and attendants have been put in the worst places or even driven away at banquets and festivals. (Barton 1989, 214)

Furthermore, "I have never requested from ministers whom I have heard suggest it, that they should pray for me or for any other person." What is more,

I am not one of those who pray or cause prayers to be made for those who are no longer in the world. I know there are those who say that everyone who is against the religion is bad. I grant that that may be so, but I do not know whether or not God may call them so. It is not my business to complain of them. . . . but God commands us to give testimony before God's creatures by our manner of living, and I am ready to do so if it please God. As to what I have heard charged upon the ministers and children of God, I have not remained silent but have taken it upon myself to defend them with more care than I have taken to defend myself. I know that there are those who threaten to banish them from the kingdom. Therefore we ought not to do so or say things that will make is possible for them to accomplish their designs. (Barton 1989, 217–18)

In the years following the assassination of the duke of Guise (1563) and the blood-shed in Orléans, and as the second religious war (1568–70) ensued, Montargis ceased to be a safe haven for the Huguenots, or even the duchess herself. In preparation for the assaults by the royal army duchess provided the escaping Huguenots (over 400 of whom had been living with her) with wagons and supplies. Following this turmoil, and in an effort to bring peace, in 1565, the wife and the mother of the murdered duke of Guise and other veiled women approached the young king Charles IX with demands for justice. A reconciliation took place in 1566 in Moulins. Coligny was deemed innocent, and Anne d'Este and Cardinal Guise promised no longer to bear malice. Not long after this Condé was assassinated and Montmorency died. Anne remarried, this time to an enemy of the Guise, Jacques de Savoie, duke of Nemours (1531–85), with whom Anne returned to the Protestant faith. A temporary peace in 1570 gave the Huguenots freedom of worship in towns in their possession. The Synod of La Rochelle in 1571 finally recognized the first Huguenot confession of faith.

The worst was not over, however. Between August 18 and 25, 1572 thousands of Huguenots would be killed in a massacre following shortly after the wedding of Marguerite de Valois (1533–1615), sister of the French king, to Henri de Navarre (1553–1610), king regnant of Navarre and the future Henri IV of France. Paris was full of noble and prominent Huguenot wedding guests and their retainers who were killed in a devious plot which spawned a blood bath that swept through the provinces in the following months. Fingers have pointed to the queen mother, Catherine de Médicis, widow of the Valois King Henri II (d.1559) as the mastermind of plot, but this remains the subject of debate. It has also been speculated that Anne de Guise may have been involved. Renée herself may have been in Paris at the time, but she was not involved in the plot.

Renée returned to Montargis and maintained a low profile, her daughter Anne begging her in vain to attend Mass. After her son Luigi, the bishop of Ferrara, became ill, he was brought to Paris and Renée returned to take care of him, until she herself collapsed with fever and had to be taken home to Montargis in April 1574, too weak to attend the funeral of Charles IX who died in the following month on May 30. Her last years in her court all but forgotten were sad. She may have been disappointed that all her children except Anne remained in the Catholic faith (Luigi even becoming a cardinal).

Renée died of pneumonia and dysentery three years after the St Batholomew's Day massacre, on June 15, 1575. She was buried at her castle at Montargis without reference to Ferrara but simply with words: "Renée de France, Duchesse de Chartres, Comtesse de Gisors et Dame de Montargis." It fell to her son Luigi to handle the delicate matter of arranging the burial of his royal mother who had been so scandalously involved with the "heretics" and the perceived enemies of the Catholic thrones of France and Italy. Her will (of which there are three versions) requested a burial with no traditional Catholic ceremonies. Her son compromised and ordered a brief mourning but omitted official mourning services. The duchess was apparently buried in a locked wooden coffin, carried without pomp and with only her servants and ladies and gentlemen of her choice present. Henry offered a brief memorial in Paris before retreating to the country to mourn his aunt.

Conclusion

Looking at Renée's lifelong involvement with the Huguenots and the Reformed faith, and the political entanglements and the multiple concerns she had to weigh in every decision she made, Renée's story unfolds as a complex history of a woman involved in the religious warfare both on private and public levels. She leaves a picture of an independent woman with tenacity and the ability to engage the broader picture in deliberating her own actions in a dangerous situation. She found a way to take the lead and remain loyal in a manner with which she was comfortable and successful.

> One may criticize Renée's inability to take an open stand for the Huguenots, who actually had her sympathies, but one cannot ignore her loyalty to the royal tradition in which she was born and raised. As hard as he tried, Calvin never succeeded in convincing Renée to declare openly for the Reformed church as her cousin Jeanne d'Albret had done. (Blaisdell 1982, 78)

Furthermore, while she was widely sought after for protection, "at the time when the Calvinist movement recruited leaders from among the members of the French nobility, Renée recoiled from leadership." Yet, in all that she did and represented, "Calvin considered her one of the key people in his plan to win over France" (ibid.).

Even if she never confessed the Protestant faith publicly in word, she did so in deeds. Her will was the last testimony of her private faith; it included a long confession of her faith in which she reveals herself to be a follower of Calvin. It also included a personal farewell to her children. She exhorted

> Messieurs and Mesdames her children, in the name of God, to read and listen to the word of God, in which they will find all manner of consolation and the true rule by which they ought to conduct their lives in order to gain that eternal life promised to us in that word, praying in the name of the Father, the Son, and the Holy Spirit that he may be gracious to all. (Renée in Barton 1989, 229).

(On the discussion of her will see Blaisdell 1972, 219–20, and for its text and further information see Fontana 1889–99 Vol. 3, 325–41.)

She died believing in God's protection and deliverance. When she was still young she had witnessed religious persecution and the price to be paid for confessing the evangelical faith in a predominantly Catholic context during the most dangerous times. She had personally experienced interrogation and imprisonment and separation from her children for the sake of her faith. She had seen people being killed for their faith. Yet she had continued to associate herself with the persecuted throughout her adult life. Her private faith, which she guarded, apparently sustained her through these difficulties and did not change with political circumstances, no matter what rituals she chose to observe.

As well as her faith, her political savvy also protected and guided her. For instance, she "openly sympathized with the Huguenot Cause, at the same time avoiding serious confrontation by quietly remaining in the background of the struggles at court between the Catholic–Guise and Protestant–Bourbon factions." (Blaisdell 1972, 220–5.) In other words,

> Renée knew exactly how far it was safe to her to venture, given her royal position and the location of her lands. While she never made a public statement of her position, she died and was buried according to the practices of the Reformed church, a personal wish that ran counter to that of her children and the royal family who tried to cover up the events of her death and burial in 1575. (Blaisdell 1982, 82)

Like Marguerite de Navarre, another powerful woman criticized for vacillating or for crypto-Protestantism, Renée could be complemented for her astute realism and survival instincts and her commitment not to allow religion to be an instrument of death, but rather of hope. In the crossfire between Calvin and Loyola and their respective disciples, she remained consistent, through the years, in her peaceful manner of living out her own faith and using her assets to defend the right of other individuals to worship, and live, as they chose.

A Word about Sources and References

See Puaux 1997, Rodocanachi 1896/1970, and Barton 1989 for core biographical informa-
tion, and the bibliography for the description of other main sources.

For biographical information and interpretation of Renée's role as a reformer, see Bainton 1971/2001 and Blaisdell 1972 and 1982. For important biographical studies in French, see Puaux 1997 and Rodocanachi 1896, reprinted in 1970. For a study in English, see Barton 1989, who focuses on the duchess' relationship with Calvin and provides most helpful translations of their correspondence. Other works with detailed facts – and at times biased interpretation – come from Fontana 1889–99 (three volumes), Bates 1872, Fawcett 1905, Ryley 1907, and Weitzel 1883, and the anonymously written *Some Memorials of Renée of France, Duchess of Ferrara* 1859. A short "ecumenical" introduction is offered by Audibert 1972, and a most interesting debate about her Huguenot status by Valeria 1969. (In the spirit of this book's agenda to highlight women's works, some of the sources that appear less academically rigorous were valuable for their insights and as being the work of women who had not benefited from the scholarly training of their male contemporaries and still were somewhat uncertain about publishing with their own name.)

CHAPTER 12

Olimpia Fulvia Morata, 1526/27– 1555 – An Italian Scholar

Olimpia Fulvia Morata

Olimpia Fulvia Morata, 1526/27–55

PARENTS
- Fulvio Pellegrino Morato (1483–1548)
- Lucrezia Gozi Morata

SIBLINGS
- Three sisters and one brother, names unknown

SPOUSE (1549 OR 1550–55)
- Andreas Grunthler (c.1518–55)

CHILDREN
- None

Introduction

She was raised in a court of unmatched splendor. She was the childhood companion of nobility. A brilliant scholar, she gave public lectures on Cicero, wrote commentaries on Homer, and composed poems, dialogues, and orations in both Latin and Greek. She was one of the most sophisticated and flexible Latin stylists of her age. She was also a Protestant in papal lands, a profound student of the Bible, who underwent a crisis of faith to emerge stronger. Thrown into disfavor at court, she married for love and love of learning. In search of religious freedom, she and her husband went over the Alps to Germany. There she communicated with leading Reformation theologians, continued her studies, wrestled with the mysteries of predestination and the Eucharist, and wrote Greek poems that won praise across Europe. (Parker 2003, 1)

Olimpia Morata's recognized gifts and laudable use of her intellect and pen set her apart among her contemporaries, men or women.

Though her gifts were undeniable, Olimpia's sex posed an obstacle for many. The epitaph on her grave, by Jérôme Angenoust, demonstrates exactly this: "Nature denied you nothing of all her gifts with one exception: that you were a woman" (Parker 2003, 213). Just like any other woman who ventured into the public forum preserved for men, despite – and because of – her learning, Olimpia needed to redefine herself as a woman:

> Never did the same thing please the hearts of all,
> And never did Zeus grant the same mind to all . . .
> And I, though born female, have left feminine things,
> yarn, shuttle, loom-threads, and work-baskets.
> I admire the flowery meadow of the Muses,
> and the pleasant choruses of twin-peaked Parnassus.
> Other women perhaps delight in other things.
> These are my glory, these my delight.
> (Olympia Morata in Parker 2003 [OM/Parker], 179)

What started under promising stars ended in tragedy with her premature death and the destruction of most of her literary works. She experienced the horrors of the Inquisition in Ferrara and was an eyewitness to the damage of religious wars in Germany. The religious wars cost her her writings, her possessions, and her strength. Her death from illness before the age of 30 was hastened by her misfortunes. "After her death she was attacked as a 'Calvinist Amazon' but other women scholars viewed her as a light shining in the darkness" (Parker 2003, 1, 2).

As a highly learned classical scholar, qualified even to teach, Olimpia Morata was a rare individual among sixteenth-century Protestant women. Learning and teaching (in private) were her passions and shaped her identity. She found solace and inspiration from literature and scholarship and wished to lead other women to similar fountains. Her life intersected with other influential women of the period, especially Renée de France and her daughter Anne d'Este (Anne de Guise by her first marriage), as well as with some of the most learned men in Italy and Germany. Olimpia's contributions as a scholar have been largely neglected, however. In Germany, her final resting place, she has of late been commemorated as one of the first learned women worthy of a teaching position. She is honored for her academic merits in, for example, the University of Heidelberg, which offers an "Olympia Morata Program," and also at the "Olympia Morata Gymnasium" in Schweinfurt (which was founded in 1878 and renamed in her honor in 1956). In her native, predominantly Catholic, Italy the memory of this learned woman is as being Catholic rather than Protestant, as is the case in Catholic Germany. Appraisals of her life reflect in many ways Olimpia's perpetual position as a member of a minority – as a woman, as a learned woman, as a Protestant, and as a foreigner. Titles such as the

"Calvinist Amazon" from her contemporaries were not flattering but indicative of her outstanding talents and exceptional standing (which evoked the admiration of such learned individuals as, Anna Maria van Schurman and Goethe).

Olimpia Fulvia Morata, a Classicist Huguenot Teacher

Olimpia was born in Ferrara in 1526 (on or after October 26), as one of the five children (four girls and one boy) of the humanist Fulvio Pellegrino Morato (1483–1548) and Lucrezia Gozi Morata. From 1522 onwards her father served as a teacher of grammar and a tutor at the court of Ferrara first under Alfonso I d'Este and later under his son Ercole II d'Este. At the peak of his career Morato was exiled from Ferrara. In the years between 1532 and 1539 he taught in Venice and Vicenza (where he established a Latin school), became increasingly influenced by Protestant teachings, mainly via Calvin's followers, and lectured on Erasmus, Luther, and Zwingli. He befriended Celio Secondo Curione (1503–69) who would become a lifelong friend also to his daughter. Upon his return in 1539, he tutored Duke Alfonso's children at the court of d'Este, and taught at the University of Ferrara from 1546 to 1548, the year of his death.

During the years he spent teaching in Ferrara, his daughter established herself as a budding scholar. Fulvio was highly devoted to his daughter's education, and as a result of early private tutoring, epecially in reading, writing and speaking in Latin and Greek, Olimpia spoke Greek fluently by the age of 12. She studied languages and grammar, history and moral philosophy. There is no concrete evidence of her knowledge of Hebrew, but it is quite probable that she did familiarize herself with the language of her interest, given her translations of the Psalms and her training as a classicist with a love for original languages and sources. (Other learned women, such as Marie Dentière, Jeanne d'Albret and Marguerite de Navarre, expressed interest in Hebrew as well and exchanged grammar books written for girls.) She was considered a child prodigy and in her youth was praised for her fluency in the classical languages.

Olimpia had first known the Ferrarese court as a young child, under Duke Alfonso. By the time Ercole II and Renée (second daughter of King Louis XII of France) succeeded to the title in 1534 following Alfonso's death, the Morato family had already been forced to leave Ferrara, but in 1539, when they returned, the duchess, who was herself versed in the humanities (and perhaps in mathematics and astronomy), and a matron of the reforms in her duchy, invited young Olimpia (aged 13 or 14, between 1539–41) to be study companion to her erudite daughter Anne (8 or 9 years old at the time). The duchess took great pains over her children's education and this opportunity to serve as intellectual pace-setter was a most significant affirmation of Olimpia's gifts, and served as a unique springboard for her (continued) academic excellence and lifelong hunger for learning; Anne also grew into an established scholar. The girls were tutored together, in particular in Greek and Latin, by the German brothers Kilian and Johann Senf (the latter a medical doctor, the duchess's personal physician). They also learned the art of translating and debating in Latin, Olympia as ever "beyond her female sex", according to Curione (Flood 1997, 178–179). (Vorländer 1970, 97; Smarr 2005b, 322.)

Olimpia benefited from the cultural life at the court and her association with erudite men who taught her and those she met through her father. She absorbed knowledge and influences not only from books but also from stimulating interactions with learned individuals interested in new ideas and religious reform. Increasingly Scripture became her primary source of interest and the main object of her work. The court at Ferrara nourished cultural life and, under the wings of the Duchess Renée, it formed the hub of the reformers' circle and a safe haven in which persecuted French Huguenots and other "dissidents" might convene. (It was probably the duchess's influence with Ercole that had made it possible for Olimpia's father to return to Ferrara.) The duchess surrounded herself with reform-minded individuals such as Celio Secundo Curione and the brothers Johann and Kilian Senf, whom we have already mentioned, with Celio Calcagnini (1479–1511), and, of course, Olimpia's father whose overall influence on Olimpia's religious formation cannot be overestimated.

During these years Olimpia befriended a courtlady named Lavinia della Rovere Orsini (the wife of Paolo Orsini) with whom she would correspond for the rest of her life. Their friendship would play a significant role in Olimpia's life and her deliberation on women's learning and identity, an issue she addressed in some of her writings. When she was still young Olimpia wrote the poem with which this chapter begins, giving insights into her awareness of the gender expectations that clashed with her own ambitions as an intellectual: she penned her experience as a young woman who yearned to learn and thus dropped the "symbols" of her sex – that is, the activities most typical of women. Her pride and delight was study, not needlework, and that is what she pursued. (Bainton 1971/2001, 253–4; King 1991, 180–1.)

In her youth most especially she felt she had to emphasize her "genderless spirit." (This was not at all uncommon. In the Middle Ages, it has been argued, "women's adhesion to intellectual or spiritual concerns was often accompanied by a negation of themselves as female, emphasizing the genderless spirit rather than the gendered body as the site of identity" [Smarr 2005a referring to Gabriella Zarri].) As she matured, she no longer saw her gender as an issue. For instance, her early dialogue (from 1530) about an imagined conversation between herself as a student and her friend Lavinia as her teacher portrays a different Olimpia from the more mature author of her second dialogue (from 1531–2) who would insist on the characters' femaleness and would portray Olimpia's character in the role of a woman and a teacher. (See Smarr 2005a, 78; Smarr 2005b, 327–9.)

While her interest in humanist and classical studies, on the one hand, and her increasing religious passion, on the other, created a tension that had to be balanced, she did not see the two as mutually incompatible, although at times she prioritized one over the other. Over the years, her interest shifted its focus from classical sources to religious pondering on Scripture. Even in her religious passion, though, she remained at heart a humanist and a classicist, which showed in her disregard for the teachers of the Church and in her intentional focus on the scriptural texts themselves. Pinpointing the period of her gradual religious awakening is difficult, but, to be sure, her time in the d'Este court, her marriage to a Protestant, and her departure from Italy serve as important landmarks in her spiritual and theological evolution.

In her teens (when she was 13 or 15) she wrote sophisticated poems in ancient, classical format (two in Greek) and letters (one out of three in Greek). She used Attic prose in her Greek composition in praise of the Roman hero Caius Mucius Scaevola. She gave public defenses in Latin of Cicero's Paradoxa Stoicorum, and would further enhance her skills in Greek in writing odes and dialogues and verses in the Homeric dialect. (Her "Defensio Ciceronis" and "Observationem in Homerum" from this period are lost

[Holzberg 1982, 144].) Her translation of the first two stories of Boccaccio's *Decameron* reveal Protestant influences even in her twenties (for instance, she omitted references to the sacrament of penance and included a story about an attack against the papal court). Even if these works already reveal her reformist interests, Olimpia's primary focus was still on humanist studies, not religion. Religion would become more important to her in the course of her marriage, relocation and the hardship she both witnessed and experienced.

During her time in Renée's court, Olimpia also witnessed the dangers of religious "dissidence" and the effects of the Inquisition: after his visit to Ferrara, Pope Paul III allied with Renée's Catholic husband and the Jesuits to eradicate heresy from the court, while in a state subject to papal power the duchess continued to offer asylum to religious refugees (including Jean Calvin). The battle between the Protestants and the Inquisition, which was in place from 1542, when Olimpia was 16, was very much alive during her stay at the court. The Inquisition brought a dark cloud over the court and Olimpia felt its effect in her own life and relationships. The first victim of the Inquisition in Ferrara to be executed, Fanino (Fannio) Fanini, was a personal acquaintance of Olimpia and her friend Lavinia della Rovere (who tried to intervene on his behalf). After Olimpia herself was effectively banished from the court she remained plagued by worry for those in Ferrara suffering from persecution.

Olimpia's life underwent dramatic changes from 1543 and especially from 1548 onwards, because of the arrival of the Inquisition and her father's fatal illness. After Pope Paul III ordered an investigation in Ferrara in 1545, considerable pressure was put on the duchess herself. Members of Renée's court were arrested and she herself was forced to attend Mass, after being separated from her family and associates. Olimpia talked about Renée's surrender in a letter to Pietro Paolo Vergerio, written in the spring of 1555 from Heidelberg (letter 62). Saddened but not surprised by it, young and unattached, lacking any intimate knowledge of Renée's ulterior motives or strategies for survival in a situation that was very precarious both to Renée personally and to all the Protestants of Ferrara, it would have been hard for Olimpia to empathize fully. Renèe's involvement with the Huguenots cast the shadow of suspicion over Olimpia too. She first spent time away from court in 1546 recuperating from illness, returning only to leave again in 1548 to take care of her terminally ill father. She would not be welcomed back again.

Upon her return after her father's death, Olimpia found few if any friends. The Inquisition was ever-present. The vital subcommunity of Protestants around the duchess had all but disappeared. Many of her Protestant friends had found safer pastures away from Ferrara (for instance, Curione had left to become a professor of Latin literature at Basel; Kilian Senf and his brother Johann had returned to Germany.) Her friend and erstwhile fellow-pupil Anne d'Este, on the other hand, had left for France and was married to the Catholic François de Lorraine, duke of Guise – the man who would notoriously lead the massacre of Huguenots at Vassy, and in so doing instigate the French Wars of Religion. The duchess, a prisoner in her own court, had cooled in her feelings towards Olimpia, who was no longer needed (Parker 2003, 20). Bereft of company in the court that had been her home, Olimpia endured her intellectual and cultural isolation and focused on educating her younger sisters and brother. Heartbroken, she wrote to Curione (October 1550) that she was deserted by her "princess" and that she was not allowed even to even read the Old and the New Testament. She felt she was "plunged into abyss," and left the court where she felt her salvation was imperiled

(Bainton 2001, 255; Flood 1997, 179–80.) From this period on she turned more seriously from "studia humanitatis" to "studia divina," and to a Calvinist faith in particular – a process only strengthened by her upcoming marriage and move to Germany. (Holzberg 1982, 145–7; Smarr 2005b, 325.)

While some mystery remains over the period of her final stay in Ferrara, the changes in religious climate and the widespread suspicion of heresy were undoubtedly factors in removing Olimpia from favor at the court. (Johann Senf wrote in 1553 to Calvin that the duke's informant Jerome Bolsec had slandered Olimpia [Bainton 2001, 256; Flood 1997, 179].) Another issue was her intellect. Olimpia experienced the not so uncommon pattern in the life of an educated woman: as a child progidy she had displayed a "brief burst of erudition, which enjoyed masculine encouragement only as long as the scholar remained a young girl. Once she became old, no longer merely a curiosity for display but a potential disturbance to the order of things, she was married off, and her talents absorbed in child rearing and domesticity." In addition, "she was in disgrace, perhaps, for the dangerous habit it seems she had acquired: reading the Old and New Testaments." She had not only read them by herself but also for herself. (King 1991, 203.)

Regardless of the pressures of gender expectations, of her religious interests, and of the Inquisition, Olimpia survived and kept on with her teaching and studies, in which she had found a fresh focus: her new Protestant faith. Two things in particular made this possible: her extraordinary talents and determination to study, and her marriage to a partner who encouraged her. In a letter (letter 19) to Celio Secundo Curione she praised God: "He has also given me as a bride to a man who greatly enjoys my studies" (OM/Parker, 106–8 at 108). (See Parker 2003, 24–5.)

Olimpia was married in 1550 (or 1549) to a friend of Johann Senf, the German doctor, Andreas Grunthler (c.1518–55) from Schweinfurt, Bavaria. Andreas was already trained in classical studies in Paris, Heidelberg, and Leipzig when he arrived in Ferrara in May 1549 to receive his laureate in medicine. The two fell in love and became engaged in 1549, marrying late the same year or early in 1550 in a Protestant ceremony. The bride composed a Greek verse to celebrate their marriage:

> Thou hast willed that fallen humanity be the mystical bride of thy Son,
> Who for her has given his life,
> Spread now harmony and peace over those united in this hour,
> For of thine ordinance is the nuptial couch.
>
> (Olimpia Morata in Bainton 2001, 258)

This was clearly a love match; letters leave no doubt about that (Parker 2003, 24), and what they tell us is reinforced by the song for four voices that Andreas composed based on a psalm when Olimpia died (Weiss 1976, 97). (On Olimpia and Andreas, see Weiss 1976, 84–99.)

Just as her parents had supported Olimpia's ambition for learning, her husband and the institution of marriage provided her with continued protection. Both society and the Church found the emancipated educated women who shunned marriage and slipped away from male control the most troubling of their sex. There was always the possibility that these intellectually independent women would extend the realm of their self control beyond the mind to the body, and seek to determine their entire social role for themselves. In an age when learning and chastity were seen as incompatible in women, and where undomesticated learned women posed a threat, the role of a Protestant wife may have actually protected Olimpia in her "anomalous position as a married scholar" and her interests (Parker 2003, 25; Lerner 1993, 222). This was not necessarily the case for most women, to whom marriage meant an end of intellectual pursuit: to marry and to study was not a probable combination for a woman. Olimpia was exceptional in this regard; exceptional also in the passion of her determination to be a scholar.

When Andreas left for Germany in search of a position soon after the wedding, Olimpia stayed with friends, grieving over his absence and writing about her longing. She wrote (in a letter from April/May 1550 [Parker 2003, 98–9]),

> I am so sad that you've left me and will be away for so long. Nothing more painful or serious could have happened to me . . . I swear by all that's holy that there is nothing dearer or sweeter to me than you. And I know you feel it too. If I ever change my mind, you'll be the first to know – just like I used to tell you openly that I had taken a dislike to you! I want, my husband, to be with you. Then you'd know clearly how great is my love for you. You can't believe how madly I love you. There's nothing so bitter, so difficult, that I wouldn't do it eagerly, if I could please you.

In yet another she urged him to write soon and return to her quickly (letter 22, from November 1550 [OM/Parker, 110]): "I hope you're well. First I want to know that you're all right, what you're doing, what's happening there, and how things are. I'm very anxious about what you think about your return or about sending for us. So, please, write to me diligently about everything: what's really happening! Don't invent anything false just to comfort me." Again, "Write, I beg you, when I am going to see you . . ." Only a month later she would beg him again (letter 23, December 1550 [ibid., 110–11]): "But I, my husband, ask you over and over again not to leave me behind . . . Please, I pray, don't forget us, and I beg you to take me from here." Finally her wishes came true.

Olimpia and Andreas left Ferrara with her 8-year-old brother Emilio in 1550 and arrived in Germany on June 12. Traveling via Augsburg to Würzburg (to stay with Johann Sinapi) they arrived in the summer of 1551 in Schweinfurt, Andreas's home-town, where he had work as a doctor. In Germany Olimpia continued to pursue her studies and writing, and tutored Emilio and the daughter of her old friend Johann Senf in Greek and Latin. During the last calm months before the struggle between the margrave of Brandenburg-Kulmbach and the emperor brought chaos and warfare to Schweinfurt (January to March 1553) she wrote her most significant *Dialogue of Theophila and Philotima*. She had already turned to religious study in 1549, but now in the German soil where Protestant theology had strong roots and was already at the stage of confessional debating, Olimpia's preoccupation and passion with religion only increased. As she deepened her knowledge in the nuances of the new theology, and studied the reformers' writings and Protestants' documents, she began to actively endorse reformation herself. For instance, she identified individuals to provide Italian translations of Protestant works that would benefit her fellow Italians. (Holzberg 1982, 146–9; Weiss 1976, 90–4; Parker 2003, 26.)

For instance, she asked Matthias Flacius Illyricus to translate a German work of Luther's into Italian – and promised to lend him, if needed, her learning, which would not disappoint him! She wrote to him from Schweinfurt in May 1553:

My dear sir . . . And since your writings have made you well-known to me, you were the first to come into my mind as one who seemed able to help my fellow Italians, who are lost in so many errors and are in need of the good things of heaven. If you were to translate into Italian any of Luther's German books in which he argues agains the general errors (for I do not yet understand German, although I have worked hard at it) or if you would write something in Italian on the same subject (you could do it far better than I, since you have unrolled the books of sacred Scripture, which I have barely touched with my lips), I am sure that you would save many pious men from the errors by which they are misled. If you are willing to do this for the sake of the church, for which we ought to lay down our lives, you will bind them to you forever by your divine kindness. I think it would be even more useful for them if you were to write in Italian, since many of them are ignorant of letters. I beg and beseech you again and again to do this through Christ . . . If you have any need of my aid, expect all the learning I have. I will not disappoint you. (OM/Parker, 133–4.)

Later she would ask Pier Paolo Vergerio to translate Luther's Large Catechism and other works into Italian. (See Rabil 1994, 271–2; Smarr 2005b, 331, 336; Vorländer 1970, 106.)

As a reforming humanist, Olimpia gravitated towards the Scriptures, "ad fontes," and took upon herself the task of retranslating Psalms into Greek (most in hexameters, one in the rarer Sapphic form), making manifest her fusion of biblical and Greco-Roman thought and with perspectives arising from her personal context in Schweinfurt. Her husband set her translations to music, and she often quoted from them and from other Psalms in her letters to her sisters. Her versions of Psalms 1, 2, 23, 34, 46, 70, 125, and 151 are still extant, but others were lost in Schweinfurt. (See Parker 2003, 184–91; Vorländer 1970, 105; Smarr 2005b, 329–30.)

Most of what is known of Olimpia after her time in Ferrara comes from her letters, the majority of which she addressed to her friends Curione and Lavinia. (Vorländer 1970, 103; Flood 1997, 179; letters from Schweinfurt, Holzberg 1982, 148.) She wrote 52 letters – 49 of those in Latin, the rest in Italian and Greek. In addition, although most of the letters she received were destroyed with the rest of her possessions during the siege, 15 letters addressed to her have survived. Her letters, which breathe humanism and portray the terror of the period (Flood 1997, 179), have been characterized as some of the most beautiful "Frauenbriefe," women's letters from the Reformation period, as "real" letters to real people, sent under the author's own name. Prosaically, the letters served as her means of communication in long-distance relations, but they were also her medium for teaching and spiritual guidance. (See Osieja 2002, 293–4.) (For editions, see Kößling and Weiss-Stählin 1990; Caretti 1940; Parker 2003.)

The 1553–4 siege of Schweinfurt dramatically changed her life. In the period between the ending of the Schmalkaldic war and before the Peace of Augsburg, Catholic and Protestant towns and princes continued to negotiate over dominance and issues of religious freedom. The little town of Schweinfurt became a scene for war horrors. During the so-called War of the Margraves, on April 22, 1553, the troops of Albert Alcibiades, margrave of Brandenburg-Kulmbach, took over the city of Schweinfurt from where he fought against the neighboring towns (Nurnberg, Braunschweig, Würzburg, and Bamberg) for nearly a year. When he had run out of supplies he authorized the pillaging of the besieged town. After he was forced to retreat, new troops entered the city, this time those of the elector Moritz von Sachsen, duke of Brunswick, and the bishops of Würzburg and Bamberg, who burned the city down. Olimpia's letters to Curione described the terror and suffering people of Schweinfurt experienced.

Facing the possibility of execution if they were caught, Olimpia and Andreas escaped Schweinfurt on foot (an ordeal Olimpia wrote about in her 1554 letter to Curione [see Parker 2003, 154–67]). They struggled to find shelter and lost everything they had, including their dear books. Andreas was even taken prisoner, but was fortunately released under Episcopal protection. The Count von Erbach and his wife Elizabeth provided shelter, food and clothes for the couple and special care for Olimpia who was ill, along with important connections to help them as they continued their journey, which is what they opted to do regardless of the countess Elizabeth von Erbach's offer to make Olimpia her lady of honor: her experiences at the Ferrarese court had made Olimpia chary of accepting such fleeting honors. So, instead of remaining in Erbach the impoverished couple traveled under the protection of the count and countess of Erbach to Heidelberg, where the count had used his influence with the Elector Palatine to secure the appointment of Andreas to the position of the chair of medicine in Heidelberg (upon the recommendation of Jacob Micyllus (Möltzer), a professor of Greek at the university). Friends attempted to at least rebuild the library of the young couple who were starting their new life with basically nothing left to their name.

The fact that Olimpia pursued her studies and tutored in Greek and Latin in private has led to the misconception that she was nominated professor at the University of Heidelberg. Competent as she was, the universities only hired men for such esteemed positions. However, it has been said that "had she lived longer, she might have become the first woman university teacher in Germany" (Flood 1997, 182). She was well-known among an international group of university men, as she corresponded not only with her friends and family, but also reformers like Luther, Melanchthon, and Flacius (even if it was atypical and risky for women to initiate such correspondence with men [Parker 2003, 27, 31, footnote 160; Vorländer 1970, 106].) She worked actively towards spreading Luther's works in Italian and requested important books for her personal library, such as Calvin's commentaries on the Lamentations of Jeremiah (letters 41, 52). Her wish to inspire and educate other women was fulfilled in the correspondence and friendships that she maintained. (Holzberg 1982, 154–5, 22–3, 27, 31.)

Olimpia stayed in touch with friends and family in Italy and abroad, especially Curione, her sister Vittoria, and her friends Cherubina Orsini and Lavinia della Rovere, and from a distance took on the role of a teacher to the women in Italy she cared for. She remained concerned about their physical health and safety, but, most of all, she cared about their intellectual and spiritual wellbeing, exhorting them to read and study diligently and remain constant in their faith. For instance, she wrote to her sister Vittoria (letter from 1554, OM/Parker, 143–4): "Make sure a day does not pass without reading with devotion and praying to God through Christ that He will illuminate things for you in the Holy Scripture with the interpretation. Get up very early, a little earlier in the morning." She wrote similarly to Cherubina Orsini: "So, My Lady Cherubina, be continually at prayer and read the Scriptures both by yourself and together . . . Pray together" (letter 46 from 1554, OM/Parker, 149; see also 147, 168). Her letter to Lavinia della Rovere Orsini (letter 28 from 1551/52, OM/Parker, 117) echoed the exhortation:

> Indeed, if Germany did not give me the comfort of being allowed to have books of theology that we could not have there, I would not be able to bear my longing for my friends, especially you, who always "remains in the depths of my being" and whom I always mention in my prayers . . . I'm also sending you some writings by Dr. Martin Luther, which I enjoyed

reading. They may be able to move and restore you, too. Work hard at these studies, for God's sake; ask that He enlighten you with true religion. You will not lose.

The issue of predestination, and the comforting message she saw imbedded in it, was increasingly present in Olimpia's writings during the time of war, which is not a surprise: she had to wonder where God was in all the suffering she witnessed! She wrote words of encouragement to Lavinia, urging her to seek for God's mercy "regardless" of the certainty of election. (She may have broken free from the rigidity of Calvinism in favor of her friend Curione's universalism [Bainton 2001, 261, 268 footnote 15].) Personally comforted by the doctrine of predestination, which she interpreted most sympathetically, she continued to worry over the acts of injustice she witnessed. She was very much aware of the situation in France, where Huguenots were being slaughtered for their faith, most dramatically in the massacre of St Bartholomew's Day. As a cry of help, she wrote to Anne d'Este, now, as Anne de Guise, married to one of the leaders of the Catholic party, exhorting her to stay strong and faithful, to take a stand and protect those persecuted for the sake of the gospel.

Given the position of Anne's husband, Olimpia's words were brave. In her letter (July 1555, from Heidelberg, OM/Parker, 169–70), she expressed her hope that Anne would devote her life to sacred studies. She also described her own conversion and the principles of her faith, thus evangelizing Anne. Reminding the duchess of the years they had passed together, she urged her to act on behalf of the innocent victims being burnt for their faith. (Bainton 2001, 262; Holzberg 1982, 154.) She wrote,

> Therefore, my sweetest lady, since God has blessed you with such kindness in order to open His truth to you, and since you know that all the men who are being burned there are innocent and are undergoing so many tortures for the sake of the gospel of Christ, it is your clear duty to show how you feel, either by pleading for them to the king or by praying for them. If you are silent or connive, allow your people to be tortured and let them be burned, and fail to show at least with words that this displeases you, you will seem by our silence to conspire in their slaughter and to agree with the enemies of Christ.

She wished to empower Anne with the idea of election and God's providence:

> Perhaps you will say, "If I do that, I may make the king or my husband angry with me and make many new enemies." Think that it is better to be hated by men than by God, Who is able to torture not just the body but also the soul in perpetual fire. But if you have Him as a friend, no one will be able to harm you, unless He permits it, in whose hands all things are. See to it that you think on these things.

How Anne received the letter and the admonishment is not known. Her problems at the time of the letter were many. A possible glimpse, however, of the effect of Olimpia's letter comes in an incident following the tragedy of the Conspiracy of Amboise in France, when the Guises took brutal revenge for a plot by the Huguenots and the house of Bourbon to seize control of France: a woman reportedly confronted Queen Catherine de Médicis, condemned the bloodshed and prophesied a misfortune to follow; it has been suggested that she may have been Anne. (Bonnet 1887, 177, 156–7; Bainton 2001, 262, 268, footnote 19.)

Because Olimpia maintained contact with her friends through letters, she left behind a unique source of information about her life and a window on to her world. For the period of her life after she left Ferrara, especially, her letters are our main resource. Letters were not only her way of communicating with people and about things that mattered to her: they were also a medium in which to present a particular woman's voice that, as if ignoring the gender framework, identified her first and foremost as an intellectual, and, next, as a Protestant. Certainly aware of the gender boundaries and of the dangers involved in her religious choice, she let herself be guided by the principles she valued beyond human conventions: learning and faith. Letters became the medium by which to share her passions and to express her lifelong vocation as a teacher.

Olimpia had the identity and ambitions of a teacher. In addition to her private tuition of young children, she assumed the role of teacher and spiritual counselor to her female correspondents. Her epistolary friendships provided that crucial "space between private and public" that allowed a creative woman to teach. (Smarr 2005a, 79–80.) To the apparently female audience for whom she wrote she, and her female characters, appeared as learned educated humanists. (Her unique combination of Ciceronian Latin and female and domestic traits and imperatives may have been her attempt to forge her own identity [Smarr 2005a, 80].) She persistently wrote about the importance of study, Scripture reading and praying together, and of the fruits of enlightening conversation; she also reminded her friends, her pupils, about the need to trust themselves into the care of their God. In the name of friendship she could exhort women to pursue these otherwise discouraged activities. Instead of composing treatises, she discussed theological matters in her letters and dialogues. (Smarr 2005a, 336, 343–4.)

The hardship that resulted from the siege of Schweinfurt depleted Olimpia's body of its resources. After she contracted fever and tuberculosis and narrowly escaped the plague, she knew she would not recover. Her death imminent, she wrote her testament, so to speak, in her letters to her friends. She died on October 26, 1555, of tuberculosis – not cholera or the plague, as some sources claim. She was 29 years old. (See letters 41, 43, in OM/Parker, 29.) Just a few weeks later she was followed by her beloved husband and little brother, both victims of the plague.

Olimpia's letters reveal how prepared she was for her death, and how her theology sustained her. "I long to be dissolved, so great is the confidence of my mind, And to be with Christ in whom my life flourished" she wrote (OM/Parker 1997, 274). Her final letter to Curione (letter 71 from 1555, OM/Parker, 176–7), written from Heidelberg shortly before her death, leaves the testimony of a woman prepared to die in the faith of the resurrection:

> I pray God to watch over you . . . My bodily strength is gone. I have no appetite for food. Congestion tries to suffocate me day and night. The fever is high and constant. There are pains throughout my body that keep me from sleeping . . . But there is still a spirit in my body that remembers all my friends and the kindness they have done. So to you and those kind men who have blessed me with so many lovely gifts, I wanted to give great thanks if the fates had allowed. I think I am going to depart soon. I comment the church to you, that whatever you do be of use to her. Be well, my dearest Calius, and don't grieve when my death is reported to you, for I know that then at last I shall live, and I desire to be dissolved and to be with Christ.

Olimpia was buried at St Peter's church in Heidelberg, where a monument to her memory was erected by a Frenchman, Guillaume Roscalon. Maybe, as some have postulated, it was the grieving Anne de Guise who paid for the memorial for her child-hood friend. Another grieving friend would leave a memorial in print: Celio Secundo Curione, now living in Basel, gathered all of Olimpia's texts that he could find for publication, an enterprise in which Andreas assisted before his own death. Unfortunately, most of Olimpia's works had already been lost. It is mostly texts from her youth that have survived; her mature works were destroyed in the siege. The first edition of 1558 (there were four editions in all) Curione dedicated to Isabella Bresegna, a prominent Italian humanist reformer. The 1562 augmented edition he dedicated to Queen Elizabeth I of England. Two more editions followed in 1570 and in 1580 (otherwise identical, the 1580 edition includes another text, not from Morata [Rabil 1994, 277]). Other than in her works, Olimpia's memory has survived in a portrait that has been traced back to Titian's school. (See Weiss 1976, 100–5, especially about the connection to Titian.)

Olimpia's letters were popular in the sixteenth century, after which they were forgot-ten until Goethe's rediscovery of her in the eighteenth century and the blooming nineteenth-century interest in Protestant "saints" (Flood 1997, 182). (For Goethe, Olimpia symbolized the Eternal Female, and someone in whose life thought and word, argument and action formed a unity; see Weiss 1976, 106–7.) The first chronology of her letters was prepared by Jules Bonnet in 1856 as along with a biography. In 1892 Giuseppe Agnelli also wrote a biography, while in 1927 Giuseppe Paladino produced a critical edition of her letters, as did Lanfranco Caretti in 1940, following it in 1954 with what has become the standard critical edition of all her writings except the translations. Paladino and Caretti also included biographies. The new English biography and edition of Olimpia and her works by Holt N. Parker (2003) is the best modern edition available. Her letters have drawn interest for the information they offer about her life and her translations have been analyzed in terms of her linguistic and literary skills. A few studies written since the late twentieth century have highlighted Olimpia's gifts and skills as a female writer, teacher, mentor, and poet, as well as her both religious and feminist maturation. Studies on Olimpia's thought and theology are still rare. (See Vorländer 1970; Holzberg 1982, 141–3; Pirovano 1998, 1997; Parker 2003, 11–12; Rabil 1994, 277.)

Olimpia's *Dialogue of Theophila and Philotima* from 1551 has been deemed her most important text, for many reasons. First of all (as demonstrated by Smarr 2005a), com-pared to the earlier dialogue between Lavinia della Rovere and Olimpia, the 1551 texts demonstrate Olimpia's maturation as a woman, scholar, and friend. The first text being more autobiographical (concerning Olimpia's lament over her earlier ignorance and lack of interest in religious matters), the second dialogue, from Germany, is more theo-logical and presents a sophisticated application of Olimpia's impulse to teach. In an imagined situation in which the female characters' husbands are absent, the women engage in an intellectual conversation for a moment of teaching and learning. The activ-ity of God is implied, but in the latter the teaching role and spiritual guidance of women are remarkably emphasized. The latter dialogue's inclusion of both male and female models for spiritual life relativized the sexual/gendered differences in faith matters, and "yet it suggests this in a gender-conscious way as an encouragement to a woman who complains of being too weak for the demands of religion" (Smarr 2005a, 76).

The dialogue also "calls attention to the learned Olimpia's real need to balance her roles of writer and housewife." She had to be creative in finding opportunities – and reasons – to follow her desire to offer spiritual counsel. The absence of men was one;

the claim that God spoke through her was another. Even a woman like Olimpia had to be careful:

> For a woman seeking to avoid the censure of making herself too public, this sense of writing to and for one's personal friends provided a space between private and public. Moreover, Olimpia knew that for her to take on the tone of authority, to preach, would be readily acceptable if her audience were at least ostensibly female and someone whom she could encounter within domestic spaces. (Smarr 2005a, 80)

(See also Smarr 2005a 72–8; Rabil 1994, 275.)

Olimpia's sense of the authority of the learned, and her education's foundational role in that comprehension, manifested itself in many ways. The fact that she wrote and published poems speaks of her exceptional gifts, as well as of her sense of authority and entitlement (Parker 19997, 248–50). Poetry and the study of the ancient Latin poets was a discipline preserved for men who needed such skills in their public roles, whereas for women poetry could be important only in teaching morality. As a public activity, poetry as such, thus, had no function in women's lives. As a matter in fact, as a public activity, it was considered unsuitable for women; as a private act, it was unnecessary. Olimpia as a poet exemplifies the emancipatory power of education in a woman's life.

From what we can tell of her life, Olimpia's sense of authority as a writer and as a teacher originated from her erudition and education; Olimpia herself traced her success and blessedness to the origins of divine grace. This may have been a rhetorical excuse: it was common for a woman writer to refer to God as the one who "made her do it." To her, learning was about divine power and God's intervention; she was as confident about the power of learning as she was about the omnipotence of God. As the development of her teaching voice coincided with her religious maturation and her growing zeal for God and godly knowledge, her intellectual exercise became her spiritual exercise and provided a mystical connection with God. She wrote, "In fact, I feel like I'm sinning if I don't spend the time God has given me . . . In these literary studies, especially since I lack all other comforts which I could use to solace the desire I have because my husband is away." She revealed she used to think she was the most learned,

> but even as I was exalted to the skies by everyone's praise, I realized that I lacked all learning and was ignorant. I had fallen, you see, into the error of thinking that everything happened by chance . . . But God began to dispel it: a little light of that unique and divine wisdom began to rise for me, and I proved in my own person that all human affairs are ruled by his wisdom.

"At last," she said, "I realized how stupid I was." And furthermore, "He gave me the mind and talent to be so on fire with love for learning that no one could keep me from it." (OM/Parker, 101–3.) Regardless of all her learning, she acknowledged that she wrote as an evangelical laywoman, and as a beginner (Vorländer 1970, 111).

Olimpia, thus, did not need mystical experiences or spiritual counsel from learned men, she was already connected with God through the words she studied and contemplated. That gave her unusual confidence, similar to the confidence of the medieval mystics empowered by their numinous experiences. "Without being a recluse or a mystic, Morata assumed for herself the right and even the duty to teach a Christian message." Confident in her understanding of the Word, "despite her deference to the learning and devotion of male reformers, she feels sure of her own religious ideas and believes she has a religious duty through letters and dialogues to urge others – especially women – to right living, the spreading of the 'true' Christianity, and the defense of its martyrs" (Smarr 2005a, 80–1). This was also the solution she found for her two dilemmas: how to meet the contemporary expectations for a woman and follow her passion in learning, and how to balance her learning ambition with her religious zeal.

A prominent theme in Olimpia's life and writing was that of suffering. During the persecutions and war, her escape and illness, she experienced suffering at first hand, as well as observing suffering in the lives of others, and it may be noted that she chose for her translation Psalms about endurance and hope in suffering (Parker 2003, 185–6; Smarr 2005b, 329–30). She pondered theologically upon the meaning of suffering. Her last letter stated her conclusion that all Christians must suffer for their faith, a conclusion close to Luther's thinking. "Her own suffering led her to identify with the suffering of others, especially those joined with her in faith." Olimpia felt a responsibility to help those who suffered for their faith, and it was for that reason she asked Anne d'Este to intercede on behalf of those persecuted in France; for her part, the solution was to use her words to alleviate distress. (See Osieja 2002, 298–300; Rabil 1994, 276.)

A factor not yet mentioned in regards to Olimpia's identity and ability to work as a scholar is the fact that she had no children. Like Katharina Schütz Zell, Olimpia had the time and luxury mothers with children rarely have to devote for reading and writing. An insight into how she understood her "motherhood" can be gained from her letter (letter 27) to Curione (OM/Parker, 114–16):

> I think I have to give the answer to one question you asked me, whether I had given birth to anything. The children I bore on the very day and hour I received your letter, I am sending to you: these poems appended here. There is also a Latin dialogue that I have just composed . . . I have borne no other children, and so far I have no expectation of bearing any.

Then she asked Celio how many children he had. To Olimpia who was still young, childlessness was not necessarily a tragedy. After all, through her writing she was constantly delivering and giving birth to new life.

Conclusion

Olimpia was a biblical humanist in the spirit of Erasmus, Calvin, Zwingli, and Melanchthon who wished to integrate biblical and theological scholarship with classical humanism. She was an educator and a proclaimer of the gospel. She was a Protestant, rejecting both the Mass and the pope. After her move to Germany, she openly broke from the Catholic church. Like Katharina Schütz Zell, Argula von Grumbach, and Marie Dentière, she called herself a Christian and identified herself as an evangelical, not as a Lutheran or a Calvinist – although she was influenced by both Luther and Calvin, and especially by the latter in the issue of the Eucharist. Her central theological concerns were those of the reformers: salvation by faith, the love of God, the work of Christ, and God's providence. She understood the debate between the reformers but refused to accept the arguments as warranting division among Christians. (On the four main identifiable themes in her works – Epicureanism, biblical humanism, evangelicalism, and Protestantism – see

Parker 2003, 31, footnote 156; 44–6.) In short, she was a humanist biblical reformer (Vorländer 1970, 113). (See on her study of Luther [letters 28, 38, 62], on Calvin [letters 43, 46], the Eucharistic debate [letter 62], and predestination [letters 28, 47], in Parker 2003, 43–4, 49–50.) (Also Rabil 1994, 274; Vorländer 1970, 111–13, 96.)

Olimpia's intellectual and religious maturation happened through the years, and the years in Germany from 1550 only deepened her religious consciousness and interest in deliberate theological reflection. In a letter dating from August 1550 or the spring of 1551 she wrote about her delight in reading religious texts every day – a change from the reading patterns she had had in Ferrara. The difficulties she encountered first in Ferrara and later in Germany, as much as her happiness in a supportive marriage with Andreas, were central factors in her growing religious devotion. (Rabil 1994, 274; Smarr 2005b, 326, 331.) Witnessing and experiencing suffering was an existential factor in her personal and spiritual development of a profundity that is hard to measure but can be read from her reflections recorded in her correspondence. Her move from a Catholic court shaken by the Inquisition to a land of vocal Protestants with acknowledged rights who were engaged in ongoing confessional debates was also an important stimulus to her existing evangelical interests.

Her marriage to Andreas (and with it the relocation to a foreign land) cannot be underestimated as a factor in Olimpia's theological development, even her survival. First of all, she and her husband shared the new faith commitment; no defense was needed on the domestic front, only encouragement could be expected. Secondly,

> as a marriage that at once rescued her from her isolation at court and made of her a Prot-
> estant (and not simply a sympathizer of reform), the break also entailed an intellectual sea
> change from a court lady involved in classical studies to an ardent Christian devoted to
> prayer and the reading of Scripture and increasingly indifferent to worldly things. (Rabil
> 1994, 273)

Throughout her short life Olimpia drew strength from her books and from her learning. "Learning was not an ornament worn by Morata; it was her identity. She was oppressed throughout her brief adult life by events that might have deterred a lesser spirit: her sickness, her father's death, her estrangement from court, the awful trials of Schweinfurt. But nothing silenced her pen." Had she lived in more peaceful times, we would have more texts from her (Rabil 1994, 277). Last but not least, Olimpia's commitment to learning had a consistent practical goal: the education of others. She carved herself a place in each context to express that vocation.

The words of her epitaph salute Olimpia with appropriate respect:

> In the name of the eternal god,
> And to the memory of OLIMPIA FULVIA MORATA
> Daughter of Peregrino Morato of Mantua
> The Beloved wife of the physician Andreas Grunthler.
> Her talent and her remarkable attainments
> In several languages
> The marvelous purity of her life, and her pity
> Elevate her above her sex
> The witness of her life was even surpassed by that of her death
> Peaceful, happy and holy

She died in the year of our lord MDLV
Ages XXIX years
In a strange land
Here she lies
With her husband and her brother Emilio
(Bonnet 1887, 193.)

A Word about Sources and References

See Parker's 2003 most recent full biographical work for the core information and interpretation of Olimpia's work, and bibliography for description of other main sources.

For an important recent study on Olimpia's "classical writing," see Smarr 2005a and 2005b. For colorful nineteenth-century biographical sources on Olimpia, see Fontana 1889–99, Bonnet 1856/1887, and Smyth 1834; these volumes offer much detail but lack constructive assessment of Olimpia's religiosity, her commitment to the Protestant cause, and her role as a woman. For the most recent, critical biography in English, providing core information and including a translation of Olimpia's texts, see Parker 2003. For other editions of Olimpia's texts, see Caretti 1940 and 1954, Kößling and Weiss-Stählin 1990. Short introductions by Rabil 1994 and Flood 1997 provide succinct biographical profiles and interpretation of Olimpia's religiosity. Foundational articles and chapters on Olimpia's contributions and identity as a learned humanist and Protestant woman writer are offered by Parker 1997, Holzberg 1982, Vorländer 1970, Weiss-Stählin 1961 and 1970, Bainton 2001, Smarr 2005b, Barton 1965, and, a celebratory book, Düchting 1998.

Conclusions and Observations on Gender and the Reformation

Reformation and Gender, Changes and Losses

The lives of the women introduced in this book have demonstrated how the Reformation's impact on the lives of members of their sex was ambiguous. In light of the gender norms prevalent in the early modern society and Church, and the theological emphases introduced by the reformers, women's responses have proven complex and surprising. Holding women up to be subjects of Reformation history and theology dethrones many of the once normative male categories and perspectives and suggests new questions, sources (as a result of resourceful digging), and horizons for its interpretation. In many ways, the work has only begun, and yet it is well under way!

It has been well established that particular gender ideologies can be detected "behind" the basic social structures and customs in the era, and as inherent in the reformers' theology. Issues regarding laws, customs, ideals, marriage, sexuality, economics, culture, and religion in this regard intertwine to a great degree. Gender awareness and gender perspectives thus necessitate interdisciplinary and holistic approaches to the study of the Reformation.

Perhaps the most important finding of the research on women and the Reformation is that women have had a central role in Reformation history, not just as "receivers" or "objects," but in action and in word, and often independently from men – and that there are exciting sources from women waiting to be perused! Instead of merely passively accepting the confessions of men or the various teachings and practices imposed upon them "from above" women had choices to make on their own, and they did. The majority of Protestant women contributed significantly in the private domain as individuals accepting the new faith and (as was expected of them) as parents of new Protestants. A small minority of exceptionally educated and positioned, or exceptionally fired up, women interpreted the principles of *sola scriptura* and the "priesthood of all believers" as entailing women's fuller inclusion in the Protestant mission: they took it upon themselves to envision new theologies, propose reforms, and write, teach, and preach – none of which was expected from women, of course.

The emancipatory potential of the reformers' preaching was realized only in part in the sixteenth century, or in the centuries following. Whether one considers the closing of convents as an act of liberation or as depriving women of an important alternative, the religious life of Protestant women did become more limited to the household. As this calling was defined in the most positive rhetoric and was held to be a vocation of equal theological importance as other calls, the majority of the women accepted it and molded the pattern to suit their own particular situation, it seems. The conspicuous lack of large-scale resistance on the part of Reformation women or of visible groundbreaking leadership either in theology and religious life or in society in general – with the notable exception of a few individuals – does speak volumes. It speaks both of women's overall content, and of their lack of power and voice as a group or class. Regardless of this, women continued to have an essential role in the Reformation and its realization in "real life." The movement(s) flourished and endured from roots that were both male and female: the product not just of the male theologians but of women, who as daughters, sisters, spouses, mothers, widows and as believers espoused the new faith and "taught" it and "preached" it in their own domains, so participating concretely in the Protestant mission.

The Reformation's impact on women was twofold and ambivalent: the exclusion of women from priestly and official leadership positions was balanced by the new vocational ethics and the stress put on the freedom of the individual Christian and the priesthood of all believers. The closing of the convents presented a definite loss for many women, but at the same time Reformation principles of the priesthood of all believers and "Scripture alone" as the clear and available authority for Christians blew wide open what it meant to have a spiritual calling, and at least in theory condoned all vocations as being equal. The sanctification of marriage and the spousal role was enormously important for women, who were traditionally expected to devote their lives to wifehood and motherhood any way. In other words, certain "losses" were balanced with certain "gains." The Reformation was neither simply a failure nor predominantly a victory for women. The "truth" was much more complex.

A general conclusion can be made that the reformers' teachings did not induce a deep cry for emancipation, liberation, or a class movement towards gender equality. The Reformation does not appear to have instigated any drastic changes in gender roles and expectations. Instead, Reformation teachings managed to give new meanings to the traditional roles of women while at the same time reinforcing a hierarchical view of human relations with a theology that taught created equality with natural differences between the sexes, as well as spiritual equality within hierarchically ordered gender roles. The reformers' convincing positive interpretation of the importance of the family and their promotion of the religious value of motherhood (the role that was considered most "normal" – and creation-based – but which, until then, had not been theologically valorized) may be one of the reasons that there was not initially a greater outcry for more options. It is ironic, that it should be the evangelical theology that was ignited by a visionary proclamation of the liberation of consciences from the oppression of religious (and secular) tyranny, and that had its premise in a most emancipatory view of the gospel, that reinforced women's theologically argued subjection and domestication via motherhood. The hierarchical ordering of family and societal relationships was not seen as contradicting the gospel of liberation, but rather as being instrumental in its successful realization.

It has been argued that at the very "crux" of Reformation theology and its implementation was a particular view of gender relations, and that "the moral ethic of the urban Reformation, both as a religious credo and a social movement, must be understood as a theology of gender." In that light, to view the Reformation's legacy as largely beneficial for women, and to ally the Reformation with "forces of progressivism, individualism, and modernization" would be "a profound misreading of the Reformation itself" (Roper 1989, 1, 5). The Reformation maintained the status quo in gender relations, and valued stability and order, all of which supported the institutionalization of the new faith in German towns, specifically through the life of the home, which was arranged according to the same patriarchal model that was at the root of the guild system. Without the continuation of the patriarchal systems embedded in both family relations and societal institutions, Reformation teachings would not have taken such a solid and swift root in German society. The Reformation needed the continuity provided by hierarchical gender relations. Marriage was of central importance; "the institutionalized Reformation was most successful when it most insisted on a vision of women's incorporation within the household under the leadership of their husbands" (ibid., 2). "In a real sense, therefore, as the Reformation was domesticated as it closed convents and encouraged nuns to marry, as it lauded the married state exemplified by the craft couple, and as it execrated the prostitute – so it was accomplished through a politics of reinscribing women within the 'family' " (ibid., 3).

By the same token, "urban Protestantism, once embedded in the certainties of household moralism, could not furnish a model for women's public action, or even at first a distinctly feminine register of piety. Women could not speak from within the intellectual heritage of urban communalism, nor could they make the language of civic righteousness their own." Just as it was the model for the private domain, the guild system provided the pattern for an ordering of public life according in which to express the mutually supportive Reformation teachings about vocation and marital life and the patriarchal arrangement of the social system were expressed in . The workshops, "where work-place and dwelling-place were identical, and where each member knew their sexual and social place, were urban Protestantism's home ground" (Roper 1989, 3). Similarly, "the sanctioning of the hierarchical ruling structure of the territorial state was a model for the organization of the household and the relationship between husband and wife" (Ozment 2001, 40–1). In other words, the Protestants' theologically-argued model for family life both reflected and reinforced the patriarchal order in Church and society.

It is possible to draw the conclusion that, on the one hand, the Reformation incorporated a vision about spiritual equality and the liberation of consciences from religious oppression, and on the other hand, it harnessed itself to a patriarchally arranged societal system and opted for continuity in social structures rather than abruptions. The integrity of the gospel proclamation was at stake in the minds of the reformers who failed to consider the issue of gender equality as a matter of integrity as well. The more liberal teachings of the reformers – and the hopes for the new theology's potential for restructuring central power relations towards a greater equality in private and public realms – were compromised for the sake of maintaining a status quo, which in its turn supported the Reformation as it gained a stronger foothold in German towns. This is hardly a coincidence: decisions in matters of theology, and most aspects of life, were made by those in the positions of privilege (in terms of wealth, education, social standing, race, and gender), who had less to loose if the societal status quo were maintained. The Reformation story might have been considerably different had those who were marginalized been the ones making decisions about how far to take the emancipatory message of the radical gospel.

Individual Choices and Women's Experiences

Women did not see themselves as a distinct class or category and thus could not have acted as a group in response to the reformers "program" of reforms. They reacted to the Reformation as individuals (Wiesner 1988, 170; also Wiesner 1989, 25). In terms of "conversions," typically women were expected to follow the decisions of their superior male kin. "Many women's response to the Protestant Reformation depended upon the commitment of their fathers or husbands – understandably, in an age which has been characterized as the zenith of the patriarchal nuclear family" (Monter 1987, 207). This does not mean that women mindlessly followed the new teachings and practices offered to them. Quite the opposite, women "continued to make personal choices about Reformation." Following "their own consciences" women could choose "what beliefs and practices made sense to them from a variety of religious options" (Wengler 1999, 282–3, 193–284). This could mean taking considerable risks, because any time that a woman challenged the prevailing teachings or practices in either religion or society she was immediately guilty of "challenging the most basic assumptions about gender roles and was doing so alone, with no official group to support here" (Wiesner 1988, 170; see also Wiesner 1989, 25).

So, while women's conversions may have typically happened within "group" conversions, mandated within regions and families, at the same time there were individual women who took enormous risks to confess their own faith, and sometimes this was distinct from that of their father or husband (see, for instance, Elisabeth von Brandenburg and Elisabeth von Braunschweig). If, however, there is no evidence of "class action" or group action from women in the Reformation (other than the occasional eruption of friction between Catholic and Protestant women), and though women were tied to the male heads of their families with no collective sense of identity and power as "we women," some could and did support each other in networks that crossed geographical and linguistic boundaries (as in the cases of Renée de Ferrara, Jeanne d'Albret, Marguerite de Navarre, Marie Dentière, Katharina Schütz Zell, Olimpia Morata, Elizabeth I, and Katharina von Bora Luther).

So, ironically, even if it was usual for women to be spoken about as one group and category, with certain ideological assumptions made about them as "the other sex/ gender," there was no widespread sharing of experiences and ideologies between women that could inspire any significant collective action. The exception was the Catholic nuns who were able to join forces as a group of women defending themselves, as they did when rising to defend their convents and celibate lifestyle, and they often did so more forcefully than their male counterparts. (Catholic city women also engaged in organized group action at times to defend their religion against the Protestants. See Davis 1975, 92–3, 85.) Among Protestant women, the only group action in which women engaged was the defense of the religious principles they had embraced, and in this they were side by side with men. For instance, Lutheran women did not agree with Calvinist women any more than women from either group agreed with the Anabaptists. Protestant women were, at least in theory, united in their rejection of the Catholic faith and thus of Catholic women's religious choices. Only in commonly condoning the persecution of radical Protestant women, Anabaptists in particular, and in their suspicion of the Jews (almost without an exception) did these opponents perversely agree. At the same time, women appear to have been generally peaceful in their relation to "others," less eager to battle in confessional wars than to seek at least for tolerance, if not even unity, and the right to live (consider, for instance, Katharina Schütz Zell, Argula von Grumbach, Jeanne d'Albret).

Women sharing "women's experiences" or addressing the women's role in the Church in particular was not common, but it did happen at times. The progressive deliberation on gender issues and women's rights of some articulate individuals would qualify them as early modern feminists. Among such women, who acted without a movement or a group around them but were connected with, and empowered, other like-minded individuals near and far, the first ones to name would be Marie Dentière, Argula von Grumbach, Marguerite de Navarre, Katharina Schütz Zell, Olimpia Morata, and Jeanne d'Albret. They articulated their gendered experiences and intentionally addressed the issue of gender and authority, they rebelliously broke gender boundaries, and they were aware of other women doing the same elsewhere; in all this they have provided inspiration and encouragement for others and thus they qualify as feminists. (See Lerner 1993 and King 1991, 238–9 about the history of feminist consciousness.)

The Options for Women

More than any other factor gender determined a woman's ability and avenues to respond to the Reformation (Wiesner 1988, 170, and Wiesner 1989, 25). "The reformers – Catholic and Protestant, magisterial and radical – all agreed on the proper avenues for female response to their ideas. The responses judged acceptable were domestic, personal, and familial: prayer, meditation, teaching the catechism to children, singing or writing hymns, entering or leaving a convent" (Wiesner 1988, 170). Public participation, dogmatic deliberation or institutional involvement, even if in agreement with the official teachings of the church, was unacceptable and an outrage. Women who stepped beyond the "acceptable" roles and understood the priesthood of all believers to enable themselves as teachers and preachers posed a serious challenge to both secular and religious authorities. Efforts were made to prevent them from even trying. Punishments came swiftly. Women discussing theology in public was to be prevented as it served no good purpose but rather presented an abomination and a seed for disorder. However, "a woman who backed the 'wrong' religion was never as harshly criticized as a man; her error was seen as simply evidence of her irrational or weak nature" (ibid.). (See Wiesner 1988, 170, 160–1; on women's options see Stupperich 1955, 205 and Davis 1975, 92–3.)

It is not a surprise that the majority of women accepted the roles offered, given the overwhelming message coming at them from all directions, from Church and society and at home, in religious teachings as well as in literature and art and legislation. Nor is it surprising that those of the women's literary contributions that are available to us. Writings of personal nature and (presumably) for private use were more acceptable for women than writings intended for a larger public. Much of women's writing throughout Christian history, and the Reformation period is no different, belongs to the autobiographical genres, letters, advice manuals, music, and devotionals. Even the few efforts at biblical exegesis and theological reflection are typically presented in a "safe" format – in personal and/or devotional writing, or imbedded in letters or advice to children and friends. Writing translations and poetry were other indirect ways to be involved in theological work without appearing to be. The scarcity of publications from Protestant women in comparison to Catholic women before and after their time is conspicuous. (See Davis 1975, 85.)

The domination of the pool of women's writings by autobiographical genres and letters has much to do with women's general exclusion from higher education, as well as with the institutional prohibition on women employing a public voice or taking a public position. Even the most highly educated women, like Olimpia Morata and Marguerite de Navarre, saw it as wise to employ indirect means to broadcast their theological work, and manipulated the conventions of writing to enter what was presumed to be the male realm of theology with their dialogues, translations, and varied treatises. What women wrote and how needs to be considered in light of what was deemed acceptable, what cultivation women had in terms of the various forms of writing, and what were the norms and ideals at the time. The images and expectations women absorbed from their culture shaped their sense of self and womanhood, and of what seemed to be feasible options for them as private believers and as writers with a potentially public voice.

Whereas literary activity was a realistic option for a few, select women, the participation of most women in the Reformation centered around their homes. It was there that women collectively made their foundational contribution to the cause of the Reformation. In their domestic realm "they carried out what might best be called domestic missionary activity, praying and reciting the catechism with their children and servants." What happened in the privacy of the home had wider ramifications. (For instance, women's decisions on the daily meals, whether to observe fasting rules or not, and whether to attend festivities or rites were far from being of purely personal or private importance.) The lines between private and public were blurred in this regard. (See Wiesner 1988, 164–5.)

Of all the women, the pastors' wives felt that the most. Women married to prominent Protestants did much more than assist their famous husbands in their ministry. These women's wifely duties, and opportunities, expanded to a degree that they could be considered a "job" and an office as a pastor's spouse and a manager of the parsonage (unpaid, of course). They served as pioneers in a role that was highly contested between those who disapproved of clergy marriage and by those who saw these women as providing a model of the ideal Protestant spouse. Pastor's wives opened their houses, provided food, care, and shelter, assisted in running hospitals, orphanages, and schools, and served as godparents and key figures in their society. They provided a cultural center in their homes, in addition to nurturing their husband and children and often extended families. They took care of the more tangible dimension of spirituality and religious life by providing for the bodies and daily needs of those under their care. Pastors' wives shone as examples of Protestant teachings about the holiness of home and fostered Protestant spirituality from the cradle. They were subject to the same rules as other women, however, and obedient meekness and total support of their spouses were expected from these groundbreaking women who were often remarkably gifted and industrious in their own right. (Clark and Richardson 1977, 133–4. Also Wiesner 1988, 164.)

Reformers' Ideas about Women

Protestant teaching on marriage and women's roles and their ideals about women raise a question about the fundamentals of Protestant anthropology: what did the reformers, implicitly and explicitly, preach about the origins, purpose, and "order" of the female species? In other words, what was the ideology that women could absorb from their culture, both secular and religious – and how did it reach women? (See King 2004, xxii, xiii–xvii.)

The forums and means through which women absorbed the anthropology and theology that would shape their self-image, public image, and range of freedom were varied. The reformers' texts circulated widely in Europe, and women in positions of wealth with powerful connections were able to stay more "up-to-date" with the reformers' treatises and read their thoughts at first hand. Most other women learned about the new theology at second hand, or from pamphlets that were available for larger audiences. They learned from family members, sometimes from other women in conversation, from tavern talks, from songs and art, paintings and woodcuts and text. The majority of Christian citizens could be reached by sermons, and, as is evident from Luther's preaching, they included much instruction about the nature, life, and purpose of women.

Luther's treatises and sermons on marriage (1519, 1522, and 1525), as well as the reformers' marriage manuals and ordinances, in many ways presented the ideal for a Protestant woman, as a spouse in particular. Anthropology and gender ideology in these works were quite homogenous, although Luther and Calvin did make attempts to view women's purpose and standing in relation to men from a more "positive" standpoint – as valuable God-willed helpmates for men, equal in creation and in justification as images of God, but different in terms of their nature and gifts. Unaware of the gender bias in their own theology and "in bondage" to the prevailing gender ideologies, they at least made an effort to deliberate on gender realities, their concern being the "order" of gender relations. The liberation of consciences was, after all, their primary concern, not gender emancipation. Thus, what women heard from the reformers was the reiteration of dogmatic statements excluding them from the ministry of the Word and sacraments and from places of public voice and authority, and affirming the traditional virtues of women and good wives. (See Wiesner 1988, 150–4, 160. Also Nowicki-Patuschka 1990, 9–12.)

Sola Scriptura, Education, and Legal Matters

Some of the most positive changes in the lives of women – and all the laity's – stemmed from the central Reformation principle of *sola sciptura*. As Church tradition and ecclesial authority were challenged with the enforced principle of Scripture being the sole authority in matters of salvation, people were invited to read the Scriptures for themselves and in their own languages. Luther himself was interested in ensuring that all people, including women, learned to read and love the Bible. The provision of vernacular translations and catechetic materials was intended to ensure that goal for the benefit of the gospel: the concerns were theological and spiritual, the goal was not emancipation via education. (Douglass 1974, 309; Blaisdell 1985, 21; Stock 1978; Green 1979.)

Women's literacy and education improved modestly. The curriculum for girls was aimed at ensuring they learned the skills needed by a pious, industrious, obedient housewife. In addition to basic reading skills, women's education stressed morality and decorum, singing, and sewing. Girls were taught submissiveness, modesty, decency, and other "womanly" virtues. Their primary education was harnessed towards producing good wives, not scholars or women with liberated minds. Women with an ambition for higher learning were suspect, and could be considered abnormal. (Blaisdell 1985, 21–2; Karant-Nunn 1982, 18.) The Protestants did promote a vision for a basic educational reform and they did proclaim (potentially) liberating theology; however, their wish was not to produce "Amazons" but, rather, pious obedient wives, practically skilled, and sexually engaged solely within marriage, without any impulse for independency in action or thought or word. The lack of higher education for women, their theologically and socially implied exclusion from public teaching roles and forums for debate, and the general culture that imposed silence on them, essentially upheld the social status quo and promoted a reality in which to be an outspoken, publicly engaged woman would be to be deemed guilty of a variety of sins (such "disobedience" at least distantly signaling spiritual or bodily un-chastity). It is hardly a surprise that so few Protestant women even tried to put their theological views in writing. Those who did left a remarkable and daring "voice of protest." (See King 2004, xxv, xxii; Blaisdell 1985, 22.)

The Protestant reformers, thus, by default, promoted the home as the main arena for women's religious expression, having barred all other forums as unacceptable. While women could exert considerable leadership in domestic matters, their spiritual and political subjection began from home – the cradle for Protestant spirituality. "Especially disturbing to a contemporary reader is the close alignment between prescriptions for women's spirituality and their oppression within their relationship with men." (Wiethaus 1993, 124.) The domestic hierarchical reality was defined theologically, and dictated legally; their spousal subjection was both a religious and a legal reality for women. It is worth asking, how that reality, in the end, shaped women's spiritual lives and expectations and their theologically perspective.

In a positive sense, home, the family, was the basic community that gave individuals tools for life in the society. The marriage was the bedrock for both family and society. As an economic basis, marriage consisted of two partners: men needed women to run the household, and women needed a provider and a legal status, which came through their spousal relations. As a wife and a mother, a woman was "somebody" and had specific roles to fill. One downside of this reality was that a woman's identity and legal status were dependent on her family, on her father and on her spouse more specifically. Her status could alter only through marriage, widowhood, remarriage and, rarely, divorce. In other words, apart from the institution of marriage, women had limited options to "be" and have a role in the society in which they were so instrumentally needed. (Wiesner 1989, 24; Clark and Richardson 1977, 132–3.)

The Reformation continued the legal and spiritual subjection of women to men. (See Witter Jr. 1997.) The theologically elevated role of mothers did not entail improved political or legal equality for women. On the contrary: in contrast to medieval society, striving for uniformity the early modern society selectively reintroduced Roman law, which meant losing the many "exceptions" that had allowed women important freedoms in legal affairs before. "The spread of Roman law thus had a largely negative effect on women's civil legal status in the early modern period both because of the views of women which jurists chose to adopt from it and the stricter enforcement of existing laws to which it gave rise" (Wiesner 2000a, 39). Laws that mostly affected women's lives were regulations about inheritance, wills, and parental authority. Legally speaking, only convent life, widowhood, or prostitution offered – ambiguous – freedom from male control; it was not a coincidence, that the reformers discouraged these options and any form of single life and offered marriage (or remarriage) as the only feasible honorable and spiritually worthy option. Even if the intent of such laws was explained as being to benefit women in need of legal protection, the actual effect of the relevant laws was to ensure that women stayed dependent on men. Needless to say, the "ideas about women and 'woman' in the abstract based on religion, biology, or tradition directly influenced the legal systems and law codes in early modern Europe" (Wiesner 2000a, 35). (See also Wiesner 2000a, 35–41; Witter Jr. 1997; Ozment 2001, 25–7.)

One of the peculiar legal changes that affected women had to do with the closing of brothels: women had practiced prostitution long before the Reformation, and continued to do so afterwards as well. Brothels had served a purpose of, supposedly, protecting respectable single and married women by meeting the needs of uncontrollable male sexuality. Prior to the Reformation, prostitution had been institutionalized and was largely accepted even if, whether she entered the business by "choice" or necessity, a prostitute's life was hardly recognized as an honorable one (although in some contexts, such as medieval Venice, it was possibly lucrative). The very existence of brothels, combined with a deep-seated fear of female sexuality (especially of women not attached to a man), however, made all single women (and especially those cohabiting) suspect of prostitution.

Prostitution itself posed a complicated reality. On the one hand, it offered women freedom from marriage and related ties with some autonomy to their bodies, on the other hand, the prostitution arrangements entailed much grief and abuse and differently (un)regulated bondage. The reformers' vigor for abolishing brothels was nevertheless as great as that for closing convents, with the result that prostitution was literally taken out of town as the women (who were obliged to wear distinctive clothing) entered the precarious world of freelancing, living without the control or the protection of the brothel outside the city walls. Prostitution as a profession did not end with the Reformation but its practice was made more difficult, and female sexuality continued to pose a threat with many unknowns. (Roper 1989, 89–131; Karant-Nunn 1982, 21–3; Monter 1987, 211.) It is interesting that the two options that had allowed women to live single and free from marital bonds, the brothels and the convents, were both abolished as harmful for women themselves, for men, and for Church and society in general.

Conclusion

The complex role of religion in women's lives has been amply documented. Equally clear is the ambivalence of the benefits the Reformation brought about.

If there is one issue on which a majority of modern historians agree, it is the detrimental effect of religion on the lives of women in the past: from the serial pregnancies and the restricted homemaking roles it decreed on the home front to the gender discrimination it sanctioned within the politics and the labor practices of public life. The Protestant Reformation and the Catholic Counter-Reformation are said to have left contemporary women only bit parts in the man's world outside the home. And entering marriages that were modeled on the "holy households" and "holy families" of the Bible, wives of both confessions could only play a subordinate role at home under the strict rule of their husbands. (Ozment 2001, 31)

That said, "women and Protestantism were brought together in two novel developments, both well established in the previous century and embraced by both sides; the rise of marriage as the dominant lifestyle for adults and the movement of the family to the center of society-sustaining work and life." (Ozment 2001, 33. See Davis, 1975, 35–7.)

While "some gender specialists reject the portrayal of European history since the fifteenth century as overwhelmingly a loss for women," as, in Heide Wunder's words, "the domestication of women through Luther," the Protestant reformers should not be blamed for all the changes or lack of them in women lives (Ozment 2001, 38, 33). It would hardly be fair either to expect from the reformers a "general disappearance of social inequality and the hierarchy of marriage" in early modern Europe. Neither should women be considered as "merely victims over centuries" (Ozment 2001, 38 quoting Wunder. See Ozment 2001, 31–2, footnote 27). The truth was much more complex, as has been demonstrated by the lives and voices of women in this book.

To conclude, the Reformation happened in the context of sixteenth-century Europe, in a religiously ordered society with social and ecclesiastical structures that had long roots and histories. The theological changes that were proposed, accompanied by both major and minor changes in religious practices and expressions of faith, were serious for men and women. The issue of gender equality and women's status was not the ultimate concern of the reformers, their interest lay in the salvation of souls and the rescue of the Christian Church. For the protection of the renewed religious values, as understood by the reformers, status quo and order in societal matters and gender relations were considered to be essential. Women too were fueled by the reform ideas, and contributed in their own ways within the existing structures, while not always abiding by the "rules." It is helpful to name the ills of sexism and the distortion of power in the evaluation of women's outcome in the process, but it is even more constructive and promising to discover the different ways in which women not only survived but did so with energetic and prominent participation – that is to say, what is of greatest importance is the recognition of women as subjects of the history they have lived and defined. The women's side of the story serves as a reminder of the blurry correlation between ideals and reality. It inspires us to a never-complete reevaluation of the core vision of the Reformation and its varied implementations and implications, as well as its theological legacies and relevance today.

Bibliography

Options and Visions for Women

Amt, Emilie. 1993. *Women's Lives in Medieval Europe: A Sourcebook*. New York and London: Routledge.

Amussen, Susan D. and Adele Seeff, eds. 1998. *Attending to Early Modern Women*. Newark: University of Delaware Press.

Bainton, Roland. 1980. "Learned Women in the Europe of the Sixteenth Century." In Patricia Labalme (ed.), *Beyond Their Sex: Learned Women of the European Past*. New York: New York University Press. Pp. 117–25.

Bainton, Roland. 2001a. *Women of the Reformation in Germany and Italy*. N.p.: Academic Renewal Press. First published 1971, Minneapolis: Augsburg Publishing House.

Bainton, Roland. 2001b. *Women of the Reformation in France and England*. N.p.: Academic Renewal Press. First published 1973, Minneapolis: Augsburg Publishing House.

Bainton, Roland. 2001c. *Women of the Reformation from Spain to Scandinavia*. N.p.: Academic Renewal Press. First published 1977, Augsburg Publishing House.

Baker, Derek, ed. 1978. *Medieval Women*. Oxford: Basil Blackwell.

Barker, Paula S. Datkso. 1995. "Caritas Pirckheimer: A Female Humanist Confronts the Reformation." *Sixteenth Century Journal* 26: 259–72.

Becker-Cantarino, Barbara. 1980. *Die Frau von der Reformation zur Romantik: Die Situation der Frau vor dem Hintergrund der Literatur- und Sozialgeschichte*. Bonn: Bouvier.

Becker-Cantarino, Barbara. 1987. *Der lange Weg zur Mündigkeit: Frau und Literatur 1500–1800*. Stuttgart: J. B. Metzler.

Beilin, Elaine V. 1996. *The Examinations of Anne Askew*. New York: Oxford University Press.

Blaisdell, Charmarie Jenkins.1982. "Calvin's Letters to Women; The Courting of Ladies in High Places." *Sixteenth Century Journal* 23: 366–83.

Blaisdell, Charmarie Jenkins. 1985. "The Matrix of Reform: Women in the Lutheran and Calvinist Movements." In Richard Greaves (ed.), *Triumph over Silence: Women in Protestant History*. Westport, CT.: Greenwood. Pp. 13–44.

Blaisdell, Charmarie. 1999. "Religion, Gender, and Class: Nuns and Authority in Early Modern France." In Michael Wolfe (ed.), *Changing Identities in Early Modern France*. Durham, NC: Duke University. Pp. 147–68.

Blamires, Alcuin. 1992. *Woman Defamed and Woman Defended: An Anthology of Medieval Texts*. Oxford: Clarendon Press.

Bornstein, Daniel and Roberto Rusconi, eds. 1996. *Women and Religion in Medieval and Renaissance Italy*. Transl. Margery J. Schneider. Chicago: University of Chicago Press.

Braght, Tieleman J. van. 1972 [1660]. *The Bloody Theater or Martyrs' Mirror of the Defenseless Christians*. 9th edn. Transl. Joseph F. Sohm. Scottdalte PA: Herald Press.

Bratt, John. H. 1976. "The Role and Status of Women in the Writings of John Calvin." In Peter de Klerk (ed.), *Renaissance, Reformation, Resurgence*. Grand Rapids: Houghton Mifflin.

Bridenthal, Renate, Claudia Koonz, and Susan Stuard, eds. 1987. *Becoming Visible: Women in European History*. 2nd edn. Boston: Houghton Mifflin.

Brink, Jean R., ed. 1980. *Female Scholars: A Tradition of Learned Women before 1800*. Montreal: Eden Press Women's Publications.

Bryant, G. 1987. "Introduction." In Katharina M. Wilson (ed.), *Women Writers of the Renaissance and Reformation*. Athens and London: The University of Georgia Press. Pp. 287–303.

Bynum, Caroline Walker. 1982. *Jesus as Mother: Studies in the Spirituality of the High Middle Ages*. Berkeley: University of California Press.

Bynum, Caroline Walker. 1987. *Holy Feast and Holy Fast: The Religious Significance of Food for Medieval Women*. Berkeley: University of California Press.

Bynum, Caroline Walker. 1991. *Fragmentation and Redemption: Essays on Gender and the Human Body in Medieval Religion*. New York: Zone Books.

Chojnacka, Monica and Merry E. Wiesner-Hanks. 2002. *Ages of Woman, Ages of Man, Sources in European Social History*. London: Pearson Education.

Chrisman, Miriam. 1972. "Women and the Reformation in Strasbourg 1490–1530. *Archiv für Reformationsgeschichte* 63: 143–68.

Chrisman, Miriam Usher. 1982. *Lay Culture, Learned Culture: Books and Social Change in Strasbourg, 1480–1599*. New Haven: Yale.

Clark, Elizabeth and Herbert Richardson, eds. 1977. "Luther and the Protestant Reformation: From Nun to Parson's Wife." In *Women and Religion: A Feminist Sourcebook of Christian Thought*. New York: Harper & Row Publishers. Pp. 131–48. Rev. and expanded edn., 1996, *The Original Sourcebook of Women in Christian Thought*. San Francisco: Harper SanFrancisco.

Classics of Western Spirituality series. Various titles (e.g., St. Birgitta of Sweden, St. Catherine of Siena, Julian of Norwich, Angela of Foligno, St. Teresa of Avila, Hildegard of Bingen, Mechtild of Magdeburg, Marguerite Porete). New York: Paulist Press Since 1979.

Conrad, Anne U. 1999. "Berlegungen zu einer Geschlechtergeschichte der Reformation und katholischen Reform." In Anne Conrad & Caroline Gritschke (eds), *"In Christo ist weder man noch weyb": Frauen in der Zeit der Reformation und der katholischen Reform*. Münster: Aschendorff. Pp. 7–22.

Conrad, Anne and Caroline Gritschke, eds. 1999. *"In Christo ist weder man noch weyb": Frauen in der Zeit der Reformation und der katholischen Reform*. Münster: Aschendorff.

Coudert, Allison P. 1989. "The Myth of the Improved Status of Protestant Women: The Case of the Witchcraze." In Jean R. Brink et al. (eds), *The Politics of Gender in Early Modern Europe*. Kirksville, MO: Sixteenth Century Journal Publishers. Pp. 61–90.

Davis, Natalie Zemon. 1975a. "City Women and Religious Change." In Natalie Zemon Davis *Society and Culture in Early Modern France*. Stanford: Stanford University Press. Pp. 65–95.

Davis, Natalie Zemon. 1975b. "Women's History in Transition: The European Case." *Feminist Studies* 3: 83–103.

Davis, Natalie Zemon. 1980. "Gender and Genre; Women as Historical Writers, 1400–1820." In Patricia Labalme *Beyond Their Sex: Learned Women of the European Past*. New York: New York University Press. Pp. 153–82.

Davis, Natalie Zemon. 1995. *Women on the Margins: Three Seventeenth-Century Lives*. Cambridge, MA: Harvard University Press.

Davis, Natalie Zemon. 1998. "Displacing and Displeasing: Writing about Women in the Early Modern Period." In Susan Amussen and Adele Seef *Attending to Early Modern Women*. Newark: University of Delaware Press. Pp. 25–37.

Deppermann, K. 1987. *Melchior Hoffman: Social Unrest and Apocalyptic Visions in the Age of Reformation*. Edinburg: T. & T. Clark.

DiCaprio, Lisa and Merry E. Wiesner. 2001. *Lives and Voices. Sources in European Women's History*. Boston: Houghton Mifflin.

Douglass, Jane Dempsey. 1974. "Women and the Continental Reformation." In Rosemary Radford Ruether (ed.), *Religion and Sexism: Images of Woman in the Jewish and Christian Traditions*. New York: Simon and Schuster. Pp. 292–318.

Douglass, Jane Dempsey. 1985. *Women, Freedom and Calvin*. Philadelphia: The Westminster Press.

Dresen-Coenders, Lene, ed. 1987. *Saints and She-Devils: Images of Women in Fifteenth and Sixteenth Centuries*. London: Rubicon. Pp. 101–27.

Duby, Georges and Michelle Perrot. 1992–3. *A History of Women in the West*, 3 vols. vol. 1 (1992), *From Ancient Goddesses to Christian Saints*. Ed. Pauline Schmitt Pantel; vol. 2 (1992), *Silences of the Middle Ages*. Ed. Christiane Klapisch-Zuber; vol. 3 (1993), *Renaissance and Enlightenment Paradoxes*. Ed. Natalie Zemon Davis and Arlette Farge. Cambridge, MA: Harvard University Press.

Eckenstein, Lina. 1963 [1896]. *Women Under Monasticism:* Chapters on Saint-Lore and Convent Life between A.D. 500 and A.D. 1500. New York: Russell and Russell.

Evangelisches Predigerseminar Luthertstadt Wittenberg. 1997 [1995]. *Frauen mischen sie ein. Katharina Luther, Katharina Melanchthon, Katharina Zell, Hille Feicken und Andere*. Wittenberger Sonntagsvorlesungen. First published 1995. 2nd print 1997. Wittenberg: Drei Kastanien Verlag.

Ezell, Margaret J. M. 1993. *Writing Women's Literary History*. Baltimore: Johns Hopkins University Press.

Faust, Ulrich, ed. 1984. *Norddeutschland*. (*Die Frauenklöster in Niedersachsen, Schleswig-Holstein und Bremen, Germania Benedictina*, vol. 11.) St Ottilien: EOS-Verlag.

Greaves, Richard, ed. 1985. *Triumph over Silence: Women in Protestant History*. Westport, CT: Greenwood Press.

Green, Lowell. 1979. "The Education of Women in the Reformation." *History of Education Quarterly* 19 (Spring): 93–116.

Halbach, Silke. 1999. "Publizistisches Engagement von Fauen in der Frühzeit der Reformation." In Anne Conrad and Caroline Gritschke (eds), *"In Christo ist weder man noch weyb": Frauen in der Zeit der Reformation und der katholischen Reform*. Pp. 49–68.

Harrison, Wes. 1992. "The Role of Women in Anabaptist Thought and Practice: The Hutterite Experience of the Sixteenth and Seventeenth Centuries." *Sixteenth Century Journal* 23/1: 49–69.

Hendrix, Scott H. 2004a. *Recultivating the Vineyard: The Reformation Agendas of Christianization*. Louisville, KY and London: Westminster John Knox Press.

Hendrix, Scott. 2004b. "Luther on Marriage." In Timothy J. Wengert (ed.), *Harvesting Martin Luther's Reflections on Theology, Ethics, and the Church*, with a Foreword by David C. Steinmetz. Grand Rapids, MI: William B. Eerdmans Publishing Company. Pp. 169–84.

Heuser, Magdalene, ed. 1996. *Autobiographien von Frauen: Beiträge zu ihrer Geschichte.* Tübingen: Max Niewmeyer.

Heutger, Nicolaus. 1981. *Evangelische Konvente in den welfischen Landen und der Grafschaft Schaumburg: Studien über ein Nachleben klösterlicher und stiftischer Former seit Einführung der Reformation.* Hildesheim.

Hull, Suzanne. 1982. *Chaste, Silent, and Obedient: English Books for Women, 1475–1640.* San Marion, CA: Huntingdon Library.

Irwin, Joyce, ed. 1979. *Women in Radical Protestantism, 1525–1675.* New York: Edwin Mellen Press.

Irwin, Joyce. 1982. "Society and Sexes." In Steven Ozment (ed.), *Reformation Europe: A Guide to Research.* St. Louis: Center for Reformation Research. Pp. 342–9.

Jacobsen, Gretha. 1989. "Nordic Women and the Reformation." In Sherrin Marshall (ed.), *Women in Reformation and Counter-Reformation Europe: Public and Private Worlds.* Bloomington and Indianapolis: Indiana University Press. Pp. 47–67.

James, Susan E. 1999. *Kathryn Parr: The Making of a Queen.* Aldershot and Brookfield, England: Ashgate Publishing Co.

Janowski, Christine J. 1984. "Umstrittene Pfarrerin. Zu einer unvollendeten Reformation der Kirche." In Martin Greiffenhagen (ed.), *Das Evangelische Pfarrfaus. Eine Kultur- und Sozialgeschichte.* Stuttgart: Kreuz Verlag. Pp. 83–107.

Jelsma, Auke. 1989. "De positie van de vrouw in de Radicale Reformatie." *Doopsgezindee Bijdragen* nieuwe reeks 15: 25–36.

Johnson, Susan M. 1992. "Luther's Reformation and (Un)holy Matromony." *Journal of Family History* 17: 271–88.

Joldersma, Hermina and Louis Grijp, eds. and transl. 2001. *Elisabeth's Manly Courage: Testimonials and Songs of Martyred Anabaptist Women in the Low Countries.* Marquette: Marquette University Press.

Jung, Martin H. 2002. *Nonnen, Prophetinnen, Kirchenmütter. Kirchen- und frömmigkeitsgeschichtliche Studien zu Frauen der Reformationszeit.* Leipzig: Evangelische Verlagsanstalt GmbH.

Jussie, Jeanne de. 1611. *Le Levain du Calvinisme, ou commencement de l'heresie de Geneve: Faict par Reverende Soeur Jeanne de Jussie, lors religieuse de Saincte Claire de Geneve, & apres sa sortie Abbesse au Convent d'Anyssi.* Chambéry: Du Four.

Jussie, Jeanne de. 1863. *Le Levain du Calvinisme, ou Commencement de l'heresie de Geneve. Faict par Reverende Soeur Jeanne de Jussie, lors religieuse à Saincte Claire de Geneve, et apres sa sortie Abbesse au Convent d'Anyssi.* Ed. Gustave Revilliod. Geneva: Jules Guillaume Fick.

Jussie, Jeanne de. 1853. *Le Levain du Calvinisme, ou commencement de l'heresie de Geneve, faict par Soeur Jeanne de Jussie. Suivi de notes justificatives et d'une notice sur l'ordre religieux de Sainte-Claire et sur la communauté des Clarisses à Genève, par Ad.-C. Grivel.* Ed. Gustave Revilliod. Geneva: Jules-Guillaume Fick.

Jussie, Jeanne de. 1996. *Kleine Chronik. Bericht einer Nonne über die Anfänge der Reformation in Genf.* Transl. and ed. Helmut Feld. Mainz: P. Von Zabern.

Jussie, Jeanne de. 1996. *Petite chronique.* Ed., introduction and commentary by Helmut Feld. Mainz: P. von Zabern.

Jussie, Jeanne de. 2006. *The Short Chronicle: A Poor Clare's Account of the Reformation of Geneva.* Ed. and transl. Carrie F. Klaus. Chicago: University of Chicago Press.

Karant-Nunn, Susan C. 1982. "Continuity and Change: Some Effects of the Reformation on the Women of Zwickau." *Sixteenth Century Journal* 12: 17–42.

Karant-Nunn, Susan. 1986. "The Transmission of Luther's Teachings on Women and Matrimony: The Case of Zwickau." *Archives for Reformation History* 77: 31–46.

Karant-Nunn, Susan C. and Merry E. Hanks-Wiesner. 2003. *Luther on Women. A Sourcebook.* Cambridge: Cambridge University Press.

Kelly, Joan. 1984. *Women, History, and Theology.* Chicago: University of Chicago.

Kelly-Gadol, Joan. 1977. "Did Women Have a Renaissance?" In Renate Bridenthal, Claudia Koonz and Susan Stuard (eds), *Becoming Visible: Women in European History*. Boston: Houghton Mifflin. Pp. 175–201. Also, with bibliography Bridenthal and Stuart 1987 2nd edn.

King, Margaret L. 1991. *Women of the Renaissance*. Chicago: University of Chicago Press. Pp. 238–9

King, Margaret L. and Albert Rabil Jr. 2004. "Series Editors' Introduction." In Mary B. McKinley (ed.), *Epistle to Marguerite de Navarre and Preface to a Sermon by John Calvin, by Marie Dentière*. Ed. and transl. Mary B. McKinley. Chicago and London: University of Chicago Press.

King, Margaret L. and Albert Rabil Jr. 2006. "The Other Voice in Early Modern Europe: Introduction to the Series." In *Katharina Schütz Zell. Church Mother: The Writings of a Protestant Reformer in Sixteenth-Century Germany*. Ed. and transl. Elsie McKee. Chicago and London: The University of Chicago Press, ix–xxix.

Kirschner, Julius and Suzanne Wemple, eds. 1985. *Women of the Medieval World: Essays in Honor of John H. Mundy*. New York and London: Basil Blackwell.

Labalme, Patricia H., ed. 1980. *Beyond Their Sex: Learned Women of the European Past*. New York: New York University Press.

Lazard, Madeleine. 1985. "Deux soeurs enemies, Marie Dentiére et Jeanne de Jussie: Nonnes et réformees à Genéve. In B. Chevalier and C. Sauzat (eds) *Les Réformes: Enracinements socio-cultures*, 25me colloque d'études humanists, Tours, 1–13 juillet 1982. Paris: La Maisnie. Pp. 233–49.

Lehmijoki-Gardner, Maiju. 2005. *Dominican Penitent Women*. Ed., transl., and introduced by Maiju Lehmijoki-Gardner with contributions by Daniel E. Bornstein and E. Ann Matter; Preface by Gabriella Zarri. Mahwah, NJ: Paulist Press.

Leicht, Irene. 1999. "Gebildet und Geistreich: Humanistinnen zwischen Renaissance und Reformation." In Anne Conrad and Caroline Gritschke, *"In Christo ist weder man noch weyb": Frauen in der Zeit der Reformation und der katholischen Reform*. Münster: Aschendorff. Pp. 29–48.

Lerner, Gerda. 1986. *The Creation of Patriarchy*. New York: Oxford University Press.

Lerner, Gerda. 1993. *The Creation of Feminist Consciousness: From the Middle Ages to Eighteen-Seventy*. Oxford: Oxford University Press.

Levin, Carole, Jo Eldridge Carney, and Debra Barrett-Graves. 1988. *Elizabeth I: Always Her Own Free Woman*. Aldershot and Burlington, VT: Ashgate Publishing Limited.

Levin, Carole, Jo Eldrige Carney, and Debra Barrett-Graves, eds. 2003. *"High and Mighty Queens" of Early Modern England: Realities and Representations*. Basingstoke and New York: Palgrave Macmillan.

Liebowitz, Ruth P. 1979. "Virgins in the Service of Christ: The Dispute over an Active Apostolate for Women During the Counter-Reformation." In Rosemary Ruether, Eleanor McLaughlin (eds), *Women of Spirit: Female Leadership in the Jewish and Christian Traditions*. New York: Simon and Schuster. Pp. 131–52.

Lindberg, Carter. 1996. *The European Reformations*. Oxford and Cambridge, MA: Blackwell Publishers.

Lindberg, Carter. 2000. "The Future of a Tradition: Luther and the Family." In Dean O. Wenthe, William C. Weinrich, Arthur A. Just Jr., Daniel Gard, and Thomas L. Olsen (eds), *All Theology is Christology, Essays in Honor of David P. Scaer*. Fort Wayne, IN: Concordia Theological Seminary Press. Pp. 133–51.

Lindsey, Karen. 1995. *Divorced Beheaded Survived: A Feminist Reinterpretation of the Wives of Henry VIII*. Reading, Mass.: Addison-Wesley Publishing Co.

Lowe, K. J. P. 2003. *Nuns' Chronicles and Convent Culture in Renaissance and Counter-Reformation Italy*. Cambridge University Press.

Luther, Martin. 1883–1993. *D. Martin Luthers Werke. Kritische Gesamtausgabe. Weimarer Ausgabe*. Weimar: Herman Böhlaus Nachfolger.

Luther, Martin. 1955–86. *Luther's Works*. American Edition. Ed. Jaroslav Pelikan. 55 vols. Phila-delphia: Fortress Press; St. Louis: Concordia Publishing House.

MacHaffie, Barbara. 2006. *Herstory: Women in Christian Tradition*. Minneapolis: Fortress Press.

McKinley, Mary B. 2004. *Epistle to Marguerite de Navarre and Preface to a Sermon by John Calvin, by Marie Dentière*. Ed. and transl. Mary B. McKinley. University of Chicago Press: Chicago, London.

Maclean, Ian. 1980. *The Renaissance Notion of Woman: A Study in the Fortunes of Scholasticism and Medical Science in European Intellectual Life*. Cambridge and New York: Cambridge University Press.

McNamara, JoAnn. 1996. *Sisters in Arms: A History of Catholic Nuns over Two Millenia*. Cambridge, MA: Harvard University Press.

Mager, Inge. 1999. "Theologenfrauen als 'Gehilfinnen' der Reformation." In Martin Treu (ed.), *Katharina von Bora, die Lutherin: Aufsätze analäßlich ihres 500. Geburtstages*. Wittenberg: Elbe-Druckerei. Pp. 113–27.

Marr, M. K. 1987. "Anabaptist Women of the North: Peers in the Faith, Subordinates in Marriage." *Mennonite Quarterly Review* 61 (October): 347–62.

Marshall, Sherrin, ed. 1989. *Women in Reformation and Counter-Reformation Europe: Public and Private Worlds*. Bloomington and Indianapolis: Indiana University Press.

Matter, Ann E. and John Coakley, eds. 1994. *Creative Women in Medieval and Early Modern Italy: A Religious and Artistic Renaissance*. Philadelphia: University of Pennsylvania Press.

Meek, Christine, ed. 2000. *Women in Renaissance and Early Modern Europe*. Dublin: Four Courts Press.

Mehlhorn, Paul. 1917. *Die Frauen unserer Reformatoren*. Tübingen: J.C. N. Mohr.

Merkel, Kertin and Heide Wunder, eds. 2000. *Deutsche Frauen der Frühen Neuzeit. Dichterinnen, Malerinnen, Mäzeninnen*. Darmstadts: Primus Verlag. Wissenschaftliche Buchgesellschaft.

Meyer, Hannah Meyer. 1960. *Gewagt auf Gottes Gnad. Frauen der Reformationszeit*. Evangelische Verlagsanstalt Berlin.

Michalove, Sharon D. 1999. "Equal in Opportunity? The Education of Aristocratic Women 1450–1540." In Barbara J. Whitehead (ed.), *Women's Education in Early Modern Europe*. (*Studies in the History of Education*, vol. 7.) Garland Publishing Inc. New York and London. Pp. 47–74.

Monter, William. 1987. "Protestant Wives, Catholic Saints, and the Devil's Handmaid: Women in the Age of Reformations." In Renate Bridenthal, Claudia Koonz, and Susan Stuard (eds.), *Becoming Visible: Women in European History*. Boston: Houghton Mifflin. Pp. 203–21.

Nielsen, Merete. 1999. "Kinder, Küche und Kirche. Pfarrfrauen der Reformationszeit in Südwest-deutschland und der Schweiz." In Martin Treu (ed.), *Katharina von Bora, die Lutherin: Auf-sätze analäßlich ihres 500. Geburtstages*. Wittenberg: Elbe-Druckerei. Pp. 128–58.

Norberg, Kathryn. 1988. "The Counter-Reformation and Women Religious and Lay." In John O'Malley, S.J. (ed.), *Catholicism in Early Modern History: A Guide to Research*. St Louis: Center for Reformation Research. Pp. 133–46.

Nowicki-Patuschka, Angelika. 1990. *Frauen in der Reformation: Untersuchungen zum Verhalten von Frauen in der Reichstädten Augsburg und Nürnberg zur reformatorischen Bewegung zwischen 1517 und 1537*. Pfaffenweiler: Centaurus-Verlagsgesellschaft.

Nussbaum, Felicity and Estelle C. Jelinek, eds. 1986. *The Tradition of Women's Autobiography from Antiquity to the Present*. Boston: Twayne.

Ozment, Steven. 1983. *When Fathers Ruled: Family Life in Reformation Europe*. Cambridge, MA: Harvard University Press.

Ozment, Steven. 2001. *Ancestors, The Loving Family in Old Europe*. Cambridge, MA and London: Harvard University Press.

Packull, Werner O. 1984. "Anna Jansz of Rotterdam, a Historical Investigation of an Early Ana-baptist Heroine? *Sixteenth Century Journal* 82: 147–73.

Partner, Nancy F. 1993. *Studying Medieval Women: Sex, Gender, Feminism*. Cambridge, MA: The Medieval Academy of America.

Perrin, David, ed. 2001. *Women Christian Mystics Speak to Our* Times. Franklin, WI: Sheet & Ward. Pp. 37–52.

Peters, Christine. 2003. *Patterns of Piety: Women, Gender and Religion in Late Medieval and Reformation England*. Cambridge: Cambridge University Press.

Petroff, Elisabeth. 1986. *Medieval Women's Visionary Literature*. New York and Oxford: Oxford University Press.

Power, Eileen. 1926. "The Position of Women." In G.C. Crump and E.F. Jacob (eds), *The Legacy of the Middle Ages*. Oxford: Clarendon Press. Pp. 401–34.

Ranft, Patricia. 1988. *Women and Spiritual Equality in Christian Tradition*. New York: St. Martin's Press.

Roper, Lyndal. 1989. *Holy Household, Women and Morals in Reformation Augsburg*. Oxford: Clarendon Press.

Roper, Lyndal. 1983. "Luther: Sex, Marriage and Motherhood." *History Today* 33 (December): 33–8.

Rossiaud, Jacques. 1988. *Medieval Prostitution: Family, Sexuality and Social Relatons in Past Times*. Oxford and Cambridge, MA: Blackwell Publishers.

Ruether, Rosemary and Eleanor McLaughlin, eds. 1979. *Women of Spirit: Female Leadership in the Jewish and Christian Traditions*. New York: Simon and Schuster.

Russell, Paul. 1986. *Lay Theology in the Reformation: Popular Pamphleteers in Southwest Germany 1521–1525*. Cambridge and New York: Cambridge University Press.

Scaraffia, Lucetta, Gabriella Zarri, eds. 1994. *Donne e fede. Santità e vita religiosa in Italia*. Roma-Bari: Editori Laterza.

Scharffenorth, Greta. 1985. "Martin Luther zur Rolle von Mann und Frau." In Hans Süssmuth (ed.), *Das Luther-Erbe in Deutschland. Vermittlung zwischen Wissenschaft und Offentlichkeit*. Düsseldorf: Droste Verlag. Pp. 111–29.

Schorn-Schütte, Louise. 1999. "Il matrimonio come professione: la moglie del pastore evangelico." In Anne Jacobson Schütte, Thomas Kuehn, and Silvana Seidel Menchi (eds), *Tempi e spazi di vita femminile tra medioevo ed èta moderna*. Bologna: Il Mulino. Pp. 255–77.

Schorn-Schütte, Louise, Walter Sparn, eds. 1997. *Evangelische Pfarrer: zur sozialen und politischen Rolle einer bürgerlichen Gruppe in der deutschen Gesellschaft des 18. bis 20. Jahrhunderts*. Stuttgart: W. Kohlhammer.

Scott, Joan. 1986. "Gender: A Useful Category of Historical Analysis." *American Historical Review* 91: 1053–1075.

Snyder, Arnold C. and Linda A. Huebert Hecht, eds. 1996. *Profiles of Anabaptist Women: Sixteenth-Century Reforming Pioneers*. Studies in Women and Religion/Etudes sur les femmes et la religion: 3. 6th impression 2002. Waterloo, ON: Wilfrid Laurier University Press.

Sommerville, Margaret R. 1995. *Sex and Subjection: Attitudes to Women in Early-Modern Society*. London: Arnold.

Sprunger, Keith L. 1985. "God's Powerful Army of the Weak: Anabaptist Women of the Radical Reformation." In Richard L. Greaves (ed.), *Triumph over Silence, Women in Protestant History*. Connecticut: Greenwood. Pp. 45–74.

Stjerna, Kirsi. 2001. "Medieval Women's Stories: Stories for Women Today." In David Perrin (ed.), *Women Christian Mystics Speak to Our Times*. Franklin, WI: Sheet & Ward. Pp. 37–52.

Stjerna, Kirsi. 2002. "Spiritual Models of Medieval Mystics Today: Rethinking the Legacy of St. Birgitta of Sweden." *Studies in Spirituality* 12: 126–40.

Stock, Phyllis. 1978. *Better than Rubies: A History of Women's Education*. New York: G. P. Putnam and Sons.

Strasser, Ulrike. 2004: "Early Modern Nuns and the Feminist Politics of Religion." *The Journal of Religion* 84 (4): 529–54.

Stuard, Susan. 1987. "The Dominion of Gender: Women's Fortunes in the High Middle Ages." In Renate Bridenthal, Claudia Koonz, and Susan Stuard (eds.), *Becoming Visible: Women in European History*. 2nd edn. Boston: Houghton Mifflin. Pp. 153–72.

Thiebaux, Marcelle, transl., ed. 1987. *The Writings of Medieval Women*. New York: Garland.

Thiele, Johannes. 1988. *Mein Herz schmiltzt wie Eis am feuer. Die religiöse Frauenbewegung des mittelalters in Porträts*. Stuttgart: Kreuz Verlag.

Thompson, John Lee. 1992. *John Calvin and the Daughters of Sarah: Women in Regular and Exceptional Roles in the Exegesis of Calvin, His Predecessors, and His Contemporaries*. Geneva: Librairie Droz S.A.

Thysell, Carol. 2000. *The Pleasure of Discernment: Marguerite de Navarre as Theologian*. Oxford: Oxford University Press.

Treu, Martin, ed. 1999. *Katharina von Bora, die Lutherin: Aufsätze analäßlich ihres 500. Geburtstages*. Martin Treu im Auftrag der Stiftung Luthergedenkstätten in Sachsen-Anhalt. Wittenberg: Elbe-Druckerei.

Umble, Jenifer. 1990. "Women and Choice: An Examination of the Martyrs' Mirror." *Mennonite Quarterly Review* 64: 135–45.

Wahl, Johannes. 1999. "'. . . sich in das dorffwesen gar nicht schicken kann.' Pfarrfrauen des 16. und 17. Jahrhunderts zwischen bürgerlicher Ehe und ländlicher Lebenswelt." In Martin Treu (ed.), *Katharina von Bora, die Lutherin: Aufsätze analäßlich ihres 500. Geburtstages*. Pp. 179–91.

Warnicke, Retha M. 1983. *Women of the English Renaissance and Reformation*. Westport, CT: Greenwood Press.

Warnicke, Retha M. 1989. *The Rise and Fall of Anne Boleyn: Family Politics at the Court of Henry VIII*. New York: Cambridge University Press.

Warnicke, Retha M. 2000. *The Marrying of Anne of Cleves: Royal Protocol in Tudor England*. New York: Cambridge University Press.

Wengler, Elisabeth M. 1999. "Women, Religion and Reform in Sixteenth-Century Geneva." PhD dissertation. Dept. of History, Boston College, Boston, MA.

Werner, Yvonne Maria, ed. 2004. *Nuns and Sisters in the Nordic Countries after the Reformation: A Female Counter-Culture in Modern Society*. Uppsala: The Authors and The Swedish Institute of Mission Research.

Whitehead, Barbara J. ed. 1999. *Women's Education in Early Modern Europe*. (Studies in the History of Education, vol. 7.) New York and London: Garland Publishing Inc.

Wiesner, Merry E. 1983. *Women in the Sixteenth Century: A Bibliography*. Sixteenth Century Bibliography, 23. St. Louis: Center for Reformation Research.

Wiesner, Merry E. 1988. "Women's Response to the Reformation." In Ronnie Po-chia Hsia (ed.), *The German People and the Reformation*. Ithaca: Cornell University Press. Pp. 148–71.

Wiesner, Merry E. 1989. "Nuns, Wives, and Mothers: Women and the Reformation in Germany." In Sherrin Marshall (ed.), *Women in Reformation and Counter-Reformation Europe: Public and Private Worlds*. Bloomington: Indiana University Press. Pp. 8–27.

Wiesner, Merry, E. 1992a. "Studies of Women, Family and Gender." In William Maltby (ed.), *Reformation Europe: A Guide to Research* II. St. Louis: Center for Reformation Research. Pp. 159–87.

Wiesner, Merry. E. 1992b. "Ideology Meets the Empire: Reformed Convents and the Reformation." In Andrew C. Fix and Susan C. Karant-Nunn (eds), *Germania Illustrata: Essays on Early Modern Germany Presented to Gerald Strauss*. Kirksville, MO: Sixteenth Century Essays and Studies. Pp. 181–95.

Wiesner, Merry E. 2000a. *Women and Gender in Early Modern Europe: New Approaches to Modern European History*. 2nd edn. Cambridge: Cambridge University Press.

Wiesner, Merry. 2000b. "Herzogin Elisabeth von Braunschweig-Lüneberg (1510–1558)." In Kerstin Merkel and Heide Wunder (eds), *Deutsche Frauen der Frühen Neuzeit: Dichterinnen, Malerinnen, Mäzeninnen*. Darmstadt: Wissenschaftliche Buchgesellschaft. Pp. 39–48.

Wiesner-Hanks, Merry, ed. 1996. *Convents Confronting Reformation: Catholic and Protestant Nuns in Germany*. Transl. Joan Skocir and Merry Wiesner-Hanks. "Introduction". Milwaukee: Marquette University Press. Pp. 11–25.

Wiesner-Hanks, Merry. 1998a. "Kinder, Kirche, Landeskinder: Women Defend their Publishing in Early Modern Germany." In R. B. Barnes, R. A. Kolb, and P. L. Presley (eds), *Habent sua fata libelli*. Kirksville, MO: Truman State University Press. Pp. 143–52.

Wiesner-Hanks, Merry. 1998b. "The Hubris of Writing Surveys, or A Feminist Confronts the Textbook." In Susan Amussen and Adele Seef (eds), *Attending to Early Modern Women*. Newark: University of Delaware Press. Pp. 297–310.

Wiesner-Hanks, Merry E. 2000. "Protestantism in Europe." In *Christianity and Sexuality in the Early Modern World: Regulating Desire, Reforming Practice*. 2nd edn. London and New York; Routledge. Pp. 59–100.

Wiesner-Hanks, Merry E. 2001. "Women's History and Social History: Are Structures Necessary?" In Anne Jacobson Schutte, Thomas Kuehn, and Silvana Seidel Menchi (eds), *Time, Space and Women's Lives in Early Modern Europe*. (*Sixteenth Century Essays & Studies*, vol. 57.) Kirksville, MO: Truman State University Press. Pp. 3–16. (Italian original: 1999. Tempi e spazi di vita femminile tra medioevo ed èta moderna. Bologna: Il Mulino.)

Wiesner-Hanks, Merry. 2003. "Reflections on a Quarter Century of Research on Women." In Lee Palmer Wandel (ed.), *History Has Many Voices: Sixteenth Century Essays and Studies*. Kirksville, MO: Truman State University Press, 2003. Pp. 93–112.

Wiethaus, Ulrike. 1993. "Female Authority and Religiosity in Letters of Katharina Zell and Caritas Pirckheimer." *Mystics Quarterly* 19 (5): 123–35.

Williams, Mary Cooper and Keever, E. F. eds. 1930. *Luther's Letters to Women*. Chicago: Wartburg.

Wilson, Katharina M. ed. 1987. *Women Writers of the Renaissance and Reformation*. "Introduction," vii–xxix. Athens and London: The University of Georgia Press.

Witte Jr., John. 1997. *From Sacrament to Contract: Marriage, Religions, and Law in the Western Tradition*. Louisville: Westminster/John Knox.

Witte Jr., John. 2002. *Law and Protestantism: The Legal Teachings of the Reformation*. Cambridge: Cambridge University Press.

Wittenmyer, Annie. 1885. *The Women of the Reformation*. New York: Phillips & Hunt. Cincinnati: Cranston & Stowe.

Wunder, Heide. 1992. "*Er ist die Sonn', sie ist der Mond.*" *Frauen in der Frühen Neuzeit*. München: Beck, 1992. English edn. 1998, *He is the Sun, She is the Moon: Women in the Early Modern Germany*, transl. Thomas Dunlap. Cambridge, MA: Harvard: University Press.

Wunder, Heide Wunder and Gisela Engel, eds. 1998. *Geschlechterperspektiven Forschungen zur Frühen Neuzeit*. Königstein: Taunus.

Zarri, Gabriella. 2000. "Living Saints: A Typology of Female Sanctity in the Early Sixteenth Century." In Letizia Panizza and Sharon Wood (eds), *A History of Women's Writing in Italy*. Cambridge: Cambridge University Press. Pp. 219–303.

Zarri, Gabriella. 2000. "Religious and Devotional Writing 1400–1600." In Letizia Panizza and Sharon Wood (eds), *A History of Women's Writing in Italy*. Cambridge: Cambridge University Press. Pp. 79–91.

Zeller, Reinmar, ed. 1982. *Luther wie ihn keiner kennt*. Freiburg im Br.: Herder. Pp. 13–27.

Zimmerli-Witschi, Alice. 1981. *Frauen in der Reformationszeit*. Zürich: aku-Fotodruck.

Åkerlund, Ingrid. 2003. "Jeanne de Jussie and Marie Dentière: Two Abbesses Persecuted for Their Religious Beliefs." In idem, *Sixteenth Century French Women Writers: Marguerite d'Angoulême, Anne de Graville, the Lyonnese School, Jeanne de Jussie, Marie Dentière, Camille de Morel*. Studies in French Literature, vol. 67. Lewiston and Lampeter: The Edwin Mellen Press. Pp. 105–26 (Marie), 106–10 (Jeanne).

Women as Models, Leaders and Teachers of the Reformation

Katharina von Bora Luther

Katharina's Letters (from Smith 1999, 769–770)

Handwritten dedication to Duchess Dorothea of Prussia. In a copy of Martin Luther's *Geistliche Lieder* (Leipzig: Valentin Bapts, 1545) University Library, Torun University, Torun, Poland. Catalogue number Cim I.180. [The only document in Katharina's own handwriting; Smith 1999, 770.] (Letter B in Smith.)

Katharina von Bora Luther, Letter to Hans von Taubenheim. Wittenberg, April 28, 1539. Thüringisches Hauptstaatsarchiv, Weimar. Catalogue number ThHStAW, Reg. Aa No. 1635–45, B. 53–53v. (Letter A in Smith.)

Letter to sister-in-law Christina von Bora after Martin Luther's death. Wittenberg, April 2, 1546. Julius Jordan (1919) "Aus den Sammlungen der Lutherhalle . . . 2. Ein Brief von Katharina von Bora, 1546." In *Lutherjahrbuch* 1: 139–43. (Letter C in Smith.)

Letter to Elector Moritz von Sachsen. Wittenberg, September 16, 1548. Staatsarchiv, Dresden. (Letter D in Smith.)

Letters to Duke Albrecht von Hohenzollern-Ansbach of Prussia. Wittenberg May 29, 1551. Staatsarchiv Berlin, Preussischer Kulturbesitz. (Letter E in Smith.)

(Two manuscript letters.)

Letters to King Christian III of Denmark, 1547–52. Statens Arkiver, Rigsarkivet, Copenhagen, Denmark. Catalogue number: Registratur 63. (Three manuscript letters from February 9, 1547, October 6, 1550, and January 8, 1552.) (Letters F1, F2, and F3 in Smith.)

[the texts above quoted from] Smith, Jeanette C. 1999. "Katharina von Bora Through Five Centuries: A Historiography." In *Sixteenth Century Journal* 30 (3): 745–4. With Katharina's Letters in Appendix.

Luther's Letters to Katharina/Luther's Conversations with and about Katharina

Luther, Martin. 1883–1993. *D. Martin Luthers Werke. Kritische Gesamtausgabe. Weimarer Ausgabe* 1883ff. Weimar: Herman Böhlaus Nachfolger. In particular in the Table Talks/Tischreden [WA Tr, esp. II, III, V, VII] and Correspondence/Briefwechsel [WA Br]. See in particular WA Br XIV [Weimar 1930–37] and WA Br VI [1912–21]. Also the Testament of Luther, in WA Br IX, no. 3699, Pp. 574–5. [In English, in Karant-Nunn and Wiesner-Hanks 2003, 196 and LW 34: 289–97.]

A Sample of Luther's Letters to Katharina, in WA Br VI, VIII, IX, X, XI/in English in Karant-Nunn and Hanks-Wiesner 2003. Pp. 186–96:

From Torgau, February 27, 1532, in WA Br VI, no. 1908, Pp. 270–1.

From Dessau July 29, 1534, in WA Br VII, no. 2130, p. 91.

From Tambach February 27, 1537, in WA Br VIII, no. 3140, Pp. 50–1.

From Eisenach July 10, 1540, in WA Br IX, no. 3511, p. 171–3.

From Eisenach July 16, 1540, in WA Br IX, no. 3512, Pp. 174–5.

From Eisenach July 26, 1540, in WA Br X, no. 3519, p. 205.

From Wittenberg September 18, 1541, in WA Br X, no. 3670, Pp. 518–19.

From Eisleben February 1, 1545, in WA Br XI no. 4195, Pp. 275–6.

From Zeitz July 28, 1545, in WA Br XI no. 4139, Pp. 149–50.

From Eisleben February 7, 1546, in WA Br XI no. 4201. Pp. 286–7.

From Eisleben February 10, WA Br XI, no. 4203, p. 291.

Luther, Martin. 1955–86. *Luther's Works*. American Edition. Ed. Jaroslav Pelikan. 55 vols. Philadelphia: Fortress Press; St. Louis: Concordia Publishing House.

References

Bainton, R. H. 2001. "Katharine von Bora." In idem, *Women of the Reformation in Germany and Italy*. Minneapolis: Augsberg Publishing House. Pp. 23–44.

Bergholtz, Detlef. 1999. *Die Heimat der Katharina Luther: Lippendorf und Zölsdorf.* 1. Aufl. Beucha: Sax-Verl.

Beste, Wilhelm. 1843. *Die Geshcichte Catharina's von Bora.* Nach den Quellen bearbeitet. Halle: Verlag von Richard Mühlmann.

Bräuer, Siegfried. 1999. "Katharina von Bora, die Lutherin – im Urteil der Zeit." In Evangelisches Predigerseminar Luthertstadt Wittenberg (ed.), *Mönschure und Morgenstern.* Wittenberger Sonntagsvorlesungen. Wittenberg: Drei Kastaninen Verlag. Pp. 75–95.

Brecht, Martin. 1994. *Shaping and Defining the Reformation, 1521–1532.* Minneapolis: Fortress Press.

Brecht, Martin. 1999. *The Preservation of the Church, 1532–1546.* Minneapolis: Fortress Press.

Deen, Edith. 1958. "Katherine von Bora – Wife of Martin Luther". In idem, *Great Women of the Christian Faith.* New York: Harper.

Delhaas, Sieth. 1995. "Katharina Luther: Wege und Entscheidungen im Zeitalter der Hexenjagd." In Evangelisches Predigerseminar Luthertstadt Wittenberg (ed.), *Frauen mischen sie ein.* Pp. 24–36.

Engelhard, Eusebius. 1747. *Lucifer Wittenbergensis oder der Morgen-Stern von Wittenberg, Das ist vollständiger Lebens-Lauff Catharinae von Bore, des . . . Ehe-Weibes D. Martini Lutheri . . .* Landsperg: Selbstverlag.

Evangelisches Predigerseminar Luthertstadt Wittenberg. 1997 [1995]. *Frauen mischen sie ein. Katharina Luther, Katharina Melanchthon, Katharina Zell, Hille Feicken und Andere.* Wittenberger Sonntagsvorlesungen. First published 1995. 2nd print 1997. Wittenberg: Drei Kastanien Verlag.

Evanglisches Predigerseminar 1999. *Mönschure und Morgenstern. Katharina von Bora, die Lutherin – im Urteil der Zeit, als Nonne, eine Frau von Adel, als Ehefrau und Mutter, eine Wirtschafterin und Saumärkterin, als Witwe.* Wittenberger Sonntagsvorlesungen. Wittenberg: Drei Kastaninen Verlag.

Evangelisches Predigerseminar Luthertstadt Wittenberg. 1999. "Katharina von Bora, die Lutherin – Ehefrau und Mutter." In *Mönchshure und Morgenstern: "Katharina von Bora, die Lutherin" – im Urteil der Zeit, als Nonne, eine Frau von Adel, als Ehefrau und Mutter, eine Wirtschafterin und Saumärkterin, als Witwe.* Wittenberg: Drei Kastanien Verlag. Pp. 9–35.

Hahn, Udo and Marlies Mügge, eds. 1999. *Katharina von Bora: Die Frau an Luthers Seite.* Stuttgart: Quell.

Hansrath, Adolf. 1993. "Luther und Käthe." In idem, *Kleine Schriften, religionsgeschichtlichen Inhalts.* Leipzig: Verlag von G Finzel. Pp. 235–98.

Ihlenfeld, Kurt. 1964. "'Meine alte arme Liebe.' Ein Blick in Luthers Briefe." *Luther Gesellschaft* 35 (3): 132–8.

Janowski, Christine J. 1984. Umstrittene Pfarrerin. Zu einer unvollendeten Reformation der Kirche. In *Das Evangelische Pfarrhaus. Eine Kultur- und Sozialgeschichte.* Hrsg. Martin Greiffenhagen. Stuttgart: Kreuz Verlag. Pp. 83–107.

Joestlel, Volkmar. 1999. Die *Nonne heiratet Mönch: Luthers Hochzeit als Scandalon: eine Textsammlung.* Wittenberg: Drei-Kastanien-Verl.

Jung, Martin H. 1999 "Zum Davonlaufen? Das Klosterleben in der frühen Reformationszeit." In Udo Hahn and Marlies Mügge (eds), *Katharina von Bora: Die Frau an Luthers Seite.* Stuttgart: Quell. Pp. 32–51.

Jung, Martin H. 2002. *Nonnen, Prophetinnen, Kirchenmütter. Kirchen- und frömmigkeitsgeschichtliche Studien zu Frauen der Reformationszeit.* Leipzig: Evangelische Verlagsanstalt GmbH.

Karant-Nunn, Susan C., and Merry E., Hanks-Wiesner. 2003. *Luther on Women: A Sourcebook.* Cambridge: Cambridge University Press.

Klepper, Jochen. 1951. *Das ewige Haus. Kap. 1: Die Flucht der Katharina von Bora oder die klugen und die törichten Jungfrauen.* Stuttgart: Dt. Verl.-Anst.

Köhler, Anne-Katrin. 2003. *Geschichte des Klosters Nimbschen.* Von der Gründung 1243 bis zu seinem Ende 1536/1542. Leipzig: Ev. Verlangsanstalt.

Kroker, Ernst. 1906. *Katharina von Bora, Martin Luthers Frau: Ein Lebens- und Charakterbild.* Leipzig: Verlag von Johannes Herrmann, Zwickau.

Lindberg, Carter. 1996. *The European Reformations.* Oxford: Basil Blackwell.

Lindberg, Carter. 2000. "The Future of a Tradition: Luther and the Family." In Dean O. Wenthe, William C. Weinrich, Arthur A. Just Jr., Daniel Gard, Thomas L. Olsen (eds), *All Theology is Christology, Essays in Honor of David P. Scaer.* Fort Wayne: Concordia Theological Seminary Press. Pp. 133–51.

Luther, Martin. 1883–1993. *D. Martin Luthers Werke: Kritische Gesamtausgabe. Weimarer Ausgabe.* Weimar: Herman Böhlaus Nachfolger.

Luther, Martin. 1955–86. *Luther's Works.* American Edition. Ed. Jaroslav Pelikan. 55 vols. Philadelphia: Fortress Press; St. Louis: Concordia Publishing House.

MacCuish, Dolinda. 1983. *Luther and His Katie.* Tain, Scotland: Christian Focus Publications.

Mager, Inge. 1999a. "Theologenfrauen als, Gehilfinnen' der Reformation." In Martin Treu (ed.) *Katharina von Bora, die Lutherin: Aufsätze analäßlich ihres 500. Geburtstages.* Wittenberg: Elbe-Druckerei. Pp. 113–27.

Mager, Inge. 1999b. "Katharina von Bora, die Lutherin – als Witwe." In Evangelisches Predigerseminar Lutherstadt Wittenberg (ed.), *Mönschure und Morgenstern.* Wittenberger Sonntagsvorlesungen. Wittenberg: Drei Kastaninen Verlag. Pp. 120–36.

Markwald, Rudolf and Marilyn Morris Markwald. 2002. *Katharina von Bora: A Reformation Life.* St Louis, MO: Concordia Publishing House.

Mayeri, Jo. Frid. 1698. *Catharina Lutheri Conjuge.* Dissertatio. Hamburgi: Typis Nicolai Spiring.

Mehlhorn, Paul. 1917. *Die Frauen unserer Reformatoren.* 1&2 Taufend. Tübingen: J.C. N. Mohr. Pp. 4–20.

Morris, John G. 1856. Catherine *de Bora: Or, Social and Domestic Scenes in the Home of Luthers.* Philadelphia: Lindsay & Blakiston.

Mügge, Marlies. 1999. "'Ich habe meine Käthe lieb' – Katharina von Bora in Briefen und Tischreden Martin Luthers." In Udo Hahn and Marlies Mügge (eds), *Katharina von Bora: Die Frau an Luthers Seite.* Stuttgart: Quell. Pp. 63–76.

Mühlhaupt, Erwin. 1986. "Sieben kleine Kapitel über die Lebenswege Luthers und Käthes." In *Zeitschrift der Luther-Gesellschft* 57 (i/): 1–18.

Müller, Gerhard. 1999. "Katharina und Martin – Das erste evangelische Pfarrhaus?" In Udo Hahn and Marlies Mügge (eds), *Katharina von Bora: Die Frau an Luthers Seite.* Stuttgart: Quell. Pp. 96–112.

Nielsen, Merete. 1999. "'Kinder, Küche und Kirche.' Pfarrfrauen der Reformationszeit in Südwestdeutschland und der Schweiz." In Martin Treu (ed.), *Katharina von Bora, die Lutherin: Aufsätze analäßlich ihres 500. Geburtstages.* Pp. 128–57.

Oehmig, Stefan. 1999. "Katharina von Bora, die Lutherin – eine Wirtschafterin und Saumärkterin." In Evangelisches Predigerseminar Lutherstadt Wittenberg (ed.), *Mönschure und Morgenstern.* Wittenberger Sonntagsvorlesungen. Wittenberg: Drei Kastaninen Verlag. Pp. 96–119.

Ozment, Steven. 1993. *Protestants: The Birth of a Revolution.* New York: Image Books, Doubleday.

Pearson, Christian. 1983. "'Line upon Line: Here a Little, There a Little' Some Letters of Martin Luther." In Peter Newman Brooks (ed.), *Seven-headed Luther: Essays in Commemoration of a Quincentenary 1483–1983.* Oxford: Clarendon Press. Pp. 275–310.

Ranft, Andreas. 1999. "Katharina von Bora, die Lutherin – eine Frau von Adel." In Evangelisches Predigerseminar Lutherstadt Wittenberg (ed.), *Mönschure und Morgenstern.* Wittenberger Sonntagsvorlesungen. Wittenberg: Drei Kastaninen Verlag. Pp. 58–74.

Rhein, Stefan. 1995. "Catharina magistri Philippi Melanchtonis Ehelich weib – ein Wittenberger Frauenschicksal der Reformationszeit, Stefan Rhein." In Evangelisches Predigerseminar Lutherstadt Wittenberg (ed.), *Frauen mischen sie ein.* Pp. 37–54.

Richer, Ludwig. 1854. *Katharina Luther.* Dresden: s.d. Microfiche.

Roper, Lyndal. 1989. *The Holy Household: Women and Morals in Reformation Augsburg*. Oxford: Clarendon Press.

Rüttgardt, Antje. 1999. "Katharina von Bora, die Lutherin – als Nonne." In Evangelisches Predigerseminar Luthertstadt Wittenberg (ed.), *Mönschure und Morgenstern*. Wittenberger Sonntagsvorlesungen. Wittenberg: Drei Kastaninen Verlag. Pp. 36–57.

Sachau, Ursula. 1991. *Das Letzte Geheimnis: Das Leben und die Zeit der Katherine von Bora*. Munich: Ehren Wirth.

Scharffenorth, Greta. 1985. "Martin Luther zur Rolle von Mann und Frau". In Hans Süssmuth (ed.), *Das Luther-Erbe in Deutschland. Vermittlung zwischen Wissenschaft und Offentlichkeit*. Dusseldorf: Droste Verlag. Pp. 111–29.

Smith, Jeanette C. 1999. "Katharina von Bora Through Five Centuries: A Historiography." *Sixteenth Century Journal* 30 (3): 745–74.

Stjerna, Kirsi. 2002. "Katie Luther: A Mirror to the Promises and Failures of the Reformation." In David Whitford (ed.), *Caritas et Reformatio: Essays on Church and Society In Honor of Carter Lindberg*. St. Louis: Concordia Publishing House. Pp. 27–39.

Stolt, Birgit. 1999. "Luthers Sprache in seinen Briefen an Käthe." In Treu, Martin, ed. *Katharina von Bora, die Lutherin: Aufsätze analäßlich ihres 500. Geburtstages*. Wittenberg: Elbe-Druckerei. Pp. 23–32.

Thoma, Albrecht. 1900. *Katharina von Bora*. Berlin.

Treu, Martin. 1995a. *Katharina von Bora*. Biographien zur Reformation. Wittenberg: Drei Kastanien Verlag.

Treu, Martin, ed. 1999a. *Katharina von Bora, die Lutherin: Aufsätze analäßlich ihres 500. Geburtstages*. Martin Treu im Auftrag der Stiftung Luthergedenkstätten in Sachsen-Anhalt. Wittenberg: Elbe-Druckerei.

Treu, Martin. 1999b. "Das Leben der Katharina von Bora – eine biografische Skizze." In Martin Treu (ed.), *Katharina von Bora, die Lutherin: Aufsätze analäßlich ihres 500. Geburtstages*. Wittenberg: Elbe-Druckerei. Pp. 11–22.

Treu, Martin. 1999c "Die Frau an Luthers Seite – Das Leben der Katharina von Bora." 32–51. In Udo Hahn and Udo and Marlies Mügge, eds. 1999. *Katharina von Bora: Die Frau an Luthers Seite*. Stuttgart: Quell. Pp. 32–51.

Treu, Martin. 1999d. "Die Frau an Luthers Seite: Katharina von Bora – Leben und Werk." *Luther* 70 (1): 10–29.

Treu, Martin. 1999e. "Katharina von Bora, the Woman at Luther's Side." *Lutheran Quarterly* 13 (2): 157–78.

Wahl, Johannes. 1999. "'. . . sich in das dorffwesen gar nicht schicken kann' Pfarrfrauen des 16. und 17. Jahrhunderts zwischen bürgerlicher Ehe und ländlicher Lebenswelt." In Martin Treu (ed.), *Katharina von Bora, die Lutherin: Aufsätze analäßlich ihres 500. Geburtstages*. Wittenberg: Elbe-Druckerei. Pp. 179–91.

Walsh, Christian Wilhelm Franz. 1752 and 1754. *Wahrhaftige Geschichte der heiligen Frau Katharina von Bora, D. Mart. Luthers Ehegattin wieder Eusebii Engelhards Morgenstern zu Wittenberg*. 2 vols. Ed. C. W. Walsh. Halle: Johann Justinus Gebauern.

Wiesner, Merry E. 1989. "Nuns, Wives, and Mothers: Women and the Reformation in Germany." In Sherrin Marshall (ed.), *Women in Reformation and Counter-Reformation Europ: Public and Private Worlds*. Bloomington: Indiana University Press, 1989, 9–27.

Wiesner-Hanks, Merry. 1996. "Introduction." In Merry Wiesner-Hanks (ed.), *Convents Confront the Reformation: Catholic and Protestant Nuns in Germany*. Milwaukee: Marquette University Press. Pp. 11–25.

Winter, Ingelore. 1990. *Katherina von Bora: Ein Leben mit Martin Luther*. Dusseldorf: Droste.

Wintersteiner, Marianne. 1983. *Luthers Frau: Katharina von Bora*. Mühlacker: Karl Elser GmbH. Stieglitz Verlag, E. Händle, Mühlhacker – Irdning/Steiermark.

Wittenmyer, Annie. 1885. "The Reformation in Germany – Catharina von Bora." In idem, *The Women of the Reformation*. New York: Phillips & Hunt. Cincinnati: Cranston & Stowe. Pp. 361–65.

Zeller, Eva. 1996. *Die Lutherin: Spurensuche nach Katharina von Bora*. Deutsche Verlags-Anstalt Stuttgart. 6th edn.

Argula von Grumbach

Argula's Works (listed after Matheson 1995, Pp. 197–9)

Argula von Grumbach. 1523. *Wie ein Christliche Fraw des adels / in // Beyern durch iren / in Gotlicher schrifft / wolgegrund // tenn Sendbrieffe/ die hohenschul zu Ingoldstat / // vmb das sie eynen Euangelischen Jungling / zu widersprechung des wort gottes. Betrangt// haben / straffet.* Actum Ingelstat. M D Xxiij. Erfurt: Matthes Maler. Köhler: Fiche 1002/2543. (Printed in 13 editions in 1523, in Nuremberg: Friedrich Peypus; Basel: Cratander; Breslau: Libisch; Augsburg: Ulhart Sr.; Zwickau: Gastel; Erfurt: Maler; Eilenburg: Stöckel and Widemar; Strasbourg: Flach; Stuttgart: Hans von Erfurt; Augsburg: Heinrich Steiner.)

Argula von Grumbach. 1523. *Ain Christennliche schrifft // ainer Erbarn frawen / vom Adel // darinn sy alle Christenliche stendt / vnd obrigkayten ermant/ Bey // der warheit / vnd dem wort // Gottes zuo bleyben / vnd // solchs auß Christlicher // pflicht zum ernstlich // sten zuo handt // haben.//* Argula Staufferin. M.D.xxii. Augsburg: Philipp Ulhart Sr. 1523. Köhler: Fiche 16/66.

(Four prints in 1523, in Bamberg, Munich, Erfurt, and in 1524 in Eilenburg.) (E.g., Argula von Grumbach. 1523. *Ein Christennliche schrifft einer erbarn frawen vom Adel/ darinn sie alle Christenliche stendt vnd obrigkeiten ermant/ Bey der warheit vnd dem wort gottes zupleiben/ vnd solchs auß Christlicher pflicht zum ernstlichsten zu handthaben.* Bamberg: Erlinger.)

Argula von Grunbach. 1523. *An ain Ersamen // Weysen Radt der stat // Ingolstat / ain sandt // brief / von Fraw // Argula von grun // bach gebore // von Stauf // fen.* Augsburg: Philipp Ulhart Sr., 1523. Köhler 5/19. (Mikrofiche der Ausg. Ausburg: Ulhart. Flugschriften des frühen 16. Jh, Ser. 1, Mikrofiche 5, Flugshr. Nr. 19. Inter Documentation Company, 1978.)

Argula von Grumbach. 1523. *Dem // Durchleüchtigen hochge // bornen Fürsten vnd herren /Herren Jo // hansen / Pfaltzgrauen bey Reyn // Hertzogen zuo Beyern / Grafen // zuo Spanheym x. Mey // nem Gnedigisten // Herren.* Argula Staufferin. Augsburg: Philipp Ulhart Sr., 1523. Köhler: Fiche 284:818. (Other prints in Bamberg 1523, and Erfurt 1524.) (E.g., Argula von Grumbach. 1523. *Ermanung an den Durchleuchtigen hochgebornen fürsten vnnd hern herren Johannsen Pfaltzgrauen bey Reyn Hertzogen in Bayrn vnd Grauen zu Spanheim etc. Das seyn F. G. ob dem wort gottis halten wöll. Von einer erbaren frawen vom Adel seinn gnaden zugeschickt*). (Mikrofiche der Ausg. Bamberg: Erlinger. Flugschriften des frühen 16. Jh, Ser. 2, Mikrofiche 566, Flugschr. Nr. 1444. Inter Documentation Company 1980.)

Argula von Grumbach. 1523?. *Dem durchleüchtigisten Hoch // gebornen Fürsten vnd herren / Herrnn Fri // derichen. Hertzogen zuo Sachssen / Des // hayligen Römischen Reychs Ertz // marschalck unnd Churfürsten / // Landtgrauen in Düringen / unnd Marggrauen zuo // Meyssen / meynem // gnedigisten // herren.//* Argula Staufferin. Augsburg: Philipp Ulhart Sr., 1523? Köhler: Fiche 10/40. (One other print in Erfurt 1524.) (Argula von Grumbach. 1524. *Dem Durchleuchtigisten Hochgebornen Fürsten vnd herren/Herren Friderichen/ Hertzogen tzu Sachssen . . . meynem Gnedigisten herren.*) (Mikrofiche der Ausg. Erfurt: Stürmer. Flugschr. Des frühen 16. Jh, Ser. 9, Mikrofiche 1808, Flugschr. Nr. 4631. Inter Documentation Company, 1987.)

Argula von Grumbach. 1523. *An den Edlen // und gestrengen he // ren / Adam von Thering // der Pfalzgrauen stat // halter zuo Newburg // x. Ain sandtbrieff // von fraw Argula // von Grumbach // geborne von // Stauf // fen.* Augsburg: Philipp Ulhart Sr., 1523. Köhler: Fiche 967: 2427.

Argula von Grumbach. 1524. *Ein Sendbrieff der edeln // Frawen Argula Staufferin / an die // von Regenßburg. //* M.D. Xxiiij. Nuremberg: Hans Hergot, 1524. Panzer 2342.

Argula von Grumbach. 1524. *Eyn Antwort in // gedichtß weiß / ainem auß d // hohen Schul zu Ingol // stat / auff ainen spruch // newlich von jm auß // gangen / welcher // hynden dabey // getruckt // steet. //* Anno. D.M. Xxiiij. // Rom. X. // So mann von hertzen glawbt / wirt // man rechtuertig / so man aber mit dem // mundt bekennet / wirt mann selig. // Argula von Grumbach / // geboren von Stauff. // Eyn Spruch von der // Staufferin / jres Dispu // tierens halben. // Nuremberg: Hieronumus Höltzel, 1524. Köhler: Fiche 285: 820.

Argula von Grumbach. A Woman's Voice in the Reformation. 1995. Ed. Peter Matheson. Edinburgh: T&T Clark.

References

Argula von Grumbach: selbst ist die Frau: Christin, Draufgängerin, Publizistin. 500? Geburtstag. 1992. Ed. Herbert Spachmüller. Veranstalter und Herausgeber: Evang.-Luth. Kirchengemeinde St. Martin (Schwabach). Ausstellug in der Schwabacher Stadtkirche. October 3–31, 1992.

Bainton, Roland. 2001. "Argula von Grumbach." In idem, *Women of the Reformation in Germany and Italy.* N.p.: Academic Renewal Press. Pp. 97–109. First published 1971, Minneapolis: Augsburg Publishing House.

Bauer, Erich. 1987. "Argula von Grumbach und ihre Flugschriften: Untersuchungen zu Leben und Wirken einer Standesfrau zu Beginn der Reformation." Unpublished dissertation. Salzburg.

Bautz, Friedrich Wilhelm. 1980. "Grumbach, Argula von." *Beiträge zur bayerischen Kirchengeschichte* 2: 370–3.

Becker-Cantarino, Barbara. 1987. "Religiöse Streiterinnen: Katharina Zell und Argula von Grumbach." In idem, *Der lange Weg zur Mündigkeit: Frau und Literatur (1500–1800).* Stuttgart: J. B. Metzler. Pp. 96–110.

Becker-Cantarino, Barbara. 1988. "Argula von Grumbach (ca. 1492–1563) und die Reformation in Bayern." In, Gisela Brinker-Gabler (ed.), *Vom Mittelalter bis zum ende des 18. Jahrhunderts.* (*Deutsche Literatur von Frauen*, vol. 1.) Munich: Beck. Pp. 155–9.

Bezzel, Irmgard. 1986. "Argula von Grumbach und Johannes aus Landshut. Zu einer Kontroverse des Jahres 1524." *Gutenberg Jahrbuch* 61: 201–7.

Bezzel, Irmgard. 1987. "Der Sendbrief Argula von Grumbachs an die Universität Ingolstadt (1523) in zwei redaktionellen Bearbeitungen." In *Gutenberg-Jahrbuch* 62: 166–73.

Chrisman, Miriam Usher. 1982. *Lay Culture, Learned Culture: Books and Social Change in Strasbourg, 1480–1599.* New Haven: Yale.

Classen, Albrecht. 1989. "Footnotes to the Canon: Maria von Wolkenstein and Argula von Grumbach." In Jean R. Brink, Allison P. Coudert, and Maryanne C. Horowitch (eds), *The Politics of Gender in Early Modern Europe.* (Sixteenth Century Essays and Studies, vol. 12.) Kirksville, MO: Sixteenth Century Journal Publishers, Pp. 131–48.

Classen, Albrecht. 1991a. "Argula von Grumbach." In Katharina M. Wilson (ed.), *An Encyclopedia of Continental Women Writers*, vol. 1. New York & London: Garland Publishing, Inc. Pp. 497–8.

Classen, Albretch. 1991b. "Woman Poet and Reformer: the 16th Century Feminist Argula von Grumbach." *Daphnis* 20 (1): 167–97.

Deubner, K. A. 1930. "Argula von Grumbach." *Die Wartburg* 29: 73–81.

Dorn, Ernst. 1902. "Argula von Grumbach, die Schloßfrau von Lenting bei Ingolstadt." *Bayerische Diasporablätter* 1: 102–5.

Engelhardt, Eduard. 1859. *Argula von Grumbach die bayerische Tabea. Ein Lebensbild aus der Reformationszeit für den christlichen Leser dargestellt.* Nuremberg.

Finauer, P. P. 1761. "Argula von Grumbach." In idem, *Allgemeines historisches Verzeichnis gelehrter Frauenzimmer.* Munich.

Halbach, Silke. 1992. *Argula von Grumbach als Verfasserin reformatorischer Flugschriften*. Europäische Hochschulschriften series 23, Theologie Bd. 468. Frankfurt am Main: Peter Lang.

Heinen, Gisela. 1981. "Bayerische Reformatorin, Argula von Grumbach." In Angelika Schmidt-Biesalski (ed.), *Lust, Liebe und Verstand: Protestantische Frauen aus fünf Jahrhunderten*. Gelnhausen, Berlin, Stein: Burckhardthaus-Laetare Verlag. Pp. 19–30.

Heinsius, Maria. 1936. "Das Bekenntnis der Frau Argula von Grumbach." *Christliche Wehrkraft* 34.

Heinsius, Maria. 1951. "Argula von Grumbach." In idem, *Das Unüberwindliche Wort: Frauen der Reformationszeit*. Munich: Kaiser. Pp. 134–59.

Heuschel, A. 1911. "Frau Argula von Grumbach, geboren von Stauffe." *Der alte Glaube* 12: 738–41.

Joldersma, Hermina. 1997. "Argula von Grumbach (1492– after 1563?)." In James Hardin and Reinhart Max (eds), *German Writers of the Renaissance and Reformation, 1280–1580*. (*Dictionary of Literary Biography*, vol. 179.). Detroit, Washington DC, and London: A Bruccoli Clark, Layman Book Gale Research. Pp. 89–96.

Jung, Martin H. 2002. *Nonnen, Prophetinnen, Kirchenmütter: Kirchen- und frömmigkeitsgeschichtliche Studien zu Frauen der Reformationszeit*. Leipzig: Evangelische Verlagsanstalt GmbH.

Kolde, Theodor. 1905. "Arsacius Seehofer und Argula von Grumbach." *Beiträge zur bayerischen Kirchengeschichte* 11: 49–77, 97–124, 149–88 (ibid. 1922 vol. 22: 162–4.)

Lehms, Georg Christian. 1715. "Argula von Grumbach." In *Teutschlands galante Poetinnen*. Frankfurt am Main: Verlegung des Autoris. Pp. 71–3.

Lipowsky, J. 1801. *Argula von Grumbach*. Munich.

Luther, Martin. 1883–1993. *D. Martin Luthers Werke. Kritische Gesamtausgabe: Weimarer Ausgabe* 1883ff. Briefwechsel. 1933ff. Weimar: Herman Böhlaus Nachfolger. Luther and Argula, Briefwechsel II, No. 509, IV, Nos 706, 713, 800, V, 1581–4.

Luther, Martin. 1955–86. *Luther's Works*. American Edition. Ed. Jaroslav Pelikan. 55 vols. Philadelphia: Fortress Press; St. Louis: Concordia Publishing House.

Matheson, Peter, ed. 1995. *Argula von Grumbach. A Woman's Voice in the Reformation*. Edinburgh: T&T Clark.

Matheson, Peter. 1996. "Breaking the Silence: Women, Censorship, and the Reformation." *Sixteenth Century Journal* 27: 97–109.

Matheson, Peter. 2002. "Argula von Grumbach." In Carter Lindberg (ed.), *The Reformation Theologians*. Oxford: Blackwell Publishers. Pp. 94–108.

Pfeilschifter, Georg. 1978. "Eine Neuentdeckun: Alte Burg in Lenting. Sitz der Argula von Grumbach." *Ingolstädter Heimatblätter* 41 (6): 21ff.

Pistorius, Hermann Alexander. 1845. *Frau Argula von Grumbach geborene von Stauffen und ihr Kampf mit der Universität zu Ingolstadt*. Magdeburg.

Reese, E. 1983. "Eine Streiterin für die Reformation. Argula von Grumbach (1492–1568)." *Lutherische Monatschefte* 22: 303–10.

Rieger, M. Georg Cunrad. 1737. *Das Leben Argulae von Grumbach, gebohrner von Stauffen. Als Einer Jüngerin Jesus, Zeugin der Warheit und Freundin Lutheri*, samt eingemengter Nachricht von Arsatio Seehofern. Stuttgart.

Russell, Paul A. 1983. "'Your Sons and Daughters shall Prophesy . . .' (Joel 2:28). Common People and the Future of the Reformation in the Pamphlet Literature of South-Western Germany to 1525." *Archiv für Reformationsgeschichte* 74: 122–40.

Russell, Paul A. 1986. *Lay Theology in the Reformation. Popular Pamphleteers in the Southwest Germany 1521–1525*. Cambridge and New York: Cambridge University Press. Pp. 185–211.

Saalfeld, H. 1960. "Argula von Grumback, die Schlossherrin von Lenting." *Sammelblätter des historischen Vereins Ingolstadt* 69: 42–53.

Schöndorf, Kurt Erich. 1983. "Argula von Grumbach, eine Verfasserin von Flugschriften in der Reformationszeit." In Jorunn Valgard and Elsbeth Wessel (eds), *Frauen und Frauenbilder Dokumentiert durch 2000 Jahre: Osloer Beiträge zur Germanistik* vol. 8. Oslo: Universitet i Oslo Germanistisk institutt. Pp. 182–202.

Söltl, J. M. 1847. "Argula von Grumbach." *Neue Jahrbücher der Geschichte und Politik* 10: 270–6.

Spohn, Georg R. 1971. "Widmungsexemplare Ulrichs von Hutten und ein Sendschreiben Argulas von Grumbach an Pfalzgraf Johann II von Pfalz-Simmern." *Archiv für Mittelrheinische Kirchengeschichte* 23: 141–6.

Stolt, Birgit. 1999. "Luthers Sprache in seinen Briefen an Käthe." In Treu, Martin, ed. *Katharina von Bora, die Lutherin: Aufsätze analäßlich ihres 500. Geburtstages.* Wittenberg: Elbe-Druckerei. Pp. 23–32.

Stupperich, Robert. 1955. "Die Frau in der Publizistik der Reformation." *Archiv für Kulturgeschichte* 37: 204–33.

Stupperich, Robert. 1956. "Eine Frau kämpft für die Reformation. Das Leben der Argula von Grumbach." *Zeitwende* 27: 676–81.

Stupperich, Robert. 1966 "Argula, geb Freiin v. Stauff. In Art. Grumbach v." *Neue Deutsche Biographie* 7: 212.

Stupperich, Robert. 1984. "Argula von Grumbach." In *Reformatorenlexikon.* Gütersloh. Pp. 90–1.

Theopald, Leonhard. 1936. "Das Sendschreiben der Stauferin Argula von Grumbach an Kammerer und Rat von Regenburg." *Zeitschrift für bayerische Kirchengeschichte* 11: 53–6.

Werner, A. Widmann. 1985. "Argula von Grumbach." *Der Turmschreiber-Kalender. Ein bayerisches Hausbuch für das Jahr 1985*: 150–3.

Wiesner, Merry E. 1988. "Women's Response to the Reformation." In Ronnie Po-chia Hsia (ed.), *The German People and the Reformation.* Ithaca: Cornell University Press. Pp. 148–71.

Wiesner, Merry E. 1989. "Nuns, Wives, and Mothers: Women and the Reformation in Germany." In Sherrin Marshall (ed.), *Women in Reformation and Counter-Reformation Europe: Public and Private Worlds.* Bloomington and Indianapolis: Indiana University Press. Pp. 8–27.

Wolff, Karin. 1983. "Argula von Grumbach und ihre reformatorischen Flugschriften." Unpublished PhD dissertation. Wissenschaftliche Prüfungsarbeit für das Lehramt an Gymnasien in Evangelischer Theologie. Mainz.

Zimmerli-Witschi, Alice. 1981. *Frauen der Reformationszeit.* Dissertation. University of Zurich. Zürich: aku-Fotodruck.

Elisabeth von Brandenburg

Bainton, Roland. 2001. "Elisabeth of Brandenburg." In idem, *Women of the Reformation in Germany and Italy.* N.p.: Academic Renewal Press, 2001. Pp. 111–24. First published 1971, Minneapolis: Augsburg Publishing House.

Baur, Wilhem. 1873. "Elisabeth, Churfürstin von Brandenburg, die Bekennerin. Ein Vortrag zum Kirchbauereins in Berlin am 11. November 1872 gehalten von Wilhelm Baur." In *Deutsche Blätter: Eine Montagschrift für Staat, Kirche und sociales Leben.* Pp. 521–40.

Becker-Cantarino, Barbara. 1983. "Die schriftstellerische tätigkeit der Elisabeth von Braunschweig-Lüneburg (1510–1558)." In idem, *Virtus et Fortuna. Zur Deutschen Literatur zwischen 1400 und 1720.* Festschrift für Hans-Gert Roloff zu seinem 50. Geburtstag. Bern, Frankfurts and New York. Pp. 237–58.

Berbig, G. 1911. "Ein Gutachten über die Flucht der Kurfürstin Elisabeth von Brandenburg aus dem Schlosse zu Berlin." *Archiv für Reformationsgeschichte* 8: 380–94.

Bornhak, Friedrich. 1889. "Elisabeth von Dänemark." In *Die Fürstinnen auf dem Throne der Hohenzollern in Brandenburg-Preussen.* Berlin. Pp. 101–28. [1907, Altenburg: S-A. Geibel]

Jakobi, Rudolf. 1909. "Die Flucht der Kurfürstin Elisabeth von Brandenburg." *Hohenzollern Jahrbuch* 8: 155–96.

Kirchner, Ernst. 1866. "Elizabeth von Dänemark." In *Die Churfürstinnen und Köninginnen auf dem Throne der Hohenzollern, im Zusamhange mit ihren Familien- und Zeit-Verhältnissen* I (Berlin). Pp. 215–90.

Lohmeyer, K. 1968 [1877]. "Elisabeth, Kurfürstin von Brandenburg." In *Allgemeine Deutsche Biographie* 6. Pp. 14–15.

Mager, Inge. 1992. "Elisabeth von Brandenburg – Sidonie von Sachsen. Zwei Frauenschicksale im Kontext der Reformation von Calenberg-Göttingen." In *450 Jahre Reformation im Calenberger Land. Festschrift zum Jubiläum im Jahr 1992.* Ev.-luth. Kirchenkreis Laatzen-Pattensen. Pp. 23–52.

Riedel, Adolf Friedrich. 1865. "Die kurfürstin Elisabeth von Brandenburg in Beziehung auf die Reformation." *Zeitschrift für Preussische Geschichte und Landeskunde* 2: 65–100, 354–55.

Schultze, Johannes. 1959. "Elisabeth, Kurfürstin von Brandenburg." *Neue Deutsche Biographie* 4: 443.

Tschackert, Paul. 1899. *Herzogin Elisabeth von Munden, geborene Markgräfin von Brandenburg: die erste Schriftstellerin aus dem Hause Brandenburg und aus dem braunschweigischen Hause, ihr Lebensgang und ihre Werke.* Berlin und Leipzig: Verlag von Gieserke & Debrient. (Also in Hohenzollern-Jahrbuch 1899, und Separatdruck 1900 mit 2 Beilagen Elisabeths . . . nach ihren Originalhandschriften zum ersten Male vollständig herausgeg. Berlin und Leipzig 1899.)

Wiesner-Hanks, Merry. 1998. "Kinder, Kirche, Landeskinder: Women Defend their Publishing in Early Modern Germany." In R. B. Barnes, R. A. Kolb, and P. L. Presley (eds), *Books Have Their Own Destiny, Habent sua fata libelli.* Kirksville, MO: Sixteenth Century Journal Publishers. Pp. 143–52.

Elisabeth von Braunschweig

Elisabeth von Brandenburg's Works

Elisabeth von Braunschweig-Lüneburg. 1542. *Der Durchleuchtigen Hochgebornen Fürstin und Frawen/Frawen Elisabetg geborne Marckgravin zu Brandenburg u. Hertzogin zu Braunschweig und Lueneburg beschlossem und verwilligtes Mandat inirem Fürstenthum Gottes Wort auffzurichten/Und irrige verfürte lerr außzurotten belangent.* Münden.

Elisabeth von Braunschweig. 1545. *Ein Christlicher Sendebrieff der Durchleuchtigen Hochgebornen Fuerstinnen und Frawen F. Elisabeth geborne Marggraffinnen zu Brandenburg, etc. Hertzoginnen zu Braunschweig und Luneburg etc. Witwen/an alle irer F. G. und irer F. G. Hertzlichen Sons Erichs Untertanen geschrieben/ Christliche besserung und newes Gottseliges leben/ so in dieser letsten bösen zeit/ Die hohe nod fordert/ belangend.* Hannover.

Elisabeth von Braunschweig. 1598. *Der Widwen Handbüchlein, durch eine hocherleuchte fürstliche Widwe/vor vielen Jahren selbst beschrieben und verfasset/Jetzt aber wiederumb auff newe gedruckt/Allen Christlichen Widwen/hohes und nieder Standes/zu besonderem Trost.* Leipzig. HAB shelfmark number YJ Helmst 8.

Elisabeth von Braunschweig. 1824. *Unterrichtung und Ordnung für Herzog Erich d.J.* In V. Friedrich Karl von Strombeck (ed.), *Deutscher Fürstenspiegel aus dem 16. Jahrhundert.*, Braunschweig: Friedrich Vieweg. Pp. 57–130.

References

Aschoff, Hans-Georg. 1984. "Herzog Heinrich der Jüngere und Herzogin Elisabeth von Braunschweig-Lüneburg." *Jahrbuch der Gesellschaft für niedersächsische Kirchengeschichte* 82: 143–73.

Bainton, Roland H. 2001. "Elisabeth of Braunschweig." In idem, *Women of the Reformation in Germany and Italy.* N.p.: Academic Renewal Press. Pp. 125–43. First published 1971, Minneapolis: Augsburg Publishing House.

Becker-Cantarino, Barbara. 1983. "Die schriftstellerische tätigkeit der Elisabeth von Braunschweig-Lüneburg (1510–1558)." In idem, *Virtus et Fortuna. Zur Deutschen Literatur zwischen 1400 und 1720*. Festschrift für Hans-Gert Roloff zu seinem 50. Geburtstag. Bern, Frankfurt, and New York. Pp. 237–58.

Brauch, Albert. 1930. *Die Verwaltung des Territoriums Calenberg-Göttingen während der Regentenschaft der Herzogin Elisabeth 1540–1546*. In Quellen und Darstellungen zur Geschichte Niedersachsens. Herausgegeben vom Historischen Verein für Niedersachsen. Band 38. Hildesheim und Leipzig: August Lax Verlagshandlung.

Brenneke, Adolf. 1924. "Die politischen Einflüsse auf das Reformationswerk der Herzogin Elisabeth in Fürstentum Calenberg-Göttingen 1538–55. *Niedersächsische Jahburch* I: 104–45.

Brenneke, Adolf. 1925. "Das Kirchenregiment der Herzogin Elisabeth während ihrer vormundschaftlichen Regierung im Fürstentum Calenberg-Göttingen." ZSRGK, Zeitschrift der Savigny-Stiftung für Rechtsgeschichte 14: 62–160.

Brenneke, Adolf. 1933. "Herzogin Elisabeth von Braunschweig-Lüneberg, die hannoverische Reformationsfürstin, als Persönlichkeit." *Zeitschrift der Gesellschaft für niedersächsische Kirchengeschichte* 38: 139–70.

Goltz-Greifswald, Freiherr von der. 1914. "Lieder der Herzogin Elisabeth von Braunschweig-Lüneburg, Gräfin von Henneberg, zu Hannover von 1553 bis 1555 Gedichtet." *Zeitschrift der Gesellschaft für Niedersächsische Kirchengeschichte* 19: 147–208.

Havemann, Wilhelm. 1839. *Elisabeth, Herzogin von Braunschweig-Lüneburg, geborene Markgräfin von Brandenburg: ein Beitrag zur Reformations- und Sittengeschichte des 16. Jahrhunderts*. Göttingen: Druck on Verlag der Dieterich f chsen Buchhandlung.

Klettke-Mengel, Ingeborg. 1958. "Elisabeth von Braunschweig-Lüneburg als reformatorische Christin." *Jahrbuch der Gesellschaft für niedersächsische Kirchengeschichte* 56: 1–16. Also in I. Klettke-Mengel 1986a, Pp. 67–81.

Klettke-Mengel, Ingerborg. 1959. "Elisabeth, Herzogin von Braunschweig-Lüneburg (Calenberg) 1510–1558." *Neue Deutsche Biographie*, 4: 443ff. Also in I. Klettke-Mengel 1986b, p. 110.

Klettke-Mengel, Ingeborg. 1973. *Die Sprache in Fürstenbriefen der Reformationszeit, untersucht am Briefwechsel Albrechts von Preussen und Elisabeths von Braunschweig-Lüneburg*. 2nd edn. Köln und Berlin: Grote'sche Verlagsbuchhandlung KG.

Klettke-Mengel, Ingeborg. 1986a. "Die Korrespondenz zwischen Albrecht in Preußen und Ernst dem Bekenner von Braunschweig-Lüneburg 1519–1546." In *Preußenland und Deusche Orden. Festschrift für Kurt Forstreuter*. Würzburg: Ostdeutsche Beiträge aus dem Göttinger Arbeitskreis IX. Pp. 90–109.

Klettke-Mengel, Ingeborg. 1986b. *Fürsten und Fürstenbriefe. Zur Briefkultur im 16. Jahrhundert an geheimen und offiziellen preußisch – braunschweigischen Korrespondenzen*, mit 4 Abbildungen und 4 faksimilierten Schrifttafeln. Köln: Grote.

Koch, Franz. 1905–6. "Briefe der Herzogin Elisabeth von Braunschweig-Lüneberg, ed. Franz Koch." *Zeitschrift der Gesellschaft für niedersächsische Kirchengeschichte* 10: 231–66, 11: 89–146.

Kurs, A. 1891. *Elisabeth, Herzogin von Braunschweig-Calenberg, geborene Prinzessen von Brandenburg. Halle: Schriften für das deutsche Volk*, Heft 4.

Liederwald, Hilde. 1931. "Das Ehe des Grafen Poppo von Henneberg mit der Herzogin Elisabeth von Braunschweig." *Neue Beiträge zur Geschichte deutscher Altertums* 36. (Schmalkaden.) Lfrg. Heft 23: 37–88.

Mager, Inge. 1992. "Elisabeth von Brandenburg – Sidonie von Sachsen. Zwei Frauenschicksale im Kontext der Reformation von Calenberg-Göttingen." In *450 Jahre Reformation im Calenberger Land. Festschrift zum Jubiläum im Jahr 1992*. Ev.-luth. Kirchenkreis Laatzen-Pattensen. Pp. 23–52.

Mager, Inge. 1994. " 'Wegert euch das lieben heiligen Creutzes nicht.' Das Witwentrostbuch der Herzogin Elisabeth von Calenberg-Göttingen." In Hartmut Boockmann (ed.), *Kirche und*

Gesellschaft im Heiligen Römischen Reich des 15. und 16. Jahrhunderts. Göttingen: Vandenhoeck & Ruprecht in Göttingen. Pp. 207–24.

Mengel, Ingeborg. 1952. "Ein bisher unbekanntes Bücherinventar der Herzogin Elisabeth von Braunschweig-Lüneburg aus dem Jahre 1539." *Jahrbuch der Gesellschaft für Niedersächsische Kirchengeschichte* 50: 51–8. Also in I. Klettke-Mengel 1986a, Pp. 82–9.

Mengel, Ingeborg. 1953. "Aktenkundliche Untersuchungen an der Korrespondenz zwischen Elisabeth von Brausnschweig-Lüneburg und Albrecht von Preussen. Ein Beitrag zur historischen Aktenkunde des 16th. Jahrhunderts." In *Archivalische Zeitschrift* 48. Band, Munich. Pp. 121–58. Also in I. Klettke-Mengel 1986a, Pp. 24–66.

Mengel, Ingeborg. 1954a. *Elisabeth von Braunschweig-Lüneburg und Albrecht von Preussen: Ein Fürstenbriefwechsel der Reformationszeit.* Göttingen, Frankfurt Berlin: Musterschmidt Wissenschaftlicher Verlag. [Veröffentlichtung der historischen Kommission für Niedersachsen 13/14.]

Mengel, Ingeborg. 1954b. "Politisch-dynastische Beziehungen zwischen Albrecht von Preussen und Elisabeth von Braunschweig-Lüneburg in den Jahren 1546–1555." In *Jahrbuch der Albertus-Universität zu Königsberg/Preussen* Band V:225–41. Also in I. Klettke-Mengel 1986a, Pp. 11–23.

Nebig, Ernst-August. 2006. *Elisabeth Herzogin von Calenberg. Regentin, Reformatorin, Schriftstellerin.* Göttingen: Matrix Media Verlag.

Quentin, Johann Ludolf. 1789. *Beschreibung der ersten Kirchen-Ordnung der Herzogin Elisabeth von Braunschweig, geborner Marggrävin von Brandenburg: Gedruckt zu Erfurt in der Arche No 1542. 4.* Göttingen: Rosenbusch.

Spengler-Ruppenthal, Anneliese. 1984. "Die Herzogin Elisabeth von Calenberg-Göttingen und der Landgraf Philipp von Hessen." *Jahrbuch der Gesellschaft für niedersächsische Kirchengeschichte* 82: 27–52.

Stelzel, Ulla. 2003. *Aufforderungen in den Schriften Herzogin Elisabeths von Braunschweig-Lüneburg. Eine Untersuchung zum wirkungsorientierten Einsatz der direktiven Sparchhandlung im Frühneuhochdeutschen.* Hildesheim, Zurich, and New York: Georg Olms Verlag.

Strombeck, V. Friedrich Karl von (ed.), *Deutscher Fürstenspiegel aus dem 16. Jahrhundert.* Braunschweig: Friedrich Vieweg. Pp. 57–130.

Tschackert, Paul. 1899. *Herzogin Elisabeth von Munden, geborene Markgräfin von Brandenburg: die erste Schriftstellerin aus dem Hause Brandenburg und aus dem braunschweigischen Hause, ihr Lebensgang und ihre Werke.* Berlin und Leipzig: Verlag von Gieserke & Debrient. Also in Paul Tschackert 1899, "Herzogin Elisabeth von Münden (gest. 1558), die erste Schriftstellerin aus dem Hause Brandenburg und aus dem braunschweigischen Hause." In *Hohenzollern Jahrbuch* 3: 49–65. (With original manuscripts.)

Tschackert, Paul. 1900. "Briefwechsel der Antoninus Corvinus." In *Quellen und Darstellungen zur Geschichte Niedersachsens* 4. Hannover, Leipzig.

Warnke, Ingo. 1994. "Elisabeth von Braunschweig-Lüneburgs Sittenspiegel. Beobachtungen zur symbolischen Interaktion." In Gisela Brandt (ed.), *Bausteine zu einer Geschichte des weiblichen Sprachgebrauchs.* Internationale Fachtagung, Rostock 6.8. 1993. Stuttgart: Verlag Hans-Dieter Heinz, Akademischer Verlag Stuttgart. Pp. 101–12.

Wiesner, Merry. 2000. "Herzogin Elisabeth von Braunschweig-Lüneberg (1510–1558)." In Kerstin Merkel and Heide Wunder (eds), *Deutsche Frauen der Frühen Neuzeit: Dichterinnen, Malerinnen, Mäzeninnen.* Darmstadt: Wissenschaftliche Buchgesellschaft. Pp. 39–48.

Wiesner-Hanks, Merry. 1998. "Kinder, Kirche, Landeskinder: Women Defend their Publishing in Early Modern Germany." In R. B. Barnes, R. A. Kolb, P. L. Presley (eds), *Habent sua fata libelli.* Pp. 143–51.

Wunder, Heide, Helga Zöttlein, and Barbara Hoffmann. 1997. "Konfession, Religiosität und politisches Handeln von Frauen vom ausgehenden 16. bis zum Beginn des 18. Jahrhunderts." *Zeitsprünge. Forschungen zur Frühen Neuzeit* 1: 75–98.

Katharina Schütz Zell

Katharina's Works (following the listing in Elsie Anne McKee, 1999b, p. 368)

Katharina Schütz Zell. 1524. *Den leydenden Christglaubigen weybern der gemain zu Kentzigen minen mitschwestern in Christo Ihesu zu handen.* Strasbourg: W. Köpffel.

Katharina Schütz Zell. 1524. *Entschuldigung Katharina Schützinn / für M. Mathes Zellen / jren Eegemahel / der ein Pfarrher und dyener ist im wort Gottes zu Straßburg. Von wegen grosser lügen uff jn erdiecht.* Strasbourg: W. Köpffel.

Katharina Schütz Zell. 1534–6. *Von Christo Jesu unserem saligmacher / seiner Menschwerdung / Geburt / Beschneidung / etc. etlich Christliche und trostliche Lobgsang / auß einem vast herrlichen Gsangbuch gezogen / Von welchem inn der Vorred weiter anzeygt würdt.* Strasbourg: J. Froelich, 1534–6.

Katharina Schütz Zell. 1548. *Klag red und ermahnung Catharina Zellin zum volk bei dem grab m. Matheus Zellen pfarer zum münster zu Straßburg / deß frommen mannß / bey und über seinem todten leib.* [The earliest extant written text in an early eighteenth-century hand was found and published in the 1880s.]

Katharina Schütz Zell. 1557. *Ein Brieff an die gantze Burgerschafft der Statt Straßburg von Katherina Zellin / dessen jetz saligen Matthei Zellen / deß alten und ersten Predigers des Evangelij diser Statt / nachgelassne Ehefraw / Betreffend Herr Ludwigen Rabus / jetz ein Prediger der Statt Ulm / sampt zweyen brieffen jr und sein / die mag mengklich lesen und urtheilen on gunst und haß / sonder allein der war heit warnemen. Dabey auch ein sanffte antwort / auff jeden Artickel / seines brieffs.* Strasbourg? 1557.

Katharina Schütz Zell. 1558. *Den Psalmen Miserere / mit dem Khünig David bedacht / gebettet / und paraphrasirt von Katharina Zellin M. Matthei Zellen seligen nachgelassne Ehefraw / sampt dem Vatter unser mit seiner erklarung / zugeschickt dem Christlichen mann Juncker Felix Armbruster / zum trost in seiner kranckheit / und andern angefochtenen hertzen und Concientzen / der sünd halben betrubt & c. in truck lassen kommen.* Strasbourg? 1558.

McKee, Elsie Anne, ed. 1999. *Katharina Schütz Zell, The Writings: A Critical Edition.* Studies in Medieval and Reformation Thought 69, vol. 2. Leiden, Boston, and Köln: E. J. Brill.

McKee, Elsie Anne, transl. 2006. *Katharina Schütz Zell, Church Mother: The Writings of a Protestant Reformer in Sixteenth-Century Germany.* Chicago and London: The University of Chicago Press.

References

Albrecht, Ruth. 1998. "Wer war Katharina Zell?" In Heide Wunder and Gisela Engel (eds), *Geschlechterperspektiven Forschungen zur Frühen Neuzeit.* Königstein: Taunus. Pp. 135–44.

Bainton, Roland. 1970. "Katharine of Zell." *Medievalia et Humanistica.* Studies in Medieval and Renaissance Culture 1: 143–68.

Bainton, Roland. 2001. "Katherine Zell." In idem, *Women of the Reformation in Germany and Italy.* N.p.: Academic Renewal Press. Pp. 55–76. First published 1971, Minneapolis: Augsburg Publishing House.

Becker-Cantarino, Barbara. 1987. "Religiöse Streiterinnen: Katharina Zell und Argula von Grumbach." In idem, *Der lange Weg zur Mündigkeit: Frau und Literatur (1500–1800).* Stuttgart: Metzler. Pp. 96–110.

Bowers, Diane. 1998. "Das Schweigen ist kein gedult, or, To Be Patient Is Not To Be Silent: The Apology of Katharina Schütz Zell, Evangelical Reformer in Strasbourg." Unpublished PhD dissertation.

Buchberger, Michael. 2001. "Zell, Katharina." In Walter Kaspar (ed.), *Lexikon für Theologie und Kirche.* Zehnter Band. [Thomaskirchen bis Žytomyr.] Freiburg: Herber. Pp. 1416–17.

Chrisman, Miriam. 1972. "Women and the Reformation in Strasbourg 1490–1530." *Archiv für Reformationsgeschichte* 63: 143–68.

Chrisman, Miriam Usher. 1982. *Lay Culture, Learned Culture: Books and Social Change in Strasbourg, 1480–1599*. New Haven: Yale.

Conrad, Anne. 1998. "'Ein männisch Abrahamisch gemuet': KZ in Kontext der Straßburger Reformations Geschichte." In Heide Wunder and Gisela Engel, *Geschlechterperspektiven Forschungen zur Frühen Neuzeit*. Königstein: Taunus. Pp. 120–39.

Davis, Natalie Zemon. 1998. "Neue Perspektiven für die Geschlechtforschung in der Frühen Neuzeit." In Heide Wunder and Gisela Engel, *Geschlechterperspektiven Forschungen zur Frühen Neuzeit*. Königstein: Taunus. Pp. 16–51.

Davis, Natalie Zemon. 2000. *The Gifts in Sixteenth-Century France*. Madison, WI: The University of Wisconsin Press. Pp. 125–6.

Evangelisches Predigerseminar Lutherstadt Wittenberg. 1997. *Frauen mischen sie ein. Katharina Luther, Katharina Melanchthon, Katharina Zell, Hille Feicken und Andere*. Wittenberger Sonntagsvorlesungen. 2nd edn. Wittenberg: Drei Kastanien Verlag.

Haase, Lisbeth. 2002. *Katharina Zell: Pfarrfrau und Reformatorin*. Stuttgart: Edition Anker im Christilichen Verlagshaus.

Heinsius, Maria. 1951. *Das Unüberwindliche Wort. Frauen der Reformationszeit*. Munich: Kaiser.

Jancke, Gabriele. 1998. "Die Kirche als Haushalt und die Leitungsrolle der Kirchenmutter." In Heide Wunder and Gisela Engel *Geschlechterperspektiven Forschungen zur Frühen Neuzeit*. Königstein: Taunus. Pp. 145–55.

Jancke-Pirna, Gabriele. 1997. "Prophetin – Pfarrfrau – Publizistin. Die Strasbourger, 'Kirchenmutter' Katharina Zell." In Evangelisches Predigerseminar Lutherstadt Wittenberg (ed.), *Frauen mischen sich sein* 1997. Pp. 55–80.

Jung, Martin. 2002. *Nonnen, Prophetinnen, Kirchenmütter: kirchen – und frömmgkeitsgeschichtliche Studien zu Frauen der Reformationszeit*. Leipzig: Evangelische Verlagsanstalt.

Kaufmann, Thomas. 1996. "Pfarrfrau und Publizistin – Das reformatorische 'Amt' der Katharina Zell." *Zeitschrift für Historiche Forschung* 23: 169–218.

Keller, Marie-Luise. 1981. "Helferin der Verfolgten, Katharina Zell." In Angelika Schmid-Biesalski (ed.), *Lust, Liebe und Verstand: Protestantische Frauen aus fünf Jahrhunderten*. Gelnhausen, Berlin, and Stein: Burckhardthaus-Laetare Verlag. Pp. 31–44.

Lienhard, Marc. 1980. "Catherine Z. née Schütz." In *Bibliotheca Dissidentium. Repertoire des non-conformistes religieux des seizième et dix-septième siècles* vol 1. Ed. Andre Séquenny. Baden-Baden: Valentin Koerner. Pp. 97–125.

Luther, Martin. 1883–1993. *D. Martin Luthers Werke, Kritische Gesamtausgabe: Weimarer Ausgabe* 1883ff. Weimar: Herman Böhlaus Nachfolger. (See Luther's letters to Katharina: December 12, 1524, WA Br 3: 405–6; January 14, 1531, WA Br 6: 26–7.)

Luther, Martin. 1955–86. *Luther's Works*. American Edition. Ed. Jaroslav Pelikan. 55 vols. Philadelphia: Fortress Press; St. Louis: Concordia Publishing House.

McKee, Elsie Anne. 1992. "The Defense of Zwingli, Schwenckfeld, and the Baptists, by Katharina Schütz Zell." In Heiko A. Oberman, Ernst Saxer, Alfred Schindler, Heinzpeter Stucki (eds), *Reformiertes Erbe: Festschrift für Gottfried W. Locher zu seinem 80. Geburtstag* vol. 1. Zurich: Theologischer Verlag. Pp. 245–64.

McKee, Elsie Anne. 1994. *Reforming Popular Piety in Sixteenth-Century Strasbourg: Katharina Schütz Zell and Her Hymnbook*. Princeton: Princeton Theological Seminary.

McKee, Elsie Anne. 1995. "Katharina Schütz Zell: A Protestant Reformer." In Timothy J. Wengert and Charles W. Brockwell, Jr. (eds), *Telling the Churches' Stories: Ecumenical Perspectives on Writing Christian History*. Grand Rapids, MI and Cambridge: William B. Eerdmans Publishing Company. Pp. 73–90.

McKee, Elsie Ann. 1997. "Speaking Out: Katharina Schütz Zell and the Command to Love One's Neighbor as an Apologia for Defending the Truth." In W. H. Neuser & H. J. Selderhuis (eds), *Ordentlich und Fruchtbar, Festschrift für Willem van't Spijker*. Leiden: J. J. Groen en Zoon. Pp. 9–22.

McKee, Elsie Anne. 1999a. *Katharina Schütz Zell: The Life and Thought of a Sixteenth-Century Reformer*. Studies in Medieval and Reformation Thought 69, vol. 1. Leiden, Boston, Koln: E. J. Brill.

McKee, Elsie Anne. 1999b. *Katharina Schütz Zell. The Writings. A Critical Edition*. Studies in Medieval and Reformation Thought 69, vol. 2. Leiden, Boston, Koln: E. J. Brill.

McKee, Elsie Anne. 1999c. "Katharina Schütz Zell and the 'Our Father.'" In Emidio Campi, Leif Grane, and Adolf Martin Ritter (eds), *Oratio: Das Gebet in patristischer und reformatorischer Sicht. Festschrift für Alfred Schindler*. Göttingen: Vandenhoeck & Ruprecht. Pp. 210–18.

McKee, Elsie Anne. 2006a. *Katharina Schütz Zell, Church Mother: The Writings of a Protestant Reformer in Sixteenth-Century Germany*, transl. Elsie McKee, Chicago and London: The University of Chicago Press.

McKee, Elsie Anne. 2006b. "Katharina Schütz Zell and Caspar Schwenckfeld: A Reassessment of Their Relationship." *Archiv für Reformationsgeshichte*. 97: 83–105.

McKee, Elsie Anne. 2007. "'A Lay Voice in Sixteenth-Century Ecumenics': Katharina Schütz Zell in Dialogue with Johannes Brenz, Conrad Pellican, and Caspar Schwenckfeld." In Mack Holt (ed.), *Adaptations of Calvinism in Reformation Europe: Essays in Honor of Brian G. Armstrong*. Burlington, VT and Aldershot: Ashgate. Pp. 81–110.

Mager, Inge. 1999a. "Katharina von Bora, die Lutherin – als Witwe." In Evangelisches Predigerseminar Lutherstadt Wittenberg (ed.), *Mönschure und Morgenstern*. Wittenberger Sonntagsvorlesungen. Wittenberg: Drei Kastaninen Verlag. Pp. 120–36.

Mager, Inge. 1999b. Unscheinbar, aber unentbehrlich – Frauen im Reformationszeitalter. In Udo Hahn and Marlies Mügge, eds. *Katharina von Bora: Die Frau an Luthers Seite*. Stuttgart: Quell. Pp. 77–95.

Mager, Inge. 1999c. "Theologenfrauen als 'Gehilfinnen' der Reformation." In Martin Treu (ed.), *Katharina von Bora, die Lutherin: Aufsätze analäßlich ihres 500. Geburtstages*. Wittenberg: Elbe-Druckerei. Pp. 113–27.

Meyer, Hannah. 1960. *Gewagt auf Gottes Gnad: Frauen der Reformationszeit*. Evangelische Verlagsanstalt Berlin. Pp. 7–25.

Moeller, Christian. 2005. "Katharina Zell (1497/98–1562): Kirchenmutter von Strassburg." In Peter Zimmerling (ed.), *Evangelische Seelsorgerinnen: biografische Skizzen, Texte und Programme*. Goettingen: Vandenhoeck & Ruprecht. Pp. 46–63.

Nielsen, Merete. 1999. "'Kinder, Küche und Kirche.' Pfarrfrauen der Reformationszeit in Südwestdeutschland und der Schweiz." In Martin Treu (ed.), *Katharina von Bora, die Lutherin: Aufsätze analäßlich ihres 500. Geburtstages*. Wittenberg: Elbe-Druckerei. Pp. 128–57.

Spellmann William. 2001. "Zell, Matthias (1477–1548)" and "Katharina (1497–1562)." In Jo Eldridge Carney (ed.), *Renaissance and Reformation 1500–1620. A Biographical Dictionary*. Westport, CT and London: Greenwood Press. Pp. 383–4.

Stupperich, Robert. 1954. "Katharina Zell, eine Pfarrfrau der Ref.-Zeit." *Zeitwende* 30: 605ff.

Wiesner-Hanks, Merry. 1995. "Katherina Zell's Ein Brieff an die ganze Bürgerschaft der Statt Strassburg as Autobiography and Theology." *Colloquia Germanica: Internationale Zeitschrift für Germanistik* 28 (3/4): 245–54.

Wiesner-Hanks, Merry. 1998. "Kinder, Kirche, Landeskinder: Women Defend Their Publishing in Early Modern Germany." In Robin B. Barnes, Robert A. Kolb, and Paula L. Presley (eds), *Books Have Their Own Destiny*. Kirksville, MS: Sixteenth Century Journal Publishers. Pp. 143–52.

Wiethaus, Ulrike. 1993. "Female Authority and Religiosity in the Letters of KZ and Caritas Pirckheimer." *Mystics Quarterly* 19: 123–35.

Wolff, Ane. 1986. *Le Recueil de cantiques de Catherine Zell, 1534–1536* 2 vols. Mémoire de Maitrise. Université des Sciences Humaines de Strasbourg, Institute d'Etudes Allemandes. Strasbourg.

Wunder, Heide and Gisela Engel, eds. 1998. *Geschlechterperspektiven Forschungen zur Frühen Neuzeit*. Königstein: Taunus.

Zimmerli-Witschi, Alice. 1981. "Frauen der Reformationszeit." Unpublished PhD Dissertation. University of Zurich, Zürich: aku-Fotodrück.

Marie Dentière

Marie Dentière's Works

Marie Dentière. 1536. *La guerre et déslivrance de la ville de Genesve de fidèlement faicte et composée par un Marchand demourant en icelle (1536)*, with excerpts from *L'Epistre tres utile*, including "Defense pour les Femmes." In Albert Rilliet, ed. 1878–88 (1881). "Restitution de l'écrit intitulé La Guerre et Deslivrance de la ville de Genesve." *Mémoires et documents publiés par la Société d'histoire et d'archéologie de Genève*, 20: 309–83. In English: *The War for and Deliverance of the City of Geneva, Faithfully Told and Written Down by a Merchant Living in That City*. Also in 1881 as *La guerre et deslivrance de la ville de Genesve composée et publiée en 1536 par Marie Dentière de Tournay, ancienne abbesse et femme d'Antoine Froment*. Geneva: Charles Schuchardt.

Marie Dentière. 1539. M[arie] D[entiere] à Marguerite de Navarre. Publiée à Genève vers la fin d'avril 1539. *Epistre tres utile faicte et composée par une femme Chrestienne de Tornay, Envoyée à la Royne de Navarre seur du Roy de France, Contre Les Turcz, Iuifz, Infideles, Faulx chrestiens, Anabaptistes, et Lutheriens, [à Anvers, chez Martin l'empereur]. (1539)*. Geneva: Jean Gérard. In Herminjard, A.-L., ed. [1866–97] 1965–6. *Correspondance des Réformateurs dans les pays de langue française: Recueillie et publiée avec d'autres letters relatives à la Réforme et des notes historiques et biographiques*. 9 vols. Nieuwkoop: B. De Graaf, (vol. 5), Pp. 295–304. In English: *A Most Beneficial Letter, Prepared and Written Down by a Christian Woman of Tournai, and Sent to the Queen of Navarre, Sister of the King of France, Against the Turks, the Jews, the Infidels, the False Christians, Anabaptists and the Lutherans (1539)*.

Marie Dentière. 1561. *Preface to a Sermon by John Calvin*. In *Les Conditions et vertus requises en la femme fidèle et bonne mesnagere: Contenues au xxxi. Chapitre des Prouerbes de Salomon. Mis en forme de Cantique, par Théodore de Besze. Plus, un Sermon de la modestie des Femmes en leurs habillemens, par. M. Iean Calvin. Outre, plusieurs chansons spirituelles, en Musique*. In English: *The Behavior and Virtues Required of a Faithful Woman and Good Housekeeper: Contained in chapter XXXI of the Proverbs of Solomon. Rendered in the form of a song by Théodore de Bèze. Plus a sermon on the modesty of Women in their Dress, by Monsiuer John Calvin. In addition, several spiritual songs with music*. M.D. LXI. s.l. See, Calvin, Jean. 1945. *Sermon où il est montré quelle doit etre la modestie des femmes en leurs habillements [sur 1 Timothèe 2: 9–11]*. Genève: Kundig. Prèface de M[arie] D[entière].

Marie Dentière. 2004. *Epistle to Marguerite de Navarre; and, Preface to a Sermon by John Calvin, by Marie Dentière*. Ed. and transl. Mary B. McKinley. Chicago and London: University of Chicago Press.

References

Backus, Irena. 1996. "Marie Dentière." In Hillerbrand, Hans J. (ed.), *Oxford Encyclopedia of the Reformation*. Oxford: Oxford University Press. Pp. 474–5.

Backus, Irena.1991. "Marie Dentière: Un cas de féminisme théologique à l'èpoque de la Rèforme?" *Bulletin de la Société de l'histoire du Protestantisme Français: Etudes historiques* 137: 177–95.

Blaisdell, Charmarie Jenkins. 1982. "Calvin's Letters to Women: The Courting of Ladies in High Places." *Sixteenth Century Journal* 13 (3): 66–83.

Blaisdell, Charmarie Jenkins. 1985. "The Matrix of Reform: Women in the Lutheran and Calvinist Movements." In Richard Greaves (ed.), *Triumph over Silence: Women in Protestant History*. Westport, CT: Greenwood. Pp. 13–44.

Blaisdell, Charmarie Jenkins. 1999. "Religion, Gender, and Class: Nuns and Authority in Early Modern France." In Michael Wolfe (ed.), *Changing Identities in Early Modern France*. Durham, NC: Duke University. Pp. 147–68.

Bothe, Catherine M. 1993. "Ecriture féminine de la Réformation: Le témoignage de Marie Dentière." *Romance Languages Annual* 5: 15–19.

Davis, Natalie Z. 1975. "City Women and Religious Change." In *Society and Culture in Early Modern France*. Stanford: Stanford University Press.

DeBoer, Willis P. 1976. "Calvin on the Role of Women." In E. Holwerda (ed.), *Exploring the Heritage of John Calvin: Essays in Honor of John H. Bratt*. Grand Rapids: Baker Book House. Pp. 236–72.

Bratt, John H. 1976. "The Role and Status of Women in the Writings of John Calvin" (with response by Charmarie Jenkins Blaisdell). In Peter DeKlerk (ed.), *Renaissance Reformation, Resurgence: Colloquium on Calvin and Calvin Studies*. Grand Rapids: Calvin Theological Seminary. Pp. 1–17.

Brink, Jean R. ed. 1980. *Female Scholars: A Tradition of Learned Women Before 1800*. Montreal: Eden P. Women's Publications.

Denommé, Isabelle C. 2004. "La vision théologique de Marie d'Ennetières et le Groupe de Neuchâtel." In Jean-François Gilmont and William Kemp (eds), Le Livre évangélique en français avant Calvin: Etudes originales, publications d'inédits, catalogues d'éditions anciennes. Proceedings of the Canadian Society for Renaissance and Reformation Studies. Turnhout: Brepols Publishers. Pp. 179–97.

Douglass, Jane Dempsey. 1985. *Women, Freedom and Calvin*. The Westminster Press: Philadelphia.

Douglass, Jane Dempsey. 1991. "Marie Dentière's Use of Scripture in Her Theology of History." In Mark Burrows and Paul Rorem (eds), *Biblical Hermeneutics in Historical Perspective: Studies in Honor of Karlfried Froelich on His Sixtieth Birthday*. Grand Rapids, MI: Wm. B. Eerdmans. Pp. 227–44.

Haag, Eugebe, ed. 1886. "Marie Dentière." In *La France protestante*. 5 vols. 2nd edn. Paris: Librairie Sandoz et Fischbacher, 1877–88. Vol. 5, Pp. 238–49.

Head, Thomas. 1987. "Marie Dentière: A Propagandist for the Reform." Katharina M. Wilson (ed.), *Women Writers of the Renaissance and Reformation*. Athens and London: The University of Georgia Press. Pp. 260–83.

Head, Thomas. 1991. "The Religion of the *Femmelettes*: Ideas and Experience among Women in Fifteenth- and Sixteenth Century France." In Lynda Coon, Katherine Haldane, and Elisabeth Sommer (eds), *That Gentle Strength: Historical Perspectives on Women in Christianity*. Charlottesville: University Press of Virginia. Pp. 149–75.

Head, Thomas. 1991. "Marie Dentière." In Katharina M. Wilson (ed.), *An Encyclopedia of Continental Women Writers*. New York and London: Garland Publishing, Inc. Pp. 303–4.

Herminjard, A.-L. 1965–6. *Correspondance des Réformateurs dans les pays de langue française: Recueillie et publiée avec d'autres lettres relatives à la Réforme et des notes historiques et biographiques*. 9 vols. Nieuwkoop: B. De Graaf. Vol. 5, Pp. 295–304. Originally published 1866–97.

Jussie, Jeanne de. 1853 [1611]. *Le levain du Calvinisme, ou Commencement de l'heresie de Geneve. Faict par Reverende Soeur Jeanne de Jussie, lors religieuse à Saincte Claire de Geneve, et apres sa sortie Abbesse au Convent d'Anyssi*. Ed: Gustave Revilliod. Geneva: Jules Guillaume Fick. Chambéry: Du Four. Reprinted with a new introduction 1865.

Jussie, Jeanne de. 1996. *Kleine Chronik: Bericht einer Nonne über die Anfänge der Reformation in Genf*. Ed. and transl. Helmut Feld. Mainz: P. Von Zabern.

Jussie, Jeanne de. 1996. *Petite chronique*. Ed., introduction, commentary, Helmut Feld. Mainz: P. von Zabern.

Jussie, Jeanne de. 2006. *The Short Chronicle: A Poor Clare's Account of the Reformation of Geneva*. Ed. and transl. Carrie F. Klaus. Chicago: University of Chicago Press.

Kemp, William and Diane Desrosiers-Bonin.1998. "Marie d'Ennetières et la petite grammaire hébraique de sa fille d'après la dédicace de l'Epistre à Marguerite de Navarre." *Bibliothèque d'Humanisme et Renaissance* 50 (1): 117–34.

Lazard, Madeleine. 1985. "Deux soeurs enemies, Marie Dentière et Jeanne de Jussie: Nonnes et réformées à Genève. In B. Chevalier and C. Sauzat (eds), *Les Réformes: Enracinements socio-cultures*. 25me colloque d'études humanists, Tours, juillet, 1–13 1982. Paris: La Maisnie. Pp. 233–49.

McKinley, Mary B. 1997. "The Absent Ellipsis: The Edition and Suppression of Marie Dentière in the Sixteenth and the Nineteenth Century." In Colette H. Winn and Donna Kuizenga (eds), *Women Writers in Pre-Revolutionary France: Strategies of Emancipation*. New York: Garland Publishing Co. Pp. 85–99.

McKinley, Mary B. ed and transl. 2004. *Epistle to Marguerite de Navarre; and, Preface to a Sermon by John Calvin, by Marie Dentière*. Chicago, London: University of Chicago Press.

Monter, E. William. 1980. "Women in Calvinist Geneva (1550–1800)." *Signs: Journal of Women in Culture and Society* 6: 189–209.

Rilliet, Albert, ed. 1878–88 (1881). "Restitution de l'ecrit intitulé La Guerre et Deslivrance de la ville de Genesve (1536)." *Mémoires et documents publiés par la Sociéte d'histoire et d'archéologie de Genève* 20: 309–83.

Roelker, Nancy. 1972. "The Appeal of Calvinism to French Noblewomen in the Sixteenth Century." *Journal of Interdisciplinary History* (Spring): 391–418.

Skenazi, Cynthia. 1997. "Marie Dentière et la prédication des femmes." *Renaissance and Reformation/Renaissance et Réforme* 21 (1): 5–18.

Stephens, Sonya, ed. 2000. *A History of Women's Writing in France*. Cambridge: Cambridge University Press.

Wengler, Elisabeth M. 1999. "Women, Religion and Reform in Sixteenth-Century Geneva." Unpublished PhD dissertation. Dept. of History, Boston College, Boston, MA.

Thompson, John Lee. 1992. *John Calvin and the Daughters of Sarah: Women in Regular and Exceptional Roles in the Exegesis of Calvin, His Predecessors, and His Contemporaries*. Geneva: Librairie Droz. Pp. 40–5, 187–226.

Åkerlund, Ingrid. 2003. "Jeanne de Jussie and Marie Dentière. Two Abbesses Persecuted for Their Religious Beliefs." In idem (ed.), *Sixteenth Century French Women Writers: Marguerite d'Angoulême, Anne de Graville, the Lyonnese School, Jeanne de Jussie, Marie Dentière, Camille de Morel*. Studies in French Literature, vol. 67. Lewiston and Lampeter: The Edwin Mellen Press. Pp. 105–26.

Marguerite de Navarre's and Jeanne d'Albret's Bibliography

Marguerite de Navarre's Works (not exhaustive)

Bideaux, Michel. 1992. *Marguerite De Navarre: "L'Heptaméron" de l'enquete au débat*. Mont-de-Marsan: Editions InterUniversitaires.

Briçonnet, Guillaume and Marguerite d'Angoulême. 1975–9. *Correspondance 1521–24*, 2 vols. Ed. Christine Martineau and Michel Veissière. Geneva and Paris, with the assistance of Henry Heller: Librairie Droz and Librairie Minard.

Herminjard, A.-L. 1886–97. *Correspondance des Réformateurs dans les pays de langue française: Recueillie et publiée avec d'autres letters relatives à la Réforme et des notes historiques et biographiques*, 9 vols. Reprinted 1965 and 1966, Nieuwkoop: B. De Graaf.

Lettres de Marguerite d'Angoulême. 1841. Ed. François Génin. Paris: Jules Renouard.

Marguerite de Navarre. 1531. *Le miroir de l'âme pêcheresse auquel elle recongnoist ses faultes et pêchiz, aussi les graces et bénéfices à elle faicts par Jesuchrist son espoux, la Marguerite très noble et précieuse s'est proposée à ceulx qui de bon cueur la cherchoient. A Alençon, chez Maistre*

Simon du Bois, *MDXXXI. (Edition at Paris, A. Augereau, 1533–1535?)*. In English: *The Mirror of the Sinful Soul. A prose translation for the French of a poem by Queen Margaret of Navarre, made in 1544, by the Princess (afterwards Queen) Elizabeth, then eleven years of Age*, facsimile edn. London 1897.

Marguerite de Navarre. 1547. *La Coche*. Critical edition by Robert Marichal, 1971. Geneva: Droz, Textes Littéraires Français.

Marguerite de Navarre. 1547. *L'Heptaméron. Marguerite, Queen, Consort of Henry II, King of Navarre 1492–1549*. Paris: M. de Roigny.

Marguerite de Navarre. 1547. *Marguerites de la Marguerite des princesses, très illustre Royne de Navarre*. Lyon: Jean de Tournes. Facsimile reprint, 1970, Ruth Thomas (ed.). The Hague: Johnson Reprint Corporation, Mouton.

Marguerite de Navarre. 1549. *Chansons spirituelles*. Critical edition by Georges Dottin, 1971. Geneva: Droz, Textes Littéraires Français.

Marguerite de Navarre. 1873. *Les Marguerites de la Marguerite des Princesses*, 4 vols. Ed. Félix Frank. Paris: Jouaust. Reprinted 1970, Geneva: Slatkine Reprints.

Marguerite de Navarre. 1842. *Nouvelles Lettres de la Reine de Navarre addressées au roi François I; son Frère*. Ed. François Génin. Paris: Chez Jules Renouard.

Marguerite de Navarre. 1880. *L'Heptaméron des Nouvelles de très haute et très illustre princesse Marguerite d'Angoulême*, 4 vols. Ed. Le Roux de Lincy and A. de Montaiglon. Paris: Auguste Etudes. Reprinted 1969, Geneva: Slatkine.

Marguerite de Navarre. 1896. *Les Dernières Poésies de Marguerite de Navarre: Publiées pour la première fois avec une introduction et des notes par Abel Lefranc*. Ed. A. Lefranc. Paris.

Marguerite de Navarre. 1926. *Dialogue en forme de vision nocturne*. Ed. Pierre Jourda. Paris.

Marguerite de Navarre. 1930. *Pater Noster de Marguerite de Navarre*. Ed. W. G. Moore. La Réforme allemande et la littérature française. Strasbourg: Publications de la Faculté des Lettres. Pp. 432–41.

Marguerite de Navarre. 1950. *L'Heptaméron*. Ed. Michel François. Paris: Classiques Garnier.

Marguerite de Navarre. 1956. *La Navire*. Ed. R. Marichal. Paris.

Marguerite de Navarre. 1960. *Petit Oeuvre dévot et contemplatif*. Ed. Hans Sckommodau. Analecta Romanica. H. 9. Frankfurt am Main: Klostermann.

Marguerite de Navarre. 1963. *Théatre Profane*. Ed. V. L. Saulnier. Geneva: Droz, Textes Littéraires Français.

Marguerite de Navarre. 1967. *Nouvelles (L'Heptaméron.)* Ed. Yves Le Hir. Paris: Presses universitaires de France.

Marguerite de Navarre. 1968. Œuvres Choisies I – I. Ed. H. P. Clive. New York.

Marguerite de Navarre. 1971 [1896]. *Les Dernières Poesies de Marguerite de Navarre*. Ed. Abel Lefranc, Paris: Colin. In *Textes litteraires Français*. Geneva: Droz.

Marguerite de Navarre. 1972. *Le Miroir de l'âme pécheresse*. Ed. Joseph L. Allaire: Munich: Wilhelm Fink Verlag.

Marguerite de Navarre. 1978. *Les Prisons*. Ed. Simone Glasson. Geneva: Droz , Textes Littéraires Français.

Marguerite de Navarre. 1979. *Le Miroir de l'âme pécheresse. Edition critique et commentaire suivis de la traduction faite par la princesse Elizabeth, future reine d'Angleterre: The Glasse of the Synnefull Soule*. Annales Academiae Scientiarum Fennicae. Par Renja Salminen. Helsinki: Suomalainen Tiedeakatemia.

Marguerite de Navarre. 1980. *Poésis inédites*. Ed. Pierre Jourda. *Revue du seiwiè, e siècle* 17: 42–63.

Marguerite de Navarre. 2000. Les Comédies bibliques. Ed. Barbara Marczuk. Geneva: Droz.

Marguerite de Navarre. 1981. *Oraison a nostre Seigneur Jésus Christ*. 1981. Ed. Renja Salminen. Suomalaisen Tiedeakatemian Toimituksia. Annales Academiae Scientiarum Fennicae. Helsinki: Suomalainen Tiedeakatemia.

Marguerite de Navarre. 1939. *Comedie de la Nativité de Jésus Christ*. Ed. Pierre Jourda. Paris.

Marguerite de Navarre. 1991–7. *L'Heptaméron. Marguerite de Navarre*. Critical edition by Renja Salminen. Helsinki: Suomalainen Tiedeakatemia.

Marguerite de Navarre. 1999. *L'Heptaméron*. Ed. Gisèle Mathieu-Castellani. Paris: Livre de Poche.

L'Heptaméron. Ed. Pierre Jourda. In Conteurs français du XVI siècle. Paris: Gallimard (Bibliothèque de la Pléiade). Pp. 701–1131.

References

Atance, Félix. 1974. "Les Religieux de l'Heptaméron: Marquerite de Navarre et les novateurs." *Archiv für Reformationsgeschichte* 65: 185–210.

Bainton, Roland. 2001. *Women of the Reformation in France and England*. N.p.: Academic Renewal Press. Pp. 13–41. First published 1973, Minneapolis: Augsburg Publishing House.

Blaisdell, Charmarie Jenkins. 1972. "*Renée* de France between Reform and Counter-Reform." *Archive for Reformation History* 63: 196–226.

Blaisdell, Charmarie Jenkins. 1980. "Marguerite de Navarre and Her Circle 1492–1549." In Jean R. Brink (ed.), *Female Scholars: A Tradition of Learned Women before 1800*. Montreal: Eden Press Women's Publications.

Blaisdell, Charmarie Jenkins. 1982. "Calvin's Letters to Women: The Courting of Ladies in High Places." *Sixteenth Century Journal* 13 (3): 66–83.

Cholakian, Patricia Francis and Rouben C. Cholakian. 2006. *Marguerite de Navarre: Mother of the Renaissance*. New York: Columbia University Press.

Clive, H. P. 1983. *Marguerite de Navarre. An Annotated Bibliography*. London: Grant & Cutler.

Collett, Barry, ed. 2000. *The Long and Troubled Pilgrimage: The Correspondence of Marguerite d'Angoulême and Vittoria Colonna, 1540–1545*. Studies in Reformed Theology and History 6. Princeton, NJ: Princeton Theological Seminary.

Cottrell, Robert D. 1986. *The Grammar of Silence: A Reading of Marguerite de Navarre's Poetry*. Washington, DC: The Catholic University of America Press.

Ferguson, Gary. 1992. *Mirroring Belief: Marguerite de Navarre's Devotional Poetry*. Edinburgh: Edinburgh University Press for the University of Durham.

Heller, Henry. 1971. "Marguerite de Navarre and the Reformers of Meaux." *Bibliothèque d'humanisme et renaissance* 33: 271–310.

International Colloquium Celebrating the 500th Anniversary of the Birth of Marguerite de Navarre. 1995. Ed. Regine Reynolds-Cornell, Birmingham, AL: Summa Publications.

Jourda, Pierre. 1930. *Répertoire analytique et chronologique de la Correspondance de Marguerite d'Angoulême, duchesse d'Alençon, reine de Navarre (1492–1549)*. Reprinted 1973, Geneva: Slatkine Reprints.

Jourda, Pierre. 1930. *Répertoire analytique et chronologique de la Correspondance de Marguerite d'Angoulême, duchesse d'Alençon, reine de Navarre (1492–1549)*. Reprinted 1973, Geneva: Slatkine Reprints.

Jourda, Pierre ed. 1930. *Correspondance de Marguerite d'Angoulême*. Paris: Honoré Champion.

Jourda, Pierre. 1930. *Marguerite d'Angoulême, duchesse d'Alençon, reine de Navarre (1492–1549): Etude biographique et littéraire*, 2 vols. Paris: Librairie Ancienne Honoré Champion. Reprinted 1978, Geneva: Slatkine Reprints.

King, Margaret. 1991. *Women of the Renaissance*. Chicago: University of Chicago Press.

Lefranc, Abel. 1897, 1889, 1898. "Marguerite de Navarre et le Platonisme de la Renaissance." In *Bibliotheque de l'Ecole des Chartres* 43 (1897) 258–92 and 59 (1889) 712–57, and *Les Idées religieuses de Marguerite de Navarre* (Paris 1898).

Lefranc, Abel Jules Maurice. 1898. *Les Idées religieuses de Marguerite de Navarre d'après son œuvre poétique les Marquerites et les Dernières poésies.* Reprinted 1969, Geneva: Slatkine Reprints.

Lerner, Gerda. 1993. *The Creation of Feminist Consciousness: From the Middle Ages to Eighteen-Seventy.* Oxford: Oxford University Press.

McKinley, Mary B., ed. and transl. 2004. *Epistle to Marguerite de Navarre; and, Preface to a Sermon by John Calvin, by Marie Dentière.* Chicago, London: University of Chicago Press.

Orth, Myra D. 1993. "Radical Beauty: Marguerite de Navarre's Illuminated Protestant Catechism and Confession." *Sixteenth Century Journal* 24 (2): 383–427.

Reynolds-Cornell, Régine, ed. 1995. *International Colloquium Celebrating the 500th Anniversary of the Birth of Marguerite de Navarre,* April 13 & 14, 1992, Agnes Scott College. Birmingham, AL: Summa Publishers.

Roelker, Nancy Lyman. 1968. *Queen of Navarre: Jeanne d'Albret 1528–1572.* Cambridge MA: Harvard University Press.

Roelker, Nancy Lyman. 1972a. "The Role of Noblewomen in the French Reformation." *Archiv für Reformationsgeschichte* 63: 168–95.

Roelker, Nancy Lyman. 1972b. "The Appeal of Calvinism to French Noblewomen in the Sixteenth Century." *Journal of Interdisciplinary History* 2 (Spring): 391–418.

Saulnier, Verdun-Louis. 1980. "Marguerite de Navarre, Vittoria Colonna et quelques autres amis italiens de 1540." In *Mélanges à la mémoire de Franco Simone; France et Italie dans la culture européenne. (Moyen Age et Renaissance,* vol. 1.). Geneva: Slatkine Reprints. Pp. 281–95.

Schroeder, Joy A. 1993. "Marguerite of Navarre Breaks Silence about the Sixteenth-Century Clergy Sexual Violence." *Lutheran Quarterly* 7 (2): 171–90.

Sckommodau, Hans. 1954. "Die religiösen Dichtungen Margarets von Navarra." In *Arbeitsgemein-schaft für Forschung des Landes Nordrhein Westfalen* 36 (Köln).

Severin, Renée M. 1996. "Union Deferred in Marguerite de Navarre's 'Oraison de l'ame fidèle.'" *Mystics Quarterly* 22 (March): 37–44.

Sommers, Paula. 1989. *Celestial Ladders: Readings in Marguerite de Navarre's Poetry of Spiritual Ascent.* Geneva: Droz.

Sommers, Paula. 1991. "Marguerite de Navarre (Marguerite d'Angoulême, Queen of Navarre)." In Katharina M. Wilson (ed.), *An Encyclopedia of Continental Women Writer.* New York & London: Garland Publishing, Inc. Pp. 903–5.

Stephenson, Barbara. 2004. *The Power and Patronage of Marguerite de Navarre.* Aldershot and Burlington, VT: Ashgate.

Suyte des Marguerites de la Marguerite des princesses, très illustre Royne de Navarre. Lyon: Jean de Tournes 1547. Facsimile reprint 1970, Ed. Ruth Thomas. The Hague: Johnson Reprint Corporation, Mouton.

Tetel, Marcel. 1987. "Marguerite of Navarre: The Heptaméron, a Simulacrum of Love." In Katharina M. Wilson (ed.), *Women Writers of the Renaissance and Reformation.* Athens and London: The University of Georgia Press. Pp. 99–131.

Thysell, Carol. 1998. "Gendered Virtue, Vernacular Theology, and the Nature of Authority in the Heptaméron." *Sixteenth Century Journal* 29 (1): 39–53.

Thysell, Carol. 2000. *Pleasure of Discernment: Marguerite de Navarre as Theologian.* New York and Oxford: Oxford University Press.

Venard, Marc. 1996. "Un catéchisme offert a Marguerite de Navarre." *Bulletin de la Sociéte de l'Histoire du Protestantisme Français* 142 (Jan–Mar): 5–32.

Vose, Heather M. 1982. "Marguerite of Navarre's Theology of the Cross." *Colloquium* 15: 6–16.

Vose, Heather M. 1985. Marguerite of Navarre: That 'righte English women.'" *Sixteenth Century Journal* 16 (3): 315–34.

Walther, Daniel. 1965. "Marguerite d'Angoulême and the French Lutherans: A Study in Pre-Calvin Reformation in France." *Andrews University Seminary Studies* 3 (Jan): 49–65.

Jeanne D'Albret

Jeanne's Works and Letters of and about Jeanne

Bonnet, Jules. ed. 1854. *Lettres de Jean Calvin*. Paris: Librairie de Ch. Meyraeis. In English, *Letters of John Calvin*, 4 vols. 1972. Ed. J. Bonnet, transl. M. R. Gilchrist. New York: Burt Franklin (reprint of 1858).

De Rochambeau, Marquis. 1877. *Lettres de Antoine de Bourbon et de Jehanne d'Albret*. Paris: Sociéte de l'Histoire de France.

De Ruble, Alphonse, see below.

Frank, Félix, ed. 1897. *La Dernier voyage de la reine de Navarre, Marguerite d'Angoulême, soeur de François Ier, avec sa fille Jeanne d'Albret, aux bains de Cauterets (1549); épîtres en vers inconnues des historiens de ces princesses et des éditeurs de leurs oeuvres; étude*. Toulouse, E. Privat: Paris, Lechevalier.

Jeanne D'Albret, Queen of Navarre, 1528–72. *Mémoires et poésies de Jeanne D'Albret*. Libraires de la Bibliotheque Nationale. Paris: Publiées par Le Baron de Ruble 1893. London: Hurst & Guillemin. Reprinted 1970, Geneva: Slatkine Reprints.

Jeanne D'Albret. 1568. *Letters originales de Jeanne d'Albret*. Ex Museo Petri Dubrowski. Copie du manuscript de Saint-Petersbourg.

Jeanne D'Albret. 1568. *Lettres de treshaute, très verteuse, & très chrétienne Princesse, Jane Royne de Navarre, au Roy, a la Royne Mère, a Monsieur frère du Roy, a Monsieur le Cardinal de Bourbon son beau frère, & a la Royne d'Angleterre*. Contenant les justes occasions de son partement, avec Monseigneur le Prince & Madame Catherine les enfans, pour venire joindre à la cause générale, avec Monseigneur le Prince de Comde son frère. La Rochelle: B. Beron.

References

Bainton, Roland. 2001. "Jeanne d'Albret." In idem, *Women of the Reformation in France and England*. N.p.: Academic Renewal Press. Pp. 43–73. First published 1973, Augsburg Publishing House.

Berdou, Bernard d'Aas. 2002. *Jeanne III d'Albret: Chronique, 1528–1572*. Biarritz: Atlantica.

Berriot-Salvadore, Evelyne, Philippe Chareyre, and Claudie Martin-Ulrich. 2004. *Jeanne d'Albret et sa cour: Actes de colloque international de Pau 17–19 mai 2001*. Paris: Honoré Champion.

Blaisdell, Charmarie. 1972. "Renee de France between Reform and Counter-Reform." *Archive for Reformation History* 63: 196–226.

Blaisdell, Charmarie. 1982. "Calvin's Letters to Women: The Courting of Ladies in High Places." *Sixteenth Century Journal* 13 (3): 66–83.

Bryson, David. 1999. *Queen Jeanne and the Promised Land: Dynasty, Homeland, Religion, and Violence in Sixteenth Century France*. Leiden, Boston, and Koln: E. J. Brill.

Bryson, David. 2004. "Jeanne d'Albret: Questions anciennes: nouvelles réponses?" In Evelyne Berriot-Salvadore, Philippe Chareyre, and Claudie Martin-Ulrich (eds), *Jeanne d'Albret et sa cour: Actes de colloque international de Pau 17–19 mai 2001*. Paris: Honoré Champion. Pp. 503–10.

Cazaux, Yves. 1973. *Jeanne d'Albret*. Paris: Editions Albin Michel.

Cocula, Anne-Marie. 2004. "Eté 1568. Jeanne d'Albret et ses deux enfants sur le chemin de la Rochelle." In Evelyne Berriot-Salvadore, Philippe Chareyre, and Claudie Martin-Ulrich (eds), *Jeanne d'Albret et sa cour: Actes de colloque international de Pau 17–19 mai 2001*. Paris: Honoré Champion. Pp. 34–57.

Coubert, E. 1904. "Jeanne d'Albret et le Heptaméron." *Bulletin du bibliophile et du bibliothecaire* 277–90.

Dartigue-Peyrou, Charles. 1934. *Jeanne D'Albret et le Béarn d'après les délibérations des ètats et les Registres du Conseil souverain (1555–1572)* [microforme] per Charles Dartigue-Peyrou. Mont-de-Marsan: Imprimerie Jean-Lacoste.

Dauvois, Nathalie. 2004. "Jeanne d'Albret et les poètes de Marot à Pay de Garros." In Evelyne Berriot-Salvadore, Philippe Chareyre, and Claudie Martin-Ulrich. (eds), *Jeanne d'Albret et sa cour: Actes de colloque international de Pau 17–19 mai 2001.* Paris: Honoré Champion. Pp. 281–95.

de Ruble, Alphonse, 1881–6. *Antoine de Bourbon et Jeanne d'Albret* [microforme]. *Suite de la marriage de Jeanne d'Albret, par le baron Alphonse de Ruble,* 4 vols. Paris: A. Labitte.

de Ruble, Alphonse, 1897. *Jeanne d'Albret et la guerre civile* [microforme]. *Suite d'Antoine de Bourbon et Jeanne d'Albret.* Vol. 1. Paris: E. Paul et Guillemin.

de Ruble, Alphonse. 1877. *Le Mariage de Jeanne d'Albret.* Paris: A. Labitte.

Desplat, Christian. 2004. "Jeanne d'Albret, un modèle d'éducation maternelle?" In Evelyne Berriot-Salvadore, Philippe Chareyre, and Claudie Martin-Ulrich. (eds), *Jeanne d'Albret et sa cour: Actes de colloque international de Pau 17–19 mai 2001.* Paris: Honoré Champion. Pp. 457–99.

Fawcett, Mrs Henry. 1905. "Jeanne d'Albret: Queen of Navarre." In idem, *Five Famous French Women.* London, Paris, New York, and Melbourne: Cassell and Company, Limited. Pp. 173–244.

Freer, Martha Walker. 1855. "Life of Jeanne d'Albret, Queen of Navarre." 2 Vols. From numerous unpublished sources, including ms. documents in the Bibliotheque Imperiale, and the Archives espagnoles de Simancas. London: Hurst and Blackett.

Kermina, Francoise. 1998. *Jeanne d'Albret: La mère passionnée d'Henri IV.* Paris: Perrin.

Kuperty-Tsur, Nadine. 2004. "Jeanne d'Albret ou la persuasion par la passion." In Evelyne Berriot-Salvadore, Philippe Chareyre, and Claudie Martin-Ulrich (eds), *Jeanne d'Albret et sa cour: Actes de colloque international de Pau 17–19 mai 2001.* Paris: Honoré Champion.

Muret, Theodore Cesar. 1862. *Histoire de Jeanne d'Albret Reine de Navarre: Precede d'une étude sur Marguerite de Valois, sa mère.* Paris: Grassart.

Nabonne, Bernard. 1945. *Jeanne d'Albret: Reine des Huguenots.* Librairie Hachette. s.l.

Pascal, Eugénie. 2004. "Lettres de la Royne de Navarre . . . avec une Ample Declaration d'icelles: autoportrait d'une femme d'exception." In *Jeanne d'Albret et sa cour.* Evelyne Berriot-Salvadore, Philippe Chareyre, and Claudie Martin-Ulrich. Paris: Honoré Champion. Pp. 243–57.

Rambeaud, Pascal. 2004. "Jeanne d'Albret et son entourage à La Rochelle (septembre 1568–aout 1571)." In Evelyne Berriot-Salvadore, Philippe Chareyre, and Claudie Martin-Ulrich (eds), *Jeanne d'Albret et sa cour: Actes de colloque international de Pau 17–19 mai 2001.* Paris: Honoré Champion. Pp. 221–9.

Roelker, Nancy Lyman. 1968. *Queen of Navarre: Jeanne d'Albret, 1528–1572.* Cambridge, MA: Belknap Press of Harvard University Press.

Roelker, Nancy Lyman. 1972. "The Appeal of Calvinism to French Noblewomen in the Sixteenth Century," *Journal of Interdisciplinary History* 2 (Spring): 391–418.

Roussel, Bernard. 2004. "Jeanne d'Albret et 'ses' théologiens." In Evelyne Berriot-Salvadore, Philippe Chareyre, and Claudie Martin-Ulrich (eds), *Jeanne d'Albret et sa cour: Actes de colloque international de Pau 17–19 mai 2001.* Paris: Honoré Champion. Pp. 13–31.

Stephenson, Barbara. 2004. *The Power and Patronage of Marguerite de Navarre.* Aldershot and Burlington, VT: Ashgate.

Vauvilliers, Mlle. 1818. *Histoire de Jeanne d'Albret, Reine de Navarre.* Paris: L. Janet.

Wittenmyer, Annie. 1885. "Jeanne d'Albret, the Illustrious Queen of Navarre." In idem, *The Women of the Reformation.* New York: Phillips & Hunt; Cincinnati: Cranston & Stowe 1885. 138–216.

Renée de France

Letters of Renée de France

A selection of Renée's scattered letters, treasured in the Archives of State, Modena, can be found in Rodocanachi 1896 and in Barton 1989, also in Fontana 1889–99, which latter also includes Vatican documents regarding the duchess.

Correspondence between Renée and Calvin, and others, can be found in various sources including those listed here.

Correspondance de Théodore de Bèze/recueillie par Hippolyte Aubert; publiée par Fernand Aubert et Henri Meylan et al. 1967. Vol. VIII. 1978. Vol. X. Genève: Librairie Droz. Pp. 155–6, 2003–4.

Bonnet, Jules, ed. 1854. *Lettres de Jean Calvin.* Paris: Librairie de Ch. Meyraeis. In English.

Letters of John Calvin, 4 vols. 1972. Ed. J. Bonnet, transl. M.R. Gilchrist. New York: Burt Franklin (reprint of 1858 edition).

Herminjard, A.-L. 1864–97. *Correspondance des réformateurs dans les pays de langue Française*, 9 vols. Geneva: H. Georg.

Jourda, Pierre. 1930. *Marguerite d'Angoulême, Duchesse d'Alençon, Reine de Navarre*, 2 vols, Paris: Librarie Ancienne Honoré Champion.

Jourda, Pierre ed. 1930. *Correspondance de Marguerite d'Angoulême.* Paris: Librairie Ancienne Honoré Champion.

Jourda, Pierre. 1930. *Répertoire analytique et chronologique de la Correspondance de Marguerite d'Angoulême, duchesse d'Alençon, reine de Navarre (1492–1549).* Reprinted, Geneva: Slatkine Reprints, 1973.

Renée's prayerbook

Petites Priéres de Renée de France. 1909. Modena: Società Tipografica Modenese. (Fontana Georges Toudouze.)

References

Audibert, Paul F. M. 1972. *Renée de France, duchesse de Ferrara: Une 'princesse oecomenique' du XVIe siècle: Renée de France, Duchesse de Ferrare.* [Carces] s.l. P. Audibert.

Bainton, Roland. 2001. "Renée of Ferrara". In idem, *Women of the Reformation in Germany and Italy.* N.p.: Academic Renewal Press. Pp. 235–51. First published 1971, Minneapolis: Augsburg Publishing House.

Barton, F. Whitfield. 1989. *Calvin and the Duchess.* Louisville, KY: WJKP.

Bates, Lizzie. 1872. *The Duchess Renée and her Court.* New York: American Tract Society.

Blaisdell, Charmarie Jenkins. 1972. "Renée de France between Reform and Counter-Reform." *Archive for Reformation History* 63: 196–226.

Blaisdell, Charmarie Jenkins. 1975. "Politics and Heresy in Ferrara, 1534–1559." *Sixteenth Century Journal* 6: 67–93.

Blaisdell, Charmarie Jenkins. 1982. "Calvin's Letters to Women: The Courting of Ladies in High Places." *Sixteenth Century Journal* 13 (3): 66–83.

Blaisdell, Charmarie J. 1992. "Calvin's and Loyola's Letters to Women: Political and Spiritual Counsel in the Sixteenth Century." In Richard C. Gamble (ed.), *Calvin's Work in Geneva.* Pp. 117–35.

Braum, Gabriel. 1988. "Le Marriage de Renée de France avec Hercule d'Este: Une inutile mesalliance, 28 juin 1528." *Histoire, Economie et Societe* 7: 147–68.

Casadei, Alfredo. 1934. "Fanino Fanini da Faenza. Episodio della Riforma protestante in Italia con documenti inediti." *Nuova Rivista Storica* 18: 168–99.

Cignoni, Mario. 1990–92. "Madame de Soubise alla corte di Ferrara.1528–1536." *Atti dell'Accademia delle scienze di Ferrara* 68–9: 91–9.

Fawcett, Mrs Henry. 1905. "Renée de France, Duchess of Ferrara." In idem, *Five Famous French Women.* London, Paris, New York, and Melbourne: Cassell and Company, Limited. Pp. 247–99.

Fontana, Bartolommeo. 1889–1899. *Renata di Francia, Duchessa di Ferrara, sui documenti dell'Archivio Estense, de' Medeceo, del Gonzaga, e dell'Archivio secreto Vaticano,* 3 vols. Rome: Forzani e C., Tipografi del Senato.

Jung, Eva-Maria. 1951. "Vittoria Colonna: Between Reformation and Counter-Reformation." *Review of Religion* 15: 144–59.

King, Margaret L. 1991. *Women of the Renaissance.* Chicago and London: The University of Chicago Press.

Puaux, Anne. 1997. *La Huguenote: Renée de France.* Collection Savoir: Letters. Editeurs des Sciences et des Arts. Paris: Hermann.

Rodocanachi, Emmanuel. 1896. *Une protetrice de la Réforme en Italie et en France: Renée de France, Duchesse de Ferrare.* Paris: Ollendorff. Reprinted 1970. Geneva: Slatkine Reprints. Microfilm: "History of Women," reel 596, no. 4712. New Haven, CT.: Research Publications, 1976.

Roelker, Nancy Lyman. 1972. "The Appeal of Calvinism to French Noblewomen in the Sixteenth Century." *Journal of Interdisciplinary History* 2 (Spring): 391–418.

Roelker, Nancy Lyman. 1972. "The Role of Noblewomen in the French Reformation." *Archiv für Reformationsgeschichte* 63: 168–95.

Roffi, Mario. 1984. "Un concorso di poesia francese a Ferrara alla corte Estense di Renata di Francia." In W. Moretti (ed), *Il Rinascimento a Ferrara e i suoi orizzoni Europei.* English version J. Salmons, J. (ed.), *The Renaissance in Ferrara and its European Horizons.* Cardiff: University of Wales Press; Ravenna: M. Lapucci, Edizioni del Girasole. Pp. 263–9.

Ryley, M. Beresford. 1907. *Queens of the Renaissance.* Boston: Small, Maynard & Company. Pp. 251–303.

Some Memorials of Renée of France, Duchess of Ferrara. 1859. 2nd edn. I. M. B. London: Bosworth and Harrison.

Valeria, Pietravalle Valeri. 1969. *Renata di Francia, duchessa di Ferrara: calvinista o no.* Studio sulle relazioni con i pontefici contemporanei e sui giudizi espresso su di lei da storici francesi ed italiani. Roma: Alfa Editoriale.

Warnicke, Retha M. 2000. *The Marrying of Anne of Cleves: Royal Protocol in Early Modern England.* Cambridge: Cambridge University Press.

Webb, Charmarie Jenkins. 1970. "Royalty and Reform: The Predicament of Renée de France, 1510–1575." Doctoral dissertation. Tufts University. Ann Arbor, MI: University Microfilms.

Weitzel, Sophie Winthrop. 1883. *Renée of France, Duchess of Ferrara.* New York: Anson D.G. Randolph & Company.

Wittenmyer, Annie. 1885. "Renée, Daughter of Louis XII, of France, Duchess of Ferrara." In idem, *The Women of the Reformation.* New York: Phillips & Hunt. Cincinnati: Cranston & Stowe. 99–137.

Olimpia Fulvia Morata

Olimpia's Works (after Holt N. Parker 2003, p. 230)

Morata, Olympia Fulvia. 1558. *Olympiae Fulviae Moratae mulieris omnium eruditissimae Latina et Graeca, quae haberi potuerunt, monumenta, eaque plane divina, cum eruditorum de ipsa iudiciis et laudibus. Hippolytae Taurellae elegia elegantissima. Ad ill. Isabellam Bresegnam. Basileae apud Petrum Pernam.* MDLVIII. Ed. Caius Secundus Curio. Basel: Petrum Pernam.

Morata, Olympia Fulvia. 1562. *Olympiae Fulviae Moratae foeminae doctissimae ac plane divinae Orationes, Dialogi, Epistolae, Carmina tam Latina quam Graecae cum eruditoru de ea testimonijs & laudibus. Hippolytae Taurellae elegia elegantissima. Ad Sereniss. Angliae reginam D. Elisabetam.* Ed. Caius Secundus Curio. 2nd. Basileae/Basel: Petrum Pernam. Also 1975, Microfilm History of Women, reel 62 no. 396. New Haven CT: Research publications.

Morata, Olympia Fulvia. 1570. *Olympiae Fulviae Moratae foeminae doctissimae ac plane divinae opera omnia quae hactenus inueniri potuerunt.* Ed. Caius Secundus Curio. 3d edn. Basileae/Basel: Petrum Pernam. Also 1975, Microfilm History of Women, reel 62, no. 397. New Haven, CT: Research Publications. (4th edn. of 1580 a reprint of this edition.)

[*Olympiae Fulviae Moratae foeminae doctissimae ac plane divinae Orationes, Dialogi, Epistolae, Carmina, tam Latina quam Graeca.* Ed. Celio Secondus Curio. 2nd. edn. Basileae/Basel: Petrum Pernam. 1558, 1562, 1570, 1580.]

Olimpia Morata Lettere. 1913–27. Ed. Giuseppe Paladino. In *Opuscoli e lettere di riformatori italiani del Cinquecento.* Bari: Laterza. Pp. 169–227, 265–79.

Olimpia Morata, Epistolario (1540–1555). 1940. Ed. Lanfranco Caretti. Ferrara: R. Deputazione di Storia Patria per l'Emilia e la Romagna, Sezione di Ferrara.

Olimpia Morata. 1954. *Opere, vol. I. Epistolae, vol. II. Orationes, Dialogi et Carmina.* Ed. Lanfranco Caretti. Ferrara: Deputazione Provinciale Ferrarese di Storia Patria.

Olimpia Morata Lettere. 1967. Ed. Giuseppe Guido Ferrero. In *Lettere del Cinquecento.* Turin: Unione tipiografico-editrice torinese. Pp. 551–64.

Olympia Fulvia Morata. 1990. *Briefe: Aus dem Lateinischen, Italienischen und Griechischen.* Transl. Rinaer Kößling and Gertrud Weiss-Stählin. Reclam-Verlag Leipzig.

Olympia Fulvia Morata, 1526–1555: The Complete Writings of an Italian Heretic. 2003. Ed. and transl. Holt N. Parker. Chicago: University of Chicago Press.

References

Bainton, Roland H. 2001. "Olympia Morata (1526–1555)." In idem, *Women of the Reformation in Germany and Italy.* N.p.: Academic Renewal Press. Pp. 253–68. First published 1971, Minneapolis: Augsburg Publishing House.

Barton, Florence Whitfield. 1965. *Olympia: A Novel of the Reformation.* Philadelphia: Fortress Press.

Benrath, Karl. 1903. "Morata, Olimpia." In *Realencyclopädie für protestantische Theologie und Kirche.* 3rd edn. Vol. 13, Pp. 461–4.

Bonnet, Jules. 1856. *Vie d'Olympia Morata: Episode de la renaissance et de la réforme en Italie.* 3rd. rev. edn. Paris: Charles Meyruels. Also 1975, Microfilm, History of Women, reel 245, no. 1634. New Haven, CT: Research Publications.

Bonnet, Jules M. 1887. *Olympia Morata.* Transl. Grace Patterson. Philadelphia: Presbyterian Board of Publication and Sabbath-School Work.

Caretti, Lanfranco. 1951. "Gli scritti di Olimpia Morata." In *Studi e ricerche di letteratura italiana.* Firenze: La Nuova Italia. Pp. 37–64.

Cignoni, Mario. 1982–4. "Il pensiero di Olimpia Morato nell'ambito della Riforma protestante." *Atti dell'Accademia delle scienze di Ferrara* 60–1 (1982–3, 1983–4): 191–204.

Cignoni, Mario. 1990–2. "Madame de Soubise alla corte di Ferrara (1528–1536)." *Atti dell'Accademia delle scienze di Ferrara* 68–9: 91–9.

Costa-Zalessow, Natalia. 1982. "Olimpia Morato." In *Scrittrici italiane dal XIII al XX secolo: Testi e critica.* Ravenna: Longo editore. Pp. 99–103.

Dizionario enciclopedico della letteratura italiana IV. 1967. Bari: LaTerza. Pp. 62.

Dizionario enciclopedico italiano VIII. 1958. Roma: Istituto Poligrafico dello Stato. Pp. 78.

Dolce, Lodovico. 1553. *Dialogo della institution delle donne.* Also 1975, Microfilm History of Women, reel 26 no. 166. New Haven CT: Research publications.

Düchting, von, Reinhard, Andrea Fleischer, Boris Körkel, Heiner Lutzmann, Werner Moritz, and Eva Näher. 1998. *Olympia Fulvia Morata: Stationem ihres Lebens: Ferrara, Schweinfurt, Heidelberg.* Katalog zur Ausstellung im Universitätsmuseum Heidelberg, 26 März – 8 Mai 1998. Ubstadt-Weiher: Verlag Regionalkultur.

Farina, Rachele, ed. 1995. "Olimpia Morata." In *Dizionario biografico delle donne lombarde 568–1968.* Milan: Baldini & Castoldi. Pp. 764–5.

Flood, John L. 1997. "Olympia Fulvia Morata." In James Hardin and Max Reinhardt (eds), *German Writers of the Renaissance 1280–1580*. Dictionary of Literary Biography 179. Detroit: Gale Research. Pp. 178–83.

Fontana, Bartolommeo. 1889–99. "Olimpia Morata." In *Renata di Francia, Duchessa di Ferrara*. 3 vols. Rome: Forzani. Vol. 2, Pp. 283–336.

Gearey, Caroline. 1886. *Daughters of Italy*. London: Simpkin, Marshall & Co.

Hare, Christopher. 1914. "Renee of Ferrara." In idem, *Men and Women of the Italian Reformation*. London: Stanley Paul & Co. Pp. 85–135.

Heinsius, Maria. 1951. *Das Unüberwindliche Wort: Frauen der Reformationszeit*. Munich: Kaiser.

Holzberg, Niklas. 1982. "Olympia Morata." In *Veröffentlichungen der Gesellschaft für Fränkische Geschichte*. Reihe 7A and Fränkische Lebensbilder. Neustadt/Aisch. NF, 10. Bd. Pp. 141–56.

Holzberg, Niklas. 1987. "Olympia Morata und die Anfänge des Griechischen an der Universität Heidelberg." *Heidelberger Jahrbücher* 31: 77–93.

King, Margaret L. 1980. "Book-Lined Cells: Women and Humanism in the Early Italian Renaissance." In Patricia Labalme (ed.), *Beyond Their Sex: Learned Women of the European Past*. New York: New York University Press. Pp. 66–90.

King, Margaret L. 1991. *Women of the Renaissance*. Chicago: University of Chicago Press.

King, Margaret L. and Albert Rabil Jr., eds. 1992. *Her Immaculate Hand: Selected Works by and about the Women Humanists of Quattrocento Italy*. 2nd rev. edn. Binghamton, NY: Center for Medieval and Early Renaissance Studies.

Lerner, Gerda. 1993. *The Creation of Feminist Consciousness: From the Middle Ages to Eighteen-Seventy*. Oxford: Oxford University Press.

Mulazzi, Virginia. 1875. *Olimpia Morato, scene della riforma: Racconto storico del secolo XVI*. 2 vols. Milan: Tipografia di Lodovico Bortolotti E. C.

Osieja, Stefan. 2002. "Die italienischen protestantischen Schriftsteller und ihr bild vom verfolgten glaubensgenossen." In idem, *Das literarische Bild des verfolgten Glaubensgenossen bei den protestantischen Schriftstellerin der Romania zur Zeit der Reformation: Studien zu Agrippa d'Aubigne, Françoisco de Enzinas, Juan Peres de Pineda, Raimundo Gonzales de Montes, Olympia Fulvia Morata, Scipione Lentolo and Taddeo Duno*. Frankfurt am Main Berlin, Bern, Bruxelles, New York, Oxford, and Wien: Peter Lang. Pp. 292–301.

Parker, Holt N. 1997. "Latin and Greek Poetry by Five Renaissance Italian Women Humanists." In Paul Allen Miller, Barbara K. Gold, and Charles Platter (eds), *Sex and Gender in Medieval and Renaissance Texts*. Albany: State University of New York Press. Pp. 247–85.

Parker, Holt N., ed. and transl. 2003. *Olympia Fulvia Morata, 1526–1555: The Complete Writings of an Italian Heretic*. Chicago: University of Chicago Press.

Parker, Holt N. 2002. "Olympia Fulvia Morata." In Anne Clark Bartlett, Laurie J. Churchill, and Jane Jeffery (eds), *Women Writing Latin: From Roman Antiquity to Early Modern Europe*. New York: Routledge. Pp. 133–65.

Pirovano, Donato. 1997. "Le edizioni cinquecentine degli scritti di Olimpia Fulvia Morata." In Fabio Danelon, Hermann Grosser, and Cristina Zampese (eds), *Le varie fila: Studi di letteratura italiana in onore di Emilio Bigi*. Milano: Principato. Pp. 96–111.

Pirovano, Donato. 1998. "Olimpia Morata e la traduzione Latina delle prime due novella del Decameron." Acme 51: 73–109. Idem, "Olimpia Morata e la traduzione latina delle prime due novelle del Decameron." *Acme: Annali della Facoltà di Lettere e Filosofia dell'Università degli Studi di Milano* LI (Gennaio–Aprile 1998): 73–109.

Rabil, Albert Jr. 1994. "Olympia Morata (1526–1555)." In Rinaldina Russell (ed.), *Italian Women Writers: A Bio-Bibliographical Sourcebook*. Westport, CT: Greenwood Press. Pp. 269–78.

Russell, Rinaldina, ed. 1994. *Italian Women Writers: A Bio-Bibliographical Sourcebook*. Westport, CT: Greenwood Press.

Smarr, Janet Levarie. 2005a. "Dialogue & Spiritual Counsel: Marguerite de Navarre, Olympia Morata, Chiara Matraini," and "Many voices, Marguerite de Navarre, Moderata Fonte." In

Joining the Conversation: Dialogues by Renaissance Women. Ann Arbor: University of Michican Press. Pp. 31–97 and 190–230.

Smarr, Janet. 2005b. "Olympia Morata: From Classicist to Reformer." In Deanne Shemek and Dennis Looney (eds), *Phaethon's Children: The Este Court and its Culture in Early Modern Ferrara.* Teme, AZ: Medieval and Renaissance Texts and Studies. Pp. 321–43.

Smyth, Amelia Gillespie. 1834. *Olympia Morata: Her Times, Life and Writings.* London: Smith, Elder & Co. [Sometimes attributed to Caroline Anne Bowles Southey.]

Turnbull, Robert. 1846. *Olympia Morata: Her Life and Times.* Boston: Sabbath School Society.

Vorländer, Dorothea. 1970. "Olympia Fulvia Morata – eine evangelische Humanistin in Schweinfurt." *Zeitschrift für Bayerische Kirchengeschichte* 39: 95–113.

Weiss-Stählin, Gertrud. 1976. "Per una biografia di Olimpia Morata." In Lucio Puttin (ed.), *Miscellanea di studi in memoria di Cesare Bolognesi nel trentacinquesimo della scomparsa.* Schio: Edizioni Ascledum. Pp. 79–107.

Weiss-Stählin, Gertrud. 1961. "Olympia Fulvia Morata und Schweinfurt: Wechselbeziehungen zwischen italienischer und deutscher Frömmigkeit im Zeitalter der Reformation." *Zeitschrift für bayerische Kirchengeschichte* 30: 175–83.

Wengler, Elisabeth M. 1999. "Women, Religion and Reform in Sixteenth-Century Geneva." Unpublished PhD dissertation. Dept. of History, Boston College, Boston, MA.

Index